USING DATA
TO IMPROVE
STUDENT LEARNING
IN HIGH SCHOOLS

VICTORIA L. BERNHARDT, Ph.D.
Executive Director
Education for the Future Initiative

Professor on Leave
Department of Professional Studies in Education
College of Communication and Education
California State University, Chico, CA

EYE ON EDUCATION
6 Depot Way West
Larchmont, NY 10538
(914) 833-0551
(914) 833-0761 Fax
www.eyeoneducation.com

For information about permission to reproduce selections from this book, write:
EYE ON EDUCATION
Permission Dept.
6 Depot Way West
Larchmont, NY 10538

Library of Congress Cataloging—in—Publication Data

Bernhardt, Victoria L., 1952-
    Using data to improve student learning in high schools / Victoria L. Bernhardt.
        p.   cm.
    Includes bibliographical references.
    ISBN 1-59667-004-5
    1. Educational evaluation--United States. 2. Educational indicators--United States.
    3. Education, Secondary--United States. I. Title.

    LB2822.75.B444 2005
    373'.021--dc22

                                                          2005002864

10 9 8 7 6 5 4 3 2 1

Also Available from Eye On Education

USING DATA TO IMPROVE STUDENT LEARNING IN MIDDLE SCHOOLS
(With CD-Rom)
Victoria L. Bernhardt

USING DATA TO IMPROVE STUDENT LEARNING IN ELEMENTARY SCHOOLS
(With CD-Rom)
Victoria L. Bernhardt

DATA ANALYSIS FOR CONTINUOUS SCHOOL IMPROVEMENT
Second Edition
Victoria L. Bernhardt

THE SCHOOL PORTFOLIO TOOLKIT:
A Planning, Implementation, and Evaluation Guide for
Continuous School Improvement (With CD-Rom)
Victoria L. Bernhardt

DESIGNING AND USING DATABASES FOR SCHOOL IMPROVEMENT
Victoria L. Bernhardt

THE EXAMPLE SCHOOL PORTFOLIO
Victoria L. Bernhardt, et. al.

THE SCHOOL PORTFOLIO:
A Comprehensive Framework for School Improvement, Second Edition
Victoria L. Bernhardt

SCHOOL LEADER'S GUIDE TO ROOT CAUSE ANALYSIS:
Using Data to Dissolve Problems
Paul Preuss

APPLYING STANDARDS-BASED CONSTRUCTIVISM:
A Two-step Guide for Motivating Middle and High School Students
Flynn, Mesibov, Vermette, and Smith

MEASUREMENT AND EVALUATION:
Strategies for School Improvement
McNamara, Erlandson and McNamara

WHAT EVERY TEACHER NEEDS TO KNOW ABOUT ASSESSMENT, Second Edition
Leslie Walker Wilson

AT-RISK STUDENTS:
Reaching and Teaching Them, Second Edition
Richard Sagor and Jonas Cox

HANDBOOK ON DIFFERENTIATED INSTRUCTION FOR MIDDLE AND HIGH SCHOOLS
Sheryn Spencer Northey

Acknowledgements

I am so lucky to have many wonderful, dedicated colleagues and friends all over the world who keep me going, and help me improve each day. I am particularly grateful for special colleagues from California, Colorado, Georgia, Iowa, Indiana, Massachusetts, Michigan, Missouri, Montana, New Jersey, New York, North Dakota, Ohio, Pennsylvania, South Carolina, Vermont, Washington, Ecuador, and Brazil who have helped make this book factual and useful. These dedicated reviewers give me powerful information for making the content useful and user-friendly. The reviewers are critical in the writing of this book for probably more reasons than they know. They give me the confidence and sense of urgency to finish.

Special mention needs to be made of Joy Rose's contributions. Joy read and edited the manuscript in every phase. Joy, as always, made herself available to help with any task, any time. Joy, my editor "extraordinaire," is unsurpassed as a supporter and encourager of high-quality work. The nature of her editing goes beyond the proper uses of verbs and commas—her knowledge of continuous school improvement provides insights and revelations that I do not always see. I know the final product is so much better because of her input. Thank you, thank you, and thank you, Joy.

Marcy Lauck's time and assistance with looking at the data was invaluable. You are so appreciated, Marcy. Thank you.

A special thanks to the school that gave me data to use in this case study. In concert with our agreement, I will not reveal who you are or your real location. We all appreciate the opportunity to learn from you. To those who used this case study in early form, thank you for your insights to continuously improve the Big River story.

I am appreciative and thankful everyday for my outstanding *Education for the Future* staff: Lynn Varicelli, Brad Geise, Alicia Warren, Sally Withuhn, Thiago Jorge, and Marcy Lauck. Brad managed the completion of the CD and graphics with his usual elegance. Alicia, Sally, and Thiago do amazing work, every day, to keep us operating and on the cutting edge. They also helped to make this book a reality. Alicia deserves special acknowledgement for help with the references and graphing, and Sally for graphing questionnaire results. Marcy, serving as our depth charge in San Jose Unified School District, helps us know that it is possible to do this on a large scale and that it can be sustained over time.

Once again, I am awestruck and indebted to Lynn Varicelli, for her careful and artistic work on the book layout and CD files. Her dedication to supporting these publications is unmatched in the history of the world! Thank you, Lynn, for your stellar work, for your commitment, loyalty, and long hours over countless days without a break. These books could never be done without you.

I am also grateful to *MC² Design Group.* Brian Curtis and Vanessa Wolfe created the CD design, artwork, and cover—I highly recommend them—and Tom Devol (that's *loved* spelled backwards), our outstanding professional photographer (even if HE cannot spell backwards).

I thank my husband, Jim Richmond, for again providing his brand of support for my work. He does a lot of what I should be doing around the house so I can pursue these publications and the work I can't not do—with few complaints.

A huge thanks to my publisher, affectionately known as *Cousin Bob*, Mr. Robert Sickles. I am grateful for all you do for us. Thank you.

This *Acknowledgement* section could not be complete without thanking you, the reader, and you, the school personnel working with continuous school improvement, who have believed in and tried *Education for the Future* products and processes.

I do hope this book exceeds your expectations and if it does, it is because of the continuous improvement that has resulted from your insights, direction, assistance, and support all along the way. Thank you.

In appreciation to all interested in continuous quality improvement, enjoy this third in a series of four books on *Using Data to Improve Student Learning.*

Vickie Bernhardt
February 2005

About the Author

Victoria L. Bernhardt, Ph.D., is Executive Director of the *Education for the Future Initiative,* a not-for-profit organization whose mission is to build the capacity of all schools at all levels to gather, analyze, and use data to continuously improve learning for all students. She is also a Professor in the Department of Professional Studies in Education, College of Communication and Education, at California State University, Chico, currently on leave. Dr. Bernhardt is the author of the following books:

▼ A four-book collection of using data to improve student learning—*Using Data to Improve Student Learning in Elementary Schools (2003); Using Data to Improve Student Learning in Middle Schools (2004); Using Data to Improve Student Learning in High Schools (2005);* and *Using Data to Improve Student Learning in School Districts (2005).* Each book shows real analyses focused on one education organizational level and provides templates on an accompanying CD-Rom for leaders to use for gathering, graphing, and analyzing data in their own learning organizations.

▼ *Data Analysis for Continuous School Improvement* (First Edition, 1998; Second Edition, 2004) helps learning organizations use data to determine where they are, where they want to be, and how to get there—sensibly, painlessly, and effectively.

▼ *The School Portfolio Toolkit: A Planning, Implementation, and Evaluation Guide for Continuous School Improvement,* and CD-Rom (2002), is a compilation of over 500 examples, suggestions, activities, tools, strategies, and templates for producing school portfolios that will lead to continuous school improvement.

▼ *The Example School Portfolio* (2000) shows what a completed school portfolio looks like and further supports schools in developing their own school portfolios.

▼ *Designing and Using Databases for School Improvement* (2000) helps schools and districts think through the issues surrounding the creation and uses of databases established to achieve improved student learning.

▼ *The School Portfolio: A Comprehensive Framework for School Improvement* (First Edition, 1994; Second Edition, 1999). This first book by the author assists schools with clarifying the purpose and vision of their learning organizations as they develop their school portfolios.

Dr. Bernhardt is passionate about her mission of helping all educators continuously improve student learning in their classrooms, their schools, their districts, and states by gathering, analyzing, and using actual data—as opposed to using hunches and "gut-level" feelings. She has made numerous presentations at professional meetings and conducts workshops on the school portfolio, data analysis, data warehousing, and school improvement at local, state, regional, national, and international levels.

Dr. Bernhardt can be reached at:

Victoria L. Bernhardt
Executive Director, *Education for the Future Initiative*
400 West First Street, Chico, CA 95929-0230
Tel: 530-898-4482 — Fax: 530-898-4484
e-mail: vbernhardt@csuchico.edu
website: *http://eff.csuchico.edu*

Table of Contents

Foreword

TetraData Corporation is a software and services company that focuses on analysis, assessment, and improvement in education. TetraData continues to be proudly associated with Victoria L. Bernhardt, one of the most dedicated, capable, and energetic leaders in school improvement today. Our firm shares a common passion, i.e., that fact-driven decision making can provide each district, each school, and each class with a reliable way to facilitate continuous school improvement. We also share a common vision of a world where education is moving toward increased knowledge, increased caring, and where we focus societal resources on our real future, i.e., the children of our world.

This book in the series of four, *Using Data to Improve Student Learning,* is an excellent addition to Dr. Bernhardt's preceding books that explain how to establish a data-driven environment and how to build the data warehouse to support the needed analysis of data. The four books in this series focus on what to do with a robust data warehouse, i.e., what analyses to prepare and how to interpret the analyses. In the several years that Dr. Bernhardt and TetraData have been building and using education specific data warehouses, the quality of the data and design of the warehouses has grown significantly. Now we have much of the data that we have been seeking to properly assemble, and the next step is addressed by this wonderful publication series.

What I enjoy immensely about these four publications is that Dr. Bernhardt has used real data from real life situations. This brings richness to the examples and the principles that Dr. Bernhardt provides since it is set forth in such a realistic environment. This realism approach has also enabled Dr. Bernhardt to provide both an insightful, as well as practical, description of how to prepare and interpret the analyses. Since there are four books, the publications deliver this information specific to the teachers and staff in elementary, middle, high school, and the district office. That was a wonderful decision by Dr. Bernhardt, as she provides very specific content for each portion of the education spectrum.

One of the major education issues that Dr. Bernhardt addresses is embodied in the word "Focus." One of the first results of the early education data warehousing and data analysis efforts was the *kid in the candy shop* syndrome. What I mean by that is the school data was finally available for examination, and educators started producing queries and analyses, many of which were useful, but not necessarily pertinent to the focus of their educational team. Dr. Bernhardt, in this work, brings focus to all of our data analysis efforts, a focus on what is important to bring about school improvement, a focus on what will bring results in our quality programs, a focus on the real challenges and opportunities, and a focus on what really can effect positive change.

This fine set of works touches the needs of numerous individuals in the education network, from the teacher who needs to understand the demographics and capabilities of her/his individual students to school principals, counselors, instructional coordinators, testing and data analysis coordinators, district researchers, and certainly the district executives. By virtue of her excellent skills, Dr. Bernhardt has given everyone in education, including the non-technologists among us, the opportunity to benefit from this fine edition. I encourage your reading of this newest edition to the library of Dr. Bernhardt's works and welcome you to embrace the passion of improving education by making objective education-enhancement decisions. Enjoy this wonderful rich material and let it drive all of us to focus on our future—our children.

Martin S. Brutosky
Chairman and CEO
TetraData Corporation
3 Independence Point, Suite 101
Greenville, SC 29615
Tel: 864-458-8243
http://www.tetradata.com

Preface

With the enactment of *No Child Left Behind,* every school and district in the country need to analyze their data to ensure adequate yearly progress. Sometimes, looking at another's analyses makes it easier to see things you would not have seen while looking only at your own analyses.

When it comes to analyzing student achievement data, the first two questions educators ask are *Now that we have the data, what analyses should we make?* and *What do the analyses tell us?*

These questions are hard to answer on the spot, so I have taken up the challenge to develop a series of books with the purposes of showing what analyses can be made, describing what these analyses are telling us, and illustrating how to use these analyses in continuous school improvement planning. This series of books includes:

▼ *Using Data to Improve Student Learning in Elementary Schools*

▼ *Using Data to Improve Student Learning in Middle Schools*

▼ *Using Data to Improve Student Learning in High Schools*

▼ *Using Data to Improve Student Learning in School Districts*

I believe that most of the time we must look at K-12 data (district level) to ensure a continuum of learning that makes sense for all students. I have purposefully separated building levels so there would be ample space to do a fairly comprehensive job of data analysis at each organizational level and to make the point about needing to understand results beyond one school level.

Each of these four publications uses real data (with some slight alterations to blur identities and to fill gaps where data are missing) and shows the actual descriptive analyses I would perform if I were the person analyzing the data at that particular level. You will see that no matter how much or how little *data* your school or district has, the *data* can tell the story. The study questions at the end of each chapter serve as guides for the reader. I have described what I saw in the analyses following the study questions for readers who want the feedback.

My goal with this book is for anyone to be able to set up these analyses, regardless of the statistical resources available. Therefore, in addition to showing the analyses in the text, the graphing templates, narratives, text templates, and supplementary tools appear on the accompanying CD.

Intended Audiences

This book is intended for school and district teachers and administrators who want to use data to continuously improve what they do for children; and for college and university professors who teach school administrators, teachers, and support personnel how to analyze school data. It is my belief that all professional educators must learn how to use data in this time of high-stakes accountability. I also believe that these practical and descriptive analyses are more important for practitioners to learn to perform than inferential statistics.

My hope is that you will find this book and the CD to be helpful as you think through the analyses of *your* data to improve learning for all students.

Victoria L. Bernhardt
Executive Director, *Education for the Future Initiative*
400 West First Street, Chico, CA 95929-0230
Tel: 530-898-4482 — Fax: 530-898-4484
e-mail: vbernhardt@csuchico.edu
website: *http://eff.csuchico.edu*

Schools that gather, analyze, and use information about their school communities make better decisions, not only about what to change but also how to institutionalize systemic change. Schools that understand the needs of their primary customers—the students—are more successful in planning changes and remain more focused during implementation. Schools that simply gather, but make no sustained effort to analyze and use, data, are at a substantial disadvantage. Schools that use data understand the effectiveness of their reform efforts; those that do not use data can only assume that effectiveness.

Schools committed to improving student learning analyze data in order to plan for the future through understanding—

▼ the ways in which the school and the community have changed and are continuing to change

▼ the current and future needs of the students, parents, teachers, school, and community

▼ how well current processes meet these customers' needs

▼ if all subgroups of students are being well-served

▼ the gaps between the results the school is getting and the results it wants

▼ the root causes for the gaps

▼ the types of education programs, expertise, and process adjustments that will be needed to alleviate the gaps and to meet the needs of all customers

▼ how well the new processes being implemented meet the needs of the students, parents, teachers, school, and community

The Importance of Data

Businesses typically use data to determine customers' wants and needs. No matter what occupation we, or our students, aspire to, everyone can appreciate that fact. We can also appreciate the fact that businesses not properly analyzing and using data, more often than not, are not successful. Those of us who work in the business of education, however, may not be as familiar with the ways that *businesses* use *educational* data.

In many states, the prison systems look at the number of students not reading on grade level in grades two, three, or four to determine the number of prison cells to build ten years hence (*Lawmakers Move to Improve Literacy,* 2001). The fact that the prison system can use this prediction formula with great accuracy should make us all cringe, but the critical point is that if businesses can use educational data for predictions, so can educators. Not only can we predict, we can use the same data to *prevent* undesirable results from happening. Nothing would make educators happier than to hear that prison systems do not need as many cells because more students are being successful in school and, therefore, in life.

Schools in the United States have a long history of adopting innovations one after another as they are introduced. Very few schools take the time to understand the needs of the children being served. Few take the time to understand the impact current processes have on these children. Few take the time to determine the root causes of recurring problems, or to measure and analyze the impact of implementing new approaches. Fewer still use sound information to build and stick with a solid long-term plan that will improve learning for all students. Across our country, we have found that schools spend an average of about two years engaged in their school improvement efforts. The sad fact is that most schools are already changing their plans before some schools in their district start implementing all plans. Is it any wonder that nothing seems to generate results for these schools?

We find a different story among the schools that measure and analyze the impact of implementing new approaches. These schools know if what they are doing is working and, if not, why not. These schools also stick with their efforts to create change long after most schools have switched to new efforts. These schools get results.

Using data can make an enormous difference in school reform efforts by improving school processes and student learning. Data can help to—

- ▼ replace hunches and hypotheses with facts concerning what changes are needed

- ▼ facilitate a clear understanding of the gaps between where the school is and where the school wants to be

- ▼ identify the root causes of these gaps, so the school can solve the problem and not just treat the symptom

- ▼ understand the impact of processes on the student population

- ▼ ensure equity in program participation

- ▼ assess needs to target services on important issues

- ▼ provide information to eliminate ineffective practices

- ▼ ensure the effective and efficient uses of dollars

- ▼ show if school goals and objectives are being accomplished

- ▼ ascertain if the school staffs are *walking the talk*

If businesses can use educational data for predictions, so can educators. Not only can we predict, we can use the same data to "prevent" undesirable results from happening.

- ▼ promote understanding of the impact of efforts, processes, and progress

- ▼ generate answers for the community related to: *What are we getting for our children by investing in the school's methods, programs, and processes?*

- ▼ continuously improve all aspects of the learning organization

- ▼ predict and prevent failures

- ▼ predict and ensure successes

Barriers to Using Data

Schools do not deliberately ignore data. Typically, schools say, "We have lots of data; we just do not know what data to use, or how or when to use them." When school personnel first get interested in data and want to do more with the data they have, they often hit the proverbial brick wall.

While many schools gather data, barriers begin with attempts to analyze the data to help improve teaching and learning. Barriers can pop-up anywhere and for a variety of reasons:

- ▼ In contrast to the work culture in business, the work culture in education usually focuses on programs, and not results data.

- ▼ Few people in schools and districts are adequately trained to gather and analyze data or to establish and maintain databases.

  - ◆ Teachers (and administrators, who are mostly former teachers) have not been trained in data analysis

  - ◆ Some teachers see data analysis as another thing that takes away from teaching

- ▼ Administrators and teachers do not see gathering and analyzing data as part of their jobs.

  - ◆ District personnel have job definitions that often do not include, as a priority, helping individual schools with data.

- ▼ Gathering data is perceived to be a waste of time (after all, we are here every day—we know what the problems are!).

- ▼ Schools do not have databases that allow for easy access and analysis of data.

  - ◆ Computer systems are outdated and inadequate; appropriate, user friendly software is not available.

- ▼ Professional learning for teachers to understand why data are important and how data can make a difference in their teaching is often sorely lacking.
- ▼ Data are not used systematically from the state to the regional and local levels, nor are they used particularly well.
  - ◆ State legislatures keeps changing the rules.
- ▼ School personnel have had only negative experiences with data.
  - ◆ There is a perception that data are collected for someone else's purposes.
  - ◆ Confusion exists regarding which data should be the focus of analyses.
- ▼ There are not enough good examples of schools gathering, maintaining, and benefiting from the use of data.

Whatever it is that keeps us from assessing our progress and products adequately, we must learn to listen, to observe, and to gather data from all sources that will help us *know* how we are doing, where we are going, and how we can get there.

> *We must learn to listen, to observe, and to gather data from all sources that will help us "know" how we are doing, where we are going, and how we can get there.*

The Purposes of this Book

This book has three purposes. The first is to provide a learning opportunity for readers. The analyses provided in these chapters are laboratories for learning— authentic tasks, if you will. The analyses are case studies, complete with study questions. The second and main purpose is to show real analyses, using a continuous school improvement planning model, that can be used to understand, explain, and continuously improve learning for students in high schools. The third purpose is to provide tools to do these analyses with your school or district. The analysis tools are found on the accompanying CD.

The Structure of this Book

Using Data to Improve Student Learning in High Schools begins with an overview of why data are important to continuous school improvement. Chapter 2 defines what data are important to have in comprehensive data analysis. It also discusses the intersections of four major data measures in terms of different levels of analyses that can be created using these measures. Chapter 3 describes how to get started and how data fit into a continuous school improvement planning model. Chapters 4 through 7 present an example school analysis using this continuous school improvement planning model, and show how the model assists in understanding what the school is doing that is working or not working for its students.

Chapter 4 focuses on the example school's demographic data to answer the question, *Who are we?*, and to establish the context of the school.

Chapter 5 uses the example school's perceptions and process data to answer the question, *How do we do business?*, in terms of its work culture and organizational climate.

Where are we now? is the heart of Chapter 6. Ways to measure student learning are defined; analyses that can be made with different measures and their uses are discussed in this chapter. The example school's data assist us with understanding how to analyze state assessment results.

Chapter 7 discusses and shows gap and root cause analyses, answering the questions, *What are the gaps?* and *What are the root causes of the gaps?*

Chapter 8 synthesizes the analyses conducted in Chapters 4 through 7 and provides implications for the example school's continuous school improvement plan. A plan that grew out of this data analysis example is shown.

Questions to guide the study of the information presented in the chapters are included at the end of chapters 2 through 8, followed by the author's analyses. These files are also found on the CD.

Chapter 9 provides a brief summary and discussion of the example school's results. As the book concludes, typical process issues, such as *who does the analysis work, the role of the administrator, databases,* and *recommendations on how to get student learning increases* are discussed.

The questionnaires, the *Continuous Improvement Continuums,* and related tools used by the example school are found on the CD, along with complete analyses, analysis templates, and questionnaire narratives, as well as other *Education for the Future* questionnaires. Whenever ⬤ appears in the text, it means that file is on the CD. The specific name of the file (in parenthesis) follows the CD icon. A list of CD files related to each chapter appears at the end of the chapter. A complete index of CD contents appears in the Appendix.

A comprehensive *Glossary of Terms* commonly used in data analysis and assessment, and other terms used in this book, is located just before the references and resources list.

Summary

Using Data to Improve Student Learning in High Schools illustrates the basic steps in conducting data analysis to inform continuous school improvement planning in high schools. Readers will understand what data to gather, how to analyze the data, what the analyses look like, and how the analyses can inform a school's continuous school improvement plan. Tools to help any school do this work, regardless of grade levels, are provided on the accompanying CD.

What Data Are Important?

If the purpose of school is to ensure that all students learn, what data will help schools understand if they are effectively carrying out their purpose? What data analyses will help schools know if all students are learning?

Chapter 2

Learning takes place neither in isolation, nor only at school. Multiple measures must be considered and used in an ongoing fashion (formative) to understand the multifaceted world of learning from the perspective of everyone involved. Using more than one method of assessment allows students to demonstrate their full range of abilities, and collecting data on *multiple occasions* provides students several opportunities to demonstrate their various abilities. If you want to know if the school is achieving its purpose and how to continually improve all aspects of the school, multiple measures—gathered from varying points of view—must be used.

The major job of every school is *student learning.* Staff must think through the factors that impact student learning to determine other data requirements. We need to ask students what they like about the way they learn at school and how they learn best. *School processes,* such as programs and instructional strategies, need to be described to understand their impact in helping all staff optimize the learning of all students.

Because students neither learn only at school nor only through teachers, we need to know about the learning environment from the parent and community perspective. Schools may also need to know employer perceptions of the abilities and skills of former students.

But will these data provide enough information to determine how well the school is meeting the needs of all students? Other factors over which we have little or no control, such as background or *demographics,* impact student learning. These data are crucial to our understanding of whom we serve, and whether or not our educational services are meeting the needs of every student.

Analyses of *demographics, perceptions, student learning,* and *school processes* provide a powerful picture that will help us understand the school's impact on student achievement. When used together, these measures give schools the information they need to improve teaching and learning and to get positive results.

In Figure 2.1, these four major categories of data are shown as overlapping circles. (MMgraphic.pdf) This figure illustrates the different types of information one can gain from individual measures and the enhanced levels of analyses that can be gained from the intersections of the measures.

Figure 2.1

Multiple Measures of Data

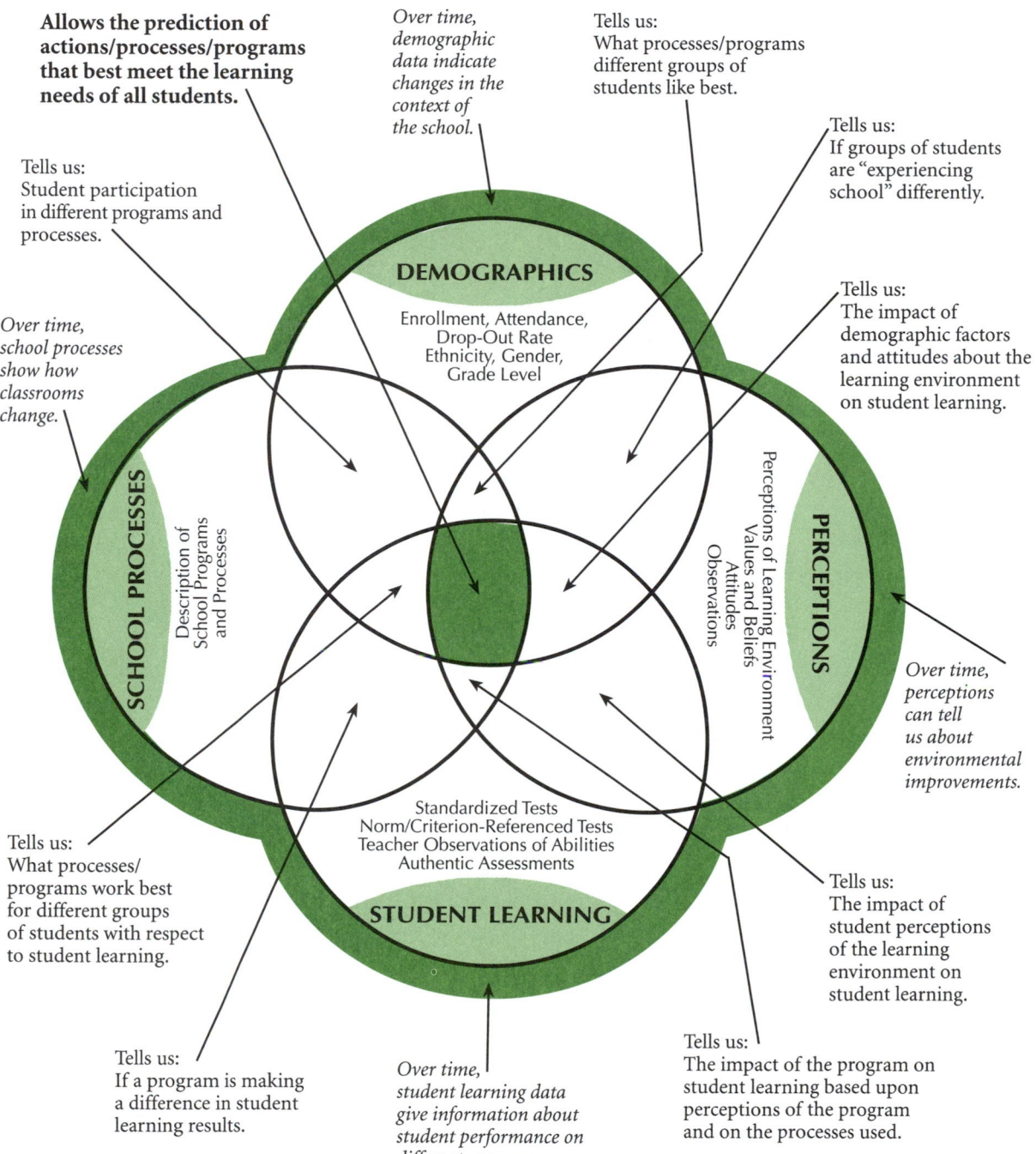

Allows the prediction of actions/processes/programs that best meet the learning needs of all students.

Over time, demographic data indicate changes in the context of the school.

Tells us:
What processes/programs different groups of students like best.

Tells us:
Student participation in different programs and processes.

Tells us:
If groups of students are "experiencing school" differently.

Over time, school processes show how classrooms change.

Tells us:
The impact of demographic factors and attitudes about the learning environment on student learning.

DEMOGRAPHICS

Enrollment, Attendance, Drop-Out Rate Ethnicity, Gender, Grade Level

SCHOOL PROCESSES

Description of School Programs and Processes

PERCEPTIONS

Perceptions of Learning Environment Values and Beliefs Attitudes Observations

Over time, perceptions can tell us about environmental improvements.

Standardized Tests
Norm/Criterion-Referenced Tests
Teacher Observations of Abilities
Authentic Assessments

STUDENT LEARNING

Tells us:
What processes/ programs work best for different groups of students with respect to student learning.

Tells us:
The impact of student perceptions of the learning environment on student learning.

Tells us:
If a program is making a difference in student learning results.

Over time, student learning data give information about student performance on different measures.

Tells us:
The impact of the program on student learning based upon perceptions of the program and on the processes used.

One measure, by itself, gives useful information. Comprehensive measures, used together and over time, provide much richer information. Ultimately, schools need to be able to predict what they must do to meet the needs of all the students they have, or will have in the future. The information gleaned from the intersections of these four measures (demographics, perceptions, student learning, and school processes), helps us to define the questions we want to ask, and focuses us on what data are necessary in order to find the answers.

Levels of Analysis

Different levels of analysis reveal answers to questions at varying depths of understanding. Each of the four measures, on its own, gives valuable descriptive information. However, more and better quality information can be found by digging deeper into the data through different levels of analysis in which one type of measure is analyzed and compared with other measures, over time.

We will discuss ten levels of analysis. Each level builds on the previous one to show how past data and intersections of measures provide more comprehensive information than a single measure of data taken one time. If you feel you are only at level one, hang in there; this book and your own work will help you get to level ten.

Note: Unless otherwise specified, *over time* refers to no less than three years. Definitions of terms appear in the Glossary at the back of the book.

Level 1: Snapshots of Measures

Level one refers to the four major measures of data, shown in Figure 2.1, in their current state and independent of each other.

Demographic data provide descriptive information about the school community, such as enrollment, attendance, grade level, ethnicity, gender, and native language. Demographic data are the part of our educational system over which we have no control. From them, however, we can observe trends and glean information for purposes of prediction and planning. Demographic data give us a glimpse of the system and how the school organizes its system.

Perceptions data help us understand what students, parents, staff, and others think about the learning environment. Perceptions can be gathered through questionnaires, interviews, focus groups, and/or observations. Perceptions are important because peoples' actions reflect what they believe, perceive, or think about different topics. Perceptions data can also tell us what is possible.

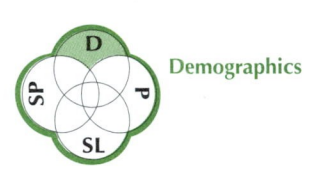

Demographics

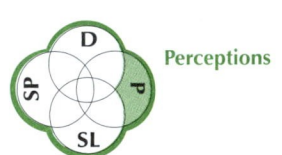

Perceptions

Student Learning describes the outcomes of our educational system in terms of standardized test results, grade point averages, standards assessments, and authentic assessments. Schools often use a variety of student learning measurements separately, sometimes without thinking about how these measurements are interrelated. Schools normally think of multiple measures as looking only at different measures of student learning, rather than including demographics, perceptions, and school processes.

School Processes define what we are doing to help students learn: how we group, teach, and assess students. School processes include programs, instruction and assessment strategies, and other classroom practices. To change the results schools are getting, teachers and school personnel must document these processes and align them with the results they are getting in order to understand what to improve to get different results, and to share their successes with others.

Looking at each of the four measures separately, we get snapshots of data in isolation from any other data at the school level. At this level we can answer questions such as—

- ▼ How many students are enrolled in the school this year? *(Demographics)*
- ▼ How satisfied are parents, students, and/or staff with the learning environment? *(Perceptions)*
- ▼ How did students at the school score on a test? *(Student Learning)*
- ▼ What programs are operating in the school this year? *(School Processes)*

Level 2: Measures, Over Time

At the second level, we start digging deeper into each of the measures by looking *over time* (i.e., at least three years) to answer questions, such as, but not limited to—

- ▼ How has enrollment in the school changed over the past five years? *(Demographics)*
- ▼ How have student perceptions of the learning environment changed, over time? *(Perceptions)*
- ▼ Are there differences in student scores on standardized tests over the years? *(Student Learning)*
- ▼ What programs have operated in the school during the past five years? *(School Processes)*

Different levels of
analysis reveal answers
to questions at varying
depths of understanding.

Level 3: Two or More Variables Within Measures

Looking at *more than one type of data* within each of the circles gives us a better view of the learning organization (e.g., one year's standardized test subscores compared with performance assessment measures). We can answer questions such as—

▼ What percentage of the students currently at the school are fluent speakers of languages other than English? *(Demographics)*

▼ Are staff, student, and parent perceptions of the learning environment in agreement? *(Perceptions)*

▼ Are students' standardized test scores consistent with teacher-assigned grades and performance assessment rubrics? *(Student Learning)*

▼ What are the processes in the school's mathematics and science programs? *(School Processes)*

Level 4: Two or More Variables Within One Type of Measure, Over Time

Level 4 takes similar measures as Level 3, *across time* (e.g., standardized test subscores and performance assessment measures compared over the past four years), and allows us to answer deeper questions such as—

▼ How has the enrollment of non-English-speaking ninth or tenth graders changed in the past three years? *(Demographics)*

▼ Are staff, students, and parents more or less satisfied with the learning environment now than they were in previous years? *(Perceptions)*

▼ Over the past three years, how do teacher-assigned grades and standardized test scores compare? *(Student Learning)*

▼ How have the processes used in the school's mathematics and science programs changed over time? *(School Processes)*

Level 5: Intersection of Two Types of Measures

Level 5 begins the *intersections across two circles* (e.g., last year's standardized test results by ethnicity). Level 5 helps us to answer questions such as—

▼ Do students who attend school every day perform better on the state assessment than students who miss more than five days per month? *(Demographics by Student Learning)*

Demographics by Student Learning

▼ How long does it take for non-English-speaking students to be redesignated as fluent English speakers? *(Demographics by School Processes)*

Demographics by School Processes

▼ Is there a gender difference in students' perceptions of the learning environment? *(Perceptions by Demographics)*

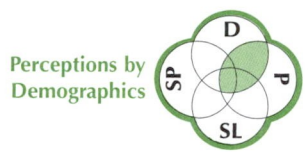
Perceptions by Demographics

▼ Do students with positive attitudes about school do better academically, as measured by the state assessment? *(Perceptions by Student Learning)*

Perceptions by Student Learning

▼ Are there differences in how students enrolled in different programs perceive the learning environment? *(Perceptions by School Processes)*

Perceptions by School Processes

▼ Do students identified as gifted get the highest scores on the state standardized test? *(Student Learning by School Processes)*

Student Learning by School Processes

Level 6: Intersection of Two Measures, Over Time

Looking at the *intersection of two of the measures over time* allows us to see trends as they develop (e.g., standardized achievement scores disaggregated by ethnicity over the past three years can help us see if the differences between scores, by ethnicity, is truly a trend or an initial fluctuation). This intersection also begins to show the relationship of the multiple measures and why it is so important to look at all the measures together.

At Level 6 we are looking at the intersection of two of the circles over time. The questions we can answer at this level include, as examples—

▼ How have students of different ethnicities scored on standardized tests over the past three years? *(Demographics by Student Learning)*

▼ Are all subgroups of students represented in special education, Title I, and gifted classes? *(Demographics by School Processes)*

▼ Have parent perceptions of the learning environment changed since the implementation of the new mathematics program? *(Perceptions by School Processes)*

Level 7: Intersection of Three Measures

As we *intersect three of the measures* at the school level (e.g., student learning measures disaggregated by ethnicity compared to student questionnaire responses disaggregated by ethnicity), the types of questions that we are able to answer include the following:

Demographics by Perceptions by Student Learning

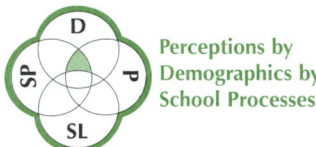

Perceptions by Demographics by School Processes

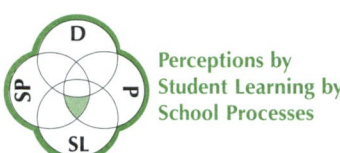

Perceptions by Student Learning by School Processes

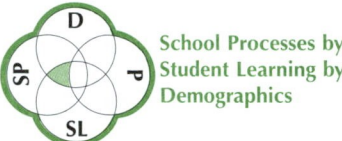

School Processes by Student Learning by Demographics

▼ Do students of different ethnicities perceive the learning environment differently, and are their scores on standardized achievement tests consistent with these perceptions? *(Demographics by Perceptions by Student Learning)*

▼ What instructional process(es) did the students who were redesignated from English-learners to English-speaking enjoy most in their all-English classrooms this year? *(Perceptions by Demographics by School Processes)*

▼ Is there a difference in students' reports of what they like most about the school by whether or not they participate in extracurricular activities? Do students who participate in extracurricular activities have higher grade-point averages than students who do not participate in extracurricular activities? *(Perceptions by Student Learning by School Processes)*

▼ Which program is making the biggest difference with respect to student achievement for at-risk students this year, and is one group of students responding "better" to the processes? *(School Processes by Student Learning by Demographics)*

Level 8: Intersection of Three Measures, Over Time

Looking at *three measures over time* allows us to see trends, to begin to understand the learning environment from the students' perspectives, and to know how to deliver instruction to get the desired results from and for *all* students.

Level 8 takes Level 7 intersections over time (e.g., standardized achievement scores disaggregated by ethnicity compared to student questionnaires disaggregated by ethnicity, for the past four years). Level 8 allows us to answer the following types of questions:

▼ What programs do all types of students like the most every year? *(Demographics by Perceptions by School Processes)*

▼ Have the processes used to teach English to English-learning students been consistent across grade levels so each student is able to build on her/his abilities? *(Demographics by Student Learning by School Processes)*

Level 9: Intersection of All Four Measures

Our ultimate analysis is the *intersection of all four measures* at the school level (e.g., standardized achievement tests disaggregated by program, by gender, within grade level, compared to questionnaire results for students by program, by gender, within grade level). These intersections allow us to answer questions such as—

▼ Given the population that attends this school, are our programs and strategies meeting their needs in every grade level, as measured by student learning results and everyone's perspective? *(Demographics by Perceptions by School Processes by Student Learning)*

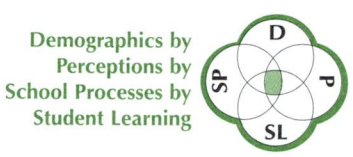

Demographics by
Perceptions by
School Processes by
Student Learning

Level 10: Intersection of All Four Measures, Over Time

It is not until we *intersect all four circles,* at the school level and *over time,* that we are able to answer questions that will predict if the actions, processes, and programs that we are establishing will meet the needs of all students. With this intersection, we can answer the ultimate question:

▼ Based on whom we have as students, how they prefer to learn, and what programs they are in, are all students learning at the same rate? *(Student Learning by Demographics by Perceptions by School Processes)*

Do note that there might not always be a way to display these intersections in one comprehensive table or graph. Often, multiple graphs and/or tables are used together to observe intersection relationships.

It is important to look at each measure by itself to understand where the school is right now and over time. Intersecting the measures can give a broader look at the data and help everyone understand all facets of the school. Figure 2.2 summarizes two, three, and four-way intersections. 📀 (IntrscTbl.pdf) On the CD are a *Data Discovery Activity* and two activities for creating questions from intersecting data, *Intersections Activity* and *Creating Intersections Activity.* 📀 (ACTDiscv.pdf, ACTIntrs.pdf, and ACTCreat.pdf) Also on the CD are the *Data Analysis Presentation,* a *Microsoft PowerPoint* slideshow overview to use with your staffs in getting started analyzing your data, and three articles entitled *Multiple Measures* (Bernhardt, 1998), *Intersections: New Routes Open when One Type of Data Crosses Another* (Bernhardt, 2000), and *No Schools Left Behind* (Bernhardt, 2003). 📀 (DASlides.ppt, MMeasure.pdf, Intersct.pdf, and NoSchls.pdf)

Figure 2.2

Summary of Data Intersections

Intersections	Can tell us —
Two-way Intersections	
◆ Demographics by student learning	◆ If subgroups of students perform differently on student learning measures
◆ Demographics by perceptions	◆ If subgroups of students are experiencing school differently
◆ Demographics by school processes	◆ If all subgroups of students are represented in the different programs and processes offered by the school
◆ Student learning by school processes	◆ If different programs are achieving similar student learning results
◆ Student learning by perceptions	◆ If student perceptions of the learning environment have an impact on their learning results
◆ Perceptions by school processes	◆ If people are perceiving programs and processes differently
Three-way Intersections	
◆ Demographics by student learning by perceptions	◆ The impact demographic factors and attitudes about the learning environment have on student learning
◆ Demographics by student learning by school processes	◆ What processes or programs work best for different subgroups of students measured by student learning results
◆ Demographics by perceptions by school processes	◆ What programs or processes different students like best, or the impact different programs or processes have on student attitudes
◆ Student learning by school processes by perceptions	◆ The relationship between the processes students prefer and learning results
Four-way Intersections	
◆ Demographics by student learning by perceptions by school processes	◆ What processes or programs have the greatest impact on subgroups of students' learning, according to student perceptions, and as measured by student learning results

Focusing the Data

Data analysis should not be about just gathering data. It is very easy to get *analysis paralysis* by spending time pulling data together and not spending time using the data. School-level data analyses should be about helping schools understand if they are achieving their guiding principles and meeting the needs of all students—and, if not, why not?

The guiding principles include the vision, created from the mission/purpose of the school and built from the values and beliefs of the school community, and standards—what we expect students to know and be able to do. Data analysis must focus on these guiding principles.

A focused data analysis process will enhance the continuous improvement process and provide comprehensive information about how the school is doing in relationship to its guiding principles.

A good way to avoid analysis paralysis is to consider using key questions that focus on the guiding principles, using the answers to these questions to guide your analyses.

The key questions used in this book are described in Chapter 3. The data we gather and analyze target the guiding principles of the school to achieve focused improvement. If this was not the case, the process could lead to nothing more than random acts of improvement, as shown in Figure 2.3.

> *Data analysis should not be about just gathering data. It is very easy to get "analysis paralysis" by spending time pulling data together and not spending time using the data.*

Figure 2.3
Focusing the Data

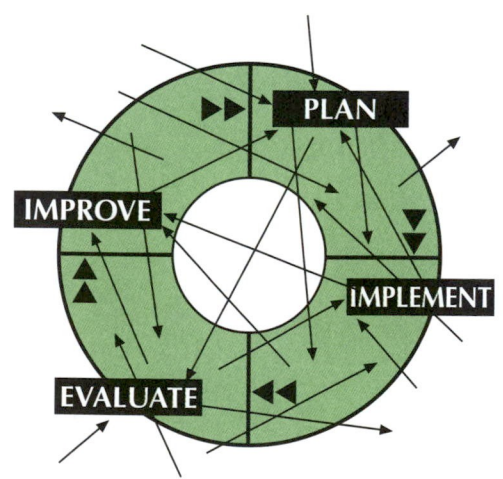

Random Acts of Improvement

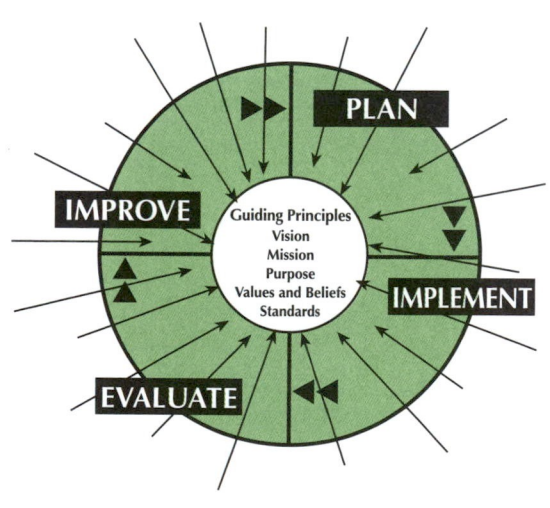

Focused Improvement

These analyses flow comfortably from questions that staff and administrators naturally ask to learn if the purpose for the school is being met. The good news is that, by looking at trends of the intersected four measures, schools will have the same information required of program evaluations and needs analyses. These intersections can tell schools just about everything they would want to know, and the intersections are easy for everyone to understand.

Study Questions for What Data Are Important?

As mentioned previously, the study questions at the end of the chapters are intended to guide your thinking about your own data analysis and/or to analyze the example school's results. (Ch2Qs.pdf) Take some time to consider these or other questions to get the maximum benefit from this publication.

Consider how you might identify intersections in your school's data and what those intersections could tell you. Use the spaces below to write at least one question you can answer about your school with these intersections, and what data you need to answer these questions. (Examples appear in the table to get you started.)

Intersections	Questions	What data do you have or need to answer the questions?
Demographics by Student Learning	*Is there a relationship between attendance and standardized test results?*	*Number of days attended and state standardized test results for each student.*
Demographics by School Processes	*Is participation in advanced placement programs representative of all students?*	*Advanced placement enrollment by gender, ethnicity, and indicators of poverty.*

Study Questions for What Data Are Important? *(Continued)*

Intersections	Questions	What data do you have or need to answer the questions?
Perceptions by Demographics	*Are all students perceiving the learning environment in the same way?*	*Student questionnaire results disaggregated by gender, by ethnicity, and/or by grade level.*
Perceptions by Student Learning	*Are the students who are getting the best grades the happiest with the learning environment?*	*Student grades by student perceptions.*
Perceptions by School Processes	*Are there differences in how students perceive the learning environment, based on whom they have as teachers?*	*Student perceptions disaggregated by teacher.*

Intersections	Questions	What data do you have or need to answer the questions?
Student Learning by School Processes	*Is there a difference in student achievement results by program participation?*	*Student achievement test results by program.*
Demographics by Perceptions by Student Learning	*What are the differences in student learning results based on whom we have as students and how they perceive the learning environment?*	*Student achievement test results disaggregated by gender and ethnicity, compared to student questionnaire results disaggregated by gender and ethnicity.*
Perceptions by Demographics by School Processes	*Are the students most satisfied with school being taught differently from students not satisfied with school, and who are they?*	*Student questionnaires disaggregated by gender, ethnicity, grade level, and program participation.*

Study Questions for What Data Are Important? *(Continued)*

Intersections	Questions	What data do you have or need to answer the questions?
Perceptions by Student Learning by School Processes	*What are the differences in student achievement results because of attitudes related to whom students have as teachers?*	*Student achievement results disaggregated by teacher, compared to student questionnaire results disaggregated by teacher.*
Demographics by Student Learning by School Processes	*What are the differences in student learning results based on who the students are and how they are taught algebra?*	*Student achievement algebra results, disaggregated by gender and ethnicity, and sorted by what program they are in and whom they have as a teacher.*
Student Learning by Demographics by Perceptions by School Processes	*What are the differences in the results we are getting, based on whom we have as students and how they are being taught? How would they prefer to learn?*	*Student achievement results, disaggregated by gender, ethnicity, grade level, and program, compared to student questionnaire results, disaggregated by gender, ethnicity, grade level, and program.*

Summary

Schools cannot use student achievement measures alone for continuous school improvement. Why? Because the *context* is missing! Relying on only one measure can mislead schools into thinking they are analyzing student learning in a comprehensive fashion. Just looking at student learning measures alone could, in fact, keep teachers from progressing and truly meeting the needs of students because they are not looking at the other elements that have a great impact on student learning and teaching.

If we want to get different results, we have to change the processes (e.g., instruction, system) that create the results. When we focus only on student learning measures, we see school personnel using their time figuring out how to look better on the student learning measures. We want school personnel to use their time to determine how to *do* better for *all* students. In order to do that, we must look at intersections of *demographic, perceptual, student learning,* and *school process* data, so we can understand the inter-relationships among these elements.

> *Just looking at student learning measures alone could, in fact, keep teachers from progressing and truly meeting the needs of students, because they are not looking at the other elements that have a great impact on student learning and teaching.*

On the CD Related to this Chapter

▼ *Multiple Measures of Data* Graphic (MMgraphc.pdf)
This is Figure 2.1 in a PDF (portable document file) for printing.

▼ *Summary of Data Intersections* (IntrscTbl.pdf)
This is Figure 2.2 in a PDF for your use with staff.

▼ *Data Discovery Activity* (ACTDiscv.pdf)
The purpose of this activity is to look closely at examples of data and to discover specific information and patterns of information, both individually and as a group.

▼ *Intersections Activity* (ACTIntrs.pdf)
The purpose of this activity is to motivate school improvement teams to think about the questions they can answer when they cross different data variables. It is also designed to help teams focus their data-gathering efforts so they are not collecting everything and anything.

▼ *Creating Intersections Activity* (ACTCreat.pdf)
This activity is similar to the *Intersections Activity.* The purpose is to have participants "grow" their intersections.

▼ *Data Analysis* Presentation (DASlides.ppt)
This *Microsoft PowerPoint* presentation is an overview to use with your staffs in getting started with data analysis.

▼ Articles (Folder)
These read-only articles, by Victoria L. Bernhardt, are useful in workshops or in getting started on data with staff.

♦ *Multiple Measures* (MMeasure.pdf)
This article summarizes why, and what, data are important to continuous school improvement.

♦ *Intersections: New Routes Open when One Type of Data Crosses Another* (Intersct.pdf)
This article, published in the *Journal of Staff Development* (Winter 2000), discusses how much richer your data analyses can be when you intersect multiple data variables.

♦ *No Schools Left Behind* (NoSchls.pdf)
This article, published in *Educational Leadership* (February 2003), summarizes how to improve learning for *all* students.

▼ Study Questions Related to *What Data are Important?* (Ch2Qs.doc)
These study questions will help you better understand the information provided in Chapter 2. This template file can be printed for use with staff members as they think through the data questions they want to answer and the data they will need to gather to answer the questions.

How does a school get started with comprehensive data analysis work? How do you and others at your school know if what you are currently doing for students is making a difference with respect to what you expect students to know and be able to do? How do you know which strategies ought to be the focus of your school improvement efforts?

If your school is like 95% of the schools in this country, my hunch is that your school improvement committee looks at student results on the state student assessment, attempts to explain the results to the school board and to the public, and then prepares school improvement plans to get better results next year. Your school might have special externally funded grants or programs that require the collection and analysis of data. Those who are providing the funds want progress described. Questionnaires are then sent out each year and are analyzed *for the funders,* not for those who implement the programs.

At the classroom level, some teachers have adopted rubrics and performance assessment measures. They might know their students are learning, but performance assessment measures are not easy to talk about in terms of an entire class, let alone schoolwide, progress. It can be done, but it is difficult.

Unfortunately, the scenarios described above are all too familiar in schools across the United States. What is starting to emerge, however, is a connection between the analysis of data and the school improvement plan to ensure that every student is learning. We want to see data about all parts of the school gathered and analyzed on a regular basis—not just when an external force requires it. We want members of the school community to understand how to use data to accurately inform their customers and other individuals of how the school is doing. Finally, we especially want schools to analyze data to understand which strategies are not working and what to do differently to get different results.

This chapter describes a process for analyzing data to plan for continuous schoolwide improvement. Data analysis in schools may be approached in many ways, and the effectiveness of school processes may be measured in many ways. The approach taken here is a systems approach: we want to gather and analyze data that will help us understand the *system that produces the results we are getting.* We also want to move our school improvement efforts from random acts of improvement to focused improvement that centers on our ultimate purpose—improving learning for *all* students.

Analyzing Data Using a Continuous School Improvement Planning Model

Data analysis is very logical. We need to think about what we want to know and why, gather the data we have or need, and analyze the data to answer the questions that will lead to understanding not only the effectiveness of what we are doing, but also what we need to do differently to get different results.

One approach to data analysis is to analyze and use data for continuous school improvement planning. The *Multiple Measures of Data,* Figure 2.1 in Chapter 2, can be reorganized into a series of logical questions that can guide the analysis, as illustrated in the flowchart in Figure 3.1. If the data that are listed next to the questions in the boxes were gathered satisfactorily, one would be on the right track toward discovering how to continuously improve the school or district. Those questions, the data required, and discussion follow the flowchart.

Continuous School Improvement Planning via The School Portfolio

Figure 3.1 shows the logical questions one could ask to plan for continuous school improvement, the data needed to answer the questions, and where that data would be housed if a school was creating a school portfolio. (CSIPlang.pdf and CSIdscr.pdf) *The School Portfolio* is a framework for continuous school improvement (Bernhardt, 1999). Gathering evidence around the seven categories of a school portfolio results in the story of your school and becomes a self-assessment. The seven categories of a school portfolio are:

- ▼ Information and Analysis
- ▼ Student Achievement
- ▼ Quality Planning
- ▼ Professional Development
- ▼ Leadership
- ▼ Partnership Development
- ▼ Continuous Improvement and Evaluation

On the CD is a *Microsoft PowerPoint* slideshow overview file, *The School Portfolio Presentation,* to use with your staffs in getting started on the school portfolio. (SPSlides.ppt)

Figure 3.1

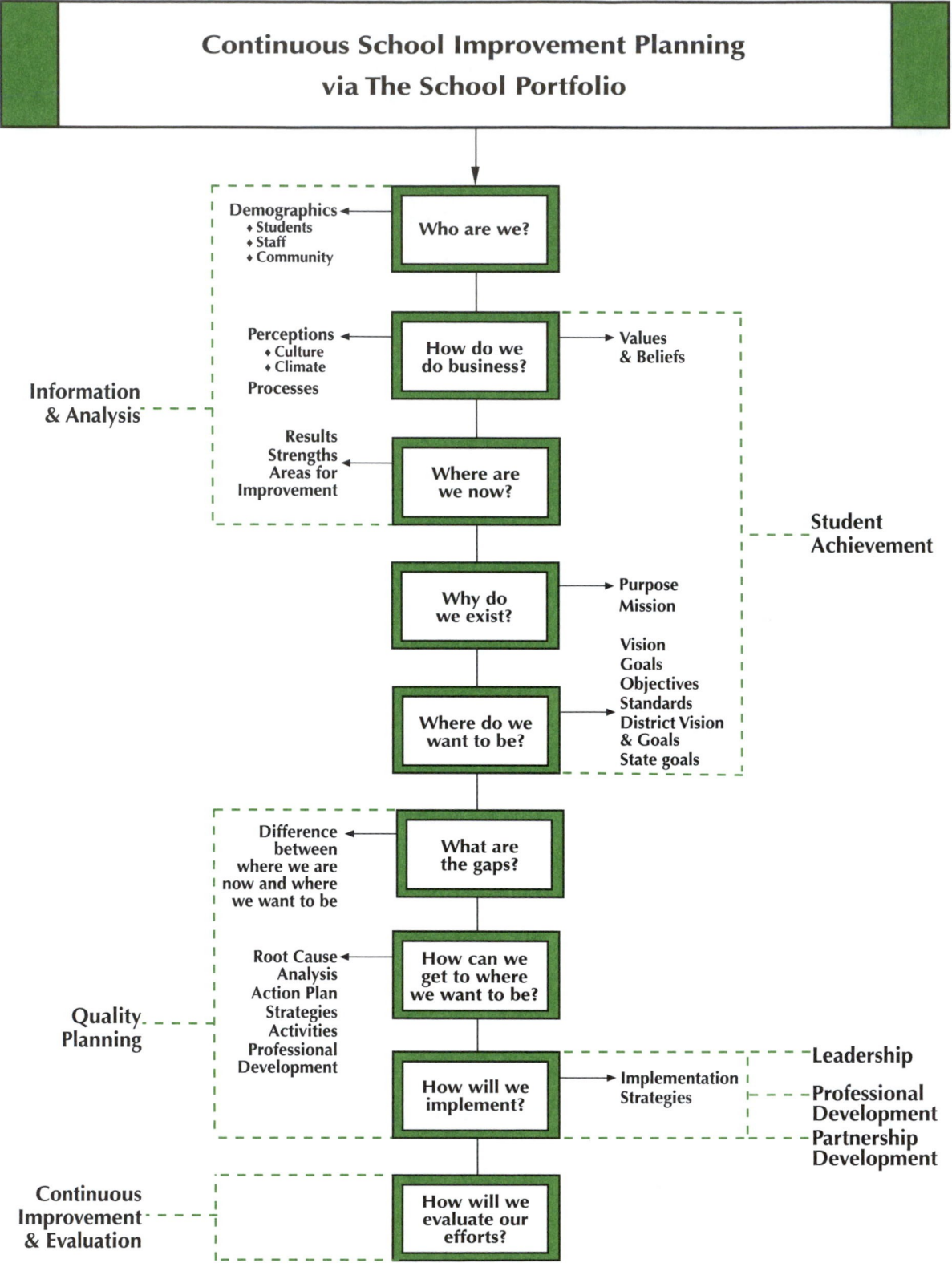

Question 1: Who are we?

Continuous school improvement planning begins by asking a question that can be answered with demographic data: *Who are we?* Specifically—

▼ *Who are the students?*

▼ *Who is the staff?*

▼ *Who is the community?*

The answers to the first questions are important in understanding the school's and district's students, staff, and community, to determine future needs. These answers are critical for continuous school improvement planning, as they establish the *context* of the classroom, school, district, and community. It is important to understand how student and community populations have changed over time, as these changes are indicators of student characteristics to plan for in the future. Staff longevity within the system and plans for retirement might lead to establishing different types of school improvement plans, as would staff experiences, certification, and levels of education. Demographic changes can also help explain results. This question is further studied in Chapter 4.

Question 2: How do we do business?

The second question, *How do we do business?*, is answered through data gathered to assess the school's culture, climate, and organizational processes. Perceptual data, school processes, and values and beliefs fall into this category. Staff values and beliefs, most often assessed through questionnaires and/or determined during visioning processes, can tell a staff what is possible to implement and if team building or specific professional learning is necessary. Student and parent questionnaires can add different perspectives to the answers generated from staff data. An assessment on the *Education for the Future Continuous Improvement Continuums*[1] can provide an overview of where the staff believes the school is and where it can go, with respect to continuous school improvement. Chapter 5 reviews more on this question.

---

[1] *Note:* The *Education for the Future Continuous Improvement Continuums* (CICs) can be found in the back of this book (Appendix B) and on the accompanying CD. The CICs are a type of assessment criteria rubric made up of seven key, interrelated, and overlapping components of systemic change, representing the theoretical flow of systemic school and/or district improvement. The *Continuums* take the theory and spirit of continuous school improvement, interweave educational research, and offer practical meaning to the components that must change simultaneously and systemically. A CIC analysis appears in Chapter 5.

Question 3: Where are we now?

The third data question, *Where are we now?*, requires a synthesis of student achievement, perceptual, demographic, and school process data to describe results and to uncover strengths and areas for improvement. We start by examining data for patterns and trends across the four multiple measures. Chapter 6 reviews the student achievement part of this question, including different types of student achievement assessments and terms associated with them.

Question 4: Why do we exist?

Question number four can be answered by determining the purpose/mission of the school. One can determine how well the school is meeting its purpose by revisiting the results collected in questions one through three. This question is answered in-depth in other resources, such as, *The School Portfolio* (Bernhardt, 1999), and *The School Portfolio Toolkit* (Bernhardt, 2002).

Question 5: Where do we want to be?

A school defines its destination through its vision, goals, and standards. The school's destination falls under the umbrella of the district's vision, goals, and standards which, in turn, are aligned with the state vision, goals, and standards. One can determine how effective the vision is being implemented through the data used to answer questions one through four. This question is answered in-depth in other resources, such as, *The School Portfolio* (Bernhardt, 1999), and *The School Portfolio Toolkit* (Bernhardt, 2002).

Question 6: What are the gaps?

Gaps are the differences between *Where are we now?* and *Where do we want to be?* Gaps are determined by synthesizing the differences in the results the school is getting with its current processes, and the results the school wants to be getting for its students. It is important to dig deeply into each gap to uncover root causes, or the gap cannot be eliminated. Gaps and root causes are studied in Chapter 7.

Question 7: How can we get to where we want to be?

The answer to *How can we get to where we want to be?* is key to unlocking how the vision will be implemented, and how gaps will be eliminated. An action plan, consisting of strategies, activities, people responsible, due dates, timelines, and resources, needs to be addressed to implement and achieve the vision and goals and to eliminate the root causes of the gaps. Chapter 8 shows how one can take the data analysis results and turn them into a continuous school improvement plan.

Question 8: How will we implement?

This question is answered in the action plan. The action plan includes how the vision will be implemented, monitored, evaluated, and improved. Action plans need to clarify how decisions will be made, identify professional learning required to learn new skills and gain new knowledge, and clarify the use of partners to achieve the vision. A school's leadership structure, professional learning strategies, and partnership development plan are important components of the answer to this question. Chapter 8 discusses what a plan would look like when it includes action for implementing, monitoring, evaluating, and improving the action plan.

Question 9: How will we evaluate our efforts?

Continuous Improvement and Evaluation are required to assess the alignment of all parts of the system to the vision and the results the learning organization is getting on an ongoing basis. All four data measures intersected to answer this question will assist with evaluating the continuously improving learning organization. Evaluation is a piece that needs to be built before implementation, not only at the end, to know if what a school is doing is making a real difference. How the action plan will be evaluated is a part of the plan which can be pulled out, enhanced, and monitored. This piece is described in Chapter 8.

The chapters that follow show how one school answered these questions with data as it conducted data analyses and built its continuous school improvement plan.

Study Questions for Getting Started

How will you get started with your school's continuous school improvement planning? What data do you have, or need to gather, to answer the questions discussed in this chapter? Fill in the blank cells in the tables that follow to guide your work. (Ch3Qs.pdf) Examples appear in the table for guidance.

Questions	What data do you have or need to answer the questions?	What other data do you have or need to gather?
Who are we?	*Student enrollment by grade, by gender, by ethnicity, by free/reduced lunch status, for five years.* *Number of teachers; number of years teaching by what grade level(s) and/or subject(s) they teach; which credentials teachers hold.*	*Information about predicted community changes.* *Administrator information, such as number of years in current position, and number of years teaching.*
How do we do business?	*Perceptions: student, staff, parent, and former student questionnaires.* *Education for the Future Continuous Improvement Continuums Assessment.*	
Where are we now?	*Student achievement results.* *Process data.*	

Questions	What data do you have or need to answer the questions?	What other data do you have or need to gather?
Why do we exist?	*Mission statement.* *Purpose of the school.*	
Where do we want to be?	*Vision.* *Goals.*	
What are the gaps? What are the root causes?	*Targeted proficiency levels for each subject area.* *Number and percentage of students not proficient in each subject area.* *Characteristics of the students not meeting proficiency.* *How these students scored.* *What they know and do not know.* *How they were taught.*	

Study Questions for Getting Started *(Continued)*

Questions	What data do you have or need to answer the questions?	What other data do you have or need to gather?
How can we get to where we want to be?	*Interventions.* *Professional learning activities.* *Timeline.*	
How will we implement?	*Implementation strategies.* *Leadership structure.* *How we meet together to talk about the vision.*	
How will we evaluate our efforts?	*Rethinking our results data.* *Monitoring and evaluating the plan.* *Understanding the effectiveness of strategies already in place.*	

Summary

Schools that are not gathering, analyzing, and using data in purposeful ways need to transform their thinking about data and start gathering, analyzing, and using data purposefully. Comprehensive data analyses focused on the continuous improvement of the entire school will result in school improvement plans that will improve learning for all students.

Logical questions can be used to guide the gathering, analysis, and use of data. Recommended questions include:

▼ *Who are we?*

▼ *How do we do business?*

▼ *Where are we now?*

▼ *Why do we exist?*

▼ *Where do we want to be?*

▼ *What are the gaps?* and *What are the root causes?*

▼ *How can we get to where we want to be?*

▼ *How will we implement?*

▼ *How will we evaluate our efforts?*

Comprehensive data analyses focused on the continuous improvement of the entire school will result in school improvement plans that will improve learning for all students.

On the CD Related to this Chapter

▼ *Continuous School Improvement Planning via the School Portfolio Graphic* (CSIPlang.pdf)
This read-only file displays the questions that can be answered to create a continuous school improvement plan. The data that can answer the questions, and where the answers would appear in the school portfolio, also appear on the graphic. In the book, it is Figure 3.1.

▼ *Continuous School Improvement Planning via the School Portfolio Description* (CSIdscr.pdf)
This read-only file shows Figure 3.1, along with its description.

▼ *The School Portfolio Presentation* (SPSlides.ppt)
This *PowerPoint* presentation is an overview to use with your staffs in getting started on *The School Portfolio.*

▼ Study Questions Related to *Getting Started* (Ch3Qs.doc)
These study questions will help you better understand the information provided in Chapter 3. This template file can be printed for use with staffs as you begin continuous school improvement planning. Answering the questions will help staffs determine the data needed to answer the questions discussed in this chapter.

Analyzing the Data:
Who Are We?

Chapter 4

Using the continuous school improvement planning model described in Chapter 3, our data analysis example begins with setting the context of the school by answering the question, *Who are we?* Demographic data are required to answer this question. Demographic data enable us to:

▼ *explain* and *understand* the school's context and results

▼ *disaggregate* other types of data, such as perceptual, process, and student learning data, to ensure all subgroups of students are being served

▼ *predict* and *prepare* for the students we will have in the near future

The demographic analyses for Big River High School are on the pages that follow. Please note the study questions on page 67 to assist in studying Big River's data. (Ch4Qs.doc) Also note that space is provided in the margins of the data pages to write your impressions about *strengths, challenges,* and *implications for the school improvement plan* as you review the data. It will help your work if you jot down your thoughts about what you are seeing in the data as you read. These first thoughts are placeholders until additional data validate the thoughts. When finished reading this chapter, think about other demographic data you wish the school would have had. At the end of the chapter, I share what I saw in the data. Graphing templates are found on the CD-ROM to help you create your school's demographic profile. (HighDemog.xls and HighProfil.doc)

Our Example School: Big River High School

Who Are We?

Big River High School is located in a metropolitan city on the west coast. The population of the city was a little less than 900,000 in the 2000 census. The median age of the residents at that time was 32.6 years. This city has approximately 276,598 households, with an average income of $70,243 per year. The unemployment rate in 2000 was 2.9%. As the economy experienced a downturn, so did the employment rate in this city. By 2003, the unemployment rate was 7%.

Industry in the area includes high technology companies. One out of every four workers in the county is employed in manufacturing. The education level of the metropolitan area workforce is one of the highest in the U.S.—67% of the workforce has some college education, and 48% have earned college degrees. This city has the lowest crime rate of any U.S. city with a population of 500,000 or more.

Ridgeview School District

Big River High School is part of the Ridgeview School District which currently serves 30,941 students in 42 schools (29 elementary, 7 middle, 6 senior high, and several alternative programs). The overall district enrollment has decreased 433 students over the past six years (Figure 4.1).

Figure 4.1

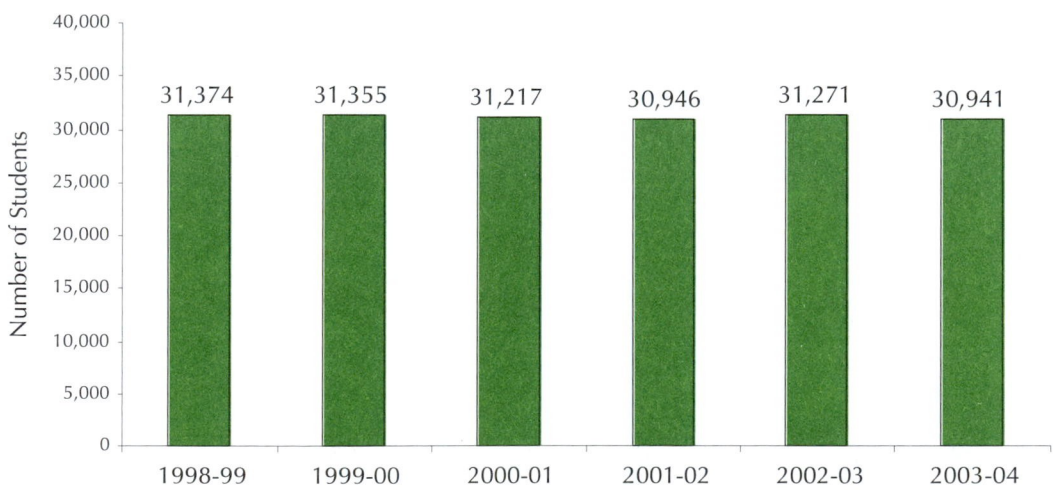

Ridgeview School District Student Enrollment
1999-00 to 2003-04

The district student enrollment by percent ethnicity for 2003-04 is shown in Figure 4.2. The pie chart shows that 51% of the district population is Hispanic. The remainder is made up of 29% White, 17% Asian, and 4% Black students.

Figure 4.2

Ridgeview School District
Student Enrollment by Percent Ethnicity[1]
2003-04 (*N*=30,941)

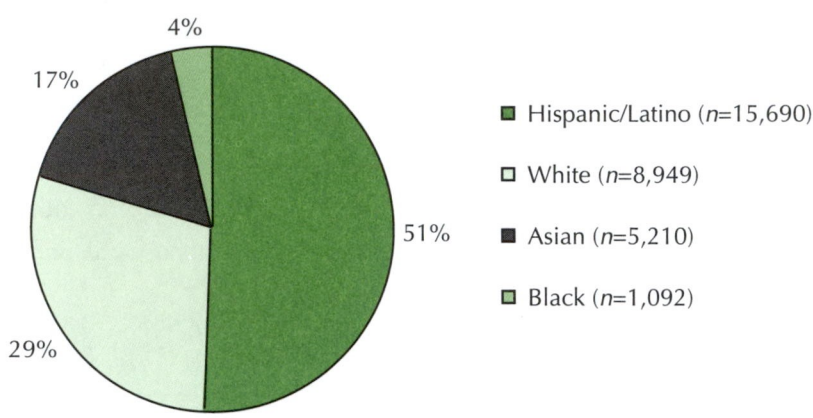

[1]The ethnicity/race categories used by this school, i.e., Black, White, Hispanic/Latino, Asian, are the federal categories used by this district and hopefully will not offend any ethnicity or race.

The district student enrollment by percent ethnicity since 1998-99 is shown in Figure 4.3. The graph shows the diversity of students has changed very little over time, overall.

Figure 4.3

Ridgeview School District
Percentage of Student Enrollment by Ethnicity
1998-99 to 2003-04

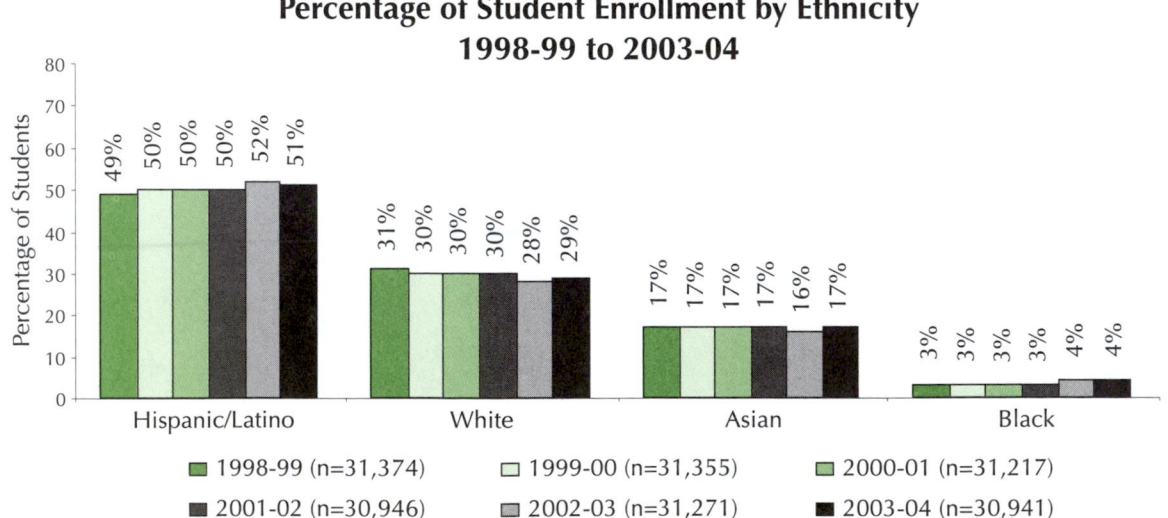

District enrollment by grade level for the past six years is shown in Figure 4.4.

Note: Looking at the same grade level over time is called grade level analysis.

Figure 4.4

**Ridgeview School District
By School Type and Grade Level, 1998-99 to 2003-04**

School Type	Grade Level	1998-99	1999-00	2000-01	2001-02	2002-03	2003-04
Preschool		195	194	196	202	217	222
Elementary	Kindergarten	2,571	2,682	2,771	2,641	2,523	2,504
	Grade 1	2,877	2,668	2,732	2,771	2,631	2,552
	Grade 2	2,713	2,799	2,664	2,670	2,588	2,527
	Grade 3	2,641	2,709	2,737	2,579	2,576	2,598
	Grade 4	2,466	2,593	2,593	2,596	2,484	2,511
	Grade 5	2,422	2,400	2,534	2,507	2,484	2,384
	Total	**15,885**	**16,045**	**16,227**	**15,966**	**15,503**	**15,293**
Middle	Grade 6	2,395	2,364	2,382	2,471	2,393	2,480
	Grade 7	2,393	2,396	2,317	2,304	2,407	2,367
	Grade 8	2,249	2,272	2,303	2,234	2,252	2,332
	Total	**7,037**	**7,032**	**7,002**	**7,009**	**7,052**	**7,179**
High	Grade 9	2,307	2,268	2,258	2,253	2,264	2,364
	Grade 10	2,264	2,316	2,185	2,282	2,344	2,377
	Grade 11	2,029	1,977	1,993	1,942	2,062	2,161
	Grade 12	1,622	1,736	1,690	1,765	1,721	1,892
	Total	**8,222**	**8,297**	**8,126**	**8,242**	**8,391**	**8,794**
District All		**31,374**	**31,355**	**31,217**	**30,946**	**31,271**	**30,941**

The percentage of district student enrollment by socio-economic status (SES) has changed very little over the past six years (Figure 4.5). There has been a higher percentage of "high SES" than "low SES" every year. "Low SES" includes students who qualify for free/reduced lunch, and/or who have parents who did not complete high school.

Figure 4.5

Ridgeview School District Student Enrollment
Percentage of Students Qualifying for Free/Reduced Lunch
1998-99 to 2003-04

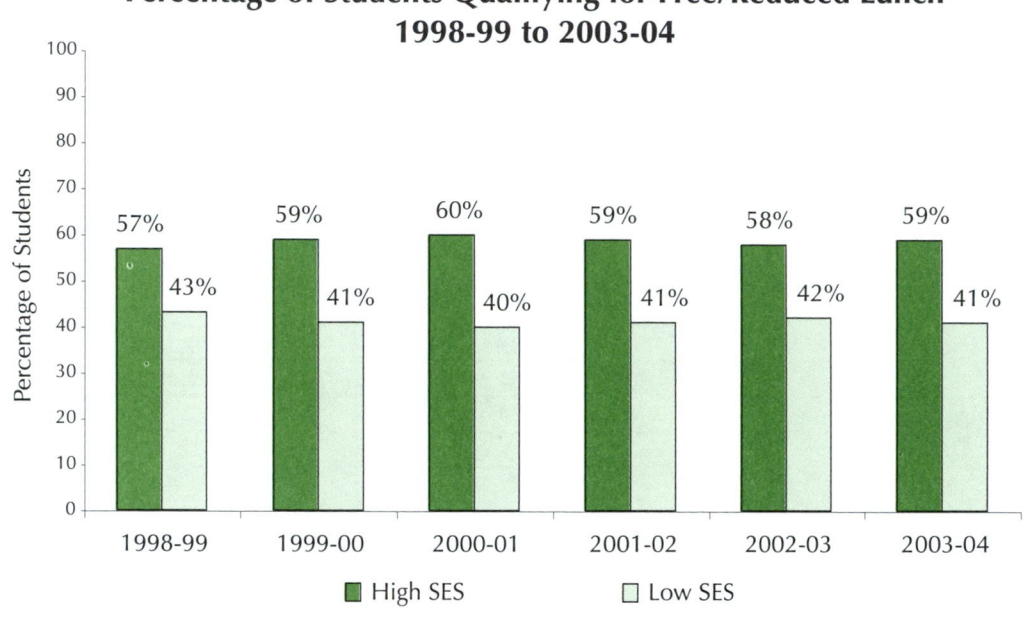

Big River High School Students

Big River High School is one of six senior high schools in Ridgeview School District. Big River currently serves 1,778 students, up 245 students from six years ago, up 140 from the previous year, and up 222 from two years before (Figure 4.6). Big River is the second largest high school in the district. The largest had 77 more students than Big River in 2003-04. The smallest had 679 fewer students than Big River in 2003-04.

Figure 4.6

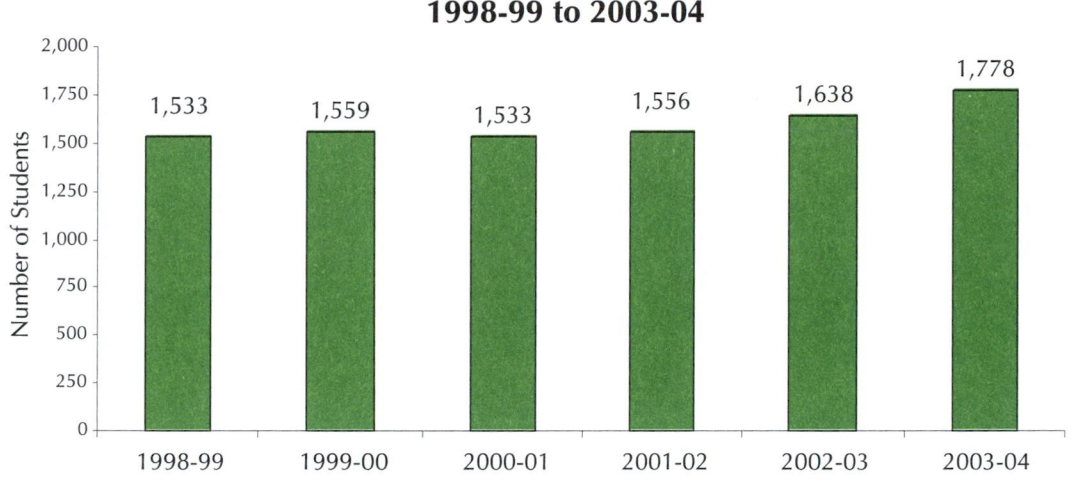

**Big River High School Student Enrollment
1998-99 to 2003-04**

Figure 4.7 shows the current student population consists of 964 Hispanics (54%), 608 Whites (34%), 161 Asians (9%), and 45 Blacks (3%).

Figure 4.7

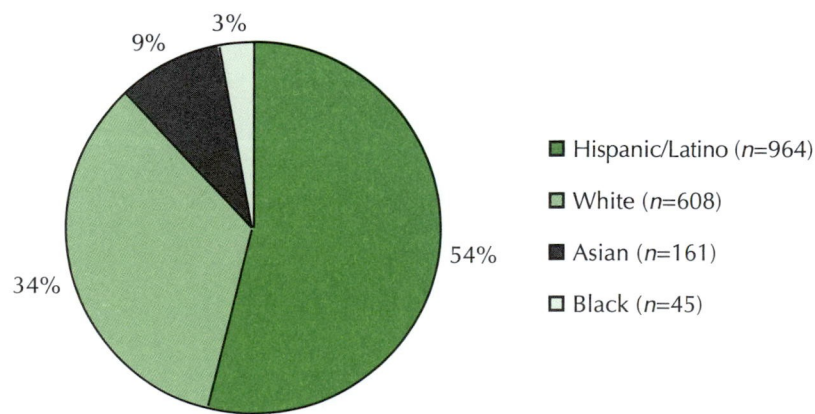

**Big River High School
Student Enrollment by Percent Ethnicity
2003-04 (N=1,778)**

Over the past six years, the Hispanic student population at Big River High School has steadily increased from 743 (49%) in 1998-99 to 964 (54%) in 2003-04 (Figure 4.8). The number of White students has increased from 594 in 1998-99, to a high of 608 in the current year, while the percentage of the White population to the total student population has decreased from 39% to 34%. The number of Asian students has decreased slightly over the six years, while the number and percentage of Black students has stayed about the same.

Figure 4.8

Big River High School
Percentage of Student Enrollment by Ethnicity
1998-99 to 2003-04

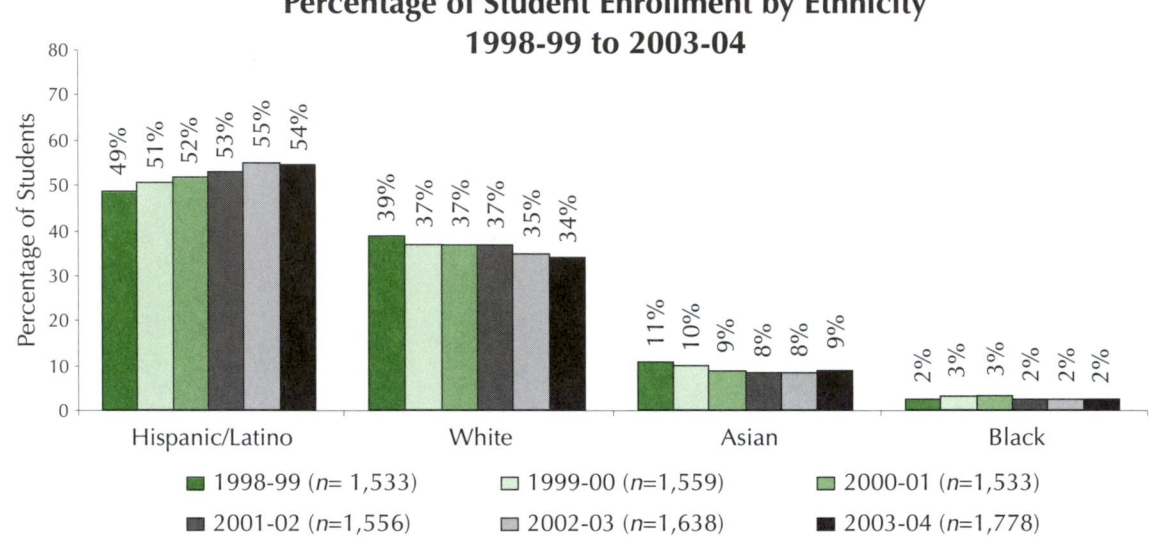

Current classes at Big River High School vary in size from a low of 24 students to a high of 29, with the average class size schoolwide of 26. The grade-level population over the last six years is shown in Figure 4.9.

Figure 4.9

**Big River High School
Student Enrollment by Grade Level
1998-99 to 2003-04**

Legend:
- 1998-99 (*n* = 1,533)
- 1999-00 (*n* =1,559)
- 2000-01 (*n*=1,533)
- 2001-02 (*n*=1,556)
- 2002-03 (*n*=1,638)
- 2003-04 (*n*=1,778)

Grade	1998-99	1999-00	2000-01	2001-02	2002-03	2003-04
Grade 9	452	459	414	437	464	526
Grade 10	379	423	407	406	426	464
Grade 11	347	360	391	379	390	416
Grade 12	355	317	321	334	359	372

The data in Figure 4.9 are reorganized by cohorts in Figure 4.10. Below the title of each cohort is a *matched cohort* number that represents the number of students who started as freshmen at Big River High School and were still there as seniors; or in the case of the class of 2005, freshmen, sophomores, and juniors; and freshmen and sophomores for the class of 2006. The mobility rate in 2003-04 was estimated to be around 30%.

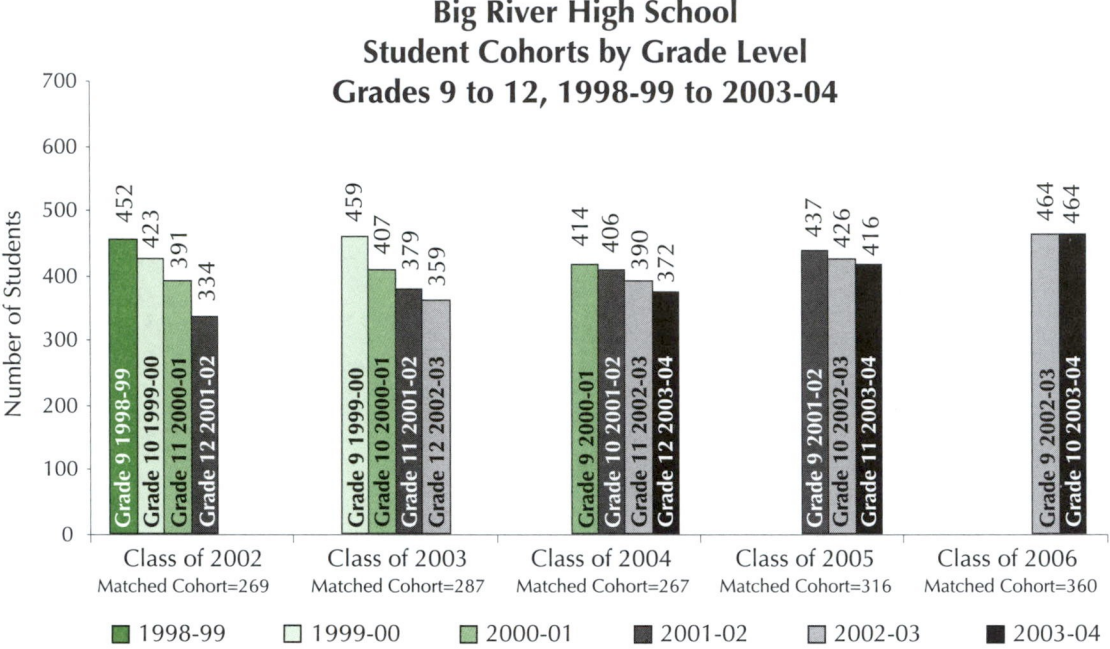

Figure 4.10

The number and percentage of males and females over time, within each grade level, are shown in Figure 4.11. The data are reorganized by cohorts in Figure 4.12. The numbers below gender in Figure 4.12 are the numbers representing matched cohorts, or the number of students who stayed at the school over the four years. Females tend to remain at Big River High School for all four years more than the males in each cohort. (*Note:* The disaggregated totals do not match the official total in Figure 4.9 because the analyses are based on two different time frames.)

Figure 4.11

Big River High School
By Grade Level and Gender, 1998-99 to 2003-04

Grade Level	Gender	1998-99		1999-00		2000-01		2001-02		2002-03		2003-04	
		Number	Percent	Number	Percent	Number	Percent	Number	Percent	Number	Percent	Number	Percent
Grade 9	Male	196	43%	201	44%	200	48%	212	49%	195	42%	198	40%
	Female	256	57%	258	56%	214	52%	225	52%	269	58%	297	60%
Grade 10	Male	166	44%	174	41%	184	45%	192	47%	198	47%	182	42%
	Female	213	56%	249	59%	223	55%	214	53%	228	54%	256	58%
Grade 11	Male	179	52%	149	42%	172	44%	176	47%	174	46%	194	48%
	Female	168	48%	210	59%	219	56%	199	53%	207	54%	211	52%
Grade 12	Male	171	48%	157	50%	129	40%	144	43%	167	47%	173	45%
	Female	184	52%	160	51%	192	60%	190	57%	192	54%	212	55%
Total	Male	712	46%	681	44%	685	45%	724	47%	734	45%	747	43%
	Female	821	54%	877	56%	848	55%	828	53%	896	55%	976	57%
	All	1,533		1,558		1,533		1,552		1,630		1,723	

Figure 4.12

Big River High School
Student Cohorts by Grade Level and Gender
Grades 9 to 12, 1998-99 to 2003-04

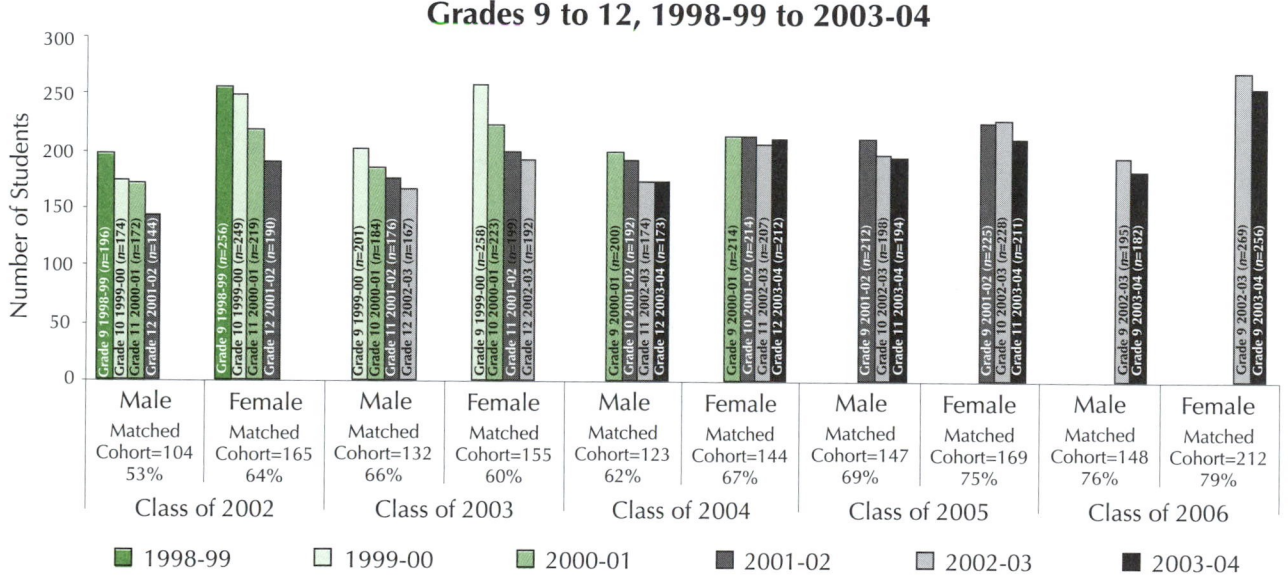

Figure 4.13 shows the number and percentage of students enrolled within each grade level by gender and ethnicity, over time.

Figure 4.13

Big River High School Students
By Grade Level, Gender, and Ethnicity, 1998-99 to 2003-04

Grade Level	Year	Gender	Hispanic		White		Asian		Black		Total
			Number	Percent	Number	Percent	Number	Percent	Number	Percent	Number
Grade 9	1998-99 (n=452)	Male	101	22.3%	69	15.3%	20	4.4%	6	1.3%	196
		Female	140	31.0%	88	19.5%	25	5.5%	3	0.7%	256
	1999-00 (n=459)	Male	107	23.3%	71	15.5%	18	3.9%	5	1.1%	201
		Female	154	33.6%	75	16.3%	22	4.8%	7	1.5%	258
	2000-01 (n=414)	Male	105	25.4%	73	17.6%	18	4.3%	4	1.0%	200
		Female	113	27.3%	77	18.6%	18	4.3%	6	1.4%	214
	2001-02 (n=437)	Male	135	30.9%	60	13.7%	13	3.0%	4	0.9%	212
		Female	119	27.2%	79	18.1%	23	5.3%	4	0.9%	225
	2002-03 (n=464)	Male	115	24.8%	63	13.6%	15	3.2%	2	0.4%	195
		Female	157	33.8%	79	17.0%	27	5.8%	6	1.3%	269
	2003-04 (n=495)	Male	120	24.2%	53	10.7%	20	4.0%	5	1.0%	198
		Female	152	30.7%	105	21.2%	27	5.5%	13	2.6%	297
Grade 10	1998-99 (n=379)	Male	78	20.6%	66	17.4%	15	4.0%	7	1.8%	166
		Female	104	27.4%	85	22.4%	16	4.2%	8	2.1%	213
	1999-00 (n=423)	Male	90	21.3%	61	14.4%	15	3.5%	8	1.9%	174
		Female	133	31.4%	85	20.1%	28	6.6%	3	0.7%	249
	2000-01 (n=407)	Male	96	23.6%	68	16.7%	14	3.4%	6	1.5%	184
		Female	133	32.7%	64	15.7%	17	4.2%	9	2.2%	223
	2001-02 (n=406)	Male	100	24.6%	74	18.2%	16	3.9%	2	0.5%	192
		Female	104	25.6%	84	20.7%	19	4.7%	7	1.7%	214
	2002-03 (n=426)	Male	128	30.0%	56	13.1%	11	2.6%	3	0.7%	198
		Female	119	27.9%	81	19.0%	24	5.6%	4	0.9%	228
	2003-04 (n=438)	Male	102	23.3%	64	14.6%	14	3.2%	2	0.5%	182
		Female	144	32.9%	79	18.0%	25	5.7%	8	1.8%	256
Grade 11	1998-99 (n=347)	Male	89	25.6%	65	18.7%	24	6.9%	1	0.3%	179
		Female	66	19.0%	77	22.2%	21	6.1%	4	1.2%	168
	1999-00 (n=359)	Male	68	18.9%	61	17.0%	13	3.6%	7	1.9%	149
		Female	99	27.6%	86	24.0%	18	5.0%	7	1.9%	210
	2000-01 (n=391)	Male	86	22.0%	65	16.6%	14	3.6%	7	1.8%	172
		Female	112	28.6%	81	20.7%	23	5.9%	3	0.8%	219
	2001-02 (n=375)	Male	85	22.7%	72	19.2%	14	3.7%	5	1.3%	176
		Female	108	28.8%	69	18.4%	15	4.0%	7	1.9%	199
	2002-03 (n=381)	Male	89	23.4%	65	17.1%	16	4.2%	4	1.0%	174
		Female	101	26.5%	82	21.5%	18	4.7%	6	1.6%	207
	2003-04 (n=405)	Male	126	31.1%	55	13.6%	10	2.5%	3	0.7%	194
		Female	106	26.2%	77	19.0%	23	5.7%	5	1.2%	211

Figure 4.13 (Continued)

Big River High School Students
By Grade Level, Gender, and Ethnicity, 1998-99 to 2003-04

Grade Level	Year	Gender	Hispanic		White		Asian		Black		Total
			Number	Percent	Number	Percent	Number	Percent	Number	Percent	Number
Grade 12	1998-99 (n=355)	Male	86	24.2%	67	18.9%	17	4.8%	1	0.3%	171
		Female	79	22.3%	77	21.7%	23	6.5%	5	1.4%	184
	1999-00 (n=317)	Male	74	23.3%	61	19.2%	21	6.6%	1	0.3%	157
		Female	64	20.2%	74	23.3%	19	6.0%	3	0.9%	160
	2000-01 (n=321)	Male	56	17.4%	52	16.2%	15	4.7%	6	1.9%	129
		Female	89	27.7%	81	25.2%	15	4.7%	7	2.2%	192
	2001-02 (n=334)	Male	73	21.9%	55	16.5%	10	3.0%	6	1.8%	144
		Female	98	29.3%	74	22.2%	17	5.1%	1	0.3%	190
	2002-03 (n=359)	Male	79	22.0%	69	19.2%	12	3.3%	7	1.9%	167
		Female	108	30.1%	63	17.5%	14	3.9%	7	1.9%	192
	2003-04 (n=385)	Male	93	24.2%	60	15.6%	16	4.2%	4	1.0%	173
		Female	106	27.5%	83	21.6%	17	4.4%	6	1.6%	212
Totals	1998-99	Male	354	23.1%	267	17.4%	76	5.0%	15	1.0%	712
		Female	389	25.4%	327	21.3%	85	5.5%	20	1.3%	821
	1999-00	Male	339	21.8%	254	16.3%	67	4.3%	21	1.3%	681
		Female	450	28.9%	320	20.5%	87	5.6%	20	1.3%	877
	2000-01	Male	343	22.4%	258	16.8%	61	4.0%	23	1.5%	685
		Female	447	29.2%	303	19.8%	73	4.8%	25	1.6%	848
	2001-02	Male	393	25.3%	261	16.8%	53	3.4%	17	1.1%	724
		Female	429	27.6%	306	19.7%	74	4.8%	19	1.2%	828
	2002-03	Male	411	25.2%	253	15.5%	54	3.3%	16	1.0%	734
		Female	485	29.8%	305	18.7%	83	5.1%	23	1.4%	896
	2003-04	Male	441	25.6%	232	13.5%	60	3.5%	14	0.8%	747
		Female	508	29.5%	344	20.0%	92	5.3%	32	1.9%	976

Nearly 70% of Big River High School students come from "High SES" families. According to student responses to questions on the state assessment, 30% of the parents of students at Big River have attended college and 26% possess a college degree. Figure 4.14 shows the estimated high and low socio-economic number and percentage over time, by ethnicity.

Figure 4.14

**Big River High School Students
By Socio-economic Status and Ethnicity, 1998-99 to 2003-04**

Year	SES Status	Hispanic		White		Asian		Black		Total	
		Number	Percent	Number	Percent	Number	Percent	Number	Percent	Number	Percent
1998-99 (n=1,559)	High SES	417	57%	546	94%	163	76%	24	69%	1,150	74%
	Low SES	312	43%	35	6%	51	24%	11	31%	409	26%
1999-00 (n=1,603)	High SES	382	48%	534	94%	150	74%	31	76%	1,097	68%
	Low SES	407	52%	37	6%	52	26%	10	24%	506	32%
2000-01 (n=1,584)	High SES	364	42%	525	94%	123	66%	32	67%	1,044	66%
	Low SES	426	49%	36	6%	62	34%	16	33%	540	34%
2001-02 (n=1,601)	High SES	445	54%	534	94%	122	71%	25	68%	1,126	70%
	Low SES	378	46%	34	6%	51	29%	12	32%	475	30%
2002-03 (n=1,676)	High SES	488	55%	520	93%	147	79%	28	72%	1,183	71%
	Low SES	403	45%	39	7%	40	21%	11	28%	493	29%
2003-04 (n=1,655)	High SES	456	49%	510	92%	102	74%	23	58%	1,091	66%
	Low SES	470	51%	42	8%	35	26%	17	43%	564	34%

Figure 4.15 shows the number and percentage of students by their home languages for the three major language groups by grade level for the past six years. Other languages in small percentages include Arabic, Assyrian, Cantonese, Cebuano, Farsi, French, German, Greek, Gujarati, Hebrew, Hindi, Hungarian, Ilocano, Italian, Japanese, Khmer, Korean, Mandarin, Portuguese, Punjabi, Romanian, Russian, Samoan, Serbo-Croatian, and Thai.

Figure 4.15

Big River High School
Number and Percentage of Students Enrolled by Grade Level and Home Language
1998-99 to 2003-04

Grade Level	Language	1998-99		1999-00		2000-01		2001-02		2002-03		2003-04	
		Number	Percent	Number	Percent	Number	Percent	Number	Percent	Number	Percent	Number	Percent
Grade 9	English	267	59%	251	55%	233	56%	243	56%	250	54%	302	57%
	Spanish	154	34%	175	38%	153	37%	166	38%	190	41%	192	37%
	Vietnamese	12	3%	15	3%	9	2%	5	1%	9	2%	10	2%
	Other	16	4%	18	4%	19	5%	23	5%	15	3%	22	4%
Grade 10	English	234	62%	251	59%	228	56%	240	59%	230	54%	257	55%
	Spanish	115	30%	144	34%	156	38%	141	35%	168	39%	184	40%
	Vietnamese	13	3%	12	3%	10	2%	8	2%	5	1%	7	2%
	Other	16	4%	16	4%	13	3%	17	4%	23	5%	16	3%
Grade 11	English	215	63%	223	62%	243	62%	227	61%	228	60%	233	56%
	Spanish	105	31%	107	30%	121	31%	130	35%	127	33%	157	38%
	Vietnamese	12	3%	12	3%	10	3%	8	2%	9	2%	5	1%
	Other	12	3%	17	5%	17	4%	10	3%	17	4%	21	5%
Grade 12	English	213	61%	198	62%	207	64%	212	63%	220	61%	228	61%
	Spanish	117	33%	95	30%	91	28%	106	32%	120	33%	118	32%
	Vietnamese	5	1%	11	3%	11	3%	4	1%	7	2%	9	2%
	Other	17	5%	13	4%	12	4%	12	4%	12	3%	17	5%
Total	English	929	61%	923	59%	911	59%	922	599%	928	57%	1,020	57%
	Spanish	491	32%	521	33%	521	34%	543	35%	605	37%	651	37%
	Vietnamese	42	3%	50	3%	40	3%	25	2%	30	2%	31	2%
	Other	61	4%	64	4%	61	4%	62	4%	67	4%	76	4%
	All	1,523		1,558		1,533		1,552		1,630		1,778	

Figure 4.16 shows the number and percentage of English Proficient and English Learner students between 1998-99 and 2003-04. Approximately 16% of the student population was English Learners in 2003-04.

Figure 4.16

Big River High School
Number and Percentage of English Proficient and English Learners
1998-99 to 2003-04

Language Proficiency	1998-99		1999-00		2000-01		2001-02		2002-03		2003-04	
	Number	Percent	Number	Percent	Number	Percent	Number	Percent	Number	Percent	Number	Percent
English Proficient	1,291	84%	1,279	82%	1,269	83%	1,317	85%	1,372	84%	1,499	84%
English Learner (EL)	242	16%	277	18%	264	17%	238	15%	266	16%	284	16%

Figure 4.17 shows the number of students classified as immigrant by grade level, for the past six years. Most of the immigrants are from Mexico. Students are identified as immigrants when they are "foreign born" and enrolled in any U.S. school for three years or less.

Figure 4.17

Big River High School
Number of Immigrant Students by Grade Level
1998-99 to 2003-04

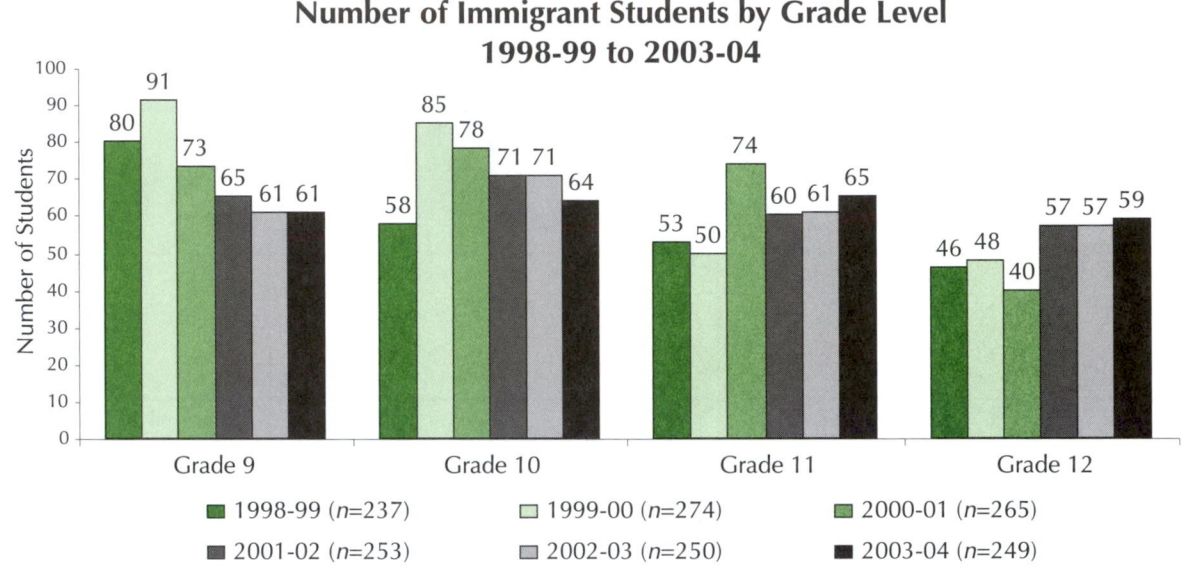

Big River High School currently has 70 students classified as migrant. Migrant students, who are identified at enrollment, have parents who are agricultural workers. Figure 4.18 displays these numbers by grade level, over time. Over ten migrant students were also identified as immigrant students in 2003-04.

Figure 4.18

Big River High School
Number of Migrant Students by Grade Level
1998-99 to 2003-04

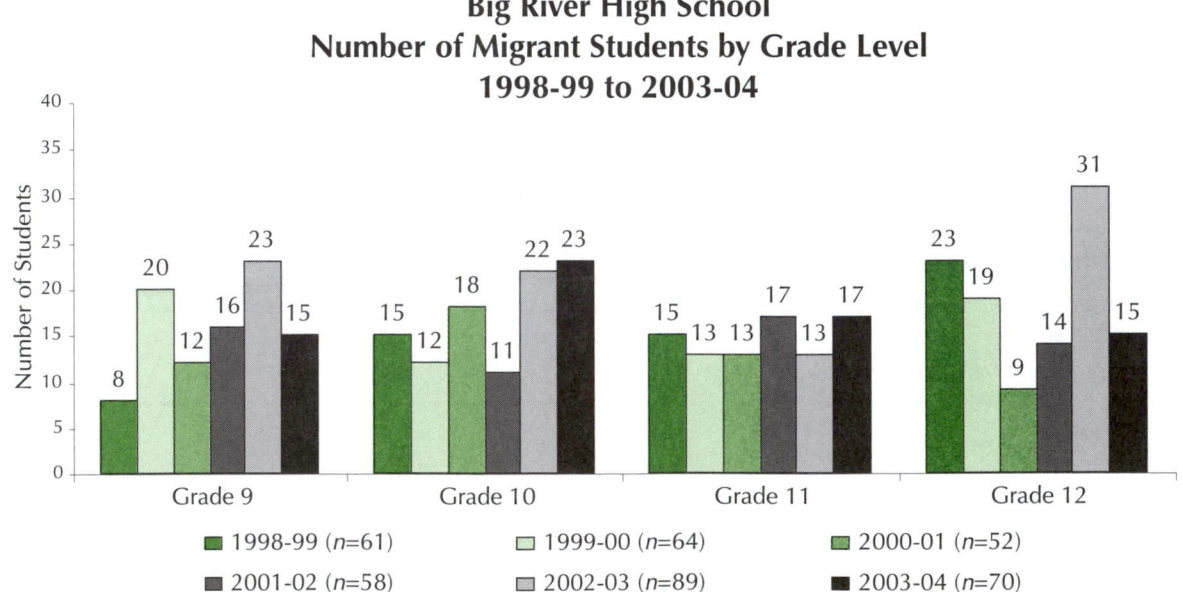

Big River High School staff believes that all students can behave appropriately in the classroom. The school discipline plan includes the regulations as outlined in the *Ridgeview School District Student Behavior and Parent Information Handbook,* and additional discipline rules and procedures are provided in the *Big River Student Handbook.* Handbooks are distributed each year to both students and parents. Student assemblies are held throughout the year to highlight changes in policy and to reinforce any urgent areas of concern. Individual teacher discipline plans are posted in each classroom. Big River has a standing *Discipline and Attendance Committee* whose charge is to communicate with the staff at large regarding procedures and policies which need revision and implementation. Parent involvement and support remains a prime deterrent to discipline problems. Figure 4.19 shows the number of student suspensions over the past six years, by grade level. Only one of the suspensions was an in-home referral in 2003-04.

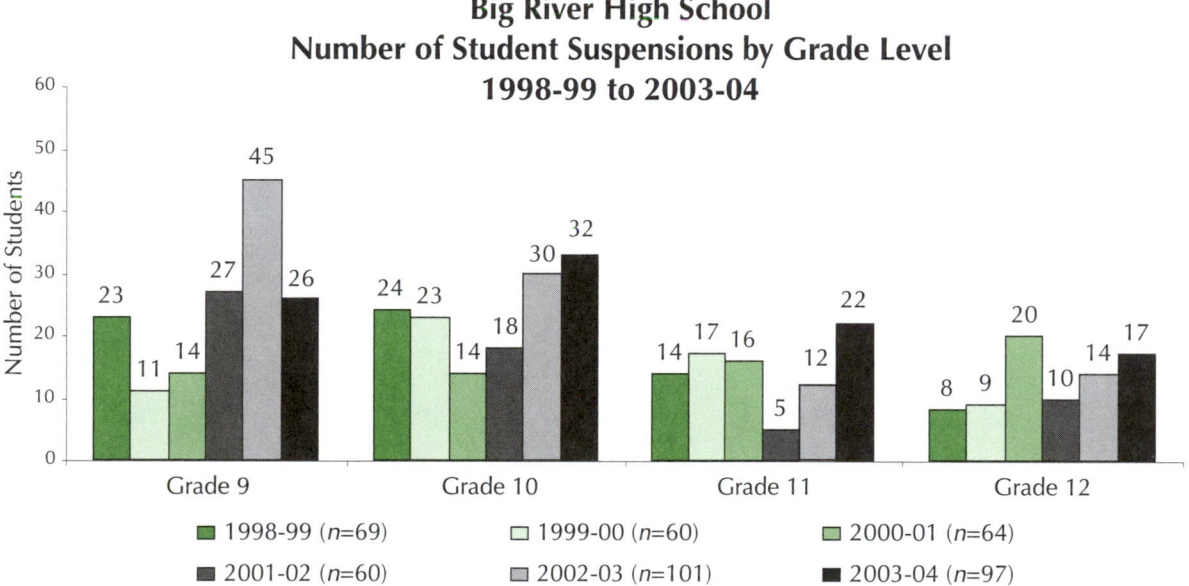

Figure 4.19

**Big River High School
Number of Student Suspensions by Grade Level
1998-99 to 2003-04**

Figure 4.20 shows the number of in-home referrals between 2001-02 and 2003-04. There were zero in-home referrals in 1998-99 through 2000-01. Figure 4.21 summarizes the number of expulsions by grade level for the past six years. There have been only five.

Figure 4.20

Big River High School
Number of In-home Referrals by Grade Level
2001-02 to 2003-04

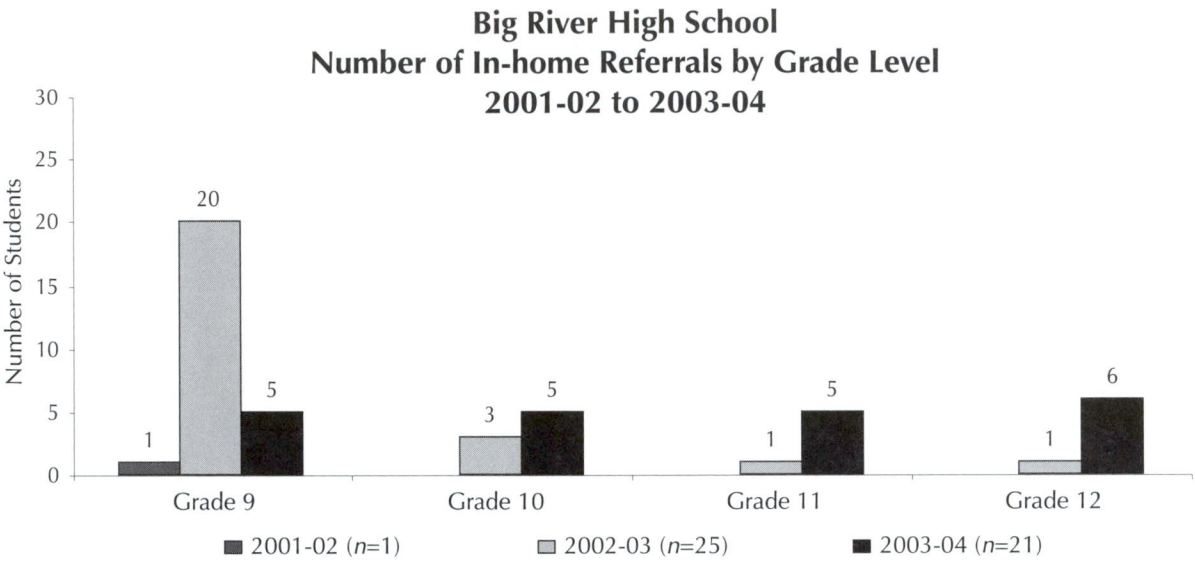

Figure 4.21

Big River High School
Number of Student Expulsions by Grade Level
1998-99 to 2003-04

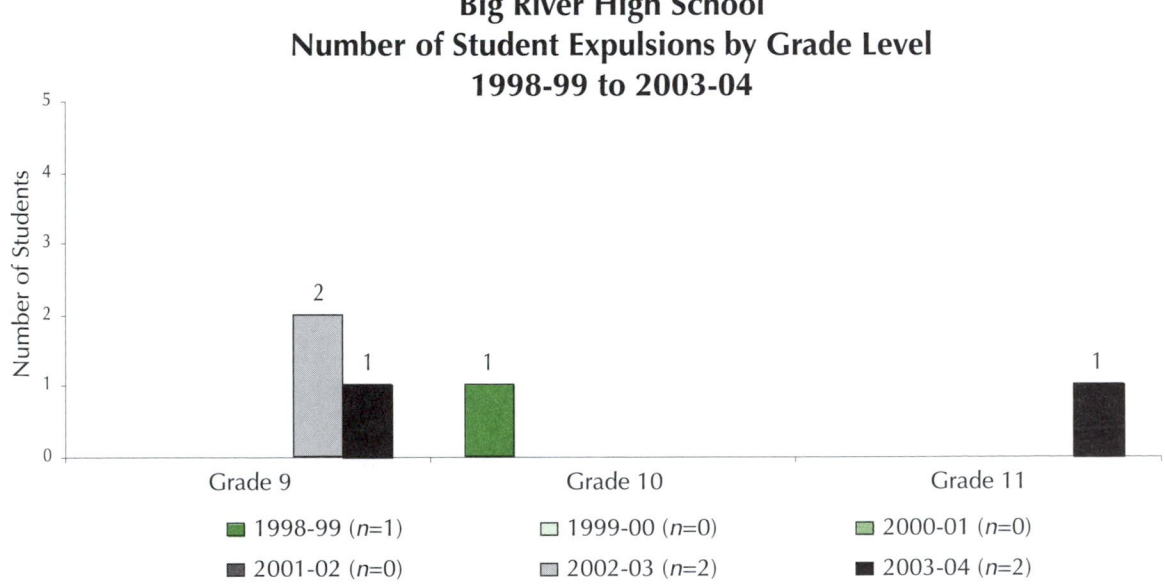

Students attending Big River High School are in attendance approximately 94% of the time, with the teacher attendance rate at about 97%.

Programs

Special Education Services

Figure 4.22 shows the number of students classified as needing special education services in each of the last six years, by grade level, gender, and ethnicity. Approximately 8% of the total student population were identified each year as qualifying for special education services.

Figure 4.22

Big River High School
Special Education Students by Grade Level, Ethnicity, and Gender
1998-99 to 2003-04

Grade Level	Ethnicity	1998-99		1999-00		2000-01		2001-02		2002-03		2003-04	
		Male	Female	Male	Female	Male	Female	Male	Female	Male	Female	Male	Female
Grade 9	Asian	2				5						1	2
	Black			3			1					2	1
	Hispanic/Latino	15	11	14	15	15	7	15	10	13	16	13	11
	White	6	7	7	5	9	5	9	5	13	2	7	4
	Total SE Grade 9	**23**	**18**	**24**	**20**	**29**	**13**	**24**	**15**	**27**	**18**	**23**	**18**
Grade 10	Asian			1	2			3		1	1	1	1
	Black			1		4			1	1	1		1
	Hispanic/Latino	14	4	12	13	13	14	14	3	15	16	11	13
	White	4	4	7	8	6	6	12	2	5	6	12	
	Total SE Grade 10	**18**	**8**	**21**	**23**	**23**	**20**	**29**	**6**	**22**	**24**	**24**	**15**
Grade 11	Asian					1	1			2		1	1
	Black			1		1		3			1	1	
	Hispanic/Latino	10	5	10	4	16	12	8	7	14	5	14	10
	White	6	4	4	5	10	7	6	5	9	2	4	5
	Total SE Grade 11	**16**	**9**	**15**	**9**	**28**	**20**	**17**	**12**	**25**	**8**	**20**	**16**
Grade 12	Asian	1							1			1	
	Black					1		1		4			1
	Hispanic/Latino	8	3	12	6	4	2	9	7	7	6	10	4
	White	7	1	9	4	3	3	5	5	5	4	7	2
	Total SE Grade 12	**16**	**4**	**21**	**10**	**8**	**5**	**15**	**13**	**16**	**10**	**18**	**7**
Total	Asian	3		1	2	6	1	3	1	3	1	4	4
	Black			5		6	1	4	1	5	2	3	3
	Hispanic/Latino	47	23	48	38	48	35	46	27	49	43	48	38
	White	23	16	27	22	28	21	32	17	32	14	30	11
	Total	**73**	**39**	**81**	**62**	**88**	**58**	**85**	**46**	**89**	**60**	**85**	**46**
	All	**112 (7%)**		**143 (9%)**		**146 (9%)**		**131 (8%)**		**149 (9%)**		**141 (8%)**	

GEAR UP *(Gaining Early Awareness and Readiness for Undergraduate Programs)* is a national program designed to increase the number of low-income students who are prepared to enter and succeed in postsecondary education. Big River had 389 participants in GEAR UP in 2003-04, down 19 from 2002-03, and up 243 from 2001-02. The number of participants by ethnicity and gender are shown in Figure 4.23 below.

Figure 4.23

Big River High School
Number of Students Participating in GEAR UP
By Gender and Ethnicity, 2001-02 to 2003-04

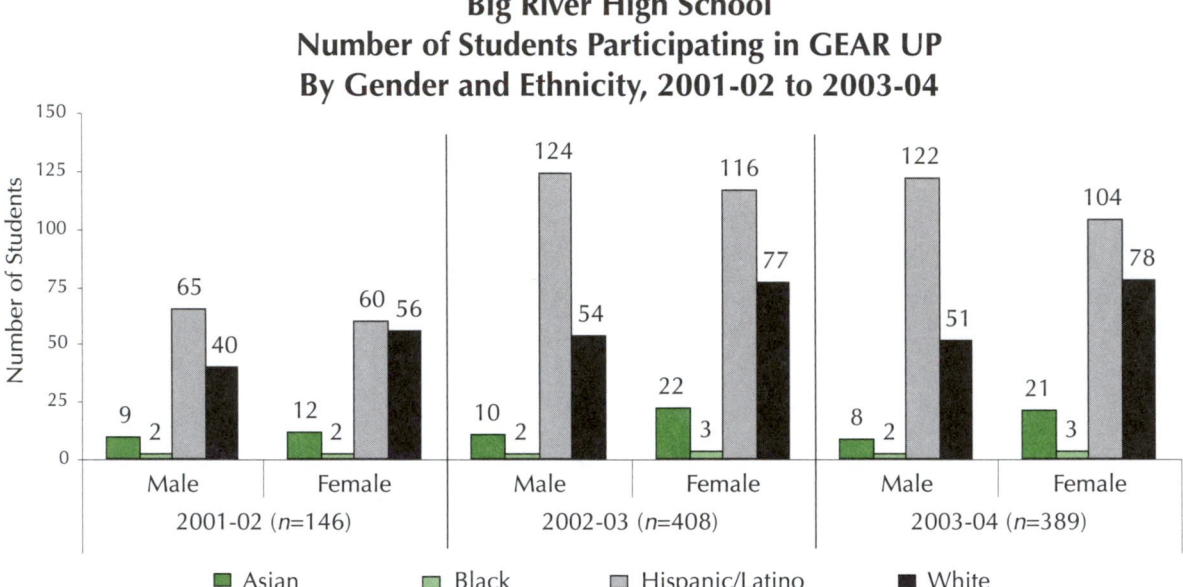

Gifted and Talented

Big River High School has a gifted program, with between 273 and 323 students enrolled each year. The number of students identified for participation in *Gifted and Talented Education* (GATE) by grade level is shown in Figure 4.24 for 1998-99 through 2003-04. Students are tested for eligibility in the program.

Figure 4.24

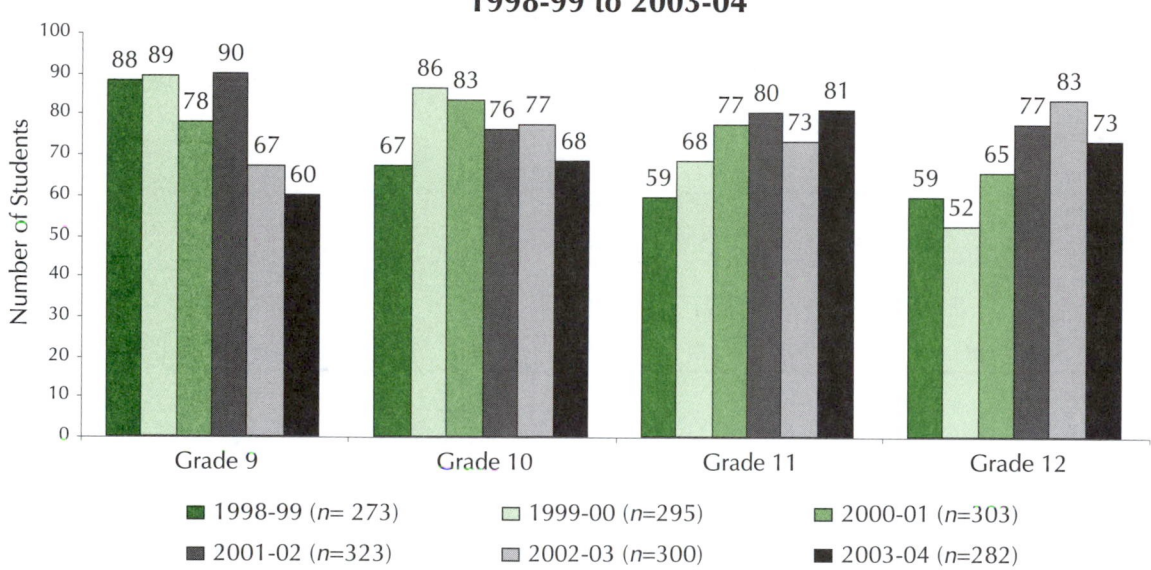

**Big River High School
Number of GATE Students by Grade Level
1998-99 to 2003-04**

Numbers of (GATE) students by grade level, ethnicity, and gender for the past six years are shown in Figure 4.25. More females than males are identified as *Gifted and Talented* in each ethnicity.

Figure 4.25

Big River High School
GATE Participation by Grade Level, Ethnicity, and Gender
1998-99 to 2003-04

Grade Level	Ethnicity	1998-99		1999-00		2000-01		2001-02		2002-03		2003-04	
		Male	Female	Male	Female	Male	Female	Male	Female	Male	Female	Male	Female
Grade 9	Asian	5	4	7	3	2	7	3	6	1	8	1	7
	Black	1	2		1	1	2	1	1			1	1
	Hispanic/Latino	13	16	10	14	11	13	17	15	12	16	7	11
	White	20	27	26	28	21	21	22	25	13	17	13	19
	Total SE Grade 9	**39**	**49**	**43**	**46**	**35**	**43**	**43**	**47**	**26**	**41**	**22**	**38**
Grade 10	Asian	1	4	5	4	6	3	2	7	3	5	1	8
	Black	1		1	2		2	1	1		1		
	Hispanic/Latino	9	12	11	16	9	14	10	10	14	13	13	15
	White	18	22	20	27	26	23	21	24	19	22	13	18
	Total SE Grade 10	**29**	**38**	**37**	**49**	**41**	**42**	**34**	**42**	**36**	**41**	**27**	**41**
Grade 11	Asian	2	6	1	5	4	4	6	4	2	7	3	5
	Black			1			2		2	1	1		1
	Hispanic/Latino	10	8	9	12	9	12	8	11	8	11	16	13
	White	15	18	17	23	20	26	27	22	20	23	20	23
	Total SE Grade 11	**27**	**32**	**28**	**40**	**33**	**44**	**41**	**39**	**31**	**42**	**39**	**42**
Grade 12	Asian	7	4	2	5	2	4	4	3	6	4	2	7
	Black					1		1	1		2	1	1
	Hispanic/Latino	8	5	9	7	8	11	10	14	8	12	8	11
	White	15	20	12	17	17	22	19	25	28	23	20	23
	Total SE Grade 12	**30**	**29**	**23**	**29**	**28**	**37**	**34**	**43**	**42**	**41**	**31**	**42**
Total	Asian	15	18	15	17	14	18	15	20	12	24	7	27
	Black	2	2	2	3	2	6	3	5	1	4	2	3
	Hispanic/Latino	40	41	39	49	37	50	45	50	42	52	44	50
	White	68	87	75	95	84	92	89	96	80	85	66	83
	Total	**125**	**148**	**131**	**164**	**137**	**166**	**152**	**171**	**135**	**165**	**119**	**163**

Graduation and Dropouts

Figure 4.26 shows the reasons students are no longer at the school from 1998-99 to 2003-04.

Figure 4.26

Big River High School
Reasons Students are No Longer at This School by Grade Level
1998-99 to 2003-04

Grade	Reason	1998-99	1999-00	2000-01	2001-02	2002-03	2003-04
Grade 9	Expelled Non-attendee				1		
	Expelled from District				1	3	3
	Guidance	1					
	Hospitalized for Rest of Year			1			
	Juvenile Court / Authority	1		2	2		
	Transfer to Independent Study				2	2	2
	Transfer to Other County District	2	1	1			1
	Transfer to Other School in District	14	4	13	27	20	23
	Transfer to Out-of-State District				1		1
	Total	**18**	**5**	**17**	**34**	**25**	**30**
Grade 10	Expelled from District	1					3
	Transfer to Other District in State	1			1	2	
	Transfer to Foreign Public School	1			1		
	Transfer to Other County District		1		1		
	Transfer to Other School in District	10	9	16	13	12	15
	Transfer to Out-of-State District				1		
	Total	**13**	**10**	**16**	**17**	**14**	**18**
Grade 11	Enrolled Non-attendee				1		
	Expelled from District						1
	Graduated During Year				1		
	Guidance			1			1
	Transfer to Foreign Public School		1	1		1	
	Transfer to Other County District	1	2	1			1
	Transfer to Other School in District	7	5	14	15	14	15
	Total	**8**	**8**	**17**	**17**	**15**	**18**
Grade 12	Expelled from District					2	
	Guidance	1					
	Juvenile Court / Authority			1			
	Over 18 to Community College	1				1	
	Transfer to Other District in State	1					2
	Transfer to Other County District			1		1	
	Transfer to Other School in District	3	2	8	17	12	15
	Total	**6**	**2**	**10**	**17**	**16**	**17**
Total	Expelled Non-attendee				2		
	Expelled from District	1			1	5	7
	Graduated During Year				1		
	Guidance	2		1			1
	Hospitalized for Remainder of Year			1			
	Juvenile Court / Authority	1		3	2		
	Over 18 to Community College	1				1	
	Transfer to Other District in State	2			1	2	2
	Transfer to Foreign Public School	1	1	1	1	1	
	Transfer to Independent Study				2	2	2
	Transfer to Other County District	3	4	3	1	1	2
	Transfer to Other School in District	34	20	51	72	58	68
	Transfer to Out-of-State District				2		1
	All	**45**	**25**	**60**	**85**	**70**	**83**

Diploma Options

There is only one path to high school graduation at Big River through completion of coursework. The Ridgeview School District put into place a dropout prevention program in 1999-00. The dropout prevention program is primarily an elementary school program that provides a counselor/liaison to help coordinate student success teams, stay on top of kids with attendance problems by making home visits, and to assist families in getting desired support/services from various county agencies.

Big River's student dropout rate for 2003-04 was 6% (n=107). In 2002-03, it was 5% (n=88), up from 2.9% in 2001-02 (n=32); 1.2% in 2000-01 (n=16); and 1.1% in 1999-00 (n=9) (Figure 4.27). Most dropouts have occurred in grade nine with the majority being male. The 2003-04 graduation rate is considered to be 94%.

Figure 4.27

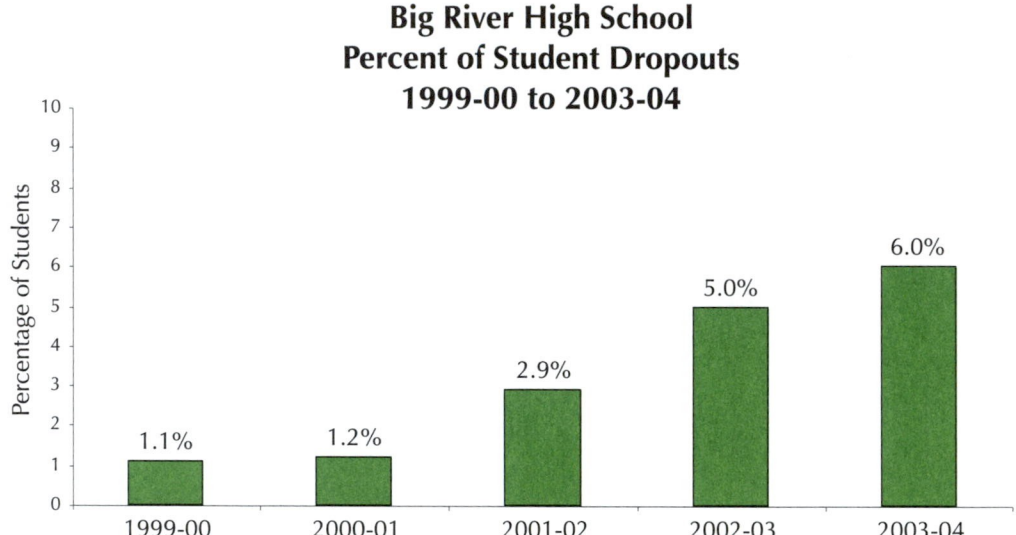

**Big River High School
Percent of Student Dropouts
1999-00 to 2003-04**

The Staff

The school employed 88 teachers in the 2003-04 school year. The number of teachers at Big River has ranged from 89 to 95 over the previous five years (Figure 4.28). The student to teacher ratio reached its highest in 2003-04 at 20 students per teacher. 2002-03 was Big River's principal's first year as a principal. The previous principal was in that position for ten years before she retired in Spring 2002. Prior to this position, the current principal was an assistant principal at the school for five years. Four assistant principals *(Curriculum, Guidance, Discipline,* and *Activities)* have helped with the transition of the new principal. Three of the assistant principals are female; two are White; one is Black; and one is Hispanic. The assistant principal for discipline is a Black male. The guidance assistant principal is a Hispanic female.

Figure 4.28

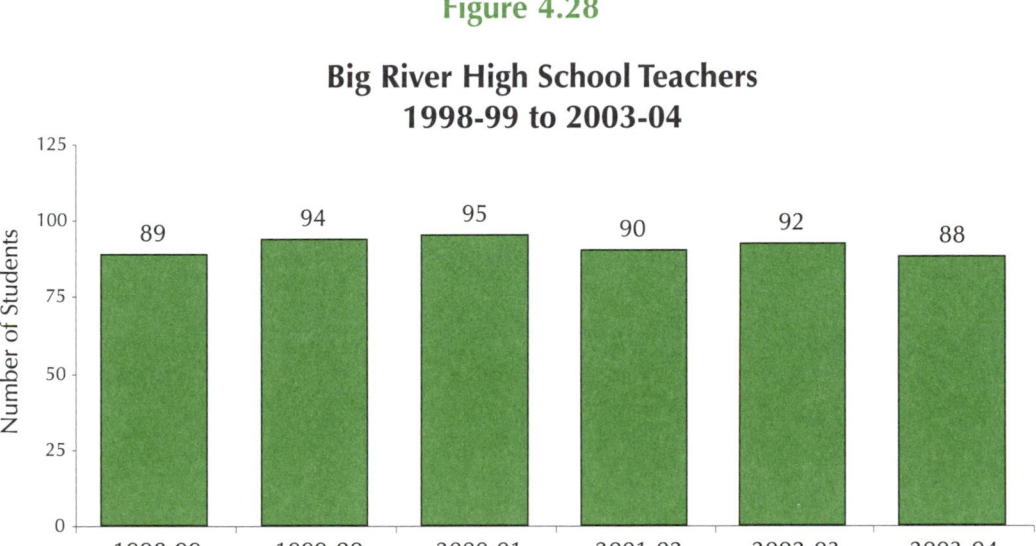

**Big River High School Teachers
1998-99 to 2003-04**

In 2003-04, 56% of the teachers at Big River were female; 44% were male. Seventy percent were White; 15% Hispanic/Latino; 9% Multi-racial; 3% Black; 1% Asian; and 1% Filipino. Figure 4.29 shows the breakdown by gender and ethnicity for the six years.

Figure 4.29

Big River High School Teachers
By Ethnicity and Gender, 1998-99 to 2003-04

Ethnicity	Gender	1998-99		1999-00		2000-01		2001-02		2002-03		2003-04	
		Number	Percent	Number	Percent	Number	Percent	Number	Percent	Number	Percent	Number	Percent
Asian	Male					1	1%			1	1%	1	1%
	Female	3	3%	1	1%	1	1%	2	2%	1	1%		
Black	Male	2	2%	1	1%	1	1%	1	1%	4	4%	3	3%
Filipino	Female			2	2%					1	1%	1	1%
Hispanic/ Latino	Male	4	4%	6	6%	6	6%	6	7%	6	7%	6	7%
	Female	8	9%	8	9%	7	7%	7	8%	6	7%	7	8%
White	Male	31	35%	28	30%	27	28%	29	32%	26	28%	25	28%
	Female	38	43%	44	47%	46	48%	42	47%	41	45%	37	42%
Multi-racial	Male	1	1%	1	1%	1	1%			3	3%	4	5%
	Female	1	1%	2	2%	1	1%	2	2%	1	1%	4	5%
	Unassigned	1	1%	1	1%	3	3%	1	1%	2	2%		
Total by Gender	Male	38	43%	36	38%	36	38%	36	40%	40	43%	39	44%
	Female	47	53%	46	60%	54	57%	51	57%	49	53%	49	56%
Total by Ethnicity	Asian	3	3%	1	1%	2	2%	2	2%	2	2%	1	1%
	Black	2	2%	1	1%	1	1%	1	1%	4	4%	3	3%
	Filipino			2	2%					1	1%	1	1%
	Hispanic/Latino	12	13%	14	15%	13	14%	13	14%	12	13%	13	15%
	White	69	78%	72	77%	73	77%	71	79%	67	73%	62	70%
	Multi-racial	3	3%	4	4%	6	6%	3	3%	6	7%	8	9%
	All	89		94		95		90		92		88	

Figure 4.30 shows the average number of years teaching for 1998-99 through 2003-04. The average number of years teaching has consistently decreased over time until 2003-04.

Figure 4.30

Big River High School
Average Number of Years Teaching Experience by Grade Level
1998-99 to 2003-04

Grade Level	1998-99	1999-00	2000-01	2001-02	2002-03	2003-04
Grade 9	11.7	11.6	9.9	9.8	5.7	6.6
Grade 10	13.4	11.8	10.1	9.9	5.5	6.3
Grade 11	14.2	13.0	11.6	10.7	5.7	6.4
Grade 12	13.8	13.0	11.3	10.7	5.8	6.5
School Average	13.3	12.4	10.7	10.2	5.7	6.4

The current average number of years of teaching is 6.4. At the end of 2002, the district offered a teacher retirement incentive plan which required the hiring of 500 new teachers and administrators. Figure 4.31 shows two things: (1) the average number of years of teaching at Big River has been lower than the district for six years, and; (2) the average number of years of teaching has decreased for both the school and the district during this same time period.

Figure 4.31

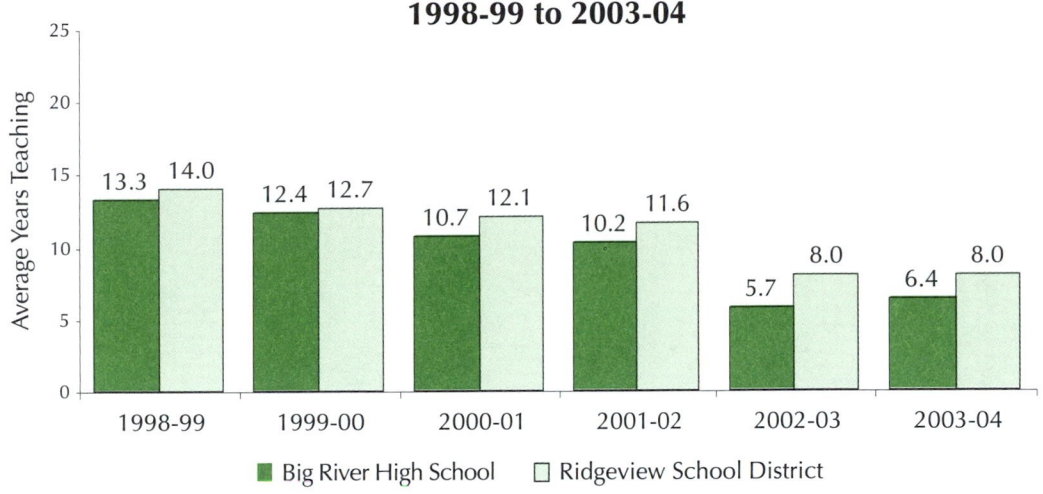

**Big River High School
Average Number of Years Teaching Compared to the District
1998-99 to 2003-04**

Figure 4.32 shows that several Big River teachers possess many years of teaching experience, while many more are still new at their profession. Sixty of the 88 teachers in 2003-04 have 0 to 7 years of teaching experience: 12 have less than one year; 33 have 1 to 3 years; 15 have 4 to 7 years.

In 2003-04, five teachers were teaching outside of their subject area; 22 were teaching with emergency credentials; and 4 were teaching with waivers—over 30%.

Figure 4.32

**Big River High School Teachers
By Years Teaching Experience
1998-99 to 2003-04**

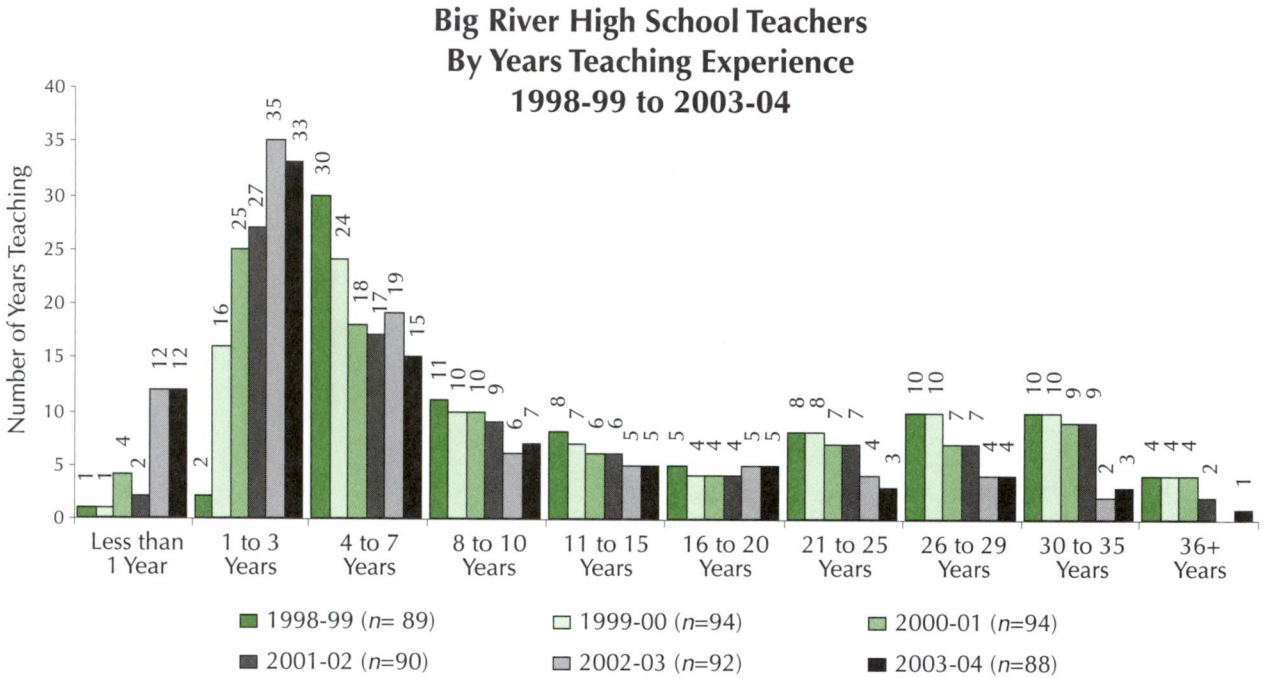

Study Questions for Who Are We?

As you review Big River's data, use either the margins in the text, this page, or print this page from the CD-ROM to write down your early thinking. (Ch4Qs.pdf) These notes, of course, are only hunches or placeholders until all the data are analyzed. If thinking about "strengths" and "challenges" is difficult, list "observations." It is important to jot down your thinking as you go through the data so you can see if additional data corroborate your first impressions.

1. What are the demographic *strengths* and *challenges* for Big River High School?

Strengths	*Challenges*
• Affluent community	• Rising unemployment
• Successful post-secondary rates	• one of 6 high schools
• class size is manageable	• population is increasing rapidly
• diverse population (ethnicity)	• disproportionate #'s in gender
• strong parental involvement deters disciplinary action	• socioeconomic status is decreasing
• disciplinary expectations are clear	• language barriers (potentially)

> staff is not representative of their student pop.

> drop out rate is increasing

> disproportionate #'s of Hispanic students in the GATE program based on population

> higher #'s of special ed. population of Hispanics

> teaching staff experience is decreasing

2. What are some *implications* for the Big River's school improvement plan?

✓ ADDRESS the issues Around staff representation in terms of ethnicity
✓ High #'s in special education
✓ hiring qualified teachers
✓ why are people leaving the ~~district~~ this school for others in the district

3. Looking at the data presented, what other demographic data would you want to answer the question *Who are we?* for Big River High School?

What I Saw in the Example: Big River High School

At the end of each chapter, I add what I saw in the data, using the study questions. (Ch4Saw.pdf) When applicable, I have referenced the figure or page number that gave me my first impression of strengths and challenges.

Demographic Strengths	Demographic Challenges
• Big River High School is located in a city with many employment options, even though it is not currently at its best. The majority of the workforce has some college education and just under half have earned college degrees. (Page 41) • District ethnicity percentages have remained consistent over time. (Figure 4.3) • The district consists of a majority of "high SES" families. (Figure 4.5) • Big River High School is a large, comprehensive school with diversity. (Figures 4.7 and 4.8) • Average class sizes are not too big at 26 students. (Page 47) • The majority of Big River students come from "high SES" families. (Figure 4.14) • With more than 40% of the students speaking a language other than English at home, only around 16% are considered limited or non-English learners. (Figure 4.16) • The numbers of immigrant students are decreasing over time. (Figure 4.17) • There is a *Student Behavior and Parent Information Handbook*, and a *Big River Handbook*. (Page 55) • Attendance rates are not bad. (Pages 56) • Special education numbers seem to be consistent over time. (Figure 4.22) • There is a good turnout for GEAR UP. (Figure 4.23) • All ethnicities are represented in the gifted program. (Figure 4.25) • The school knows the reasons students are no longer at the school, by grade level. (Figure 4.26) • The dropout rate is low for an urban setting. (Figure 4.27) • The graduation rate is good at 94%. (Page 62) • The student-to-teacher ratio is good. (Page 63) • There are four assistant principals. The assistant principal for discipline is Black and the AP for guidance is Hispanic. (Page 63) • There is an increasing percentage of male teachers. (Figure 4.29) • The average number of years of teaching is pretty consistent across grade levels. The average increased last year at the school, while the district stayed the same. (Figure 4.30)	• The unemployment rate in the city is currently high: more than double what it was three years earlier. (Page 41) • Ridgeview School District is large, with a slightly decreasing enrollment. (Page 4.1) • There is diversity in the district and school. The majority population is Hispanic, possibly with English learning needs. (Figure 4.2 and 4.7) • Big River High School enrollment is increasing; however, grade level enrollment appears to drop-off by grade twelve each year. (Figures 4.9 and 4.10) • There are more females than males in each grade level and year. (Figure 4.11 and 4.13) • Mobility, at 30%, is fairly high. (Page 48) • The gap between the number of high and low SES students is closing. (Figure 4.14) • A majority of White and Asian students come from high SES families, while Hispanic and Black families are both high SES and low SES. (Figure 4.14) • Over 40% of the Big River students have a home language other than English. Thirty-seven percent speak Spanish at home. (Figure 4.15) • The numbers of suspensions and expulsions have increased in the past two years. (Figures 4.19 and 4.21) • It appears that more males than females get referred to special education, and mostly Hispanic. (Figure 4.22) • There is an increase in students leaving Big River in the past three years. Most transfer to another school in the district and most seem to do so in grade nine. (Figure 4.26) • There is an increase in Dropouts. (Figure 4.27) • Seventy percent of the teachers are White, while only 34% of the students are White. (Figures 4.7 and 4.29) • There are a lot of new teachers at Big River. Many more teachers may be retiring in the next few years. (Pages 64-65) • Thirty-one teachers were teaching without full credentials in 2003-04. (Page 66)

Implications for Big River's school improvement plan

- Do teachers have the professional learning opportunities needed to work with students with ethnic, language, school experience, and SES backgrounds different from their own? With the unemployment rate increasing, perhaps there will be an even higher need for understanding how to work with students who live in poverty.
- Are the new teachers and those not fully credentialed well supported to becoming effective teachers?
- The school needs to recruit more ethnic teachers, particularly Hispanics.
- Big River would do well to make sure teachers, by average years of teaching, are mixed by grade and content area.
- With an assumed shortage of Hispanic teachers, it might be good for the school district to have a future teacher program.
- The behavior program and the dropout prevention program need to be evaluated, as does GEAR UP.

Other desired demographic data or information

- Who are the migrant students? Where do they come from, and where do they go? At what rate do they come back?
- Why is there an increase in suspensions and expulsions? What are the causes?
- It would be good to know more about how students are treated, with respect to discipline.
- It would be good to know *attendance by grade levels.*
- What about mobility? How many of these students become dropouts? Why do they transfer to another school?
- Are there after-school programs, summer school, adult education, and/or community English as a Second Language programs?
- What about the parents? How many of these students are in single parent families or living with unemployed parents? Are there homeless families?
- What happens to the students after high school?
- What languages do the teachers speak?
- Why do students dropout: what is the effectiveness of the dropout prevention program in preventing dropouts?
- It would be good to know *special education numbers by disabilities.* How are students identified for special education?
- What were the policy changes that may have contributed to increases in behavior issues and dropouts? Are they effective changes?
- How many years of teaching do most teachers have, by courses taught?

> *With demographic data, we are answering the basic question, "Who are we?" The answers to the question, "Who are we?", set the context for the school, have huge implications for the direction the continuous school improvement plan will take, and can help explain how the school gets the results it is getting.*

Summary

The first data required for continuous school improvement planning are demographic data. With demographic data, we are answering the basic question, *Who are we?* The answers to the question, *Who are we?*, set the context for the school, have huge implications for the direction the continuous school improvement plan will take, and can help explain how the school gets the results it is getting. Our example school, Big River High School, showed how a demographic analysis could look. The accompanying CD-ROM has tools and templates to help your school create a comprehensive demographic profile.

Typical Demographic Data to Gather to Answer the Question, *Who Are We?*  (DemoData.pdf)

Community

▼ Location and history
▼ Economic base, population trends, and community resources (*www.census.gov* is a great resource for getting information about the community, as is your local chamber of commerce)
▼ Community involvement
▼ Business partnerships

School District

▼ Description and history
▼ Number of schools, administrators, students and teachers over time, and by grade level

School

▼ Description and history, attendance area, location
▼ Type of school, e.g., magnet, alternative, charter, private, private management
▼ Number of administrators, students and teachers over time, and by grade level
▼ Number of students electing to come to the school from out of the attendance area
▼ Grants and awards received
▼ Title 1/Schoolwide
▼ Safety/crime data
▼ *State designation as a dangerous school
▼ Uniqueness and strengths
▼ Class sizes
▼ After-school programs/summer school

- ▼ Extracurricular activities
- ▼ Advisors for extracurricular activities
  - ◆ Are they teachers on staff who receive extra pay?
  - ◆ Are they teachers in district, but at other schools, who receive extra pay?
  - ◆ Are they non-teachers paid to be advisors?
- ▼ Tutoring/peer mentoring
- ▼ Community support-services coordinated
- ▼ Counseling opportunities
- ▼ *Facilities: equipped for networked computers and handicapped
- ▼ Facilities: age, capacity, maintenance
- ▼ Availability of necessities and other supplies

Students Over Time, and by Grade Level

- ▼ Living situation/family structure/family size
- ▼ Preschool/Head Start/Even Start
- ▼ Preschool attendance
- ▼ *Number of students
- ▼ Gender of students
- ▼ *Race/ethnicity numbers and percentages
- ▼ Free/reduced lunch numbers and percentages
- ▼ *Language fluency by language
- ▼ *Migrant/immigrants by country, home languages
- ▼ *Homeless
- ▼ *Special Education by disability, gender, ethnicity, language fluency, free/reduced lunch
- ▼ *Attendance/tardies
- ▼ Mobility (where students go/come from)
- ▼ Retention rates by gender, ethnicity, language fluency, free/reduced lunch
- ▼ *Dropout rates by gender, ethnicity, free/reduced lunch, migrant, special education (where students go/what they do)
- ▼ Number of students leaving school overall by gender, ethnicity, language fluency, free/reduced lunch
- ▼ Extracurricular activity participation/clubs/service learning by gender, ethnicity, language fluency, free/reduced lunch
- ▼ Number of participants in programs, such as AP, IB, Honors, Upward Bound, GEAR UP, college-prep, vocational
- ▼ Number of home schoolers associated with school, along with how they are associated with the school
- ▼ Number of students electing to come to the school from out-of-the-attendance area
- ▼ Number of bus riders and distances they ride

- ▼ Student employment
- ▼ *Discipline indicators (e.g., suspensions, referrals, types of incidences, number of students carrying weapons on school property)
- ▼ *Number of drugs on school property (offered, sold, or given illegal drugs)
- ▼ *Graduation rates by gender, ethnicity, language proficiency, free/reduced lunch, migrant, and special education (where students go/what they do)
- ▼ Number of high school students concurrently enrolled in college courses
- ▼ Number of students meeting college course entrance requirements by gender, ethnicity, language fluency, free/reduced lunch
- ▼ Number of middle students concurrently enrolled in high school courses
- ▼ Number of scholarships by gender, ethnicity, language proficiency, free/reduced lunch
- ▼ Number of students completing GEDs
- ▼ Adult education programs
- ▼ Number and percentage of students going on to college, post-graduate training, and/or employment
- ▼ Grade-point average in college
- ▼ Number of graduates ending up in college remedial classes

Staff Over Time

- ▼ *Number of teachers, administrators, instructional specialists, support staff by roles
- ▼ *Years of experience, by grade level and/or role, in this school/in teaching
- ▼ Ethnicity, gender, languages spoken
- ▼ Retirement projections
- ▼ *Types of certifications/licenses/teacher qualifications/percentage of time teaching in certified area(s)
- ▼ Grades/subjects teachers are teaching
- ▼ Degrees
- ▼ *Educational training of paraprofessionals
- ▼ Teacher-student ratios by grade level
- ▼ Teacher turnover rates
- ▼ Attendance rates
- ▼ Teacher involvement in extracurricular activities, program participation
- ▼ *Number of teachers receiving high-quality professional development
- ▼ *Percent of teachers qualified to use technology for instruction
- ▼ National Board for Professional Teaching Standards (NBPTS) teachers

Parents

- ▼ Educational levels, home language, employment, socioeconomic status
- ▼ Involvement with their child's learning
- ▼ Involvement in school activities
- ▼ Incarceration

*Required for *No Child Left Behind* (includes the numbers required to understand the disaggregated numbers required by NCLB).

On the CD Related to This Chapter

▼ Study Questions Related to *Who are we?* (Ch4Qs.doc)
These study questions will help you better understand the information provided in Chapter 4. This template file can be printed for use as you study the case study or to use with staff as you study your own demographic data.

▼ Demographic Graphing Templates (HighDemog.xls)
All of the *Microsoft Excel* files that were used to create the demographic graphs in the Big River High School example (Chapter 4) appear on the CD. Use these templates by putting your data in the data source table and changing the title/labels to reflect your data. Your graphs will build automatically. This file also explains how to use the templates.

▼ *School Data Profile Template* (HighProfil.doc)
This *Microsoft Word* file provides a template for creating your own school data profile like the one for Big River High School, using the graphing and table templates provided. Create your graphs in the graphing and table templates, then copy and paste them into the *School Data Profile Template*.

▼ The following profile templates for gathering and organizing data, prior to graphing, can be adjusted to add data elements you feel are important to fully complete the profile. If you just need to graph your data, use the graphing templates. These are for optional use.

- ◆ *School Profile* (ProfilSc.doc)
  The *School Profile* is a template for gathering and organizing data about your school, prior to graphing. Please adjust the profile to add data elements you feel are important for describing the context of your school. This information is then graphed and described in narrative form. If creating a school portfolio, the data graphs and narrative will appear in *Information and Analysis*. (If you already have your data organized and just need to graph it, you might want to skip this step and use the graphing templates, described above.)

- *Community Profile* (ProfilCo.doc)

  The *Community Profile* is a template for gathering and organizing data about your community, prior to graphing. Please adjust the profile to add data elements you feel are important for describing the context of your community. It is important to describe how the community has changed over time, and how it is expected to change in the near future. This information is then graphed and written in narrative form. If creating a school portfolio, the data graphs and narrative will appear in *Information and Analysis*. (If you already have your data organized and just need to graph it, you might want to skip this step and use the graphing templates described on the previous page.)

- *Administrator Profile* (ProfilAd.doc)

  The *Administrator Profile* is a template for gathering and organizing data about your school administrators, prior to graphing. Please adjust the profile to fully describe your administrators. This information is then graphed and written in narrative form. If creating a school portfolio, the data graphs and narrative will appear in the *Information and Analysis* and *Leadership* sections. (If you already have your data organized and just need to graph it, you might want to skip this step and use the graphing templates described on the previous page.)

- *Teacher Profile* (ProfilTe.doc)

  The *Teacher Profile* is a template for gathering and organizing data about your school's teachers, prior to graphing. Please adjust the profile to fully describe your teachers. The synthesis of this information is then graphed and written in narrative form. If creating a school portfolio, the data graphs and narrative will appear in *Information and Analysis*. (If you already have your data organized and just need to graph it, you might want to skip this step and use the graphing templates described on the previous page.)

- *Staff (other than teacher) Profile* (ProfilSt.doc)

  The *Staff (Other than Teacher) Profile* is a template for gathering and organizing data about school staff who are not teachers, prior to graphing. Please adjust the profile to fully describe your non-teaching staff. The synthesis of this information is then graphed and written in narrative form. If creating a school portfolio, the data graphs and narrative will appear in *Information and Analysis*. (If you already have your data organized and just need to graph it, you might want to skip this step and use the graphing templates described on the previous page.)

▼ *History Gram Activity* (ACTHstry.pdf)

A team-building activity that will "write" the history of the school, which could help everyone see what staff has experienced since coming to the school and how many school improvement initiatives have been started over the years. It is helpful for understanding what it will take to keep this current school improvement effort going.

▼ *Questions to Guide the Analysis of Demographic Data* (QsDemogr.doc)

This *Microsoft Word* file provides a guide for interpreting your demographic data. Adjust the questions to better reflect the discussion you would like to have with your staff about the gathered demographic data.

▼ *What I Saw in the Example* (Ch4Saw.pdf)

What I Saw in the Example is a file, organized by the demographic study questions, that summarizes what the author saw in the demographic data provided by Big River High School.

▼ *Demographic Data to Gather to Create the Context of the School* (DemoData.pdf)

This file defines the types of demographic data that are important to gather to create the context of the school and describe *Who are we?*

Analyzing the Data:
How Do We Do Business?

Chapter 5

> *How a school does business can be ascertained through studying student, staff, and parent questionnaire results, and through assessing with tools that can tell how staff works together and with the larger school community.*

The second question in our continuous school improvement planning model, described in Chapter 3, is *How do we do business?* This question helps us understand organizational culture, shared assumptions, beliefs, and typical behavior. How a school does business can be ascertained through studying student, staff, and parent questionnaire results, and through assessing with tools that can tell how staffs work together and with the larger school community. The answers to this question can inform school staff members of what is possible as they plan for the future, and what it will take to systemically improve how they work together.

Humans cannot act any differently from what they value, believe, or perceive. Since we all want staff to act as the vision directs, it seems wise to understand what staff is perceiving about the learning environment and what staff believes will improve student learning. Staff questionnaire results can tell us about needs for professional learning, team building, and motivation. Parent and student questionnaire results can point to needs that must also be considered in the continuous school improvement plan.

The example school in this book used the student, staff, and parent questionnaires to assess how it does business. (These files are not on the CD, as the questionnaires have been upgraded to the *Education for the Future* questionnaires, which *are* on the CD.) (EFF_Qs Folder) The school also used the *Education for the Future Continuous Improvement Continuums* (CICs). The CICs are powerful tools for assessing the health of a school as a system. (CICs.doc) (A version for the district is also found on the CD.)

As we start on *How do we do business?* with Big River High School, please note the study questions on page 119 to assist in studying the Big River data. (Ch5Qs.pdf) There is space in the margins on the data pages to write your impressions as you review the data. At the end of the chapter, I share what I saw in the data. (Ch5Saw.pdf) For reviewing your own data, you might want to use a comparison table to look across student, staff, and parent questionnaire results. (QTable.doc) You are welcome to use this as well as the study questions.

Our Example School: Big River High School
How Do We Do Business?

To get a better understanding of the learning environment, Big River administered the same student, staff, and parent questionnaires for the past five years. In October 2004, they administered a different staff questionnaire to see if they could get different information, including an understanding of the degree to which standards are being implemented in the school. Staff also assessed where it felt the school ranked on the *Education for the Future Continuous Improvement Continuums* (CICs). Summaries of the results follow, starting with the CICs.

School Processes

Big River High School Continuous Improvement Continuum Baseline Results

In February 2001, Big River High School staff conducted its baseline assessment on the *Education for the Future Continuous Improvement Continuums.* 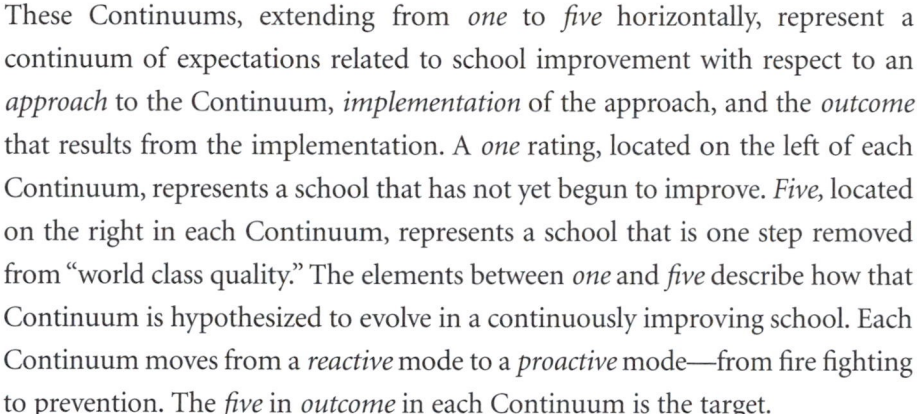 (BRbase.pdf)

These Continuums, extending from *one* to *five* horizontally, represent a continuum of expectations related to school improvement with respect to an *approach* to the Continuum, *implementation* of the approach, and the *outcome* that results from the implementation. A *one* rating, located on the left of each Continuum, represents a school that has not yet begun to improve. *Five,* located on the right in each Continuum, represents a school that is one step removed from "world class quality." The elements between *one* and *five* describe how that Continuum is hypothesized to evolve in a continuously improving school. Each Continuum moves from a *reactive* mode to a *proactive* mode—from fire fighting to prevention. The *five* in *outcome* in each Continuum is the target.

Vertically, we have *Approach, Implementation,* and *Outcome,* for any number *one* through *five,* as hypotheses. In other words, the *implementation* statement describes how the *approach* might look when *implemented,* and the *outcome* is the "pay-off" for *implementing* the *approach.* If the hypotheses are accurate, the *outcome* will not be realized until the *approach* is actually *implemented.*

After reading a Continuum, each staff member placed a dot on the Continuum to represent where she/he thought the school was with respect to *Approach, Implementation,* and *Outcome.* Staff members discussed why they thought their school was where they rated it. Following the discussion, the staff came to consensus on a number that represented where the school was for each element, and created *Next Steps* for moving up the Continuums.

In November 2002, staff reassessed to see progress. It wasn't until May 2004 that staff came back to the CICs for a follow-up assessment. The comparison ratings for 2001 and 2002, and brief discussions from their 2004 report, follow.

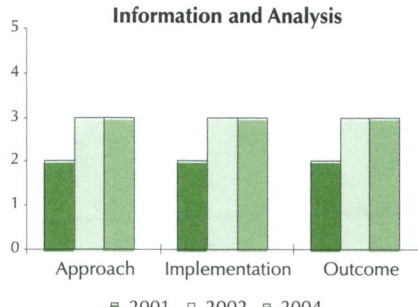

Information and Analysis

2001 □ 2002 ▣ 2004

Information and Analysis

Collectively, staff members believe that Big River High School was a 3 in *Approach,* 3 in *Implementation,* and 3 in *Outcome* with respect to *Information and Analysis* in 2004. Schoolwide data are being collected on student performance, attendance, and achievement; and student, staff, and parent questionnaires are being administered annually. The data are being used for planning. These data have been extremely valuable. The district helped considerably by purchasing and establishing a data warehouse.

2004 Next Steps:

▼ We need to pull our data together in a systematic way to help us plan strategically, and to continuously improve.

▼ We need to make sure that we are using complete data, and looking at what all the data are telling us, not just one questionnaire item as we used to do.

▼ We need to better use these data to feed the systemic plan, to analyze information to get to the root causes of problems, and to track data for improvement.

▼ We need to get ourselves rejuvenated for continuous improvement.

INFORMATION AND ANALYSIS—2004

	One	Two	Three	Four	Five
Approach	Data or information about student performance and needs are not gathered in any systematic way; there is no way to determine what needs to change at the school, based on data.	There is no systematic process, but some teacher and student information is collected and used to problem-solve and establish student learning standards.	School collects data related to student performance (e.g., attendance, achievement) and conducts surveys on student, teacher, and parent needs. The information is used to drive the strategic quality plan for school change.	There is systematic reliance on hard data (including data for subgroups) as a basis for decision making at the classroom level as well as at the school level. Changes are based on the study of data to meet the needs of students and teachers.	Information is gathered in all areas of student interaction with the school. Teachers engage students in gathering information on their own performance. Accessible to all levels, data are comprehensive in scope and an accurate reflection of school quality.
Implementation	No information is gathered with which to make changes. Student dissatisfaction with the learning process is seen as an irritation, not a need for improvement.	Some data are tracked, such as drop-out rates and enrollment. Only a few individuals are asked for feedback about areas of schooling.	School collects information on current and former students (e.g., student achievement and perceptions), analyzes and uses it in conjunction with future trends for planning. Identified areas for improvement are tracked over time.	Data are used to improve the effectiveness of teaching strategies on all student learning. Students' historical performances are graphed and utilized for diagnostics. Student evaluations and performances are analyzed by teachers in all classrooms.	Innovative teaching processes that meet the needs of students are implemented to the delight of teachers, parents, and students. Information is analyzed and used to prevent student failure. Root causes are known through analyses. Problems are prevented through the use of data.
Outcome	Only anecdotal and hypothetical information is available about student performance, behavior, and satisfaction. Problems are solved individually with short-term results.	Little data are available. Change is limited to some areas of the school and dependent upon individual teachers and their efforts.	Information collected about student and parent needs, assessment, and instructional practices is shared with the school staff and used to plan for change. Information helps staff understand pressing issues, analyze information for "root causes," and track results for improvement.	An information system is in place. Positive trends begin to appear in many classrooms and schoolwide. There is evidence that these results are caused by understanding and effectively using data collected.	Students are delighted with the school's instructional processes and proud of their own capabilities to learn and assess their own growth. Good to excellent achievement is the result for all students. No student falls through the cracks. Teachers use data to predict and prevent potential problems.

Student Achievement

Staff rated the school a 3 in *Approach, Implementation,* and *Outcome* with respect to *Student Achievement*. The rationale follows. There has been a lot of effort to track data, which has led to an increase in communication among students and teachers regarding student learning. Staff is happy with the progress being made. However, staff believes it needs to crank up the heat.

2004 Next Steps:

▼ A district data warehouse has been established that allows a more systematic look at student achievement data and a closer look at classroom data.

▼ More staff members need to learn how to use the data warehouse to dig deeper into the data to prevent student achievement failures.

▼ We need to continue to make further progress in developing a comprehensive and consistent view of how students are evaluated.

▼ We need to continue to look at the vision and mission of the school and determine the most effective design for the master schedule.

▼ We need to do more work with the middle and elementary schools to ensure a continuum of learning that makes sense for the students.

▼ We need to reinforce the teaching of standards through professional learning, communication, and collaboration.

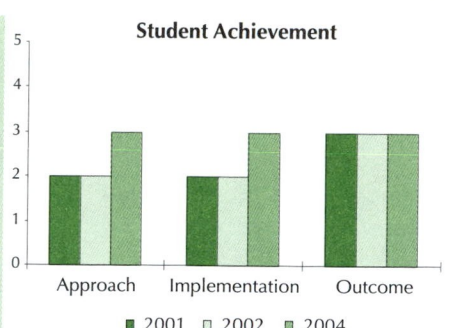

Student Achievement

■ 2001 □ 2002 ■ 2004

STUDENT ACHIEVEMENT—2004

	One	Two	Three	Four	Five
Approach	Instructional and organizational processes critical to student success are not identified. Little distinction of student learning differences is made. Some teachers believe that not all students can achieve.	Some data are collected on student background and performance trends. Learning gaps are noted to direct improvement of instruction. It is known that student learning standards must be identified.	Student learning standards are identified, and a continuum of learning is created throughout the school. Student performance data are collected and compared to the standards in order to analyze how to improve learning for all students.	Data on student achievement are used throughout the school to pursue the improvement of student learning. Teachers collaborate to implement appropriate instruction and assessment strategies for meeting student learning standards articulated across grade levels. All teachers believe that all students can learn.	School makes an effort to exceed student achievement expectations. Innovative instructional changes are made to anticipate learning needs and improve student achievement. Teachers are able to predict characteristics impacting student achievement and to know how to perform from a small set of internal quality measures.
Implementation	All students are taught the same way. There is no communication with students about their academic needs or learning styles. There are no analyses of how to improve instruction.	Some effort is made to track and analyze student achievement trends on a school-wide basis. Teachers begin to understand the needs and learning gaps of students.	Teachers study effective instruction and assessment strategies to implement standards and to increase their students' learning. Student feedback and analysis of achievement data are used in conjunction with implementation support strategies.	There is a systematic focus on implementing student learning standards and on the improvement of student learning schoolwide. Effective instruction and assessment strategies are implemented in each classroom. Teachers support one another with peer coaching and/or action research focused on implementing strategies that lead to increased achievement and the attainment of the shared vision.	All teachers correlate critical instructional and assessment strategies with objective indicators of quality student achievement. A comparative analysis of actual individual student performance to student learning standards is utilized to adjust teaching strategies to ensure a progression of learning for all students.
Outcome	There is wide variation in student attitudes and achievement with undesirable results. There is high dissatisfaction among students with learning. Student background is used as an excuse for low student achievement.	There is some evidence that student achievement trends are available to teachers and are being used. There is much effort, but minimal observable results in improving student achievement.	There is an increase in communication between students and teachers regarding student learning. Teachers learn about effective instructional strategies that will implement the shared vision, including student learning standards, and meet the needs of their students. They make some gains.	Increased student achievement is evident schoolwide. Student morale, attendance, and behavior are good. Teachers converse often with each other about preventing student failure. Areas for further attention are clear.	Students and teachers conduct self-assessments to continuously improve performance. Improvements in student achievement are evident and clearly caused by teachers' and students' understandings of individual student learning standards, linked to appropriate and effective instructional and assessment strategies. A continuum of learning results. No students fall through the cracks.

Quality Planning

Quality Planning

Big River staff rated itself 3s in *Approach, Implementation,* and *Outcome* for *Quality Planning.* The school plan needs to become a comprehensive representation of the vision for the school so that improvement can be systematic and schoolwide.

2004 Next Steps:

▼ We need to ensure that we work from one plan that describes how we carry out our vision. This plan needs to be based on the facts (data) and truly implemented.

▼ We need to put the plan into action and include time for evaluation and continuous improvement.

QUALITY PLANNING—2004

	One	Two	Three	Four	Five
Approach	No quality plan or process exists. Data are neither used nor considered important in planning.	The staff realize the importance of a mission, vision, and one comprehensive action plan. Teams develop goals and timelines, and dollars are allocated to begin the process.	A comprehensive school plan to achieve the vision is developed. Plan includes evaluation and continuous improvement.	One focused and integrated schoolwide plan for implementing a continuous improvement process is put into action. All school efforts are focused on the implementation of this plan that represents the achievement of the vision.	A plan for the continuous improvement of the school, with a focus on students, is put into place. There is excellent articulation and integration of all elements in the school due to quality planning. Leadership team ensures all elements are implemented by all appropriate parties.
Implementation	There is no knowledge of or direction for quality planning. Budget is allocated on an as-needed basis. Many plans exist.	School community begins continuous improvement planning efforts by laying out major steps to a shared vision, by identifying values and beliefs, the purpose of the school, a mission, vision, and student learning standards.	Implementation goals, responsibilities, due dates, and timelines are spelled out. Support structures for implementing the plan are set in place.	The quality management plan is implemented through effective procedures in all areas of the school. Everyone commits to implementing the plan aligned to the vision, mission, and values and beliefs. All share responsibility for accomplishing school goals.	Schoolwide goals, mission, vision, and student learning standards are shared and articulated throughout the school and with feeder schools. The attainment of identified student learning standards is linked to planning and implementation of effective instruction that meets students' needs. Leaders at all levels are developing expertise because planning is the norm.
Outcome	There is no evidence of comprehensive planning. Staff work is carried out in isolation. A continuum of learning for students is absent.	The school community understands the benefits of working together to implement a comprehensive continuous improvement plan.	There is evidence that the school plan is being implemented in some areas of the school. Improvements are neither systematic nor integrated schoolwide.	A schoolwide plan is known to all. Results from working toward the quality improvement goals are evident throughout the school. Planning is ongoing and inclusive of all stakeholders. Evidence of effective teaching	and learning results in significant improvement of student achievement attributed to quality planning at all levels of the school organization. Teachers and administrators understand and share the school mission and vision. Quality planning is seamless and all demonstrate evidence of accountability.

Professional Development

Staff assessed the school on *Professional Development* as 3s in *Approach, Implementation,* and *Outcome.* Staff feels that the school plan and analysis of student needs continues to be used to target appropriate professional development for teachers. Inservices are helping staff think about the entire school and to rethink the types of professional learning that the entire staff needs to engage in in order to implement the vision. The 3s in 2001 and the 3s in 2004 are different. We have not done enough to warrant 4s.

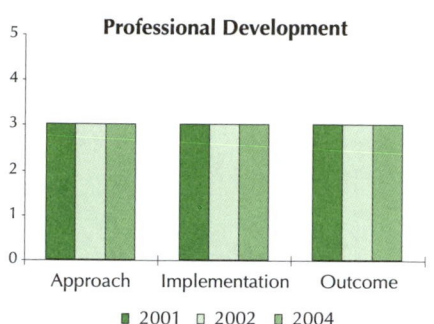

Professional Development

■ 2001　□ 2002　■ 2004

2004 Next Steps:

▼ Our professional development needs to become professional learning that is embedded into the work week and include collaboration, peer coaching, demonstration lessons, and strong accountability to implement the vision and standards.

▼ Our professional learning needs to focus on teaching students who live in poverty and who are not fluent speakers of English. Our professional development also needs to include studying student data and student work.

▼ We need to allocate more time for cross-curricular planning.

▼ We need to evaluate professional learning activities to make sure that they are getting us to our goals.

▼ We need to support our new teachers as much as we can.

PROFESSIONAL DEVELOPMENT—2004

	One	Two	Three	Four	Five
Approach	There is no professional development. Teachers, principals, and staff are seen as interchangeable parts that can be replaced. Professional development is external and usually equated to attending a conference alone. Hierarchy determines "haves" and "have-nots."	The "cafeteria" approach to professional development is used, whereby individual teachers choose what they want to take, without regard to an overall school plan.	The shared vision, school plan and student needs are used to target focused professional development for all employees. Staff is inserviced on relevant instructional and leadership strategies.	Professional development and data-gathering methods are used by all teachers and are directed toward the goals of the shared vision and the continuous improvement of the school. Teachers have ongoing conversations about student achievement data. Other staff members receive training in their content areas. Systems thinking is considered in all decisions.	Leadership and staff continuously improve all aspects of the learning organization through an innovative, data-driven, and comprehensive continuous improvement process that prevents student failures. Effective job-embedded professional development is ongoing for implementing the vision for student success. Traditional teacher evaluations are replaced by collegial coaching and action research focused on student learning standards. Policies set professional development as a priority budget line-item. Professional development is planned, aligned, and lead to the achievement of student learning standards.
Implementation	Teacher, principal, and staff performance is controlled and inspected. Performance evaluations are used to detect mistakes.	Teacher professional development is sporadic and unfocused, lacking an approach for implementing new procedures and processes. Some leadership training begins to take place.	Teachers are involved in year-round quality professional development. The school community is trained in shared decision making, team building concepts, effective communication strategies, and data analysis at the classroom level.	Teachers, in teams, continuously set and implement student achievement goals. Leadership considers these goals and provides necessary support structures for collaboration. Teachers utilize effective support approaches as they implement new instruction and assessment strategies. Coaching and feedback structures are in place. Use of new knowledge and skills is evident.	Teams passionately support each other in the pursuit of quality improvement at all levels. Teachers make bold changes in instruction and assessment strategies focused on student learning standards and student learning styles. A teacher as action researcher model is implemented. Staffwide conversations focus on systemic reflection and improvement. Teachers are strong leaders.
Outcome	No professional growth and no staff or student performance improvement. There exists a high turnover rate of employees, especially administrators. Attitudes and approaches filter down to students.	The effectiveness of professional development is not known or analyzed. Teachers feel helpless about making schoolwide changes.	Teachers, working in teams, feel supported and begin to feel they can make changes. Evidence shows that shared decision making works.	A collegial school is evident. Effective classroom strategies are practiced, articulated schoolwide, and are reflective of professional development aimed at ensuring student achievement, and the implementation of the shared vision, that includes student learning standards.	True systemic change and improved student achievement result because teachers are knowledgeable of and implement effective, differentiated teaching strategies for individual student learning gains. Teachers' repertoire of skills are enhanced and students are achieving. Professional development is driving learning at all levels.

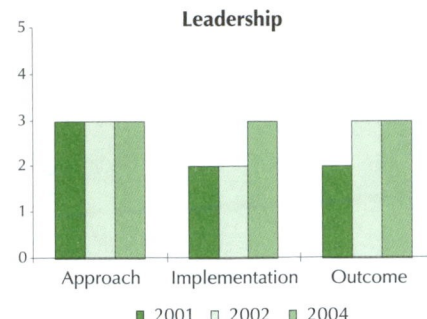

Leadership

2001 ■ 2002 □ 2004 ■

Leadership

Big River staff rated the school 3s in *Approach*, *Implementation*, and *Outcome* with respect to *Leadership*. We have come a long way in this category, but we have a long way to go.

2004 Next Steps:

▼ Our steering committees need to make recommendations from their research to the staff concerning leadership for the comprehensive plan for school improvement based on the school's mission.

▼ Continuous efforts to keep everyone informed are essential to effective implementation of the plan.

▼ We must continue to meet regularly to ensure the implementation of the vision, plan, and standards. Our early release days have been invaluable, although we need to focus the time more on reviewing student work and student data.

LEADERSHIP—2004

	One	Two	Three	Four	Five
Approach	Principal as decision maker. Decisions are reactive to state, district, and federal mandates. There is no knowledge of continuous improvement.	A shared decision-making structure is put into place and discussions begin on how to achieve a school vision. Most decisions are focused on solving problems and are reactive.	Leadership team is committed to continuous improvement. Leadership seeks inclusion of all school sectors and supports study teams by making time provisions for their work.	Leadership team represents a true shared decision making structure. Study teams are reconstructed for the implementation of a comprehensive continuous improvement plan.	A strong continuous improvement structure is set into place that allows for input from all sectors of the school, district, and community, ensuring strong communication, flexibility, and refinement of approach and beliefs. The school vision is student focused, based on data and appropriate for school/ community values, and meeting student needs.
Implementation	Principal makes all decisions, with little or no input from teachers, the community, or students. Leadership inspects for mistakes.	School values and beliefs are identified; the purpose of school is defined; a school mission and student learning standards are developed with representative input. A structure for studying approaches to achieving student learning standards is established.	Leadership team is active on study teams and integrates recommendations from the teams' research and analyses to form a comprehensive plan for continuous improvement within the context of the school mission. Everyone is kept informed.	Decisions about budget and implementation of the vision are made within teams, by the principal, by the leadership team, and by the full staff as appropriate. All decisions are communicated to the leadership team and to the full staff.	The vision is implemented and articulated across all grade levels and into feeder schools. Quality standards are reinforced throughout the school. All members of the school community understand and apply the quality standards. Leadership team has systematic interactions and involvement with district administrators, teachers, parents, community, and students about the school's direction. Necessary resources are available to implement and measure staff learning related to student learning standards.
Outcome	Decisions lack focus and consistency. There is no evidence of staff commitment to a shared vision. Students and parents do not feel they are being heard. Decision-making process is clear and known.	The mission provides a focus for all school improvement and guides the action to the vision. The school community is committed to continuous improvement. Quality leadership techniques are used sporadically.	Leadership team is seen as committed to planning and quality improvement. Critical areas for improvement are identified. Faculty feel included in shared decision making.	There is evidence that the leadership team listens to all levels of the organization. Implementation of the continuous improvement plan is linked to student learning standards and the guiding principles of the school. Leadership capacities for implementing the vision among teachers are evident.	Site-based management and shared decision making truly exists. Teachers understand and display an intimate knowledge of how the school operates. Teachers support and communicate with each other in the implementation of quality strategies. Teachers implement the vision in their classrooms and can determine how their new approach meets student needs and leads to the attainment of student learning standards. Leaders are standards-driven at all levels.

Partnership Development

Collectively, the staff believes that, with respect to *Partnership Development*, Big River currently is a 4 in *Approach*, a 4 in *Implementation*, and 4 in *Outcome*. In the past couple of years, Big River's partnerships have become more systematically defined in their support of the school mission and student achievement. Our community mentoring program for *At Risk Kids* continues to be strong, as well as our performing arts partnerships.

2004 Next Steps:

▼ We need to evaluate our partnerships and encourage new ones to help students achieve and exceed learning standards.

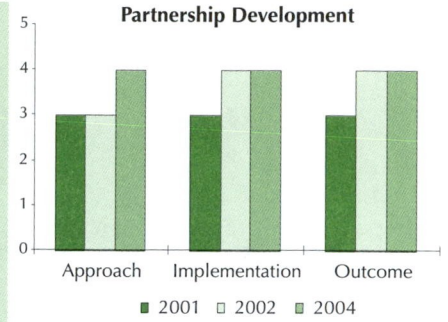

Partnership Development

■ 2001 □ 2002 ■ 2004

PARTNERSHIP DEVELOPMENT—2004

	One	Two	Three	Four	Five
Approach	There is no system for input from parents, business, or community. Status quo is desired for managing the school.	Partnerships are sought, but mostly for money and things.	School has knowledge of why partnerships are important and seeks to include businesses and parents in a strategic fashion related to student learning standards for increased student achievement.	School seeks effective win-win business and community partnerships and parent involvement to implement the vision. Desired outcomes are clearly identified. A solid plan for partnership development exists.	Community, parent, and business partnerships become integrated across all student groupings. The benefits of outside involvement are known by all. Parent and business involvement in student learning is refined. Student learning *regularly* takes place beyond the school walls.
Implementation	Barriers are erected to close out involvement of outsiders. Outsiders are managed for least impact on status quo.	A team is assigned to get partners and to receive input from parents, the community, and business in the school.	Involvement of business, community, and parents begins to take place in some classrooms and after school hours related to the vision. Partners begin to realize how they can support each other in achieving school goals. School staff understand what partners need from the partnership.	There is a systematic utilization of parents, community, and businesses schoolwide. Areas in which the active use of these partnerships benefit student learning are clear.	Partnership development is articulated across all student groupings. Parents, community, business, and educators work together in an innovative fashion to increase student learning and to prepare students for the 21st Century. Partnerships are evaluated for continuous improvement.
Outcome	There is little or no involvement of parents, business, or community at-large. School is a closed, isolated system.	Much effort is given to establishing partner-ships. Some spotty trends emerge, such as receiving donated equipment.	Some substantial gains are achieved in implementing partnerships. Some student achievement increases can be attributed to this involvement.	Gains in student satisfaction with learning and school are clearly related to partnerships. All partners benefit.	Previously non-achieving students enjoy learning with excellent achievement. Community, business, and home become common places for student learning, while school becomes a place where parents come for further education. Partnerships enhance what the school does for students.

Continuous Improvement and Evaluation

Continuous Improvement and Evaluation

Staff rated the school 3s in *Approach, Implementation,* and *Outcome* with respect to *Continuous Improvement and Evaluation.*

2004 Next Steps:

▼ Identify root causes of problems and plan improvement based on the results.

▼ Explore alternative ways to prevent student failure.

▼ Define assessment parameters.

▼ Define data to be used (e.g., classroom grades, assessments, etc.).

▼ Seek information about client perceptions.

CONTINUOUS IMPROVEMENT AND EVALUATION—2004

	One	Two	Three	Four	Five
Approach	Neither goals nor strategies exist for the evaluation and continuous improvement of the school organization or for elements of the school organization.	The approach to continuous improvement and evaluation is problem-solving. If there are no problems, or if solutions can be made quickly, there is no need for improvement or analyses. Changes in parts of the system are not coordinated with all other parts.	Some elements of the school organization are evaluated for effectiveness. Some elements are improved on the basis of the evaluation findings.	All elements of the school's operations are evaluated for improvement and to ensure congruence of the elements with respect to the continuum of learning students experience.	All aspects of the school organization are rigorously evaluated and improved on a continuous basis. Students, and the maintenance of a comprehensive learning continuum for students, become the focus of all aspects of the school improvement process.
Implementation	With no overall plan for evaluation and continuous improvement, strategies are changed by individual teachers and administrators only when something sparks the need to improve. Reactive decisions and activities are a daily mode of operation.	Isolated changes are made in some areas of the school organization in response to problem incidents. Changes are not preceded by comprehensive analyses, such as an understanding of the root causes of problems. The effectiveness of the elements of the school organization, or changes made to the elements, is not known.	Elements of the school organization are improved on the basis of comprehensive analyses of root causes of problems, client perceptions, and operational effectiveness of processes.	Continuous improvement analyses of student achievement and instructional strategies are rigorously reinforced within each classroom and across learning levels to develop a comprehensive learning continuum for students and to prevent student failure.	Comprehensive continuous improvement becomes the way of doing business at the school. Teachers continuously improve the appropriateness and effectiveness of instructional strategies based on student feedback and performance. All aspects of the school organization are improved to support teachers' efforts.
Outcome	Individuals struggle with system failure. Finger pointing and blaming others for failure occurs. The effectiveness of strategies is not known. Mistakes are repeated.	Problems are solved only temporarily and few positive changes result. Additionally, unintended and undesirable consequences often appear in other parts of the system. Many aspects of the school are incongruent, keeping the school from reaching its vision.	Evidence of effective improvement strategies is observable. Positive changes are made and maintained due to comprehensive analyses and evaluation.	Teachers become astute at assessing and in predicting the impact of their instructional strategies on individual student achievement. Sustainable improvements in student achievement are evident at all grade levels, due to continuous improvement.	The school becomes a congruent and effective learning organization. Only instruction and assessment strategies that produce quality student achievement are used. A true continuum of learning results for all students and staff. The impact of improvements is increasingly measurable.

Perceptions

Big River High School students, staff, and parents completed the same questionnaires, designed by a district committee, over the past five years. Students and staff also answered two open-ended questions. Since the results over the five years were nearly identical, only data for 2004 is shown here.

Note: The narratives of these results are located on the CD. (StuNarr.doc, StfNarr.doc, ParNarr.doc) *Education for the Future* questionnaires and tools used to gather and assess perceptions, *similar* to the ones used by Big River High School, can be downloaded from the *Education for the Future* website: *http://eff.csuchico.edu/questionnaire_resources/.* For more information about *designing* questionnaires, see *Data Analysis for Continuous School Improvement,* Second Edition (Bernhardt, 2004).

The icons in the graphs that follow show the average responses to each item by disaggregation indicated in the legend. The lines join the icons to help the reader know the distribution results for each disaggregation. The lines have no other meaning.

Note: Some of the subgroup numbers do not add up to the total number of respondents because some respondents did not identify themselves by this demographic, or identified themselves by more than one demographic.

Comparison of Student, Staff, and Parent Responses

Student (n=1,353), staff (n=50), and parent (n=418) responses for 2003-04 were graphed by the totals and compared in Figure 5.1. In general, staff and parents were more positive than students when responding to the questionnaire items.

Figure 5.1

Big River High School Student, Staff, and Parent Responses
May 2004

5 Strongly Agree   4   3   2   Strongly Disagree 1

Students know what they are to learn in each class this year

Students have to work hard to do well in their classes

Students receive help with homework at school outside of class

Students' time is spent waiting for other students to behave

There is a regular schoolwide program to reward students for good work at this school

Teachers help students to look at their work to learn from their mistakes

Students evaluate their work using scoring guides or examples of already completed model assignments

Students are practicing different kinds of writing such as letters, reports, poetry, stories, etc.

Teachers have challenging activities for students to do if they finish their classwork early

Teachers motivate students to do their best work

Parents and teachers work together to help students do well in school

Students respect one another at this school

Students respect teachers at this school

Teachers respect students at this school

Teachers contact parents about student progress in school

I know what activities are going on at school

Students' parents help regularly with their students' schoolwork

When parents have a problem at the school they know who to call

Students (n=1,353)
Staff (n=50)
Parents (n=418)

Figure 5.1 (Continued)

Big River High School Student, Staff, and Parent Responses
May 2004

This can be used .....

22 questions

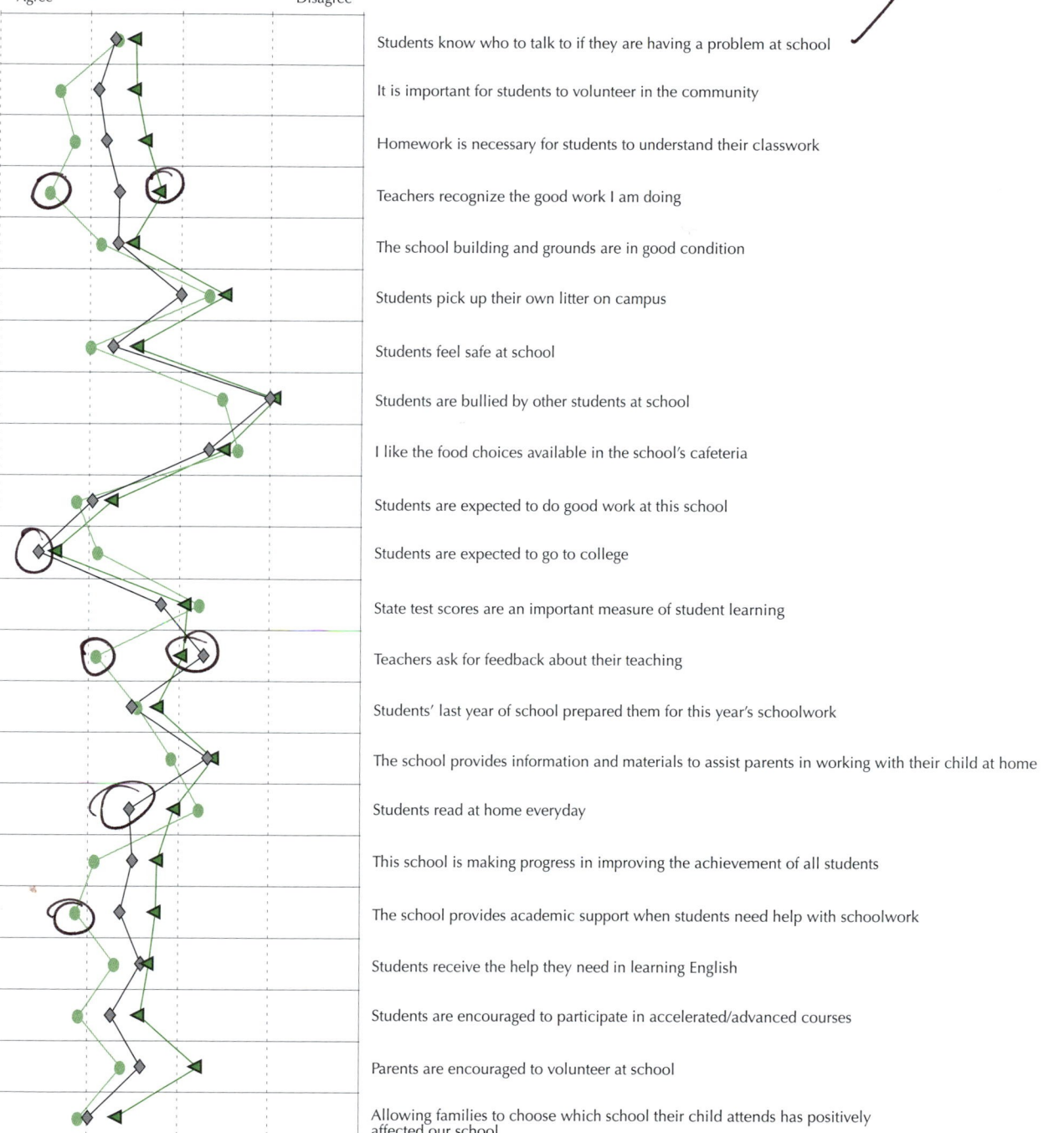

Students know who to talk to if they are having a problem at school

It is important for students to volunteer in the community

Homework is necessary for students to understand their classwork

Teachers recognize the good work I am doing

The school building and grounds are in good condition

Students pick up their own litter on campus

Students feel safe at school

Students are bullied by other students at school

I like the food choices available in the school's cafeteria

Students are expected to do good work at this school

Students are expected to go to college

State test scores are an important measure of student learning

Teachers ask for feedback about their teaching

Students' last year of school prepared them for this year's schoolwork

The school provides information and materials to assist parents in working with their child at home

Students read at home everyday

This school is making progress in improving the achievement of all students

The school provides academic support when students need help with schoolwork

Students receive the help they need in learning English

Students are encouraged to participate in accelerated/advanced courses

Parents are encouraged to volunteer at school

Allowing families to choose which school their child attends has positively affected our school

Legend:
- Students (*n*=1,353)
- Staff (*n*=50)
- Parents (*n*=418)

Scale: 5 Strongly Agree, 4, 3, 2, 1 Strongly Disagree

Student Questionnaire Results

Students in grades nine through twelve at Big River High School responded to a questionnaire designed to measure how they feel about their learning environment in May 2000 (n=1,363), May 2001 (n=1,254), May 2002 (n=1,328), May 2003 (n=1,374), and May 2004 (n=1,353). Students were asked to respond to items using a five-point scale: 1 = strongly disagree; 2 = disagree; 3 = neutral; 4 = agree; and, 5 = strongly agree.

Average responses to each item on the questionnaire were graphed by the totals for the five years and disaggregated by gender, grade level, and ethnicity. In general, the average responses revealed few differences over time. Some of the graphs are shown on the pages that follow. A summary of results is shown below. (StuNarr.doc)

Student Responses by Gender

When the 2004 data were disaggregated by gender (562 female; 791 male), student responses to the items on the questionnaire revealed that responses clustered around the overall average. (Graph not shown.)

Student Responses by Grade Level

The questionnaire results were also disaggregated by grade level. In May 2004, there were 394 ninth graders (29%); 341 tenth graders (25%); 327 eleventh graders (24%); and 291 twelfth graders (21%) responding. The graph revealed few differences when disaggregated by grade level. No significant distinguishing pattern emerged when looking at the data by these subgroups. (Graph not shown.)

Student Responses by Ethnicity

Student questionnaire data were also disaggregated by ethnicity (Figure 5.2). In 2004, 91 Black students; 319 Asians; 483 Whites; and 715 Hispanics responded. (*Note:* Ethnicity numbers add up to more than the total number of respondents because some students identified themselves by more than one ethnicity.)

Figure 5.2 shows that all but Black student averages cluster around the overall average. Blacks were in disagreement with the following items, while the other students were neutral:

▼ My teachers help me to look at my work to learn from my mistakes.

▼ I evaluate my work using scoring guides or examples of already completed model assignments.

▼ My parents and teachers work together to help me do well in school.

▼ Students respect one another at this school.

Figure 5.2

Big River High School Student Responses By Ethnicity
May 2004

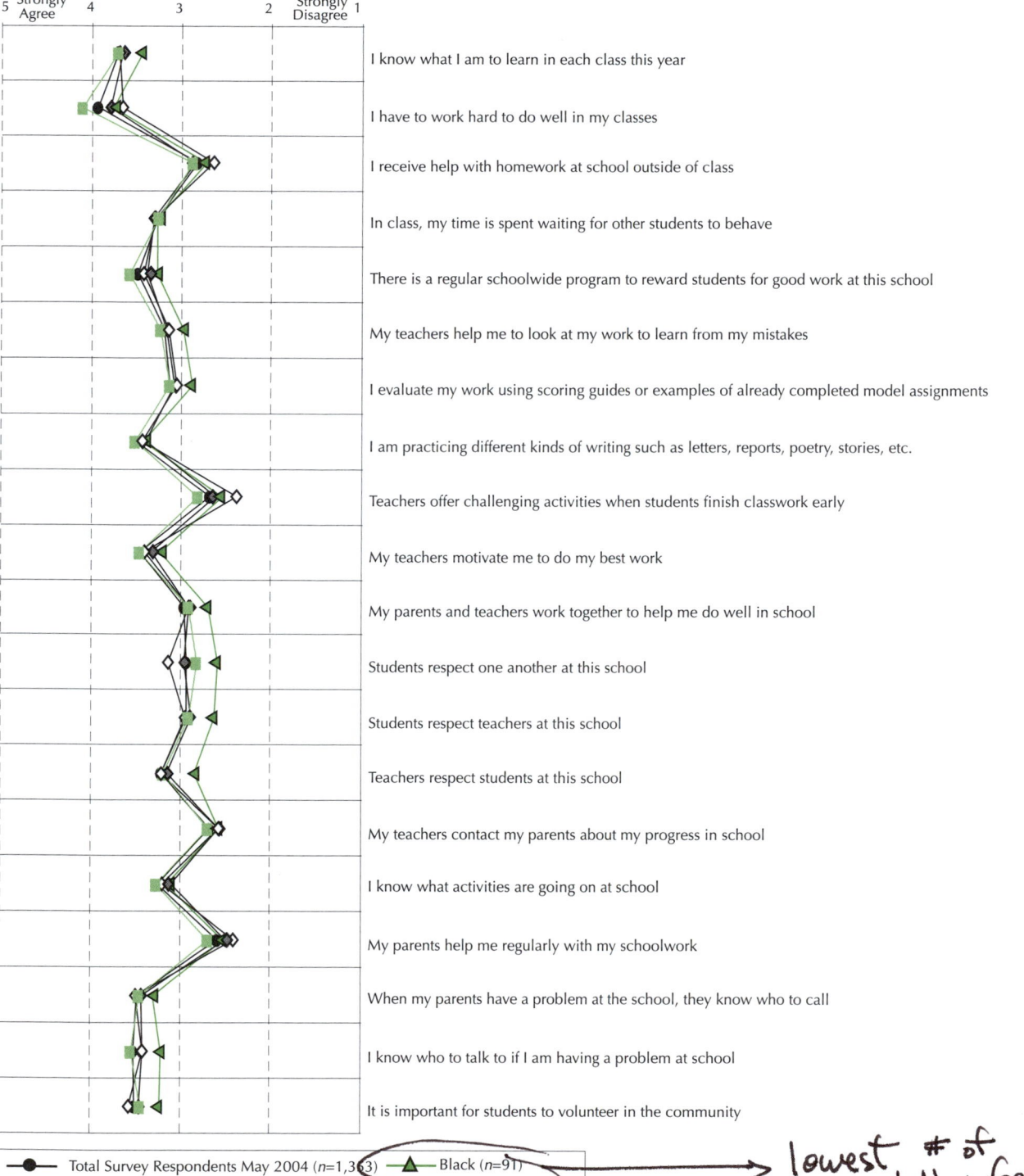

5 Strongly Agree	4	3	2	Strongly Disagree 1

I know what I am to learn in each class this year

I have to work hard to do well in my classes

I receive help with homework at school outside of class

In class, my time is spent waiting for other students to behave

There is a regular schoolwide program to reward students for good work at this school

My teachers help me to look at my work to learn from my mistakes

I evaluate my work using scoring guides or examples of already completed model assignments

I am practicing different kinds of writing such as letters, reports, poetry, stories, etc.

Teachers offer challenging activities when students finish classwork early

My teachers motivate me to do my best work

My parents and teachers work together to help me do well in school

Students respect one another at this school

Students respect teachers at this school

Teachers respect students at this school

My teachers contact my parents about my progress in school

I know what activities are going on at school

My parents help me regularly with my schoolwork

When my parents have a problem at the school, they know who to call

I know who to talk to if I am having a problem at school

It is important for students to volunteer in the community

● Total Survey Respondents May 2004 (*n*=1,363) ▲ Black (*n*=91)
◆ Asian (*n*=319) ◇ White (*n*=483) ■ Hispanic/Latino (*n*=715)

lowest # of representation feels the most slighted

Figure 5.2 (Continued)

Big River High School Student Responses By Ethnicity
May 2004

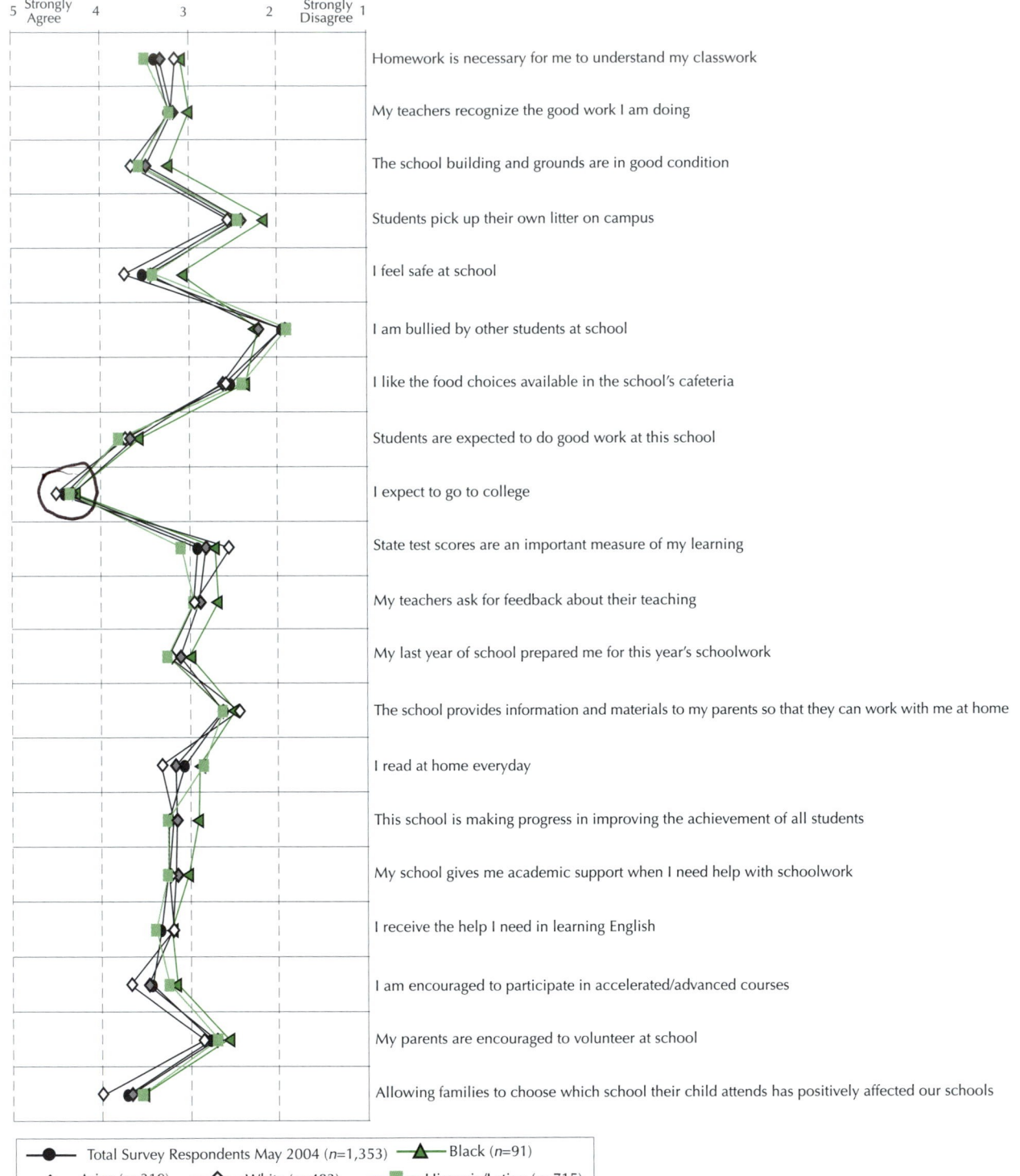

- ▼ Students respect teachers at this school.

- ▼ Teachers respect students at this school.

- ▼ Students pick up their own litter on campus.

- ▼ My teachers ask for feedback about their teaching.

- ▼ This school is making progress in improving the achievement of all students.

Black students were in lower agreement, although still in agreement, with:

- ▼ I know what I am to learn in each class this year.

- ▼ When my parents have a problem at the school, they know who to call.

- ▼ I know who to talk to if I am having a problem at school.

- ▼ It is important for students to volunteer in the community.

- ▼ My teachers recognize the good work I am doing.

- ▼ The school building and grounds are in good condition.

- ▼ I feel safe at school.

- ▼ My school gives me academic support when I need help with schoolwork.

- ▼ I am encouraged to participate in accelerated/advanced courses.

Student Open-ended Responses

In May 2004, Big River School students were asked to respond to two open-ended questions: *What do you like about your school?* and *What do you wish was different at your school?* The top ten responses are shown below. (*Note:* When analyzing open-ended results, one must keep in mind the number of responses that were written-in. Open-ended responses often help us understand the multiple choice responses, although caution must be exercised around small numbers of respondents. A file to help you analyze open-ended responses is on the CD.) (OEanalz.pdf)

What do you like about your school?	What do you wish was different at your school?
• The teachers (they care about me, they are fun, they want me to do well) (574) • The visual and performing arts (554) • It is fun (311) • The sports (200) • My friends (150) • The diversity (146) • Nothing (62) • There are a lot of classes to choose from (60) • The spirit squad (47) • The computers (38)	• Less homework (367) • Better food (232) • More time for lunch (211) • Some teachers (79) • Everything (75) • The dances (we need more of them and they need to be better (66) • More interesting ways to earn (61) • Nothing (54) • The principal (34) • Less testing (29)

Staff Questionnaire Results

Big River High School staff members responded to a questionnaire designed to measure their perceptions of the school environment in May 2000 ($n=47$), May 2001 ($n=39$), May 2002 ($n=36$), May 2003 ($n=51$), and May 2004 ($n=50$). Members of the staff were asked to respond to items using a five-point scale: 1 = strongly disagree; 2 = disagree; 3 = neutral; 4 = agree; and 5 = strongly agree.

Average responses to the items on the questionnaire were graphed by the totals for the five years and disaggregated by gender, teaching team participation, and number of years teaching. In general, the average responses revealed no differences over time. (Graph not shown.) A summary of results is shown below. (StfNarr.doc)

Staff Responses by Gender

When the 2004 data were disaggregated by gender (28 female; 22 male), staff responses to the items on the questionnaire revealed essentially no differences. (Graph not shown.)

Staff Responses by Teaching Team Participation

Staff questionnaire data were also disaggregated by teaching team participation (staff members who are part of a formal teaching team, $n=16$; and staff members who are not part of a formal teaching team, $n=32$). Results graphed by this demographic revealed that responses clustered around the overall average. (Graph not shown.)

Staff Responses by Number of Years Teaching

Staff questionnaire data were also disaggregated by the number of years teaching (one to three years, $n=9$; four to six years, $n=14$; seven to ten years, $n=6$; and eleven or more years, $n=21$). Results graphed by this demographic reveal some differences in responses (Figure 5.3).

Figure 5.3

Big River High School Staff Responses by Number of Years Teaching
May 2004

Figure 5.3 (Continued)

Big River High School Staff Responses by Number of Years Teaching
May 2004

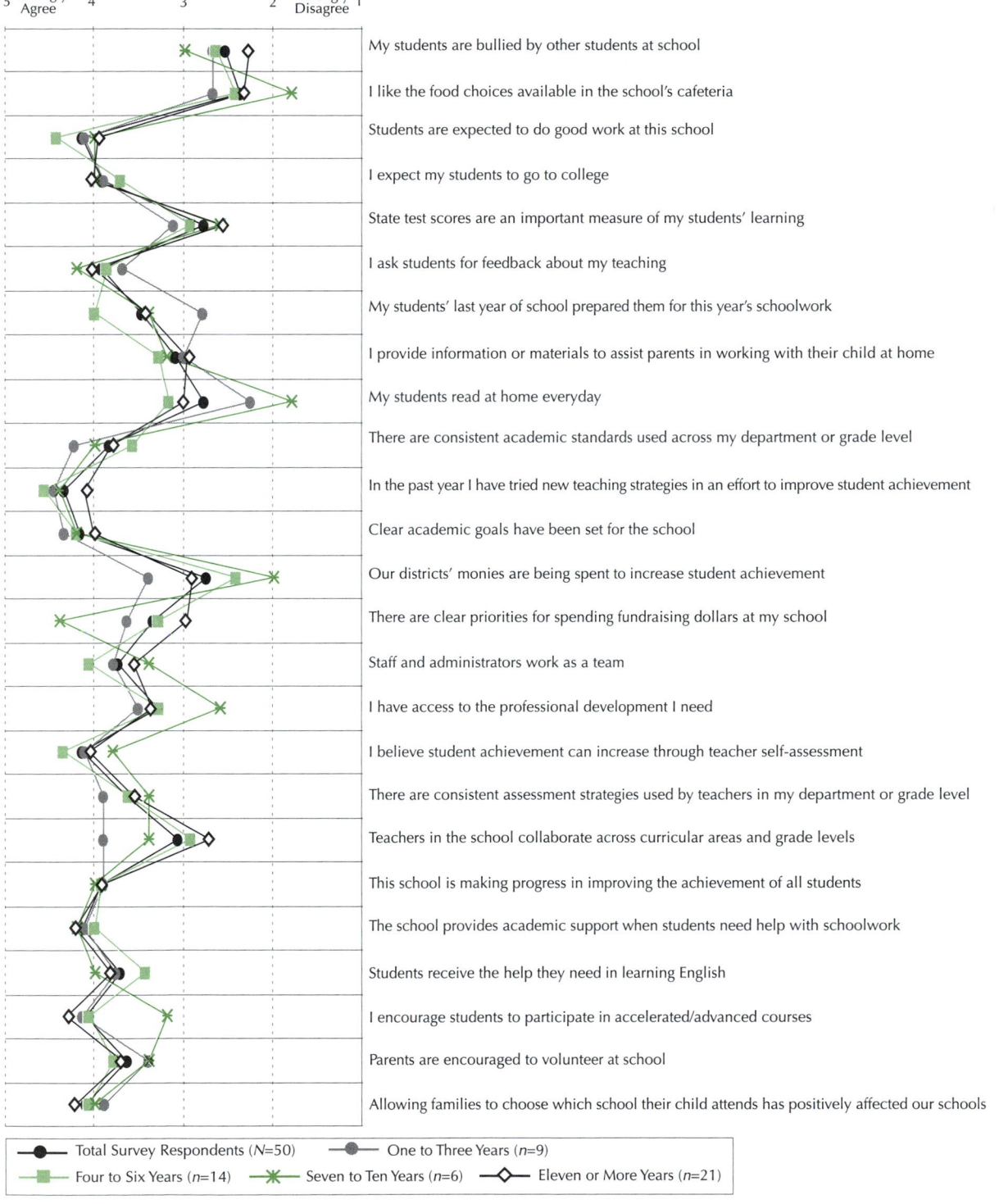

5 Strongly Agree 4 3 2 Strongly Disagree 1

My students are bullied by other students at school

I like the food choices available in the school's cafeteria

Students are expected to do good work at this school

I expect my students to go to college

State test scores are an important measure of my students' learning

I ask students for feedback about my teaching

My students' last year of school prepared them for this year's schoolwork

I provide information or materials to assist parents in working with their child at home

My students read at home everyday

There are consistent academic standards used across my department or grade level

In the past year I have tried new teaching strategies in an effort to improve student achievement

Clear academic goals have been set for the school

Our districts' monies are being spent to increase student achievement

There are clear priorities for spending fundraising dollars at my school

Staff and administrators work as a team

I have access to the professional development I need

I believe student achievement can increase through teacher self-assessment

There are consistent assessment strategies used by teachers in my department or grade level

Teachers in the school collaborate across curricular areas and grade levels

This school is making progress in improving the achievement of all students

The school provides academic support when students need help with schoolwork

Students receive the help they need in learning English

I encourage students to participate in accelerated/advanced courses

Parents are encouraged to volunteer at school

Allowing families to choose which school their child attends has positively affected our schools

— ● — Total Survey Respondents (*N*=50)   — ● — One to Three Years (*n*=9)

— ■ — Four to Six Years (*n*=14)   — ✶ — Seven to Ten Years (*n*=6)   — ◇ — Eleven or More Years (*n*=21)

Staff Open-ended Responses

Big River High School staff responded to two open-ended questions in May 2004: *What are the strengths of this school?* and *What needs to be improved?* The top ten responses are shown below.

What are the strengths of this school?	What needs to be improved?
• The dedicated teachers (70) • The arts program (67) • Course offerings (51) • The vision for the school is a strong focus (50) • Staff really helps to make things happen (46) • A great group of students (45) • The school facilities (32) • Dedicated administrators (32) • Creativity of the staff (17) • Student performances (12)	• Professional development that helps us know how to better meet diverse student needs (69) • Student motivation (67) • Communication among staff members (62) • Staff and administration need to work as team (58) • Our students need better support services (47) • Make every teacher teach to the standards and the curriculum (45) • Get all the new teachers on board with what we are trying to do here (45) • Better services for English learners (42) • More parents need to be involved (37) • Public relations with our community (34)

Parent Questionnaire Results

Parents of students attending Big River High School completed a questionnaire designed to measure their perceptions of the school environment in May 2000 (*503*), May 2001 (*n=656*), May 2002 (*n=744*), May 2003 (*n=674*), and May 2004 (*n=418*). Parents were asked to respond to items using a five-point scale: 1 = strongly disagree; 2 = disagree; 3 = neutral; 4 = agree; and, 5 = strongly agree.

Average responses to each item on the questionnaire were graphed by the totals for the five years and disaggregated by ethnicity, native language, children's grade levels, number of children in the household, and number of children in the school. In general, the average responses revealed no differences over time. (Graph not shown.) A summary of results is shown below. (ParNarr.doc)

Parent Responses by Ethnicity

When 2004 parent questionnaire data were disaggregated by ethnicity (10 Blacks; 75 Asians; 153 Whites; and 168 Hispanics), the graph revealed some differences (Figure 5.4). Black parent responses resemble student responses.

Figure 5.4

Big River High School Parent Responses by Ethnicity
May 2004

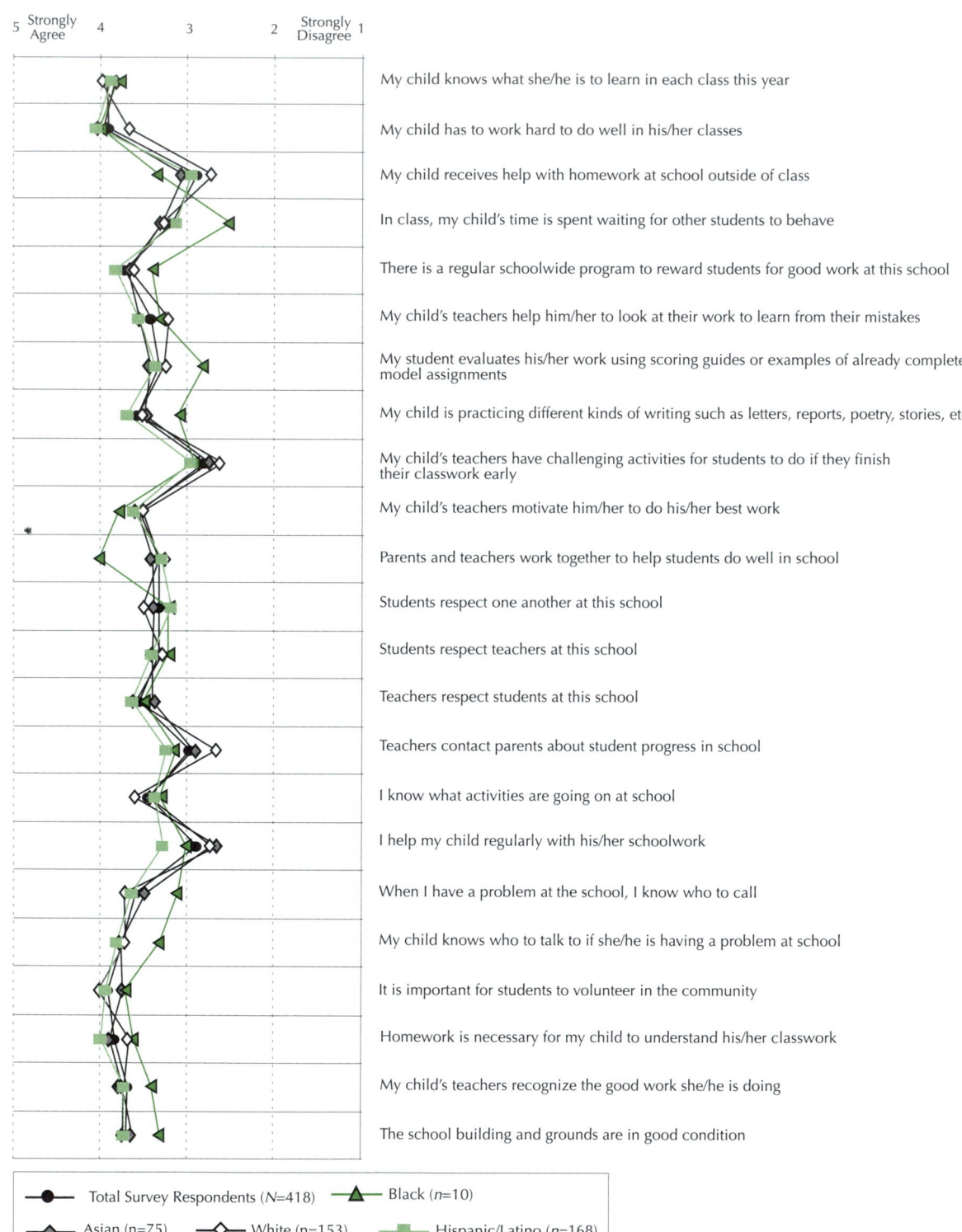

Figure 5.4 (Continued)

Big River High School Parent Responses by Ethnicity
May 2004

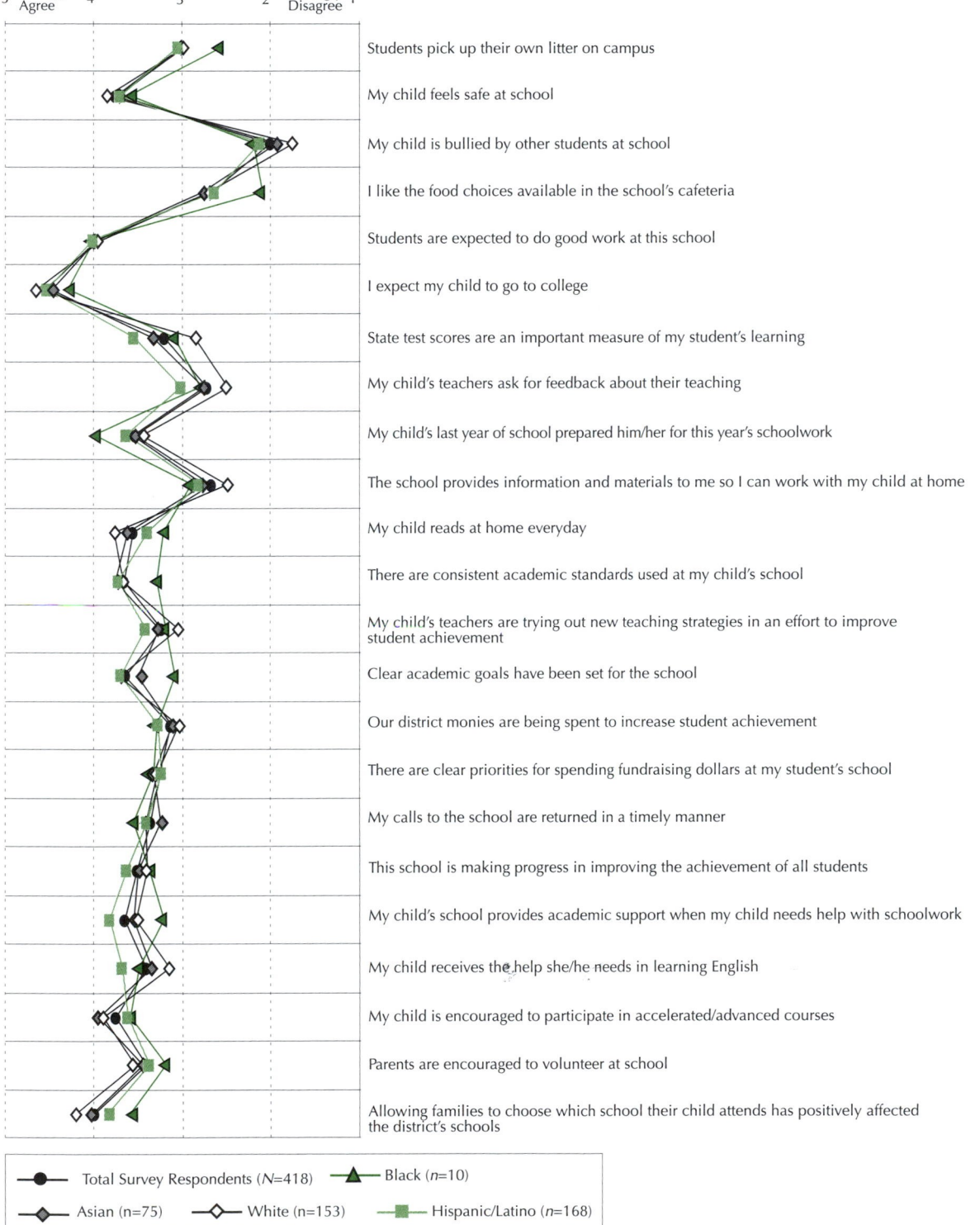

| 5 Strongly Agree | 4 | 3 | 2 | Strongly Disagree 1 |

Students pick up their own litter on campus

My child feels safe at school

My child is bullied by other students at school

I like the food choices available in the school's cafeteria

Students are expected to do good work at this school

I expect my child to go to college

State test scores are an important measure of my student's learning

My child's teachers ask for feedback about their teaching

My child's last year of school prepared him/her for this year's schoolwork

The school provides information and materials to me so I can work with my child at home

My child reads at home everyday

There are consistent academic standards used at my child's school

My child's teachers are trying out new teaching strategies in an effort to improve student achievement

Clear academic goals have been set for the school

Our district monies are being spent to increase student achievement

There are clear priorities for spending fundraising dollars at my student's school

My calls to the school are returned in a timely manner

This school is making progress in improving the achievement of all students

My child's school provides academic support when my child needs help with schoolwork

My child receives the help she/he needs in learning English

My child is encouraged to participate in accelerated/advanced courses

Parents are encouraged to volunteer at school

Allowing families to choose which school their child attends has positively affected the district's schools

Legend:
- ● Total Survey Respondents (N=418)
- ▲ Black (n=10)
- ◆ Asian (n=75)
- ◇ White (n=153)
- ■ Hispanic/Latino (n=168)

Parent Responses by Children's Grade Levels

When data were disaggregated by children's grade levels (139 ninth graders, 112 tenth graders, 102 eleventh graders, and 114 twelfth graders), the graph revealed few differences. No significant distinguishing pattern emerged when looking at the data by these subgroups. (Graph not shown.)

Parent Responses by Native Language

Parent questionnaire data were also disaggregated by native language (English, n=220; Spanish, n=110; Vietnamese, n=15; Other, n=19). Results graphed by native language revealed few differences in responses (Graph not shown).

Parent Responses by Number of Children in the School

Parent questionnaire data disaggregated by the number of children in the school (one child, n=276; two children, n=86; three children, n=15), revealed few differences in responses. (Graph not shown.)

Parent Responses by Number of Children in the Household

Parent questionnaire data were also disaggregated by the number of children in the household (one child, n=71; two children, n=153; three children, n=89; four children, n=33; and five children, n=10). Results graphed by this demographic revealed almost no differences in responses. (Graph not shown.)

Staff Questionnaire and Standards Assessment

Staff members did not feel that their current questionnaires helped them know about their system. In October 2004, they also completed the *Education for the Future* staff questionnaire. The questionnaire asks questions about the learning environment and the alignment of their system. The questionnaire also contains questions about standards: how well teachers know content standards, and to what degree they are implementing the standards. A total of 71 teachers at Big River High School responded (81%). A summary of the results follow.

Staff Responses by Teaching Qualifications

When the data were disaggregated by teaching qualifications (Secondary Credential, $n=53$; Special Education, $n=8$; Elementary Credential, $n=4$; Emergency Credential, $n=4$; Other, $n=9$), staff responses to the items on the questionnaire revealed some differences (Figure 5.5).

Figure 5.5

Big River High School Staff Responses
By Teaching Qualifications, October 2004

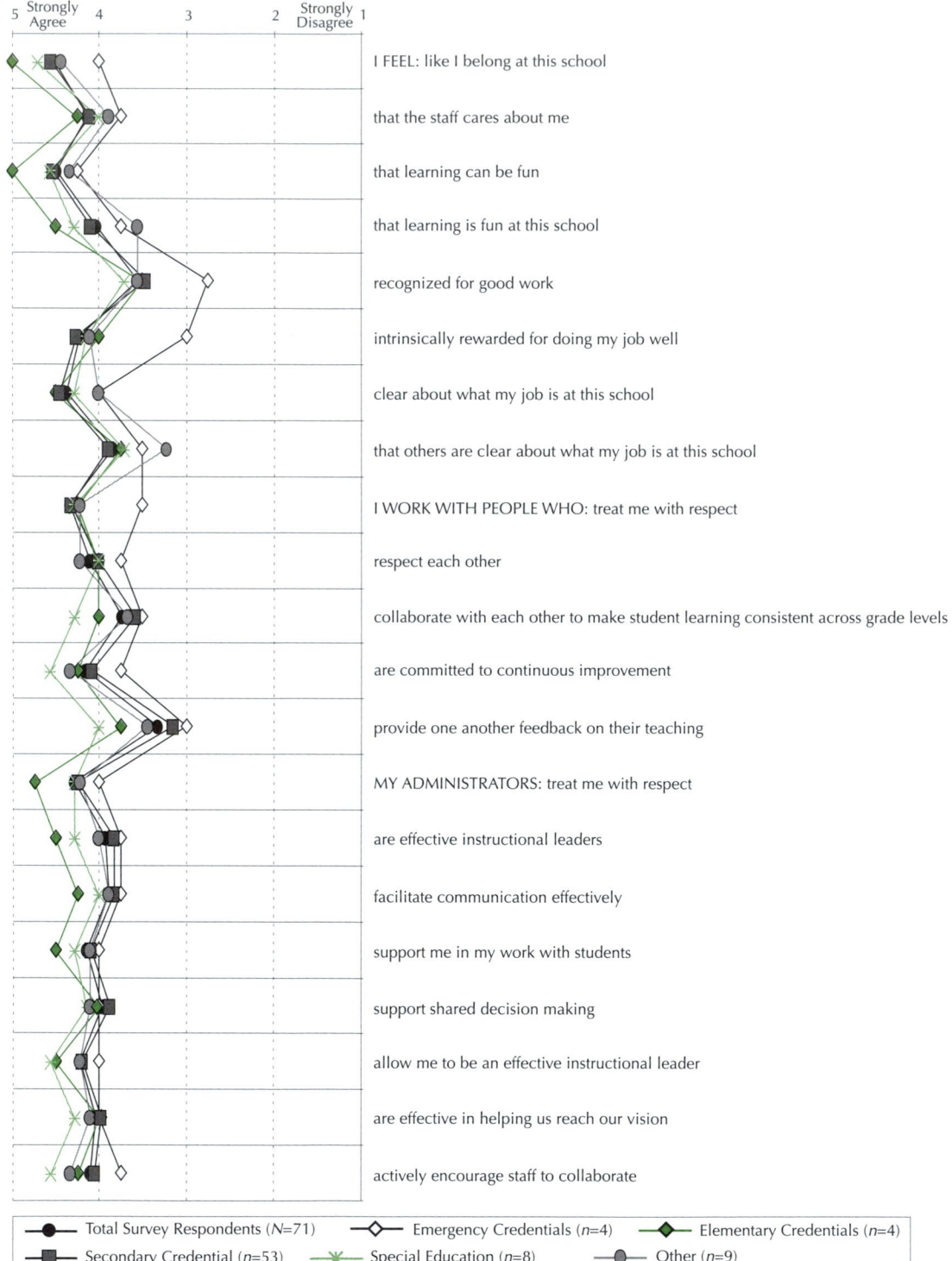

Figure 5.5 (Continued)

Big River High School Staff Responses
By Teaching Qualifications, October 2004

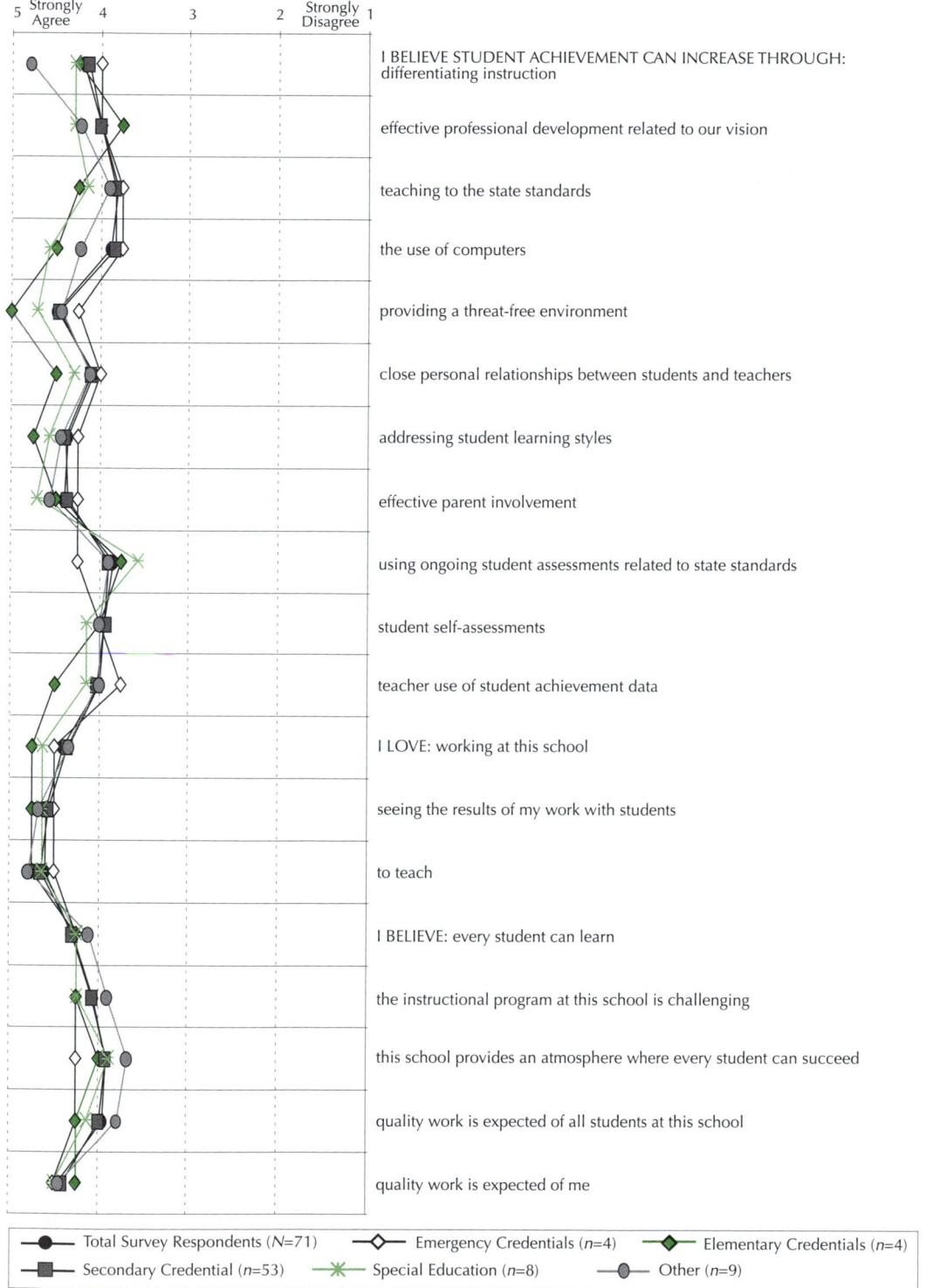

Figure 5.5 (Continued)

Big River High School Staff Responses
By Teaching Qualifications, October 2004

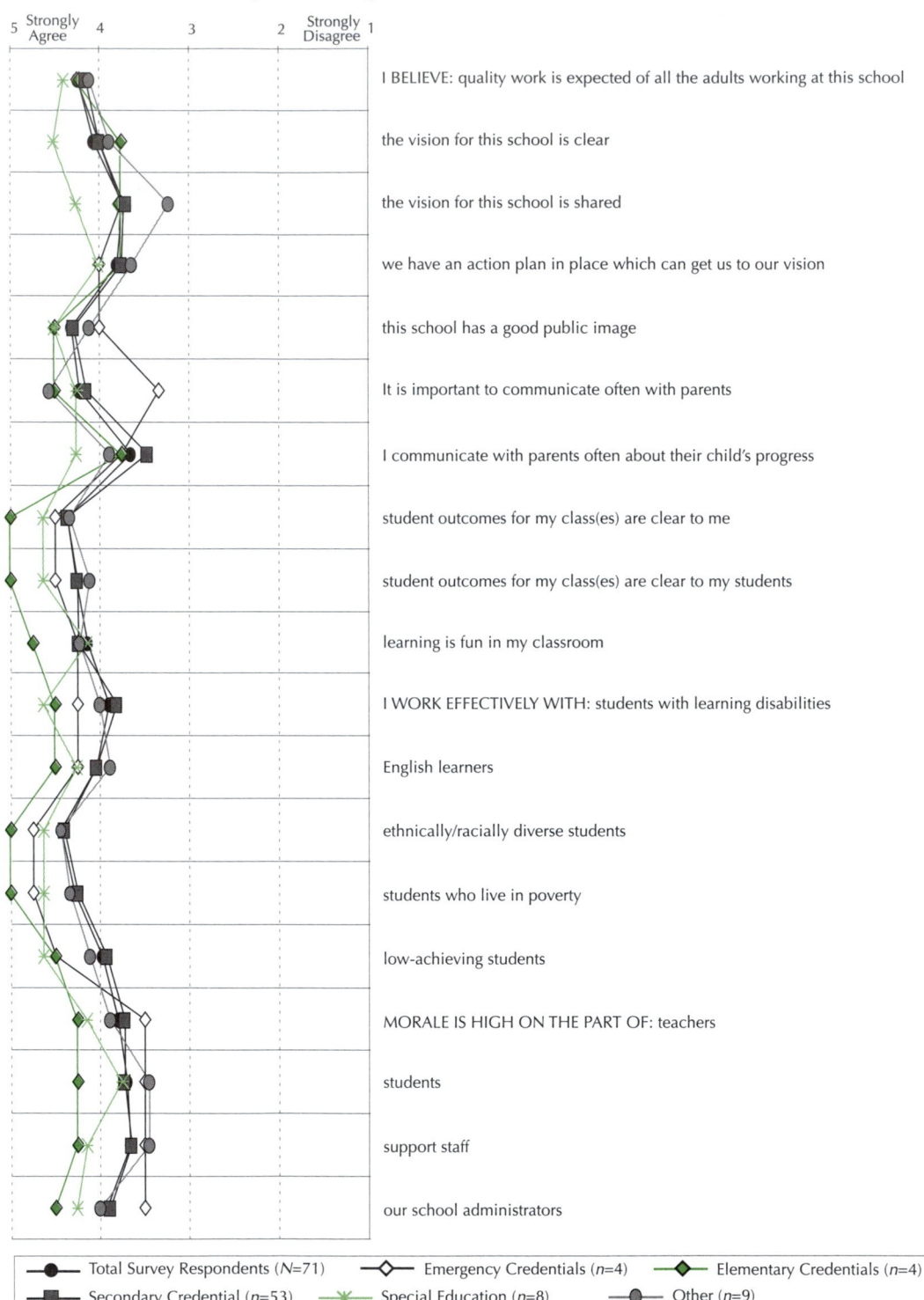

Staff Responses by Number of Years Teaching Experience

Staff questionnaire data were also disaggregated by number of years teaching experience (first year, $n=8$; two to three years, $n=8$; four to six years, $n=15$; seven to ten years, $n=12$; eleven to fourteen years, $n=8$; fifteen to twenty years, $n=7$; twenty-six plus years, $n=8$). Results graphed by this demographic revealed some differences in responses (Figure 5.6).

(*Note:* Since the size of the subgroups is very small, members of the groups might be identifiable. Therefore, these graphs would be used for inhouse analysis only.)

Figure 5.6

Big River High School Staff Responses
By Number of Years Teaching, October 2004

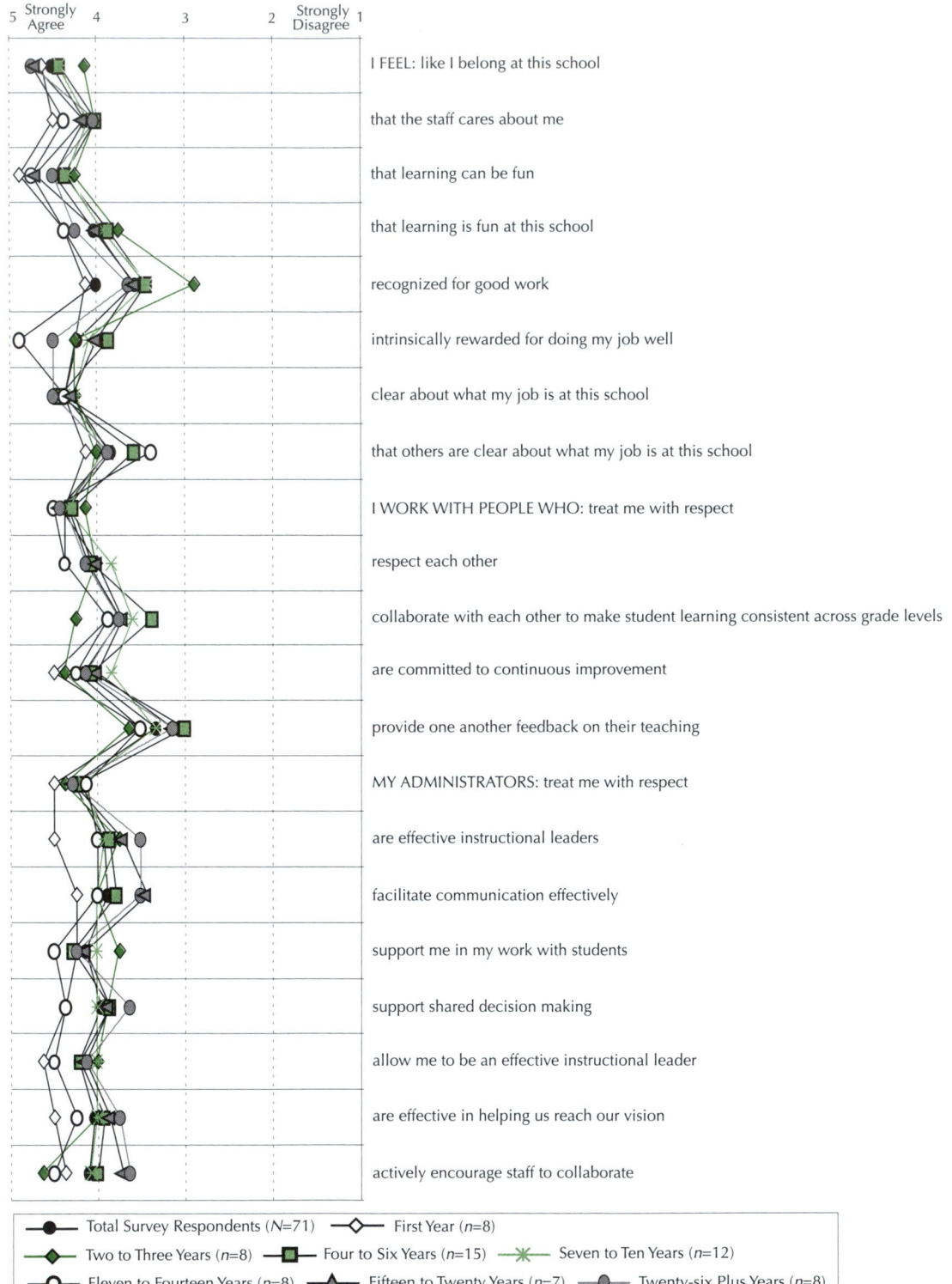

Figure 5.6 (Continued)

Big River High School Staff Responses
By Number of Years Teaching, October 2004

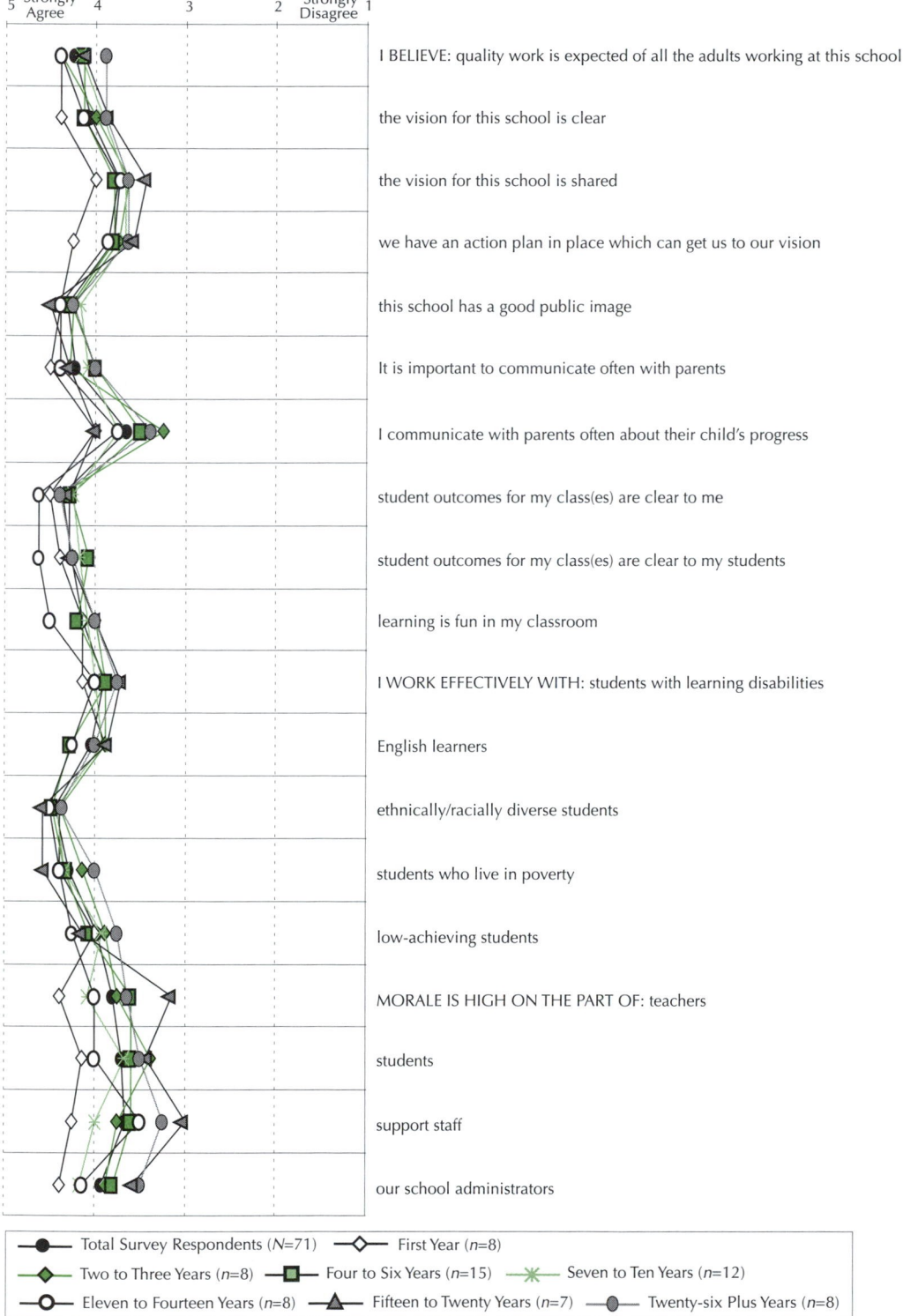

Figure 5.6 (Continued)

Big River High School Staff Responses
By Number of Years Teaching, October 2004

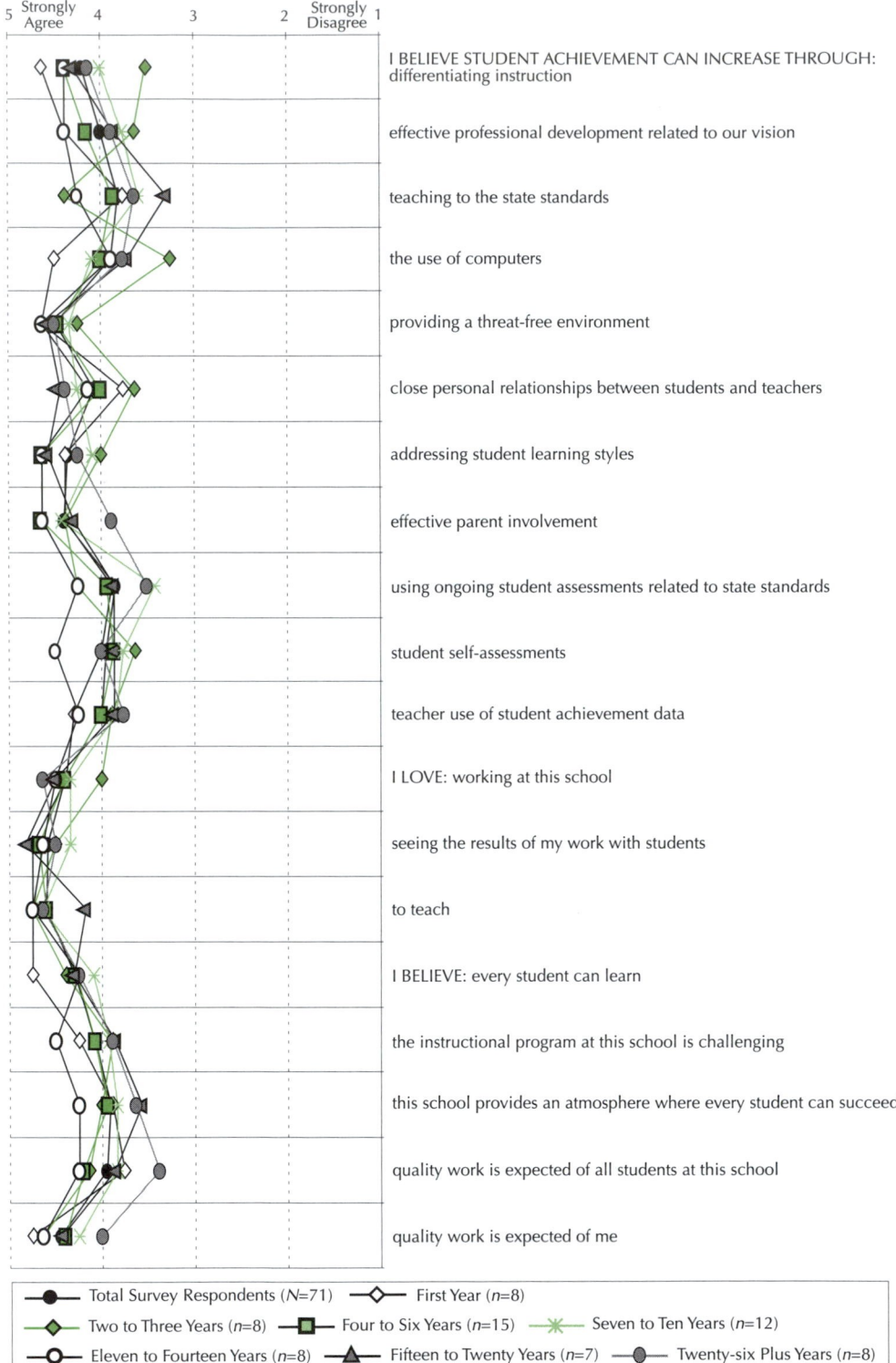

Staff Open-ended Responses

Big River High School staff responded to three open-ended questions in October 2004: *What would it take to improve student learning in this school?*, *What are the strengths of this school?*, and *What needs to be improved?* The top ten responses are shown below.

What would it take to improve student learning in this school?

- Teachers, who are not expecting excellence from their students should be observed and given constructive, but measurable, expectations from an administrator. We still have too many students who are being taught by mediocre teachers who are not committed to pushing students to achieve. (10)
- Fast action to restore a good learning environment when a teacher leaves suddenly, for whatever reason. (9)
- More time for small group tutoring and one-on-one instruction, possibly imbedded in the school day. (9)
- Smaller class sizes. (8)
- Increased parent involvement and accountability. (6)
- There needs to be more support from the administration in supporting teachers. (5)
- More challenging and interesting classes. (5)
- Each student brings necessary materials to class and that they learn to be responsible for their education. (4)
- More time to prepare lessons, communicate and work with each other, and assess student learning. (4)
- Fast and effective support and action in dealing with rude or disruptive students who prevent others from learning. (5)

What are the strengths of this school?

- The staff/faculty are caring. (27)
- Students. (14)
- The administration. (14)
- The arts magnet program/activities. (12)
- Good environment/climate. (10)
- Community involvement and good ties. (9)
- Strong academic program. (7)
- Parent support. (5)
- Varied curriculum/selection of classes. (5)
- Activities. (3)

What needs to be improved?

- Communication, collaboration, and rapport among teachers and administration, and support staff with teachers and administration. (9)
- Suggestions and opportunities for each teacher to learn and grow regarding the standards and instruction. (6)
- Morale. (5)
- Facilities. (5)
- Different schedules for events so that all students can participate. (4)
- Parental involvement. (4)
- More money, especially for supplies. (3)
- Services: photocopying, places to meet. (3)
- Smaller class sizes. (3)
- More support from administration. (2)

The questionnaire also contained ten questions about how well teachers know content standards, and to what degree they are implementing the standards. A summary of the results for questions 1 through 7 are shown in two different ways—(A) shows average responses disaggregated by teaching qualifications and by number of years teaching experience, followed by (B), percentage responding to each response option for the questions (Figures 5.7 A and B).

Figure 5.7 A

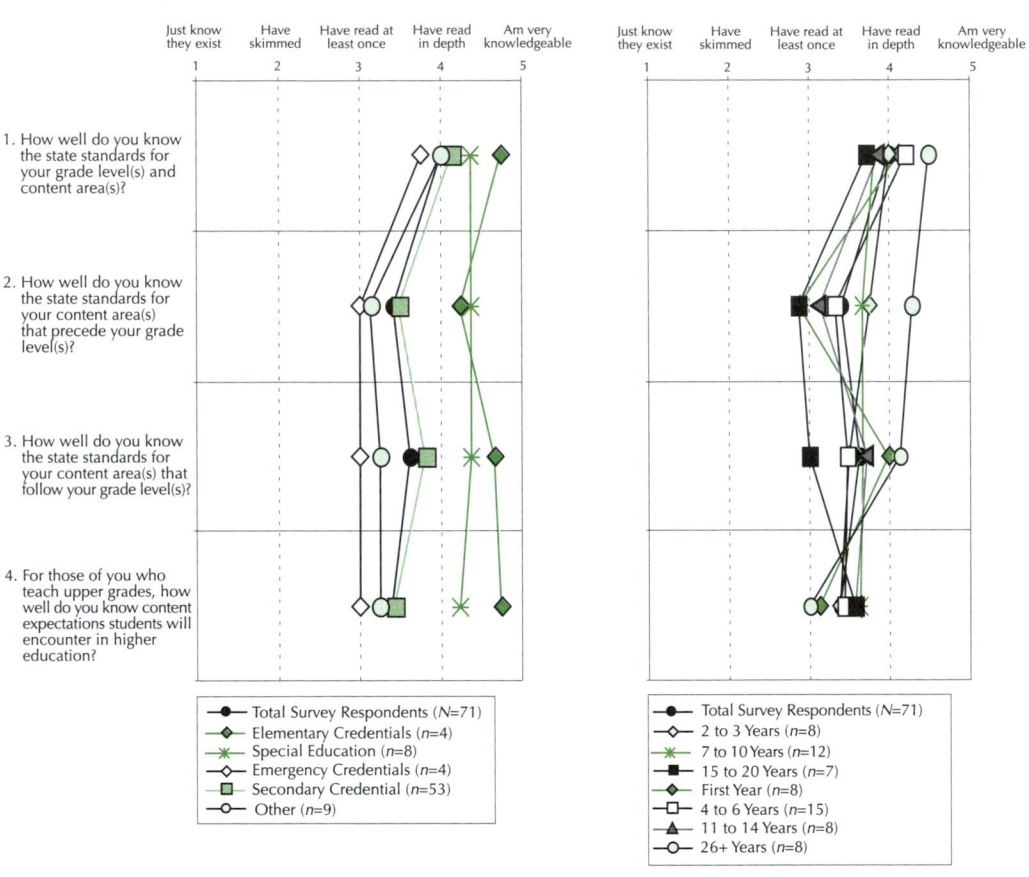

Figure 5.7 B

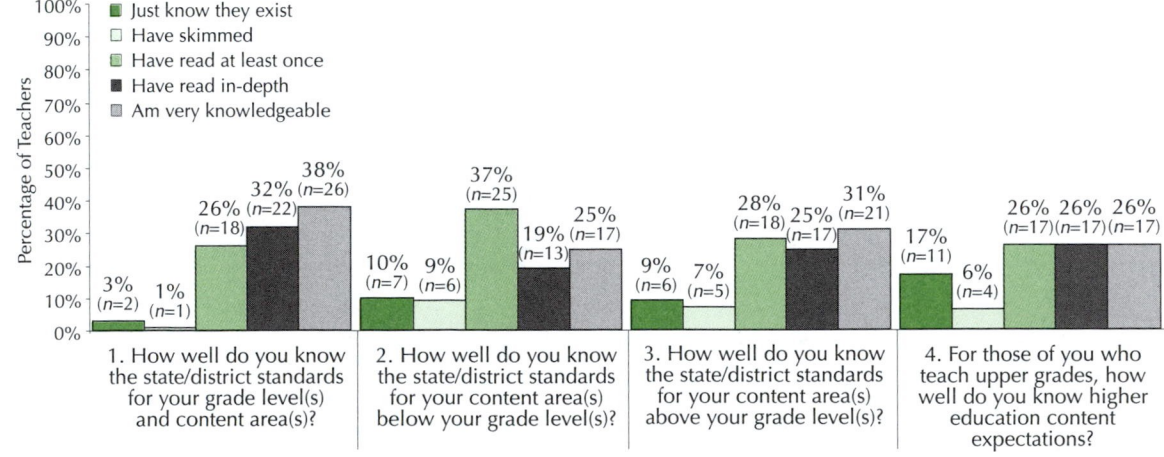

5. Big River teachers were asked what would help them better know the standards for their grade level(s). They were asked to select all statements that apply. Results follow (Figures 5.8 A and B).

Figure 5.8 A

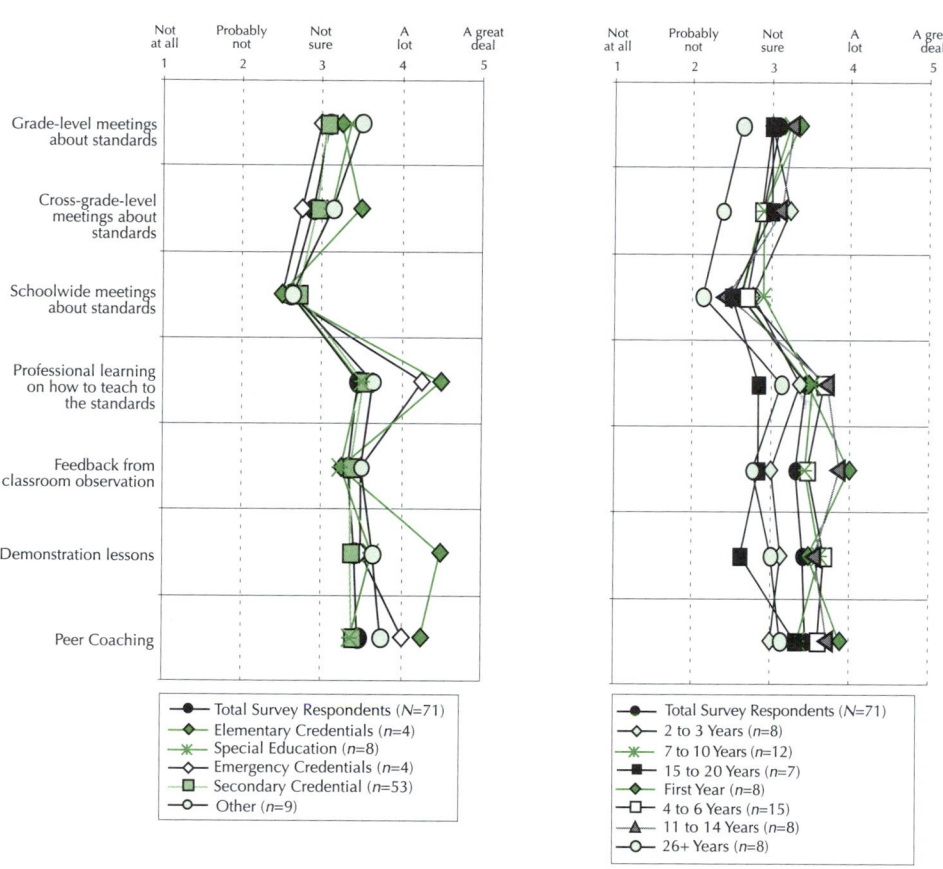

Figure 5.8 B

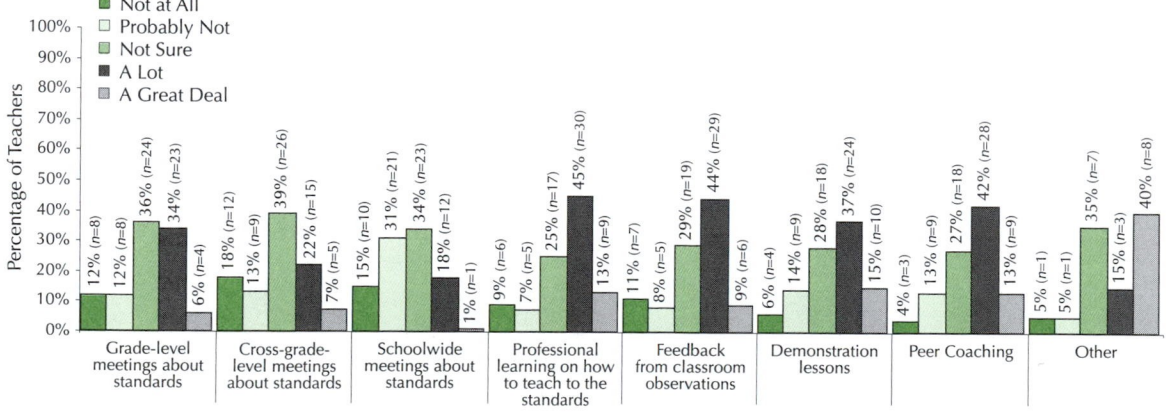

6. Big River High School teachers were asked how much support they receive from their school administrator to ensure that standards are being implemented. Results follow (Figures 5.9 A and B).

Figure 5.9 A

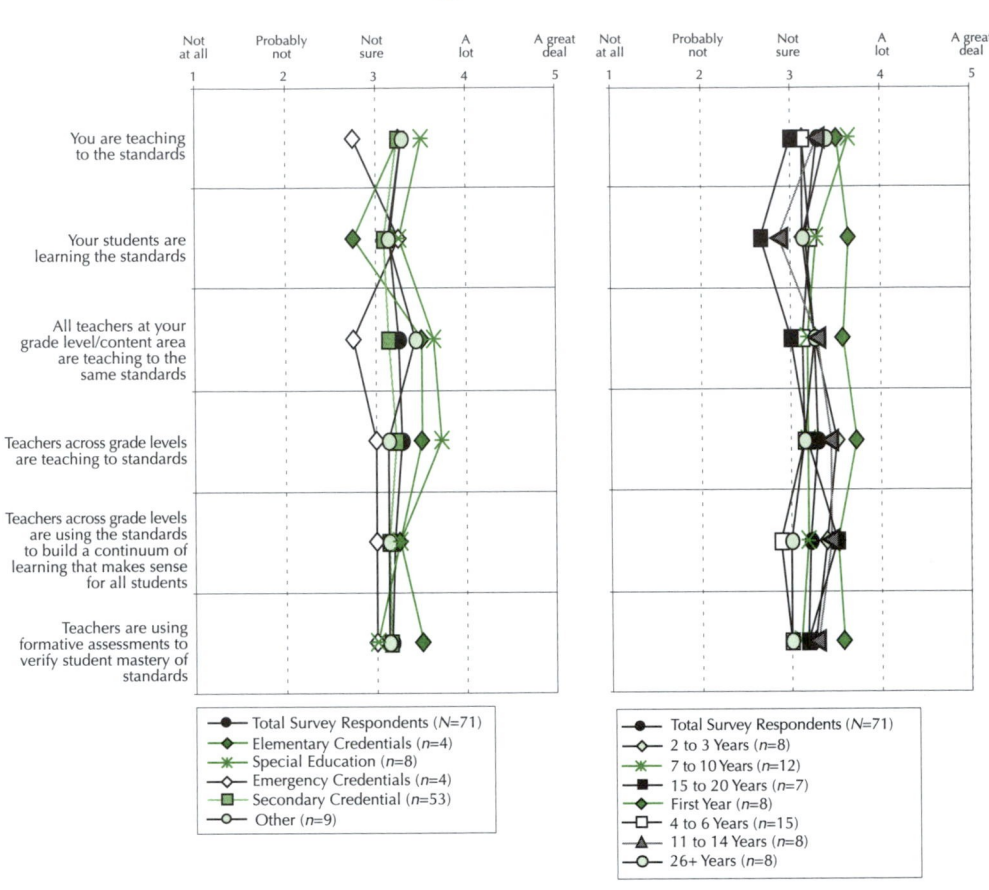

Figure 5.9 B

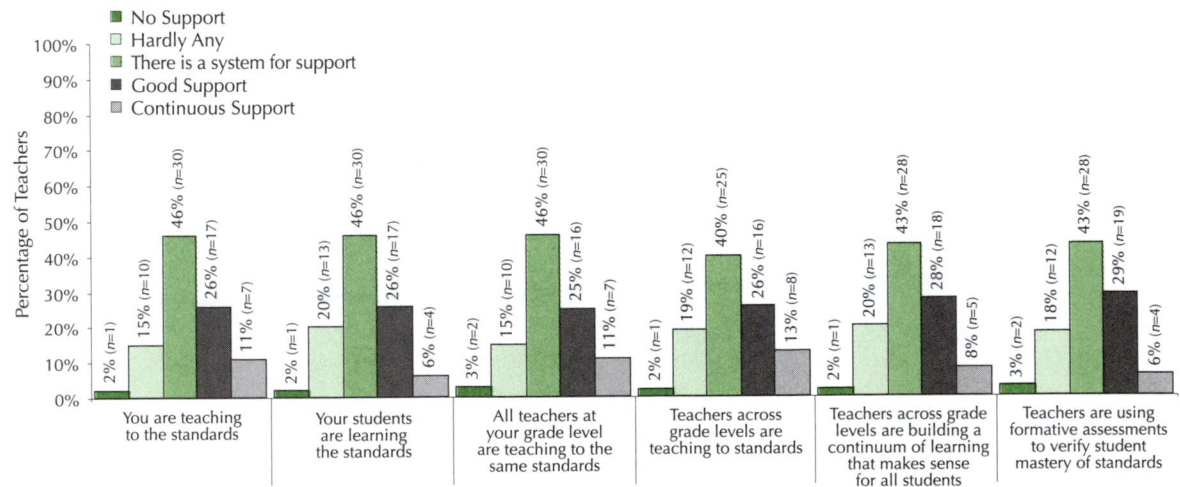

7. Big River teachers were asked how much support they receive from their colleagues to ensure that standards are being implemented. Results follow (Figures 5.10 A and B).

Figure 5.10 A

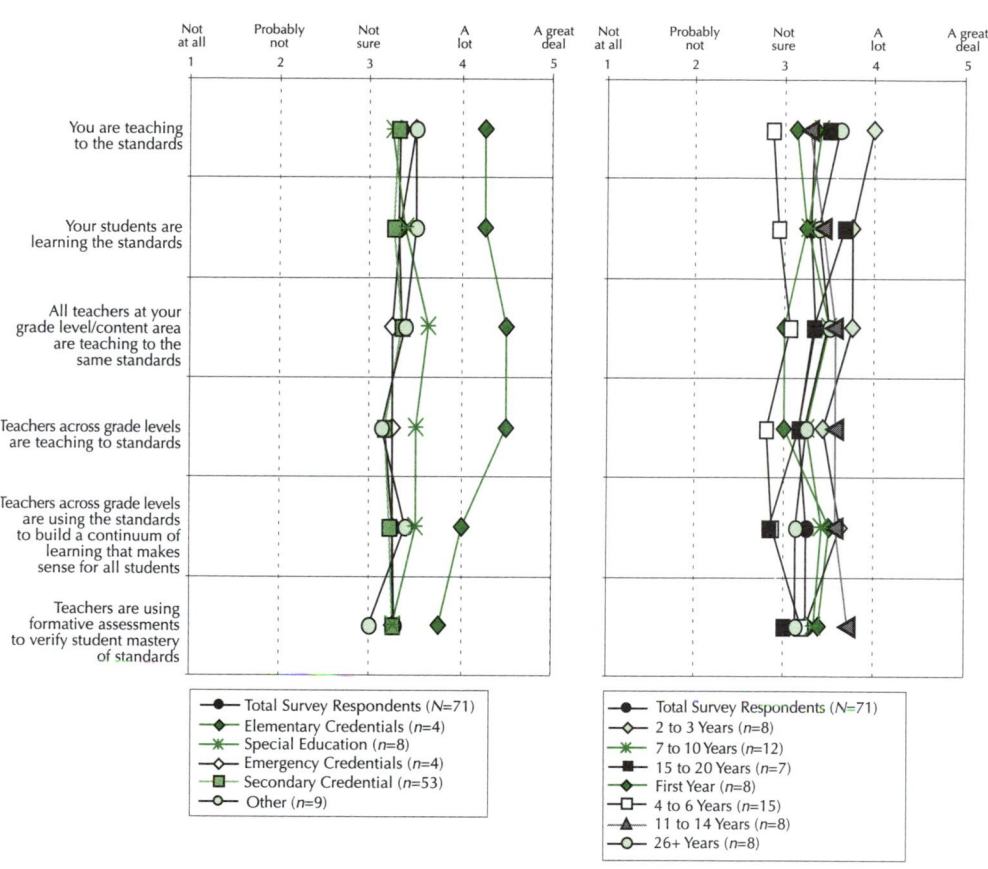

Figure 5.10 B

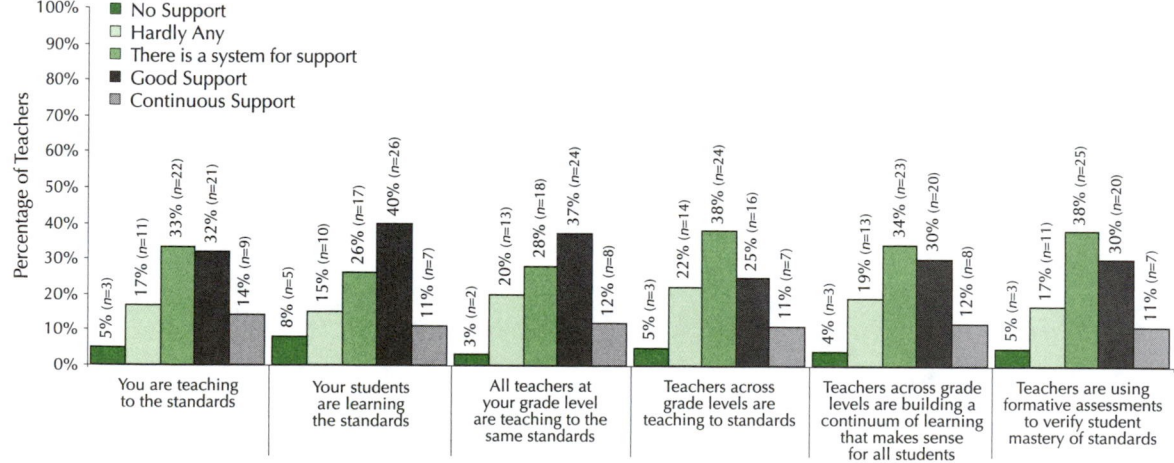

8. Big River High School teachers were asked how well they would say they know what it would look like and feel like if they were teaching to the standards 100% of the time. Results follow (Figure 5.11).

Figure 5.11

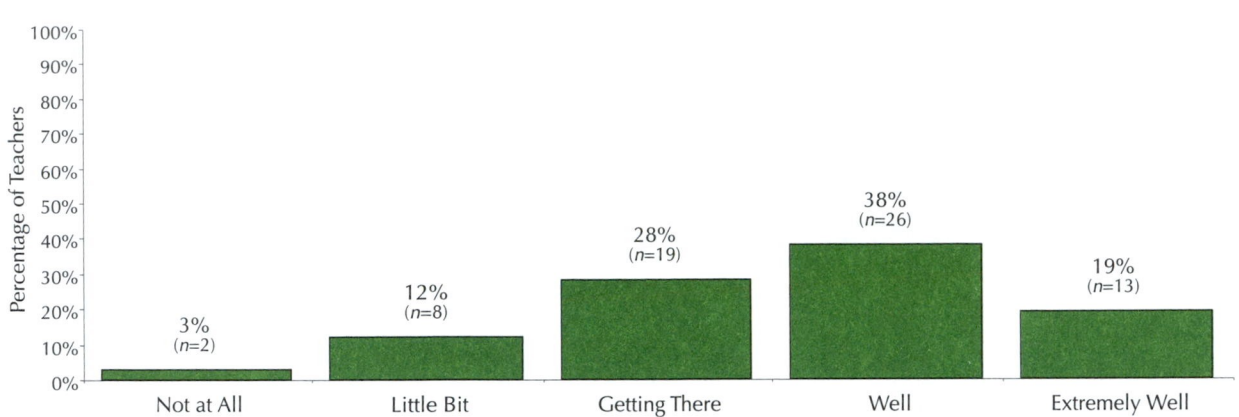

9. Teachers were asked to indicate which statements best describe how they use standards to design instruction. Results follow (Figure 5.12).

Figure 5.12

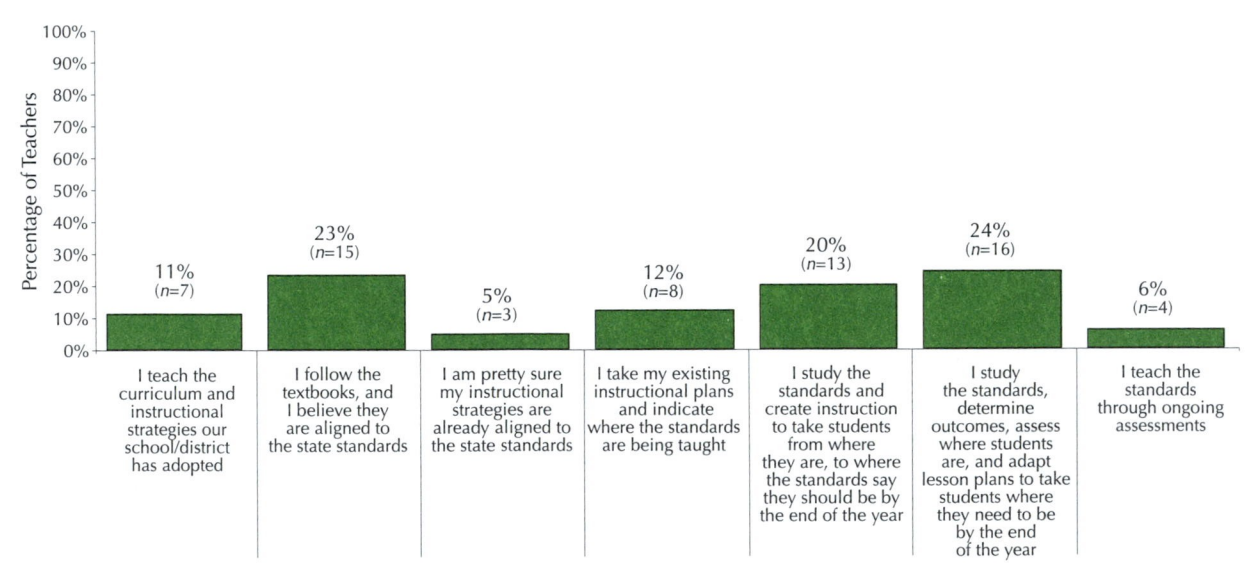

10. Teachers were asked to what extent they believe teachers and instructional staff or school leadership can make the necessary changes to improve student learning. Results follow (Figure 5.13).

Figure 5.13

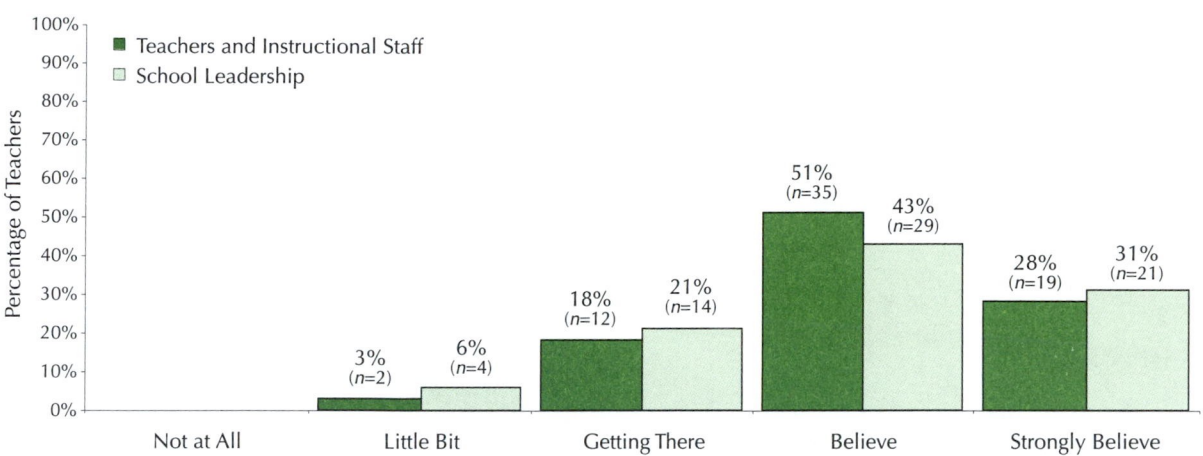

11. Teachers were asked how committed they are to making necessary changes to improve student learning. Results follow (Figure 5.14).

Figure 5.14

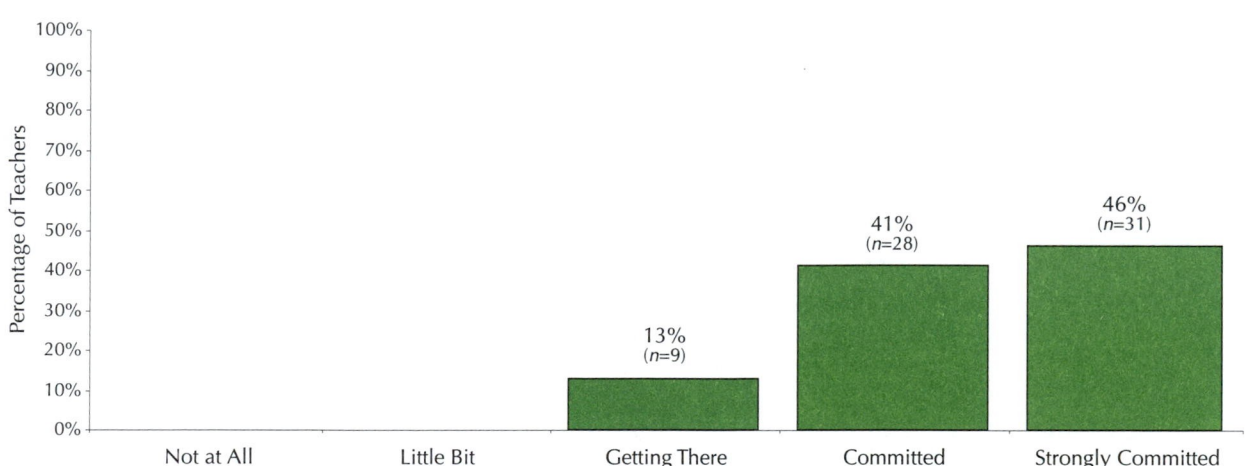

12. Big River teachers were asked what percentage of their students will meet the standards by the end of the school year. Results follow (Figure 5.15).

Figure 5.15

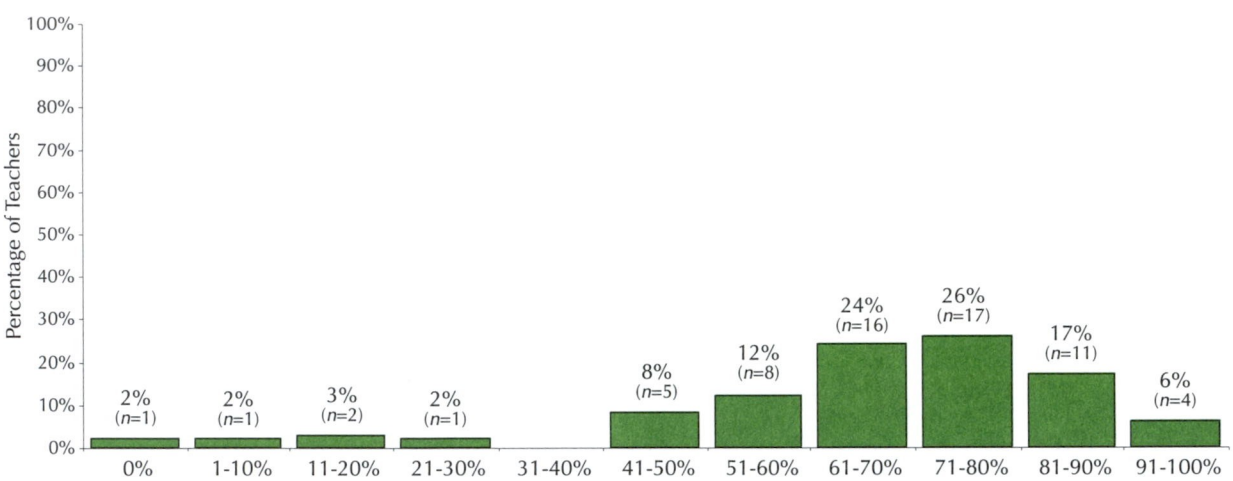

Study Questions for How Do We Do Business?

As you review Big River's perceptual data, use either the margins in the text, this page, or print this page from the CD to write down your early thinking. (Ch5Qs.pdf) These notes, of course, are only hunches or placeholders until all the data are analyzed.

1. What are the perceptual *strengths* and *challenges* for Big River High School?	
Strengths	*Challenges*

2. What are some *implications* for the Big River school improvement plan?

3. Looking at the data presented, what other perceptual data would you want to answer the question *How do we do business?* for Big River High School?

What I Saw in the Example: Big River High School

Using the study questions as an outline, what I saw in the data for Chapter 5 appears below. (Ch5Saw.pdf) When applicable, I have referenced the figure or page number that gave me my first impression of strengths and challenges.

Continuous Improvement Continuums Assessment

CIC Strengths	CIC Challenges
◆ It is great that the Big River staff assessed on the CICs three times and got back to the assessment after some time had passed. (Pages 79-86) ◆ Data are being used for planning. (Page 80) ◆ The district purchased a data warehouse that will help the school with data analysis. (Page 81) ◆ Big River High School staff has an early release day on Mondays to plan and work together. (Page 83) ◆ The mentoring program sounds strong. (Page 85)	◆ It appears that by taking some time away from the Continuums, staff is still about where they were two years ago, which makes sense with the leadership and teacher changes. ◆ Communication needs to improve, especially with all the new teachers at the school. ◆ The staff needs to renew the vision and mission, and reinforce the teaching of standards. ◆ All aspects of the school need to be evaluated.

Implications for Big River's school improvement plan

- Staff needs to review the mission and vision of the school, and bring the new staff along.
- Staff needs to use the data warehouse to dig deeper to prevent student failures, and also to pull the data together in a systematic and systemic way for planning.
- Staff needs to continue to clarify and communicate student evaluation procedures.
- Staff needs to reinforce the teaching of standards.
- Staff needs to implement and evaluate the plan, and implement powerful professional development, partnership development, and leadership strategies.
- Staff needs to continue to meet regularly to ensure the implementation of the vision and plan, for cross-curricular planning, for collaboration and communication, and to ensure that new teachers are supported and feeling supported, to reinforce the teaching of standards, and to study student work and student data.
- Staff needs to do more work with the elementary and middle schools to create a continuum of learning that makes sense for the students.
- Staff needs professional learning related to teaching students who live in poverty and who are not native speakers of English, also related to studying student work and student data. The professional learning needs to be imbedded into the work week.
- Staff needs to evaluate partnerships and encourage new ones.

Other desired perceptual data or information

- How many partnerships are there, what are they, and how many students are involved? Do these partners volunteer at the school?
- Did all respondents or participants think the school was in the same place as they rated themselves on the *Continuous Improvement Continuums,* or was there a wide disparity of responses? (Digital photos of the posters with dots would be nice.)
- Do new teachers rate the school in the same way experienced teachers do?

Questionnaire Data

Perceptual Strengths	Perceptual Challenges

Student questionnaires
• There was an "okay" response rate for each of the five years the questionnaire was given. (Figures 5.1 and 5.2)
• Students strongly agree that—
  * They expect to go to college.
  * They are not bullied.
• Student believe they are expected to do good work and that they have to work hard to do well in their classes.
• Students know what they are to learn in each class this year.
• Students know there is a regular schoolwide program to reward students for good work at this school.
• Students are practicing different kinds of writing.
• Students feel teachers motivate students to do their best work.
• Students know what activities are going on at school.
• Students feel it is important to volunteer in the community.
• Students feel safe at school.
• In the open-ended responses, students mentioned that what they like the most about the school are the teachers and the visual and performing arts opportunities.
• Students also think that school is fun.
	Student questionnaires
	• There were not many changes in student perceptions of the learning environment over the past five years.
	• Students do not like the food choices at the school.
	• Students do not feel that students are picking up their own litter on campus.
	• Students do not feel teachers ask for feedback about their teaching.
	• Students do not think state test scores are an important measure of their learning.
	• Students do not feel the school provides information and materials to their parents to help them at home.
	• Students are not reading at home every day.
	• Students do not feel teachers contact their parents about progress in school.
	• Students think parents do not help them regularly with schoolwork.
	• Students do not believe parents are encouraged to volunteer at the school.
	• Black students' perceptions fall into disagreement around respect of students for one another, student respect for teachers, and teacher respect for students.
	• Black students do not evaluate their work using scoring guides, etc.
	• Black students were in most disagreement with respect to teachers asking for feedback about their teaching.
	• Black students were lowest around thinking that the school is making progress in improving the achievement of all students, and that they got academic support when it is needed.
	• In the open-ended responses, students mentioned they would like less homework, better food, and more time for lunch.

Staff questionnaires • Teachers do not think students are bullied or that student time is spent waiting for other students to behave. • Teachers feel that students know what they are to learn in class. • Teachers feel that students are recognized for good work and that they have to work hard to do well in their classes. • Teachers are trying new teaching strategies to improve student learning. • Teachers believe it is important for students to volunteer in the community. • Teachers expect students to go to college (although not as much as students and parents).	*Staff questionnaires* • Staff needs to get all teachers to respond to the questionnaire. • Teachers do not think students' parents help with schoolwork outside of the classroom. • Teachers do not like the food choices in the cafeteria. • There is disagreement regarding teachers collaborating across curricular areas and grade levels. • Teachers disagree in the past two years that district monies are spent to increase student achievement. • Teachers do not think the state test scores are an important measure of their students' learning. • Teachers do not feel that students read at home every day. • Some of the newer teachers' perceptions are lower than the other teachers' perceptions. • Teachers with seven to ten years of teaching were in most disagreement with a number of items. • In the open-ended responses, teachers know they need professional development that helps them know how to better meet diverse student needs. • Teachers feel student motivation needs to be improved and that communication among staff members and staff and administration needs to be improved. • In the open-ended responses, teachers mentioned that all teachers need to teach to the standards and the curriculum, and that more parents need to be involved.

What I Saw in the Example: Big River High School *(Continued)*

Questionnaire Data

Perceptual Strengths	*Perceptual Challenges*
Parent questionnaires • Parents expect their child to go to college. • Parents believe their child is expected to do good work at this school. • Parents do not feel that their child is bullied by other students at the school, or that time is spent in classes waiting for students to behave. • Parents feel that their child knows what they are supposed to learn in each class and that the child has to work hard to do well. • Parents feel it is important for students to volunteer in the community. • Parents believe that last year of school prepared their child for this year's school work.	*Parent questionnaires* • Parents do not feel that their child likes the food choices in the cafeteria. • Parents do not feel that their child's teachers ask for feedback about their teaching, or that the school provides information and materials for them to work with their child at home. • Parents do not feel teachers contact parents about their child's progress in school. • Parents do not feel that their child receives help with homework at school outside of class. • Black parents concerns are similar to the students' concerns.

Implications for Big River's school improvement plan

* Getting the same results for five years implies that either the questionnaires need to be improved, or the results need to be implemented.
* Teachers should be using the expectations of parents and students to go to college as a means of improving student achievement results.
* Teachers need to ask students for feedback about their teaching.
* Teachers need to think about adding more challenging classroom activities.
* Teachers need to make sure all student populations are being treated with respect (pay attention to the Black students).
* Staff needs to make sure Black students are feeling that they are being assisted with their learning.
* All staff have to make the state test more important to students and to teachers.
* New teachers might need some support with classroom management.
* Staff needs to collaborate within and across curricular areas and grade levels.
* Staff wants communication to be improved across staff and between staff and administration.
* Staff needs to look at ways to increase parent contact regarding student progress, and to help parents know how to help their children learn at home.
* Staff needs to develop a system to get more parents to complete the questionnaire.

Other desired perceptual data or information

* How effective is homework? Are there other more effective approaches to getting the work done?
* Do students know what it takes to go to college?
* Can the food be improved?

Staff Questionnaire and Standards Assessment Data

Perceptual Strengths	Perceptual Challenges

• Teachers took it upon themselves to administer another questionnaire when the results of their current one did not tell them enough.
• In the main questionnaire, staff was in agreement with the items.
• In the standards assessment, staff (overall) was in strong agreement with the following:
  * Teachers seem to be knowledgeable of the standards.
  * Staff knows there is a system of support for standards.
• Almost 80% of the staff believes teachers and instructional staff can make the necessary changes to improve student learning.
• Seventy-four percent of the staff believes school leadership can facilitate the necessary changes to improve student learning.
• Special education and emergency credentialed teachers, and those with 26+ years of teaching experience, seem to be the most knowledgeable of standards.
• Staff believes staff and administration are strengths.
	• Staff members on emergency credentials do not feel recognized for good work, intrinsically rewarded for doing their job well, or that they work with people who provide one another feedback on their teaching.
	• *I believe all students can learn* was not one of the staffs' highest scoring items.
	• Teachers with two to three years of teaching experience do not feel recognized for good work.
	• Morale is lowest for teachers with 15 to 20 years of teaching experience.
	• Teachers with 26+ years of teaching experience were in least agreement that quality work is expected of all students at the school.
	• Staff members feel that schoolwide meetings about standards probably would not help them better know the standards.
	• Twenty-three percent of the teachers follow textbooks as a means of teaching to standards.
	• Thirteen percent of staff are less than committed to making necessary changes to improve student learning.
	• Teachers feel more support from colleagues than administrators in teaching standards.
	• In open-ended remarks, staff implied that teachers need to care more and improve their teaching.

Implications for Big River's school improvement plan

• Staff needs to communicate and collaborate to make learning consistent across grade levels, to remember why they got into teaching in the first place, and to provide feedback on their teaching with one another.
• Staff seems to think professional development on how to teach to the standards, feedback from classroom observations, demonstration lessons, and peer coaching will help them better know the standards.
• Staff would like all staff to care more about students and teach to the standards.
• Staff would like time to work with each other and students, and more administrative support.
• Staff wants more ways to improve students' basic skills.

Other desired perceptual data or information

• Classroom observation data would be helpful.

Understanding how we do business can help a school know what is possible, what is appropriate, and what is needed in the continuous school improvement plan.

Summary

The second question, *How do we do business?*, tells us about perceptions of the learning environment from student, staff, and parent perspectives. Multiple-choice questionnaires can give us a quick snapshot of different groups' perspectives. Open-ended responses, used with the multiple choice responses, help paint the picture of the school. Understanding how we do business can help a school know what is possible, what is appropriate, and what is needed in the continuous school improvement plan.

The *Education for the Future Continuous Improvement Continuums* are also a valuable assessment tool for understanding the system.

On the CD Related to this Chapter

▼ *Continuous Improvement Continuums* for Schools (CICs.pdf)
This read-only file contains the seven *School Portfolio Continuous Improvement Continuums* for schools. These can be printed as is and also enlarged for posting individual staff opinions during staff assessments.

▼ *Continuous Improvement Continuums* for Districts (CICsDstrct.pdf)
This read-only file contains the seven *School Portfolio Continuous Improvement Continuums* for assessing the district level. These can be printed as is and also enlarged for posting individual staff opinions during staff assessments.

▼ *Big River High School Baseline CIC Results* (BRBase.pdf)
This read-only file is the summary of Big River's baseline assessment on the *School Portfolio Continuous Improvement Continuums.*

▼ *Continuous Improvement Continuum* Tools Folder
These files are tools for assessing on the CICs and for writing the CIC report.

◆ *Continuous Improvement Continuums Self-Assessment Activity* (ACTCIC.pdf)
Assessing on the *Continuous Improvement Continuums* will help staffs see where their systems are right now with respect to continuous improvement and ultimately will show they are making progress over time. The discussion has major implications for the *Continuous School Improvement (CSI) Plan.*

◆ *Coming to Consensus* (Consenss.pdf)
This read-only file provides strategies for coming to consensus, useful when assessing on the *Continuous Improvement Continuums.*

- *Continuous Improvement Continuums Report Example* (ExReprt1.pdf)
  This read-only file shows a real school's assessment on the *School Portfolio Continuous Improvement Continuums,* as an example.

- *Continuous Improvement Continuums Report Example for Follow-up Years* (ExReprt2.pdf)
  This read-only file shows a real school's assessment on the *School Portfolio Continuous Improvement Continuums* over time, as an example.

- *Continuous Improvement Continuums Baseline Report Template* (ReptTemp.doc)
  This *Microsoft Word* file provides a template for writing your school's report of its assessment on the *School Portfolio Continuous Improvement Continuums.*

- *Continuous Improvement Continuums Graphing Templates* (CICGraph.xls)
  This *Microsoft Excel* file is a template for graphing your assessments on the seven *School Portfolio Continuous Improvement Continuums.*

▼ Study Questions Related to *How Do We Do Business?* (Ch5Qs.doc)
These study questions will help you better understand the information provided in Chapter 5. This template file can be printed for use with staffs as you answer the question, *How do we do business?,* through analyzing Big River's perceptual data.

▼ *What I Saw in the Example* (Ch5Saw.pdf)
What I Saw in the Example is a file, organized by the perceptual study questions, that summarizes what the author saw in the perceptual data provided by Big River High School.

▼ *Analysis of Questionnaire Data Table* (QTable.doc)
This *Microsoft Word* file is a tabular guide for interpreting your student, staff, and parent questionnaires, independently and interdependently. It will help you see the summary of your results and write the narrative.

▼ Full Narratives of Questionnaire Results Used in the Big River Example:
  - *Big River Student Questionnaire Results* (StuNarr.doc)
  - *Big River Staff Questionnaire Results* (StfNarr.doc)
  - *Big River Parent Questionnaire Results* (ParNarr.doc)

◆ *Education for the Future* Questionnaires:
These PDF files are for content review purposes only—*not* intended for use in questionnaire administration. For more information about administering and analyzing *Education for the Future* questionnaires, please visit *http://eff.csuchico.edu/questionnaire_resources/*.

* *Student (Kindergarten to Grade 3) Questionnaire* (StQKto3.pdf)
* *Student (Grades 1 to 12) Questionnaire* (StQ1to12.pdf)
* *Student (Middle/High School) Questionnaire* (StQMidHS.pdf)
* *Teaching Staff Questionnaire* (TeachStaffQ.pdf)
* *Organizational Learning Questionnaire* (OrgLearnQ.pdf)
* *Administrator Questionnaire* (AdminQ.pdf)
* *Parent Questionnaire* (ParntK12Q.pdf)
* *High School Parent Questionnaire* (ParntHSQ.pdf)
* *Alumni Questionnaire* (AlumniQ.pdf)

▼ *How to Analyze Open-ended Responses* (OEanalz.pdf)
This read-only file discusses how to analyze responses to the open-ended questions on questionnaires.

▼ *Questions to Guide the Analysis of Perceptions Data* (PerceptQ.doc)
This *Microsoft Word* file is a tabular guide for interpreting your perceptions data. You can change the questions if you like or use the file to write in the responses. It will help you write the narrative for your results.

Visit *http://eff.csuchico.edu* for information about questionnaire tools and *Education for the Future* questionnaires.

Analyzing the Data:
Where Are We Now?

What are the results of current processes? Where are we now? The results from the demographic data collection and analysis, reviewed in Chapter 4, provide a framework for understanding student performance data. Further, the understanding of school culture developed through the analyses of beliefs, values, and perceptions contribute to a richer understanding of the environment within which student learning takes place. We must remember, however, that the overall purpose of the continuous school improvement model is to *get results:* to improve student learning.

Chapter 6

Most often, schools determine their results through student learning measures only. More often than not, schools use a simple student learning measure, usually a state-required assessment. While this is clearly a good starting point, generating a sound understanding of how well students are learning *requires multiple measures* that are disaggregated, across demographic groups over time. Only by understanding the different type of assessment data, analyzed for detail, can we get to a real understanding of what we need to do to continuously improve our results.

Why do we measure student learning?
We measure student learning to know—

- ▼ if students have particular skills and knowledge
- ▼ if students have attained a level of proficiency/competence/mastery
- ▼ if instructional strategies are making a difference for all students
- ▼ the effectiveness of instructional strategies and curricula
- ▼ how to improve instructional strategies
- ▼ how to classify students into instructional groups
- ▼ that students are ready to graduate or proceed to the next level of instruction
- ▼ if school processes are making the intended progress

Unfortunately, student learning results are not always used in these ways. Most of the time it is because school personnel struggle with the way student learning is measured and the analyses to display the results. The purpose of this chapter is to show different ways of measuring, analyzing, and reporting student learning results.

We start with discussions of different ways to measure student learning in high schools; then the example, Big River High School, is shown. Please note the study questions on page 175 to assist in interpreting the data. (Ch6Qs.pdf) Also note that there is space in the margins on the data pages to write your impressions as you review the data. At the end of the chapter, I have shared what I saw in the data.

month work. It only means that the student obtained the same score that one would expect average tenth grade students to score if they took the same ninth-grade test during the eighth month of grade nine. Grade-level equivalent scores are okay for a snapshot in time, but they should not be averaged or taken literally.

Standard Scores. Standard scores, or scaled scores, refer to scores that have been *transformed* for reasons of convenience, comparability, and ease of interpretation. Ranges vary depending upon the test, and sometimes even the subtest. The best uses of standard scores are averages calculated over time allowing for the study of change. These scores are good to use for calculations because of their equal intervals and their easy conversions to other score types. The downsides are that, with the various ranges, it is difficult to look across subtests, grade levels, and years. It is often hard for the layperson to create meaning from these scores. The normal curve is needed to interpret the results with respect to other scores and people. The NCE is a standard score and probably one of the best to use because of the constant range and mean.

Anticipated Achievement/Cognitive Abilities Scores. Occasionally, norm-referenced tests provide indicators of ability, such as anticipated achievement scores, cognitive abilities, or cognitive skills indexes. The anticipated achievement score is an estimate of the average score for students of a similar age, grade, and academic aptitude. It can be computed in grade-level equivalents, normal curve equivalents, standard scores, and national percentiles. The higher the student scores on sequences, analogies, memory, and verbal reasoning tests, the higher the student is expected to score on standardized tests.

A cognitive abilities or cognitive skills index is also created from the same four tests mentioned above, and assesses the student's academic aptitude. The range of this scale is 58 to 141, with a mean of 100. Two-thirds of the scores will fall between 84 and 118. Anticipated Achievement/Cognitive Abilities scores can tell teachers if they are teaching to students' potential.

> *Grade-level equivalent scores are okay for a snapshot in time, but they should not be averaged or taken literally.*

> *The best uses of standard scores are averages calculated over time allowing for the study of change.*

> *Anticipated Achievement/ Cognitive Abilities scores can tell teachers if they are teaching to the students' potential.*

> *Criterion-referenced assessments tell us how well students are performing on specific criteria, goals, or standards.*

Criterion-referenced Tests

Criterion-referenced tests compare an individual's performance to a specific learning objective or performance standard and not to the performance of other test takers. Criterion-referenced assessments tell us how well students are performing on specific criteria, goals, or standards. For school level analyses, criterion-referenced tests are usually scored in terms of the number or percentage of students meeting the standard or criterion, or the number or percentage of students falling in typical descriptive categories, such as *far below basic, below basic, basic, proficient,* and *advanced.* Criterion-referenced tests can be standardized or not, and they can also have norming groups.

Diagnostic Tests

> *Diagnostic tests can help teachers know the nature of students' difficulties, but not the cause of the difficulty.*

Diagnostic tests, usually standardized and normed, are given before instruction begins to help the instructor(s) understand student learning needs. Diagnostic tests can help teachers know the nature of students' difficulties, but not the cause of the difficulty. Many different score types are used with diagnostic tests.

These tests, score types, and other frequently used terms are defined in Figure 6.3, along with a description of most effective uses and cautions for use. (TestTerm.pdf)

Figure 6.3

	Standardized Test Score Terms, Their Most Effective Uses, and Cautions for Their Uses		
Score	**Definition**	**Most Effective Uses**	**Cautions**
Anticipated Achievement Scores	A student's anticipated achievement score is an estimate of the average score for students of similar ages, grade levels, and academic aptitude. It is an estimate of what we would expect the student to score on an achievement test.	Anticipated achievement scores can be used to see if a student is scoring "above" or "below" an expected score, indicating whether or not she/he is being challenged enough, or if her/his needs are being met.	It is easy to think of these scores as "IQ" scores. They are just achievement indicators on a standardized test.
Cognitive Abilities or Skills Index	The cognitive skills index is an age-dependent normalized standard score based on a student's performance on a cognitive skills test with a mean of 100 and standard deviation of 16. The score indicates a student's overall cognitive ability or academic aptitude relative to students of similar age, without regard to grade level.	Cognitive skills index scores can be used to see if a student is scoring "above" or "below" an expected score, indicating whether or not she/he is being challenged enough, or if her/his needs are being met.	It is easy to think of these scores as "IQ" scores. They are just achievement indicators on a standardized test.
Criterion-referenced Tests	Tests that judge how well a test-taker does on an explicit objective relative to a predetermined performance level.	Tell us how well students are performing on specific criteria, goals, or standards.	CRTs test only what was taught, or planned to be taught. CRTs can not give a broad estimate of knowledge.
Deciles	Deciles divide a distribution into ten equal parts: 1–10; 11–20; 21–30; 31–40; 41–50; 51–60; 61–70; 71–80; 81–90; 91–99. Just about any scale can be used to show deciles.	Deciles allow schools to show how all students scored throughout the distribution. One would expect a school's distribution to resemble a normal curve. Watching the distribution move to the right, over time, could imply that all students in the distribution are making progress.	One must dig deeper to understand if all students and all groups of students are moving forward.
Diagnostic Tests	Diagnostic tests, usually standardized and normed, are given before instruction begins to help the instructor(s) understand student learning needs. Many different score types are used with diagnostic tests.	Help teachers know the nature of students' difficulties, but not the cause of the difficulty.	Make sure the diagnostic test is measuring what you want it to measure and that it can be compared to formative and summative assessments used.

Figure 6.3 (Continued)

<table>
<tr><th colspan="4">Standardized Test Score Terms,
Their Most Effective Uses, and Cautions for Their Uses</th></tr>
<tr><th>Score</th><th>Definition</th><th>Most Effective Uses</th><th>Cautions</th></tr>
<tr>
<td>Grade-level Equivalents</td>
<td>Grade-level equivalents indicate the grade and month of the school year for which a given score is the actual or estimated average. Based on a ten-month school year, scores would be noted as 9.1 for ninth grade, first month, or 11.10 for eleventh grade, tenth month.</td>
<td>Grade-level equivalents are most effectively used as a snapshot in time.
Scores are comparable across subtests.</td>
<td>These scores should not be taken literally. If a ninth grader scored a 11.8 on a subtest, that does not mean that she/he should be doing eleventh grade, eighth-month work. It only means that the student obtained the same score that one would expect average eleventh-grade students in their eighth month of school to score if they took the ninth-grade test.</td>
</tr>
<tr>
<td>Latent-trait Scale</td>
<td>A latent-trait scale is a scaled score obtained through one of several mathematical approaches collectively known as Latent-Trait Procedures or Item Response Theory. The particular numerical values used in the scale are arbitrary, but higher scores indicate more knowledgeable students or more difficult items.</td>
<td>Latent-trait scales have equal intervals allowing comparisons over time.</td>
<td>These are scores set up by testing professionals. Laypeople typically have difficulty understanding their meaning.</td>
</tr>
<tr>
<td>NCE (National or Local)</td>
<td>Normal Curve Equivalent (NCE) scores are standard scores with a mean of 50, a standard deviation of 21.06, and a range of 1 to 99.
The term National would indicate that the norming group was national; local usually implies a state or district norming group.</td>
<td>NCEs have equal intervals so they can be used to study gains over time. The scores have the same meaning across subtests, grade levels, and years.
A 50 is what one would expect in an average year's growth.</td>
<td>This score, just like all scores related to norm-referenced tests, cannot be taken literally. The score simply shows relative performance of a student group or of students to a norming group.</td>
</tr>
<tr>
<td>Percent Passing</td>
<td>Percent passing is a calculated score implying the percentage of the student group meeting and exceeding some number, usually a cut score, proficiency/mastery level, or a standard.</td>
<td>With standards-based accountability, it is beneficial to know the percentage of the population meeting and exceeding a standard and to compare a year's percentages with the previous year(s) to understand progress being made.</td>
<td>This is a very simple statistic, and its interpretation should be simple as well. Total numbers (n=) of students included in the percentage must always be noted with the percentage to assist with the understanding.</td>
</tr>
</table>

Figure 6.3 (Continued)

	Standardized Test Score Terms, Their Most Effective Uses, and Cautions for Their Uses		
Score	**Definition**	**Most Effective Uses**	**Cautions**
Percentile / Percentile Rank (PR) (National or Local)	Percentile ranks indicate the percentage of students in a norm group (e.g., national or local) whose scores fall below a given score. The range is from 1 to 99. 50th percentile ranking would mean that 50 percent of the scores in the norming group fall below a specific score. The term National would indicate that the norming group was national; local usually implies a state or district norming group.	One-year comparison to the norming group. Schools can see the relative standing of a student or group in the same grade to the norm group who took the test at a comparable time.	Percentile rank is not a score to use over time to look for gains because of unequal intervals, unless the calculations are made with equal interval scores and then converted to percentile ranks. One cannot calculate averages using NPR because of the unequal intervals. Medians are the most appropriate statistic to use.
Quartiles	There are three quartiles points—Q1, Q2, Q3 — that divide a distribution into four equal groups: Q1=25th percentile Q2=50th percentile (Median) Q3=75th percentile	Quartiles allow schools to see the distribution of scores for any grade level, for instance. Over time, schools trying to increase student achievement would want to monitor the distribution to ensure that all students are making progress.	With quartiles, one cannot tell if the scores are at the top of a quartile or the bottom. There could be "real" changes taking place within a quartile that would not be evident.
Raw Scores	Raw scores are the number of questions answered correctly on a test or subtest. A raw score is simply calculated by adding the number of questions answered correctly. The raw score is a person's observed score.	The raw score provides information about the number of questions answered correctly. To get a perspective on performance, raw scores must be used with the average score for the group and/or the total number of questions. Alone, it has no meaning.	Raw scores do not provide information related to other students taking the test or to other subtests. One needs to keep perspective by knowing the total number possible. Raw scores should never be used to make comparisons between performances on different tests unless other information about the characteristics of the tests are known and identical.
RIT Scale Scores	RIT scores, named for George Rasch who developed the theory of this type of measurement, are scaled scores that come from a series of tests created by the Northwest Evaluation Association (NWEA). The tests, which draw from an item bank, are aligned with local curriculum and state/local standards.	RIT scores provide ongoing measurement of curriculum standards and a way for students to see progress in their knowledge. The scores can also be shown as percentiles to know performance related to other students of similar ages and/or grades. You will most probably see gains each time a measurement is taken with a group of students.	RIT scores are great as long as the test was carefully designed to measure standards.

Figure 6.3 (Continued)

Standardized Test Score Terms, Their Most Effective Uses, and Cautions for Their Uses			
Score	**Definition**	**Most Effective Uses**	**Cautions**
Scaled Scores	A scaled score is a mathematical transformation of a raw score, resulting in interval scores within a defined range. Scaled scores take item difficulty into account.	The best uses of scaled scores are averages and averages calculated over time allowing for the study of change. These scores are good to use for calculations because of equal intervals. The scores can be applied across subtests within most tests. Scaled scores facilitate conversions to other score types.	Ranges vary, depending upon the test. Watch for the minimum and maximum values. It is sometimes hard for laypeople to create meaning from these scores. The normal curve is needed to interpret the results with respect to other scores and people.
Standard Scores	Standard score is a general term referring to scores that have been "transformed" for reasons of convenience, comparability, ease of interpretation, etc., to have a predefined mean and standard deviation. z-scores and T-scores are standard scores.	The best uses of standard scores are averages and averages calculated over time, allowing for the study of change. These scores are good to use for calculations because of equal intervals. The scores can be applied across subtests on most tests. Standard scores facilitate conversions to other score types.	Ranges vary, depending upon the test. Watch for the minimum and maximum values. It is sometimes hard for laypeople to create meaning from these scores. The normal curve is needed to interpret results with respect to other scores and people.
Standards-based Assessments	Standards-based assessments measure students' progress toward mastering local, state, and/or national content standards.	The way standards-based assessments are analyzed depends upon the scales used. The most effective uses are in revealing the percentage of students achieving a standard.	One has to adhere to the cautions of whatever test or score type used. It is important to know how far from mastering the standard the students were when they did not meet the standard.
Stanines	Stanines are a nine-point standard score scale. Stanines divide the normal curve into nine equal points: 1 to 9.	Stanines, like quartiles, allow schools to see the distribution of scores for any grade level, for instance. Over time, schools trying to increase student achievement would want to monitor the distribution to ensure that all student scores are improving.	Often, the first three stanines are interpreted as "below average," the next three as "average," and the top three as "above average." This can be misleading. As with quartiles, one cannot tell if the scores are at the top of a stanine or the bottom. There could be "real" changes taking place within a stanine that would not be evident.

Figure 6.3 (Continued)

Standardized Test Score Terms, Their Most Effective Uses, and Cautions for Their Uses			
Score	**Definition**	**Most Effective Uses**	**Cautions**
T-scores	A T-score is a standard score with a mean of 50 and a standard deviation of 10. T-scores are obtained by the following formula: $$T = 10z + 50$$	The most effective uses of T-scores are averages and averages calculated over time. T-scores are good to use for calculations because of their equal intervals. T-scores can be applied across subtests on most tests because of the forced mean and standard deviation.	T-scores are rarely used because of the lack of understanding on the part of most test users.
z-scores	A z-score is a standard score with a mean of zero and a standard deviation of one. z-scores are obtained by the following formula: $$z = \frac{\text{raw score } (x) - \text{mean}}{\text{standard deviation (sd)}}$$	z-scores can tell one how many standard deviations a score is away from the mean. z-scores are most useful, perhaps, as the first step in computing other types of standard scores.	z-scores are rarely used by the lay public because of the difficulty in understanding the score.

> *The term "performance assessment" refers to assessments that measure skills, knowledge, and ability directly—such as through "performance."*

Performance Assessments

The term *performance assessment* refers to assessments that measure skills, knowledge, and ability directly—such as through *performance*. In other words, if you want students to learn to write, you assess their ability on a writing activity. One must find a way to score these results and make sense for individual students and groups of students. Some of the arguments for and against performance assessments are listed in Figure 6.4. (PerfArgu.pdf) (See *References* for sources.)

Figure 6.4

Arguments For and Against Performance Assessments

Arguments For Performance Assessments

+ Performance assessments can be designed to measure performance, thinking, problem solving, and communication skills.
+ Performance assessments can be used to measure the process students use to solve problems.
+ Performance assessments can be developed to match state standards.
+ Many schools, districts, and states have seen achievement levels rise in recent years, which they attribute to higher expectations of students and what they can do, attributed to the use of performance assessments.
+ Performance assessments provide data that show what students are lacking, giving educators the information necessary to tailor classes and instructional strategies to student needs.
+ Students can learn during a performance task.
+ Some teachers believe that when students participate in developing a rubric for evaluating their performance, they come to appreciate high-quality work.
+ Performance assessments provide opportunities for students to reflect on their own work.
+ Performance assessments can allow students to work until standards are met—to ensure quality work from all students.
+ Performance assessments can help the teacher improve instructional strategies.
+ Performance assessments allow students to perform in the learning style that suits them best.

Arguments Against Performance Assessments

+ Designing good performance assessments that accurately measure performance, thinking, problem solving, and communication skills is difficult.
+ Designing good performance assessments that accurately measure performance, thinking, problem solving, and communication skills is very costly.
+ Some performance tasks require long periods of time to complete, such as graduation or end-of-course exhibitions.
+ To be effective, skills and performances being assessed should be taught in the same way they are measured.
+ The quality of performance assessments is a concern.
+ It is not fair to hold students accountable on one test when the schools might not be providing students with quality teachers, curricula, and time to master concepts.
+ Scoring criteria requires analyzing performance into its components, such as breaking out the craft of writing into developmental elements.
+ Many scoring criteria are no different from giving grades or norm-referenced scoring.
+ Good scoring criteria could take a long time to develop.
+ It is very difficult to design performance assessments that can be compared across grade levels in other than descriptive terms.

Grades

Teachers use number or letter grades to judge the quality of a student's performance on a task, unit, or during a period of time. Grades are most often given as A, B, C, D, F, with pluses and minuses given by some teachers for the first four to distinguish among students. Grades mean different things to different teachers. Needless to say, grades can be subjective. "It appears that teachers consider grading to be a private activity, thus 'guarding practices with the same passion with which one might guard an unedited diary' (Kain, 1996, p. 569)" (O'Connor, 2000, p. 11). Some of the arguments for and against teacher grading are shown in Figure 6.5. (GradeArg.pdf)

Figure 6.5

Arguments For and Against Teacher Grading

Arguments For Teacher Grading

- Grades can be designed to reflect performance, thinking, problem solving, and communication skills.
- Teachers can grade the process students use to solve a problem, rather than just the result.
- Grades can communicate to students, parents, and administrators the student's level of performance.
- Grading can allow teachers to be very flexible in their approaches to assessing student performance.
- Grades can match teaching.
- Grades can be given for team work and not just individual work.
- Grades can be effective if students are aware of expectations.
- Grades can cover multiple standards.
- Certain teacher-developed tests can be graded quickly.
- Most people believe they know what grades mean.

Arguments Against Teacher Grading

- It is difficult to convert activities, such as performance, thinking, and problem solving, into numbers or letters and have them hold true for all students in a class.
- Grading can be very subjective.
- Grading can be distorted by effort, extra credit, attendance, behavior, etc.
- To be beneficial, students must trust the grader and the grading process, have time to practice and complete an assessment, and have choices in how they are assessed—all of which make it time-consuming for teachers to do this type of assessment well.
- To be beneficial, grading assessments must be meaningful and promote learning.
- Grades must include a variety of assessment techniques to get to all areas of student understanding and performance.
- Often parents, students, and teachers focus on grades and not on learning.
- Grading is not reflective of instructional strategies.
- Grades are not always motivators; in fact, they can demoralize students on the low end, and on the high end.
- Grades tell little about student strengths and areas for improvement.
- Grading can mean many different things within a grade level, across grade levels by teacher, subject area, and school.
- Some teachers' highest priorities with grading are to use techniques where the grades can be calculated quickly.
- Grading is not always compatible with all instructional strategies.
- Grades often are given for more than achievement.
- Grading is not essential for learning.

Analyzing the Results, Descriptively

Descriptive statistics (i.e., mean, median, percent correct) can give schools very powerful information. It is imperative that the appropriate analyses be used for the specific score type. Figure 6.6 summarizes terms of analyses, their definitions, their most effective uses, and cautions for their uses in analyzing student achievement scores descriptively. (SAterms1.pdf) Descriptive statistics are used in the examples in this chapter largely because they can show a school how its students are doing, and because anyone can do the calculations.

Descriptive statistics summarize the basic characteristics of a particular group of students, without making any inferences about any larger group that may include the one from which the scores are taken. Graphing the information can also be considered descriptive.

Descriptive statistics summarize the basic characteristics of a particular distribution, without making any inferences about population parameters.

Figure 6.6

	Terms Related to Analyzing Student Achievement Results, Descriptively, Their Most Effective Uses, and Cautions for Their Uses		
Term	**Definition**	**Most Effective Uses**	**Cautions**
Disaggregate	Disaggregation is breaking a total score into groups for purposes of seeing how subgroups performed. One disaggregates data to make sure all subgroups of students are learning.	Disaggregating student achievement scores by gender, ethnicity, backgrounds, etc., can show how different subgroups performed.	Disaggregations are for helping schools understand how to meet the needs of all students, not to say, "This group always does worse than the other group and always will." We must exercise caution in reporting disaggregations with small numbers in a subgroup.
Gain	Gain scores are the change or difference between two administrations of the same test. Gain scores are calculated by subtracting the previous score from the most recent score. One can have negative gains, which are actually losses.	One calculates gains to understand improvements in learning for groups of students and for individual students.	Gain scores should not be calculated using unequal interval scores, such as percentiles. The quality of gain score results is dependent upon the quality of the assessment instrument; the less reliable the assessment tool, the less meaningful the results. One needs to make sure the comparisons are appropriate, e.g., same students, same score types.
Maximum	A maximum is the highest score achieved, or the highest possible score on a test.	Maximum possible scores and highest received scores are important for understanding the relative performance of any group or individual, especially when using scaled or standard scores.	A maximum can tell either the highest score possible or the highest score received by a test-taker. One needs to understand which maximum is being used in the analysis. It is best to use both.
Mean	A mean is the average score in a set of scores. One calculates the mean, or average, by summing all the scores and dividing by the total number of scores.	A mean can be calculated to provide an overall average for the group, and/or student, taking a specific test. One can use any equal interval score to get a mean.	Means should not be used with unequal interval scores, such as percentile ranks. Means are more sensitive to extreme results when the size of the group is small.
Median	A median is the score that splits a distribution in half: 50 percent of the scores fall above and 50 percent of the scores fall below the median. If the number of scores is odd, the median is the middle score. If the number of scores is even, one must add the two middle scores and divide by two to calculate the median.	Medians are the way to get a midpoint for scores with unequal intervals, such as percentile ranks. The median splits all scores into two equal parts. Medians are not sensitive to outliers, like means are.	Medians are relative. Medians are most effectively interpreted when reported with the possible and actual maximum and minimum.
Minimum	A minimum is the lowest score achieved, or the lowest possible score on the test.	Minimum possible scores and lowest received scores are important for understanding the relative performance of any group or individual.	A minimum tells either the lowest score possible or the lowest score received by a test-taker. One needs to understand which minimum is being used. It is best to use both.

Figure 6.6 (Continued)

	Terms Related to Analyzing Student Achievement Results, Descriptively, Their Most Effective Uses, and Cautions for Their Uses		
Term	**Definition**	**Most Effective Uses**	**Cautions**
Mode	The mode is the score that occurs most frequently in a scoring distribution.	The mode basically tells which score or scores appear most often.	There may be more than one mode. The mode ignores other scores.
Percent Correct	Percent correct is a calculated score implying the percentage of students meeting and exceeding some number, usually a cut score, or a standard.	This calculated score can quickly tell educators how well the students are doing with respect to a specific set of items. It can also tell educators how many students need additional work to become proficient.	Percent correct is a calculated statistic, based on the number of items given. When the number of items given is small, the percent correct can be deceptively high or low.
Percent Proficient *Percent Passing* *Percent Mastery*	Percent proficient, passing, or mastery represent the percentage of students who passed a particular test at a "proficient," "passing," or "mastery" level, as defined by the test creators or the test interpreters.	With standards-based accountability, it is beneficial to know the percentage of the population meeting and exceeding the standard and to compare a year's percentage with the previous year(s) to understand progress being made.	This is a very simple statistic, and its interpretation should be simple as well. Total numbers (N=) of students included in the percentage must always be noted with the percentage to assist in understanding the results. Ninety percent passing means something very different for 10 or 100 test-takers.
Range	Range is a measure of the spread between the lowest and the highest scores in a distribution. Calculate the range of scores by subtracting the lowest score from the highest score. Range is often described as end points also, such as the range of percentile ranks is 1 and 99.	Ranges tell us the width of the distribution of scores. Educators working on continuous improvement will want to watch the range, of actual scores, decrease over time.	If there are outliers present, the range can give a misleading impression of dispersion.
Raw Scores	Raw scores refer to the number of questions answered correctly on a test or subtest. A raw score is simply calculated by adding the number of questions answered correctly. The raw score is a person's observed score.	The raw score provides information only about the number of questions answered correctly. To get a perspective on performance, raw scores must be used with the average score for the group and the total number of questions. Alone, raw scores have little meaning.	Raw scores do not provide information related to other students taking the test or to other subtests or scores. One needs to keep perspective by knowing the total number possible. Raw scores should never be used to make comparisons between performances on different tests unless other information about the characteristics of the tests are known and identical.

Figure 6.6 (Continued)

Terms Related to Analyzing Student Achievement Results, Descriptively, Their Most Effective Uses, and Cautions for Their Uses			
Term	**Definition**	**Most Effective Uses**	**Cautions**
Relationships	Relationships refer to looking at two or more sets of analyses to understand what they mean to each other without using extensive statistical techniques.	Descriptive statistics lend themselves to looking at the relationships of different analyses to each other; for instance, student learning results disaggregated by ethnicity, compared to student questionnaire results disaggregated by ethnicity.	This type of analysis is general and the results should be considered general as well. This is not a "correlation."
Rubric	A rubric is a scoring tool that rates performance according to clearly stated levels of criteria. The scales can be numeric or descriptive, or both.	Rubrics are used to give teachers, parents, and students an idea of where they started, where they want to be with respect to growth, and where they are right now.	Students need to know what the rubrics contain or, even better, help with the development of the rubrics.
Standard Deviation	The standard deviation is a measure of variability in a set of scores. The standard deviation indicates how far away scores are from the mean. The standard deviation is the square root of the variance. Unlike the variance, the standard deviation is stated in the original units of the variable. Approximately 68 percent of the scores in a normal distribution lie between plus one and minus one standard deviation of the mean. The more scores cluster around the mean, the smaller the variance.	Tells us about the variability of scores. Standard deviations indicate how spread-out the scores are without looking at the entire distribution. A low standard deviation would indicate that the scores of a group are close together. A high standard deviation would imply that the range of scores is wide.	Often this is a confusing statistic for laypeople to understand. There are more descriptive ways to describe and show the variability of student scores, such as with a decile graph. Standard deviations only make sense with scores that are distributed normally.
Triangulation	Triangulation is a term used for combining three or more measures to get a more complete picture of student achievement.	If students are to be retained based on standards proficiency, educators must have more than one way of knowing if the students are proficient or not. Some students perform well on standardized measures and not on other measures, while others do not do well with standardized measures. Triangulation allows students to display what they know on three different measures.	It is sometimes very complicated to combine different measures to understand proficiency. When proficiency standards change, triangulation calculations will need to be revised. Therefore, all the calculations must be documented so they can be recalculated when necessary.

Analyzing the Results, Inferentially

Many school administrators and teachers have taken statistics courses that taught them that it is important to have control groups, experimental designs, and to test for significant differences. These terms fall in the category of *inferential statistics.* Inferential statistics are concerned with measuring a sample from a population, and then making estimates, or inferences, about the population from which the sample was taken. Inferential statistics help generalize the results of data analysis, when one is not using the entire population in the analysis.

The main purpose of this book is to model analyses that school personnel can perform *without* the assistance of statisticians. Descriptive analyses provide helpful and useful information and can be understood by a majority of people. When using the entire school population in your analyses, there is no need to generalize to a larger population—you have the whole population. There is no need for inferential statistics.

Inferential statistical methods, such as analyses of variance, correlations, and regression analyses, are complex and require someone who knows statistics to meet the conditions of the analyses. Since there are times when a statistician is available to perform inferential statistics, some of the terms the statistician might use with tests include those listed in Figure 6.7. (SAterms2.pdf)

A Note About "Scientifically-based Research." With the passage of the *No Child Left Behind* (NCLB) *Act of 2001,* which reauthorized the *Elementary and Secondary Education Act of 1965,* school districts and schools are required to gather, analyze, and use data to ensure adequate yearly progress (AYP). While increased accountability is just one part of NCLB, all schools must gather data and overcome the barriers to analyzing and using the data.

Figure 6.7

Terms Related to Analyzing Student Achievement Results, Inferentially, Their Most Effective Uses, and Cautions for Their Uses			
Term	**Definition**	**Most Effective Uses**	**Cautions**
Analysis of Variance (ANOVA)	Analysis of variance is a general term applied to the study of differences in the application of approaches, as opposed to the relationship of different levels of approaches to the result. With ANOVAs, we are testing the differences of the means of at least two different distributions.	ANOVAs can be used to determine if there is a difference in student achievement scores between one school and another, keeping all other variables equal. It cannot tell you what the differences are, per se, but one can compute confidence intervals to estimate these differences.	Very seldom are the conditions available to study differences in education in this manner. Too many complex variables get in the way, and ethics may be involved. There are well-defined procedures for conducting ANOVAs to which we must adhere.
Correlation Analyses	Correlation is a statistical analysis that helps one understand the relationship of scores in one distribution to scores in another distribution. Correlations show magnitude and direction. Magnitude indicates the degree of the relationship. Correlation coefficients have a range of -1.0 to +1.0. A correlation of around zero would indicate little relationship. Correlations of .8 and higher, or -.8 and lower would indicate a strong relationship. When the high scores in one distribution are also high in the comparing distribution, the direction is positive. When the high scores in one distribution are related to the low scores in the other distribution, the result is a negative correlational direction.	Correlations can be used to understand the relationship of different variables to each other, e.g., attendance and performance on a standardized test; .40 to .70 are considered moderate correlations. Above .70 is considered to be high correlations.	It is wise to plot the scores to understand if the relationship is linear or not. One could misinterpret results if the scores are not linear. Pearson correlation coefficient requires linear relationships. A few outliers could skew the results and oppositely skewed distributions can limit how high a Pearson coefficient can be. Also, one must remember that correlation does not suggest causation.
Regression Analyses	Regression analysis results in an equation that describes the nature of the relationship between variables. Simple regression predicts an object's value on a response variable when given its value on one predictor variable. Multiple regression predicts an object's value on a response variable when given its value on each of several predictor variables. Correlation tells you strength and direction of relationship. Regression goes one step further and allows you to predict.	A regression equation can be used to predict student achievement results, for example. Regression can determine if there is a relationship between two or more variables (such as attendance and student background) and the nature of those relationships. This analysis helps us predict and prevent student failure, and predict and ensure student successes.	One needs to truly understand the statistical assumptions that need to be in place in order to perform a regression analysis. This is not an analysis to perform through trial and error.

Figure 6.7 (Continued)

Term	Definition	Most Effective Uses	Cautions
Terms Related to Analyzing Student Achievement Results, Inferentially, Their Most Effective Uses, and Cautions for Their Uses			
Control Groups	During an experiment, the control group is studied the same as the experimental group, except that it does not receive the treatment of interest.	Control groups serve as a baseline in making comparisons with treatment groups. Control groups are necessary when the general effectiveness of a treatment is unknown.	It may not be ethical to hold back from students some method of learning that we believe would be useful.
Experimental Design	Experimental design is the detailed planning of an experiment, made beforehand, to ensure that the data collected are appropriate and obtained in a way that will lead to an objective analysis, with valid inferences.	Experimental designs can maximize the amount of information gained, given the amount of effort expended.	Sometimes it takes statistical expertise to establish an experimental design properly.
Tests of Significance	Tests of significance use samples to test claims about population parameters.	Tests of significance can estimate a population parameter, with a certain amount of confidence, from a sample.	Often laypeople do not know what *statistically significant* really means.

The term *scientifically-based research* (Title IX, General Provisions, Part A, Section 9101, Definitions) means (A) research that involves the application of rigorous, systematic, and objective procedures to obtain reliable and valid knowledge relevant to education activities and programs; and (B) includes research that:

▼ employs systematic, empirical methods that draw on observation or experiment

▼ involves rigorous data analyses that are adequate to test the stated hypotheses and justify the general conclusions drawn

▼ relies on measurements or observational methods that provide reliable and valid data across evaluators and observers, across multiple measurements and observations, and across studies by the same or different investigators

▼ is evaluated using experimental or quasi-experimental designs in which individuals, entities, programs, or activities are assigned to different conditions and with appropriate controls to evaluate the effects of the condition of interest, with a preference for random-assignment experiments, or other designs to the extent that condition controls

▼ ensures that experimental studies are presented in sufficient detail and clarity to allow for replication or, at a minimum, offer the opportunity to build systematically on their findings

▼ has been accepted by a peer-reviewed journal or approved by a panel of independent experts through a comparably rigorous, objective and scientific review

While NCLB calls for scientific and experimental procedures, such as control groups and experimental designs, in reality, they are not always possible. Over time, well-documented case studies have become accepted as powerful designs as well.

The Big River High School example that follows shows a sampling of descriptive analyses the school performed using its state criterion-referenced test.

Our Example School: Big River High School

What are our results?

Big River High School participates in the mandated state *High School Standards Test* (HSST), a test that is standardized, normed for the state, criterion-referenced, and analyzed by proficiency levels for grades nine, ten, and eleven in English Language Arts and Mathematics.

Student results are provided in scaled score analyses and reports by proficiency levels. The definition of the proficiency levels follow:

▼ *Below Basic*

   A student who performs at the *Below Basic* level on the HSST has not met minimum expectations for student performance based on the curriculum standards approved by the State Board of Education. The student is not prepared for work at the next grade.

▼ *Basic*

   Performance at the *Basic* level means a student has passed the test. A student who performs at the *Basic* level on the HSST has met minimum expectations for student performance based on the curriculum standards approved by the State Board of Education. The student is minimally prepared for work at the next grade.

▼ *Proficient*

   A student who performs at the *Proficient* level on the HSST has met expectations for student performance based on the curriculum standards approved by the State Board of Education. The student is well prepared for work at the next grade. The *Proficient* level represents the long-term goal for student performance.

▼ *Advanced*

   A student who performs at the *Advanced* level on the HSST has exceeded expectations for student performance based on the curriculum standards approved by the State Board of Education. The student is very well prepared for work at the next grade.

In this state, students are considered "proficient" when they score in the *Proficient* or *Advanced* levels of each test.

Proficiency Levels

The first analysis of Big River's most recent proficiency results compares Big River's results to the district (Figures 6.8 and 6.9). The graphs show the percentage of students scoring in English Language Arts (ELA) and Mathematics proficiency levels for grades nine, ten, and eleven, over time. While four years of ELA data are shown, only three years of Big River's Mathematics data were available since the Math test was available a year after the ELA test.

(*Note:* This is called *trend analysis*—looking at the same grade levels over time.)

Figure 6.8

Big River High School Compared to the District
State High School Standards Test Proficiency Percentages
2000-01 to 2003-04

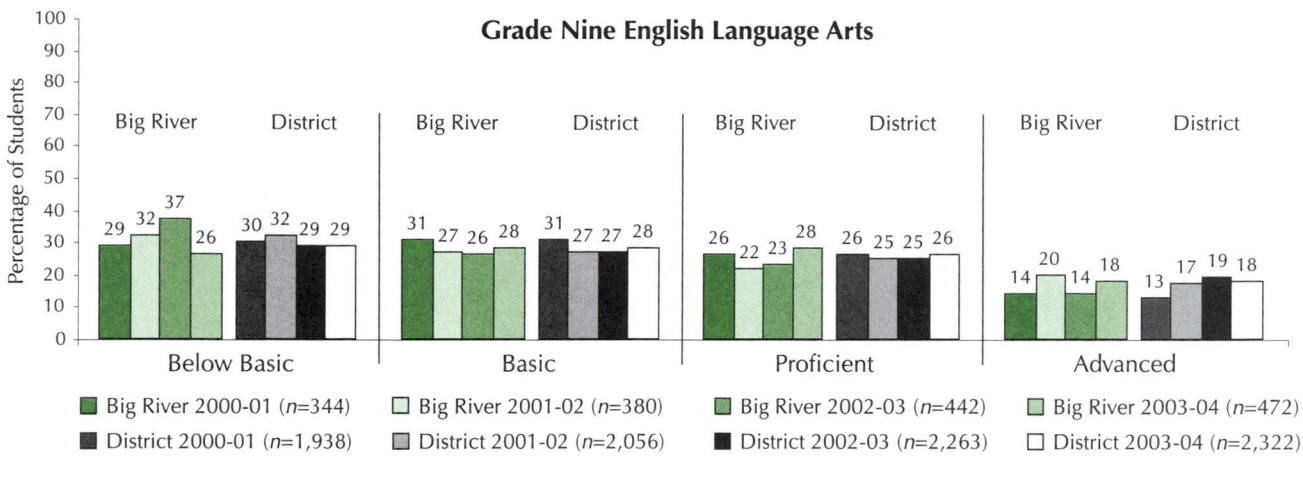

Grade Nine English Language Arts

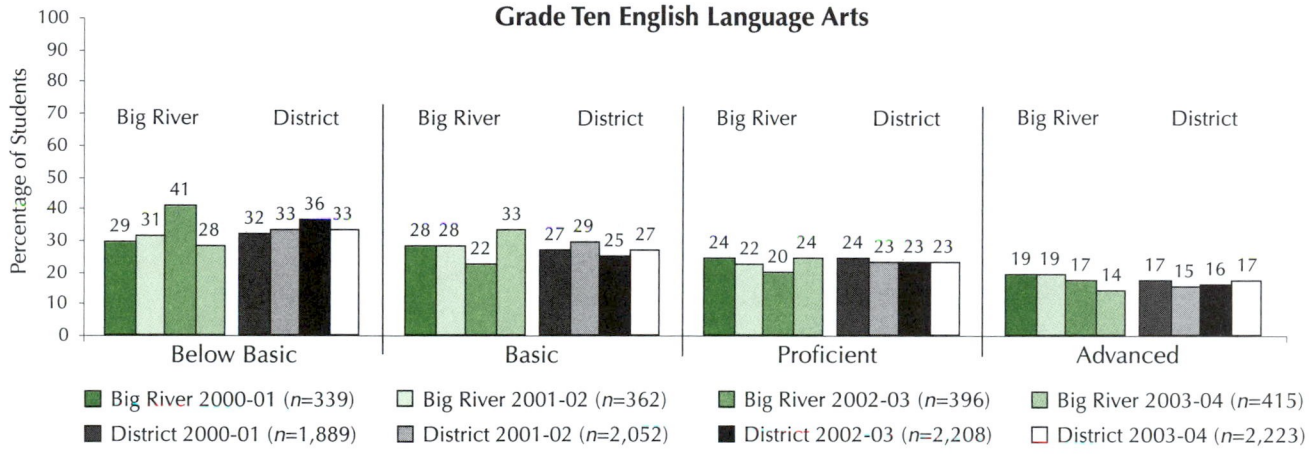

Grade Ten English Language Arts

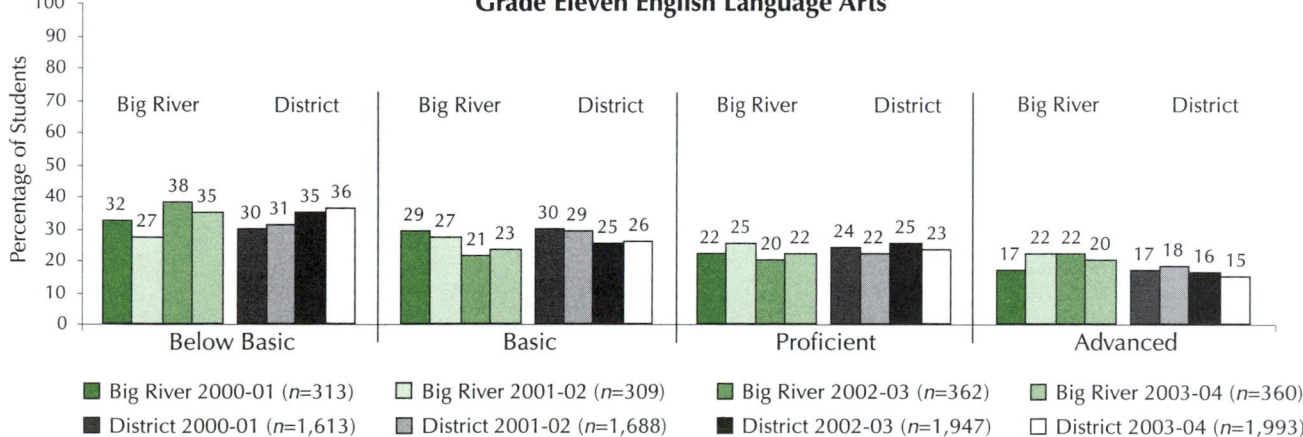

Grade Eleven English Language Arts

Figure 6.9

Big River High School Compared to the District
State High School Standards Test Proficiency Percentages
2001-02 to 2003-04

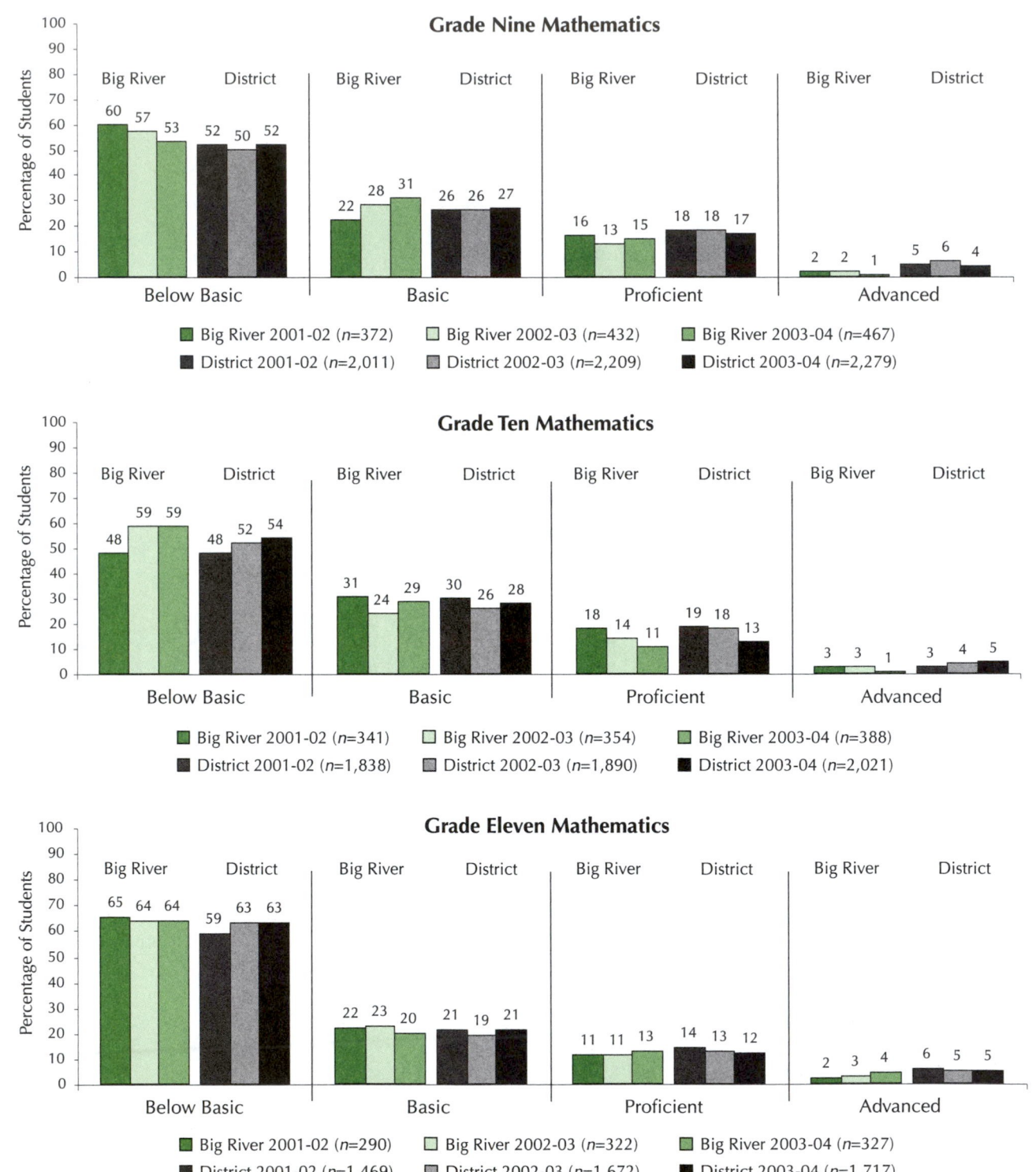

HSST English Language Art (ELA) Scores

The next eight figures are related to English Language Arts (ELA), followed by the same displays for Mathematics.

Cohort analysis reorganizes the trend data to follow the same *groups* of students (unmatched) progressing through the grades, over time. Figure 6.10 shows the percentage of Big River students scoring in ELA proficiency levels by cohorts for four years.

Figure 6.10

**Big River High School
HSST ELA Proficiency by Cohorts
2000-01 to 2003-04**

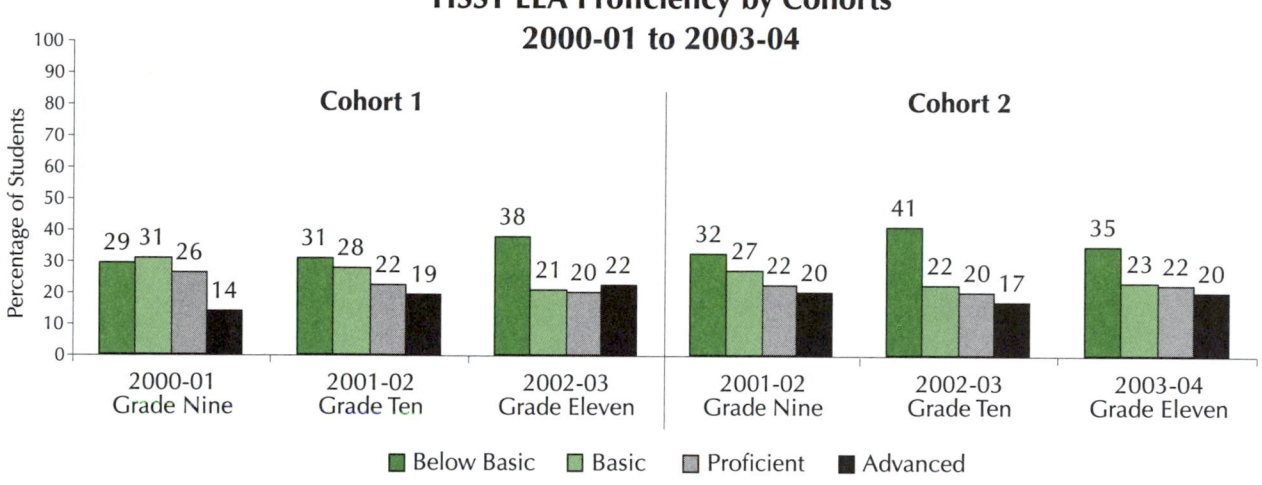

Figures 6.11 through 6.25 show proficiency disaggregations for student groups and grade levels for four years. The number of students in some subgroupings is very small. Caution should be taken in interpreting the results. These analyses would be used inhouse, only. Figure 6.11 shows the ELA results by gender.

Figure 6.11

Big River High School HSST ELA Proficiency Levels
By Grade Level and Gender, 2000-01 to 2003-04

Grade Level	Year	Gender	Below Basic		Basic		Proficient		Advanced		% Proficient	
			Number	Percent	Number	Percent	Number	Percent	Number	Percent	Number	Percent
Grade 9	2000-01	Male (*n*=165)	61	37%	54	33%	33	20%	17	10%	50	30%
		Female (*n*=179)	39	22%	52	29%	56	31%	32	18%	88	49%
	2001-02	Male (*n*=181)	74	41%	47	26%	31	17%	29	16%	60	33%
		Female (*n*=199)	46	23%	54	27%	53	27%	46	23%	99	50%
	2002-03	Male (*n*=185)	94	51%	38	21%	34	18%	19	10%	53	29%
		Female (*n*=257)	71	28%	76	30%	69	27%	41	16%	110	43%
	2003-04	Male (*n*=185)	67	36%	60	32%	41	22%	17	9%	58	31%
		Female (*n*=287)	55	19%	74	26%	92	32%	66	23%	158	55%
Grade 10	2000-01	Male (*n*=151)	51	34%	38	25%	36	24%	26	17%	62	41%
		Female (*n*=188)	48	26%	57	30%	44	23%	39	21%	83	44%
	2001-02	Male (*n*=167)	66	40%	49	29%	25	15%	27	16%	52	31%
		Female (*n*=195)	46	24%	52	27%	56	29%	41	21%	97	50%
	2002-03	Male (*n*=185)	102	55%	27	15%	32	17%	24	13%	56	30%
		Female (*n*=211)	61	29%	60	28%	46	22%	44	21%	90	43%
	2003-04	Male (*n*=169)	62	37%	55	33%	36	21%	16	9%	52	31%
		Female (*n*=246)	56	23%	82	33%	65	26%	43	17%	108	44%
Grade 11	2000-01	Male (*n*=130)	46	35%	38	29%	31	24%	15	12%	46	35%
		Female (*n*=183)	55	30%	52	28%	39	21%	37	20%	76	42%
	2001-02	Male (*n*=141)	45	32%	30	21%	36	26%	30	21%	66	47%
		Female (*n*=168)	37	22%	53	32%	41	24%	37	22%	78	46%
	2002-03	Male (*n*=165)	79	48%	32	19%	24	15%	30	18%	54	33%
		Female (*n*=197)	58	29%	43	22%	48	24%	48	24%	96	49%
	2003-04	Male (*n*=170)	76	45%	31	18%	34	20%	29	17%	63	37%
		Female (*n*=190)	51	27%	51	27%	45	24%	43	23%	88	46%

Figure 6.12 shows the ELA proficiency results for Big River by grade level and ethnicity for the four years.

Figure 6.12

Big River High School HSST ELA Proficiency Levels By Grade Level and Ethnicity, 2000-01 to 2003-04

Grade Level	Ethnicity	Year	Below Basic		Basic		Proficient		Advanced		% Proficient	
			Number	Percent	Number	Percent	Number	Percent	Number	Percent	Number	Percent
Grade 9	Black	2000-01 (*n*=8)	3	38%			3	38%	2	25%	5	63%
		2001-02 (*n*=6)	3	50%			1	17%	2	33%	3	50%
		2002-03 (*n*=8)	3	38%	2	25%	3	38%			3	38%
		2003-04 (*n*=17)	4	24%	5	29%	6	35%	2	12%	8	47%
	Asian	2000-01 (*n*=32)	9	28%	12	38%	6	19%	5	16%	11	34%
		2001-02 (*n*=34)	2	6%	8	24%	11	32%	13	38%	24	71%
		2002-03 (*n*=39)	7	18%	10	26%	14	36%	8	21%	22	56%
		2003-04 (*n*=44)	9	20%	10	23%	14	32%	11	25%	25	57%
	White	2000-01 (*n*=139)	16	12%	32	23%	53	38%	38	27%	91	65%
		2001-02 (*n*=122)	16	13%	23	19%	35	29%	48	39%	83	68%
		2002-03 (*n*=128)	25	20%	24	19%	42	33%	37	29%	79	67%
		2003-04 (*n*=148)	16	11%	33	22%	46	31%	53	36%	99	67%
	Hispanic/Latino	2000-01 (*n*=165)	72	44%	62	38%	27	16%	4	2%	31	19%
		2001-02 (*n*=218)	99	45%	70	32%	37	17%	12	6%	49	22%
		2002-03 (*n*=267)	130	49%	78	29%	44	16%	15	6%	59	22%
		2003-04 (*n*=263)	93	35%	86	33%	67	25%	17	6%	84	32%
Grade 10	Black	2000-01 (*n*=11)	4	36	3	27%	2	18%	2	18%	4	36%
		2001-02 (*n*=7)	1	14%	3	43%	1	14%	2	29%	3	43%
		2002-03 (*n*=6)	3	50%	1	17%	2	33%			2	33%
		2003-04 (*n*=8)	3	38%	5	63%					0	0%
	Asian	2000-01 (*n*=31)	5	16%	12	39%	5	16%	9	29%	14	45%
		2001-02 (*n*=28)	5	18%	11	39%	5	18%	7	25%	12	43%
		2002-03 (*n*=34)	3	9%	6	18%	12	35%	13	38%	25	74%
		2003-04 (*n*=37)	6	16%	15	41%	9	24%	7	19%	16	43%
	White	2000-01 (*n*=119)	15	13%	18	15%	41	34%	45	38%	86	72%
		2001-02 (*n*=147)	17	12%	29	20%	44	30%	57	39%	101	69%
		2002-03 (*n*=128)	28	22%	20	16%	34	27%	46	36%	80	63%
		2003-04 (*n*=132)	17	13%	33	25%	46	35%	36	27%	82	62%
	Hispanic/Latino	2000-01 (*n*=178)	75	42%	62	35%	32	18%	9	5%	41	23%
		2001-02 (*n*=180)	89	49%	58	32%	31	17%	2	1%	33	18%
		2002-03 (*n*=228)	129	57%	60	26%	30	13%	9	4%	39	17%
		2003-04 (*n*=238)	92	39%	84	35%	46	19%	16	7%	62	26%

Figure 6.12 (Continued)

Big River High School HSST ELA Proficiency Levels
By Grade Level and Ethnicity, 2000-01 to 2003-04

Grade Level	Ethnicity	Year	Below Basic		Basic		Proficient		Advanced		% Proficient	
			Number	Percent	Number	Percent	Number	Percent	Number	Percent	Number	Percent
Grade 11	Black	2000-01 (n=8)	3	38%	1	13%	2	25%	2	25%	4	50%
		2001-02 (n=9)	2	22%	4	44%	2	22%	1	11%	3	33%
		2002-03 (n=9)	3	33%			4	44%	2	22%	6	67%
		2003-04 (n=7)	4	57%	2	29%		0%	1	14%	1	14%
	Asian	2000-01 (n=30)	10	33%	7	23%	10	33%	3	10%	13	43%
		2001-02 (n=27)	4	15%	7	26%	5	19%	11	41%	16	59%
		2002-03 (n=32)	12	38%	9	28%	4	13%	7	22%	11	34%
		2003-04 (n=31)	2	6%	6	19%	12	39%	11	35%	23	74%
	White	2000-01 (n=123)	18	15%	31	25%	34	28%	40	33%	74	60%
		2001-02 (n=124)	18	15%	21	17%	39	31%	46	37%	85	69%
		2002-03 (n=141)	24	17%	22	16%	37	26%	58	41%	95	67%
		2003-04 (n=120)	14	12%	23	19%	32	27%	51	43%	83	69%
	Hispanic/ Latino	2000-01 (n=152)	70	46%	51	34%	24	16%	7	5%	31	20%
		2001-02 (n=149)	58	39%	51	34%	31	21%	9	6%	40	27%
		2002-03 (n=180)	98	54%	44	24%	27	15%	11	6%	38	21%
		2003-04 (n=202)	107	53%	51	25%	35	17%	9	4%	44	22%

Figure 6.13 displays the four years of ELA proficiency results by grade level, ethnicity, and gender.

Figure 6.13

Big River High School HSST ELA Proficiency Levels
By Grade Level, Ethnicity, and Gender, 2000-01 to 2003-04

Grade Level	Ethnicity	Gender	Year	Below Basic		Basic		Proficient		Advanced		% Proficient	
				Number	Percent	Number	Percent	Number	Percent	Number	Percent	Number	Percent
Grade 9	Black	Male	2000-01 (*n*=3)	1	33%			2	67%			2	67%
			2001-02 (*n*=3)	3	100%							0	0%
			2002-03 (*n*=2)	1	50%			1	50%			1	50%
			2003-04 (*n*=4)	1	25%	1	25%			2	50%	2	50%
		Female	2000-01 (*n*=5)	2	40%			1	20%	2	40%	3	60%
			2001-02 (*n*=3)					1	33%	2	67%	3	100%
			2002-03 (*n*=6)	2	33%	2	33%	2	33%			2	33%
			2003-04 (*n*=13)	3	23%	4	31%	6	46%			6	46%
	Asian	Male	2000-01 (*n*=15)	6	40%	7	47%		0%	2	13%	2	13%
			2001-02 (*n*=12)	1	8%	1	8%	3	25%	7	58%	10	83%
			2002-03 (*n*=13)	4	31%	4	31%	3	23%	2	15%	5	38%
			2003-04 (*n*=19)	7	37%	4	21%	5	26%	3	16%	8	42%
		Female	2000-01 (*n*=17)	3	18%	5	29%	6	35%	3	18%	9	53%
			2001-02 (*n*=22)	1	5%	7	32%	8	36%	6	27%	14	64%
			2002-03 (*n*=26)	3	12%	6	23%	11	42%	6	23%	17	65%
			2003-04 (*n*=25)	2	8%	6	24%	9	36%	8	32%	17	68%
	White	Male	2000-01 (*n*=67)	14	21%	17	25%	22	33%	14	21%	36	54%
			2001-02 (*n*=54)	11	20%	11	20%	12	22%	20	37%	32	59%
			2002-03 (*n*=57)	19	33%	9	16%	16	28%	13	23%	29	51%
			2003-04 (*n*=47)	9	19%	14	30%	12	26%	12	26%	24	51%
		Female	2000-01 (*n*=72)	2	3%	15	21%	31	43%	24	33%	55	76%
			2001-02 (*n*=68)	5	7%	12	18%	23	34%	28	41%	51	75%
			2002-03 (*n*=71)	6	8%	15	21%	26	37%	24	34%	50	70%
			2003-04 (*n*=101)	7	7%	19	19%	34	34%	41	41%	75	74%
	Hispanic/ Latino	Male	2000-01 (*n*=80)	40	50%	30	38%	9	11%	1	1%	10	13%
			2001-02 (*n*=112)	59	53%	35	31%	16	14%	2	2%	18	16%
			2002-03 (*n*=113)	70	62%	25	22%	14	12%	4	4%	18	16%
			2003-04 (*n*=115)	50	43%	41	36%	24	21%			24	21%
		Female	2000-01 (*n*=85)	32	38%	32	38%	18	21%	3	4%	21	25%
			2001-02 (*n*=106)	40	38%	35	33%	21	20%	10	9%	31	29%
			2002-03 (*n*=154)	60	39%	53	34%	30	19%	11	7%	41	27%
			2003-04 (*n*=148)	43	29%	45	30%	43	29%	17	11%	60	41%

Figure 6.13 (Continued)

Big River High School HSST ELA Proficiency Levels
By Grade Level, Ethnicity, and Gender, 2000-01 to 2003-04

Grade Level	Ethnicity	Gender	Year	Below Basic		Basic		Proficient		Advanced		% Proficient	
				Number	Percent	Number	Percent	Number	Percent	Number	Percent	Number	Percent
Grade 10	Black	Male	2000-01 (*n*=3)	1	33%	1	33%	1	33%			1	33%
			2001-02 (*n*=1)							1	100%	1	100%
			2002-03 (*n*=2)	2	100%							0	0%
			2003-04 (*n*=2)	1	50%	1	50%					0	0%
		Female	2000-01 (*n*=8)	3	38%	2	25%	1	13%	2	25%	3	38%
			2001-02 (*n*=6)	1	17%	3	50%	1	17%	1	17%	2	33%
			2002-03 (*n*=4)	1	25%	1	25%	2	50%			2	50%
			2003-04 (*n*=6)	2	33%	4	67%					0	0%
	Asian	Male	2000-01 (*n*=14)	2	14%	6	43%	3	21%	3	21%	6	43%
			2001-02 (*n*=13)	3	23%	7	54%	1	8%	2	15%	3	23%
			2002-03 (*n*=10)	1	10%			4	40%	5	50%	9	90%
			2003-04 (*n*=14)	3	21%	6	43%	4	29%	1	7%	5	36%
		Female	2000-01 (*n*=17)	3	18%	6	35%	2	12%	6	35%	8	47%
			2001-02 (*n*=15)	2	13%	4	27%	4	27%	5	33%	9	60%
			2002-03 (*n*=24)	2	8%	6	25%	8	33%	8	33%	16	67%
			2003-04 (*n*=23)	3	13%	9	39%	5	22%	6	26%	11	48%
	White	Male	2000-01 (*n*=62)	11	18%	11	18%	21	34%	19	31%	40	65%
			2001-02 (*n*=68)	13	19%	15	22%	17	25%	23	34%	40	59%
			2002-03 (*n*=54)	16	30%	8	15%	14	26%	16	30%	30	56%
			2003-04 (*n*=56)	12	21%	15	27%	18	32%	11	20%	29	52%
		Female	2000-01 (*n*=57)	4	7%	7	12%	20	35%	26	46%	46	81%
			2001-02 (*n*=79)	4	5%	14	18%	27	34%	34	43%	61	77%
			2002-03 (*n*=74)	12	16%	12	16%	20	27%	30	41%	50	68%
			2003-04 (*n*=76)	5	7%	18	24%	28	37%	25	33%	53	70%
	Hispanic/ Latino	Male	2000-01 (*n*=72)	37	51%	20	28%	11	15%	4	6%	15	21%
			2001-02 (*n*=85)	50	59%	27	32%	7	8%	1	1%	8	9%
			2002-03 (*n*=119)	83	70%	19	16%	14	12%	3	3%	17	14%
			2003-04 (*n*=97)	46	47%	33	34%	14	14%	4	4%	18	19%
		Female	2000-01 (*n*=106)	38	36%	42	40%	21	20%	5	5%	26	25%
			2001-02 (*n*=95)	39	41%	31	33%	24	25%	1	1%	25	26%
			2002-03 (*n*=109)	46	42%	41	38%	16	15%	6	6%	22	20%
			2003-04 (*n*=141)	46	33%	51	36%	32	23%	12	9%	44	31%

Figure 6.13 (Continued)

Big River High School HSST ELA Proficiency Levels
By Grade Level, Ethnicity, and Gender, 2000-01 to 2003-04

Grade Level	Ethnicity	Gender	Year	Below Basic		Basic		Proficient		Advanced		% Proficient	
				Number	Percent	Number	Percent	Number	Percent	Number	Percent	Number	Percent
Grade 11	Black	Male	2000-01 (*n*=5)	2	40%	1	20%	2	40%			2	40%
			2001-02 (*n*=2)			1	50%	1	50%			1	50%
			2002-03 (*n*=4)	1	25%			2	50%	1	25%	3	75%
			2003-04 (*n*=3)	2	67%	1	33%					0	0%
		Female	2000-01 (*n*=3)	1	33%					2	67%	2	67%
			2001-02 (*n*=7)	2	29%	3	43%	1	14%	1	14%	2	29%
			2002-03 (*n*=5)	2	40%			2	40%	1	20%	3	60%
			2003-04 (*n*=4)	2	50%	1	25%			1	25%	1	25%
	Asian	Male	2000-01 (*n*=13)	4	31%	3	23%	6	46%			6	46%
			2001-02 (*n*=13)	2	15%	3	23%	3	23%	5	38%	8	62%
			2002-03 (*n*=14)	7	50%	4	29%	1	7%	2	14%	3	21%
			2003-04 (*n*=9)					4	44%	5	56%	9	100%
		Female	2000-01 (*n*=17)	6	35%	4	24%	4	24%	3	18%	7	41%
			2001-02 (*n*=14)	2	14%	4	29%	2	14%	6	43%	8	57%
			2002-03 (*n*=18)	5	28%	5	28%	3	17%	5	28%	8	44%
			2003-04 (*n*=22)	2	9%	6	27%	8	36%	6	27%	14	64%
	White	Male	2000-01 (*n*=53)	13	25%	15	28%	11	21%	14	26%	25	47%
			2001-02 (*n*=62)	11	18%	12	19%	18	29%	21	34%	39	63%
			2002-03 (*n*=62)	16	26%	9	15%	13	21%	24	39%	37	60%
			2003-04 (*n*=51)	4	8%	14	27%	13	25%	20	39%	33	65%
		Female	2000-01 (*n*=70)	5	7%	16	23%	23	33%	26	37%	49	70%
			2001-02 (*n*=62)	7	11%	9	15%	21	34%	25	40%	46	74%
			2002-03 (*n*=79)	8	10%	13	16%	24	30%	34	43%	58	73%
			2003-04 (*n*=69)	10	14%	9	13%	19	28%	31	45%	50	72%
	Hispanic/ Latino	Male	2000-01 (*n*=59)	27	46%	19	32%	12	20%	1	2%	13	22%
			2001-02 (*n*=64)	32	50%	14	22%	14	22%	4	6%	18	28%
			2002-03 (*n*=85)	55	65%	19	22%	8	9%	3	4%	11	13%
			2003-04 (*n*=107)	70	65%	16	15%	17	16%	4	4%	21	20%
		Female	2000-01 (*n*=93)	43	46%	32	34%	12	13%	6	6%	18	19%
			2001-02 (*n*=85)	26	31%	37	44%	17	20%	5	6%	22	26%
			2002-03 (*n*=95)	43	45%	25	26%	19	20%	8	8%	27	28%
			2003-04 (*n*=95)	37	39%	35	37%	18	19%	5	5%	23	24%

Figure 6.14 displays the differences in results by grade level and high and low socio-economic status. Nearly 70% of Big River High School students were designated "high SES" families.

Figure 6.14

Big River High School HSST ELA Proficiency Levels
By Grade Level and Socio-economic Status, 2000-01 to 2003-04

Grade Level	SES	Year	Below Basic		Basic		Proficient		Advanced		% Proficient	
			Number	Percent	Number	Percent	Number	Percent	Number	Percent	Number	Percent
Grade 9	High SES	2000-01 (*n*=231)	50	22%	62	27%	73	32%	46	20%	119	52%
		2001-02 (*n*=252)	59	23%	59	23%	67	27%	67	27%	134	53%
		2002-03 (*n*=266)	69	26%	64	24%	78	29%	55	21%	133	50%
		2003-04 (*n*=345)	67	19%	94	27%	107	31%	77	22%	184	53%
	Low SES	2000-01 (*n*=113)	50	44%	44	39%	16	14%	3	3%	19	17%
		2001-02 (*n*=128)	61	48%	42	33%	17	13%	8	6%	25	20%
		2002-03 (*n*=176)	96	55%	50	28%	25	14%	5	3%	30	17%
		2003-04 (*n*=127)	55	43%	40	31%	26	20%	6	5%	32	25%
Grade 10	High SES	2000-01 (*n*=232)	43	19%	59	25%	67	29%	63	27%	130	56%
		2001-02 (*n*=252)	61	24%	59	23%	67	27%	65	26%	132	52%
		2002-03 (*n*=277)	90	32%	57	21%	66	24%	64	23%	130	47%
		2003-04 (*n*=292)	62	21%	92	32%	84	29%	54	18%	138	47%
	Low SES	2000-01 (*n*=107)	56	52%	36	34%	13	12%	2	2%	15	14%
		2001-02 (*n*=110)	51	46%	42	38%	14	13%	3	3%	17	15%
		2002-03 (*n*=114)	71	62%	29	25%	10	9%	4	4%	14	12%
		2003-04 (*n*=120)	53	44%	45	38%	17	14%	5	4%	22	18%
Grade 11	High SES	2000-01 (*n*=218)	42	19%	67	31%	60	28%	49	22%	109	50%
		2001-02 (*n*=231)	40	17%	59	26%	68	29%	64	28%	132	57%
		2002-03 (*n*=272)	86	32%	50	18%	64	24%	72	26%	136	50%
		2003-04 (*n*=284)	88	31%	62	22%	66	23%	68	24%	134	47%
	Low SES	2000-01 (*n*=272)	59	62%	23	24%	10	11%	3	3%	13	14%
		2001-02 (*n*=78)	42	54%	24	31%	9	12%	3	4%	12	15%
		2002-03 (*n*=90)	51	57%	25	28%	8	9%	6	7%	14	16%
		2003-04 (*n*=74)	38	51%	20	27%	12	16%	4	5%	16	22%

Results for students identified as requiring special education services are shown below in Figure 6.15.

Figure 6.15

**Big River High School HSST ELA Proficiency Levels
By Grade Level and Special Education Identified, 2000-01 to 2003-04**

Grade Level	Year	Below Basic		Basic		Proficient		Advanced		% Proficient	
		Number	Percent	Number	Percent	Number	Percent	Number	Percent	Number	Percent
Grade 9	2000-01 (*n*=21)	11	52%	6	29%	4	19%			4	19%
	2001-02 (*n*=29)	23	79%	6	21%					0	0%
	2002-03 (*n*=42)	34	81%	4	10%	3	7%	1	2%	4	10%
	2003-04 (*n*=37)	26	70%	9	24%	2	5%			2	5%
Grade 10	2000-01 (*n*=16)	13	81%	2	13%	1	6%			1	6%
	2001-02 (*n*=23)	16	70%	5	22%	1	4%	1	4%	2	9%
	2002-03 (*n*=39)	33	85%	6	15%					0	0%
	2003-04 (*n*=36)	30	83%	4	11%	2	6%			2	6%
Grade 11	2000-01 (*n*=23)	18	78%	4	17%	1	4%			1	4%
	2001-02 (*n*=14)	11	79%	1	7%	2	14%			2	14%
	2002-03 (*n*=27)	23	85%	3	11%	1	4%			1	4%
	2003-04 (*n*=29)	23	79%	4	14%	2	7%			2	7%

As shown in the demographics section, Big River has a gifted program. Figure 6.16 displays the ELA proficiency results for the gifted students, by grade level, compared to those not in the program.

Figure 6.16

Big River High School HSST ELA Proficiency Levels
By Grade Level and Gifted Designation, 2000-01 to 2003-04

Grade Level	Ability	Year	Below Basic		Basic		Proficient		Advanced		% Proficient	
			Number	Percent	Number	Percent	Number	Percent	Number	Percent	Number	Percent
Grade 9	Gifted	2000-01 (n=74)	3	4%	17	23%	25	34%	29	39%	54	73%
		2001-02 (n=83)	4	5%	16	19%	22	27%	41	49%	63	76%
		2002-03 (n=64)	8	13%	10	16%	21	33%	25	39%	46	72%
		2003-04 (n=90)	2	2%	9	10%	47	52%	32	36%	79	88%
	Not Gifted	2000-01 (n=270)	97	36%	89	33%	64	24%	20	7%	84	31%
		2001-02 (n=297)	116	39%	85	29%	62	21%	34	11%	96	32%
		2002-03 (n=378)	157	42%	104	28%	82	22%	35	9%	117	31%
		2003-04 (n=465)	120	26%	125	27%	169	36%	51	11%	220	47%
Grade 10	Gifted	2000-01 (n=80)			11	14%	31	39%	38	48%	69	86%
		2001-02 (n=71)	1	1%	14	20%	21	30%	35	49%	56	79%
		2002-03 (n=74)	8	11%	10	14%	20	27%	36	49%	56	76%
		2003-04 (n=89)	6	7%	9	10%	49	55%	25	28%	74	83%
	Not Gifted	2000-01 (n=259)	99	38%	84	32%	49	19%	27	10%	76	29%
		2001-02 (n=291)	111	38%	87	30%	60	21%	33	11%	93	32%
		2002-03 (n=322)	155	48%	77	24%	58	18%	32	10%	90	28%
		2003-04 (n=385)	112	29%	128	33%	111	29%	34	9%	145	38%
Grade 11	Gifted	2000-01 (n=73)			16	22%	27	37%	30	41%	57	78%
		2001-02 (n=78)	2	3%	11	14%	25	32%	40	51%	65	83%
		2002-03 (n=73)	9	12%	10	14%	14	19%	40	55%	54	74%
		2003-04 (n=114)	8	7%	13	11%	55	48%	38	33%	93	82%
	Not Gifted	2000-01 (n=240)	101	42%	74	31%	43	18%	22	9%	65	27%
		2001-02 (n=231)	80	35%	72	31%	52	23%	27	12%	79	34%
		2002-03 (n=289)	128	44%	65	22%	58	20%	38	13%	96	33%
		2003-04 (n=318)	119	37%	69	22%	96	30%	34	11%	130	41%

Figure 6.17 shows the proficiency results for students classified as English Proficient, English Learners, and those newly redesignated as English Proficient, by grade level.

Figure 6.17

Big River High School HSST ELA Proficiency Levels
By Grade Level and Language Proficiency, 2000-01 to 2003-04

Grade Level	Language Proficiency	Year	Below Basic		Basic		Proficient		Advanced		% Proficient	
			Number	Percent	Number	Percent	Number	Percent	Number	Percent	Number	Percent
Grade 9	English Proficient	2000-01 (n=294)	59	20%	97	33%	89	30%	49	17%	138	47%
		2001-02 (n=329)	76	23%	94	29%	84	26%	75	23%	159	48%
		2002-03 (n=277)	73	26%	64	23%	88	32%	52	19%	140	51%
		2003-04 (n=386)	58	15%	73	19%	178	46%	77	20%	255	66%
	English Learner	2000-01 (n=50)	41	82%	9	18%					0	0%
		2001-02 (n=51)	44	86%	7	14%					0	0%
		2002-03 (n=82)	68	83%	14	17%					0	0%
		2003-04 (n=78)	54	69%	22	28%	2	3%			2	3%
	Redesignated Proficient	2002-03 (n=83)	24	29%	36	43%	15	18%	8	10%	23	28%
		2003-04 (n=91)	10	11%	39	43%	36	40%	6	7%	42	46%
Grade 10	English Proficient	2000-01 (n=283)	53	19%	86	30%	79	28%	65	23%	144	51%
		2001-02 (n=299)	58	19%	93	31%	80	27%	68	23%	148	49%
		2002-03 (n=273)	86	32%	61	22%	63	23%	63	23%	126	46%
		2003-04 (n=319)	62	19%	59	18%	131	41%	67	21%	198	62%
	English Learner	2000-01 (n=56)	46	82%	9	16%	1	2%			1	2%
		2001-02 (n=63)	54	86%	8	13%	1	2%			1	2%
		2002-03 (n=64)	58	91%	6	9%					0	0%
		2003-04 (n=52)	44	85%	6	12%	2	4%			2	4%
	Redesignated Proficient	2002-03 (n=59)	19	32%	20	34%	15	25%	5	8%	20	34%
		2003-04 (n=61)	21	34%	17	28%	18	30%	5	8%	23	38%
Grade 11	English Proficient	2000-01 (n=265)	59	22%	85	32%	70	26%	51	19%	121	46%
		2001-02 (n=264)	42	16%	79	30%	76	29%	67	25%	143	54%
		2002-03 (n=250)	66	26%	52	21%	58	23%	74	30%	132	53%
		2003-04 (n=317)	56	18%	77	24%	133	42%	51	16%	184	58%
	English Learner	2000-01 (n=42)	36	86%	5	12%			1	2%	1	2%
		2001-02 (n=44)	39	89%	4	9%	1	2%			1	2%
		2002-03 (n=65)	59	91%	4	6%	2	3%			2	3%
		2003-04 (n=65)	47	72%	17	26%	1	2%			1	2%
	Redesignated Proficient	2002-03 (n=54)	19	35%	19	35%	12	22%	4	7%	16	30%
		2003-04 (n=92)	15	16%	43	47%	26	28%	8	9%	34	37%

HSST Mathematic Scores

Figure 6.18 shows the percentage of students scoring in Mathematics proficiency levels by unmatched cohorts. Figures 6.19 through 6.25 show disaggregations for student groups and grade levels for three years. Figure 6.19 shows Math results by gender.

Figure 6.18

**Big River High School
HSST Mathematics Proficiency by Cohorts
2001-02 to 2003-04**

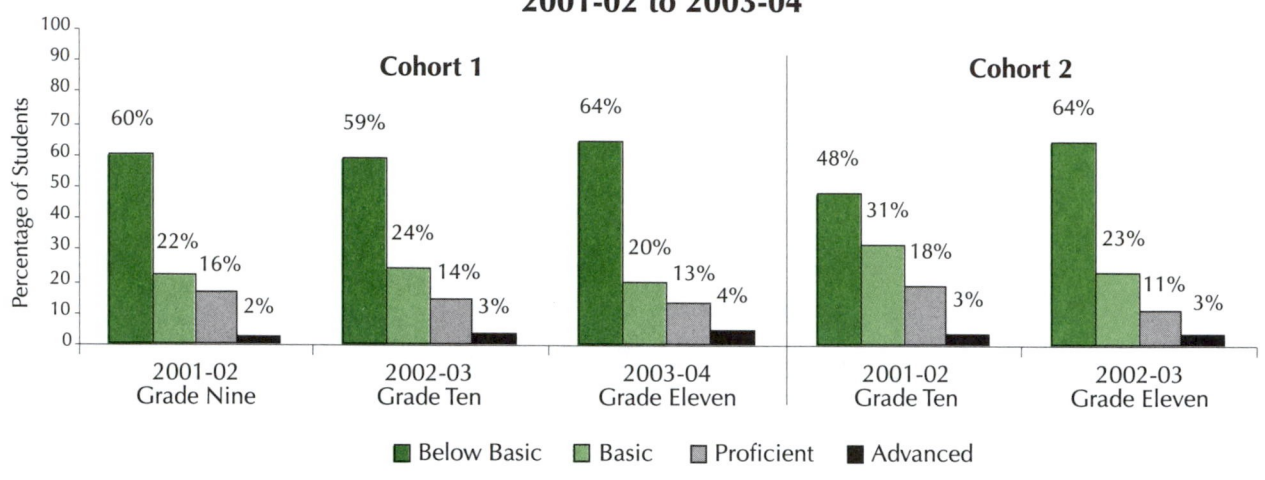

Figure 6.19

Big River High School HSST Mathematics Proficiency Levels
By Grade Level and Gender, 2001-02 to 2003-04

Grade Level	Year	Gender	Below Basic		Basic		Proficient		Advanced		% Proficient	
			Number	Percent	Number	Percent	Number	Percent	Number	Percent	Number	Percent
Grade 9	2001-02	Male (*n*=181)	121	67%	30	17%	25	14%	5	3%	30	17%
		Female (*n*=191)	102	53%	50	26%	35	18%	4	2%	39	20%
	2002-03	Male (*n*=181)	115	64%	42	23%	16	9%	8	4%	24	13%
		Female (*n*=251)	131	52%	79	31%	39	16%	2	1%	41	16%
	2003-04	Male (*n*=183)	119	65%	39	21%	22	12%	3	2%	25	14%
		Female (*n*=284)	129	45%	104	37%	48	17%	3	1%	51	18%
Grade 10	2001-02	Male (*n*=154)	81	53%	36	23%	33	21%	4	3%	37	24%
		Female (*n*=187)	82	44%	71	38%	29	16%	5	3%	34	18%
	2002-03	Male (*n*=168)	108	64%	32	19%	24	14%	4	2%	28	17%
		Female (*n*=186)	100	54%	53	28%	26	14%	7	4%	33	18%
	2003-04	Male (*n*=155)	98	63%	44	28%	11	7%	2	1%	13	8%
		Female (*n*=233)	130	56%	70	30%	32	14%	1	0.4%	33	14%
Grade 11	2001-02	Male (*n*=137)	89	65%	27	20%	16	12%	5	4%	21	15%
		Female (*n*=153)	100	65%	36	24%	15	10%	2	1%	17	11%
	2002-03	Male (*n*=136)	91	67%	28	21%	14	10%	3	2%	17	13%
		Female (*n*=186)	115	62%	45	24%	20	11%	6	3%	26	14%
	2003-04	Male (*n*=155)	102	66%	27	17%	21	14%	5	3%	26	17%
		Female (*n*=172)	107	62%	38	22%	20	12%	7	4%	27	16%

Figure 6.20 shows the Mathematics proficiency results for each grade level, disaggregated by ethnicity. Figure 6.21 displays the three years of Mathematics proficiency data for Big River students by grade level, ethnicity, and gender.

Figure 6.20

Big River High School HSST Mathematics Proficiency Levels By Grade Level and Ethnicity, 2001-02 to 2003-04

Grade Level	Ethnicity	Year	Below Basic		Basic		Proficient		Advanced		% Proficient	
			Number	Percent	Number	Percent	Number	Percent	Number	Percent	Number	Percent
Grade 9	Black	2001-02 (n=6)	3	50%	2	33%	1	17%			1	17%
		2002-03 (n=8)	6	75%	2	25%					0	0%
		2003-04 (n=15)	7	47%	6	40%	2	13%			2	13%
	Asian	2001-02 (n=31)	7	23%	9	29%	15	48%			15	48%
		2002-03 (n=40)	21	53%	11	28%	8	20%			8	20%
		2003-04 (n=44)	21	48%	15	34%	8	18%			8	18%
	White	2001-02 (n=121)	48	40%	36	30%	30	25%	7	6%	37	31%
		2002-03 (n=129)	54	42%	41	32%	26	20%	8	6%	34	26%
		2003-04 (n=147)	57	39%	50	34%	34	23%	6	4%	40	27%
	Hispanic/ Latino	2001-02 (n=212)	165	78%	33	16%	14	7%			14	7%
		2002-03 (n=255)	165	65%	67	26%	21	8%	2	1%	23	9%
		2003-04 (n=261)	163	62%	72	28%	26	10%			26	10%
Grade 10	Black	2001-02 (n=6)	3	50%	2	33%	1	17%			1	17%
		2002-03 (n=5)	2	40%	2	40%	1	20%			1	20%
		2003-04 (n=8)	8	100%							0	0%
	Asian	2001-02 (n=27)	10	37%	9	33%	7	26%	1	4%	8	30%
		2002-03 (n=32)	8	25%	16	50%	6	19%	2	6%	8	25%
		2003-04 (n=37)	17	46%	14	38%	6	16%			6	16%
	White	2001-02 (n=138)	42	30%	48	35%	41	30%	7	5%	48	35%
		2002-03 (n=117)	45	38%	33	28%	32	27%	7	6%	39	33%
		2003-04 (n=125)	52	42%	49	39%	21	17%	3	2%	24	19%
	Hispanic/ Latino	2001-02 (n=170)	108	64%	48	28%	13	8%	1	1%	14	8%
		2002-03 (n=200)	153	77%	34	17%	11	6%	2	1%	13	7%
		2003-04 (n=218)	151	69%	51	23%	16	7%			16	7%
Grade 11	Black	2001-02 (n=9)	7	78%	2	22%					0	0%
		2002-03 (n=7)	5	71%	1	14%	1	14%			1	14%
		2003-04 (n=5)	2	40%	3	60%					0	0%
	Asian	2001-02 (n=25)	11	44%	7	28%	6	24%	1	4%	7	28%
		2002-03 (n=32)	13	41%	8	25%	9	28%	2	6%	11	34%
		2003-04 (n=28)	7	25%	13	46%	5	18%	3	11%	8	29%
	White	2001-02 (n=116)	61	53%	31	27%	20	17%	4	3%	24	21%
		2002-03 (n=128)	63	49%	38	30%	20	16%	7	5%	27	21%
		2003-04 (n=113)	56	50%	23	20%	28	25%	6	5%	34	30%
	Hispanic/ Latino	2001-02 (n=140)	110	79%	23	16%	5	4%	2	1%	7	5%
		2002-03 (n=155)	125	81%	26	17%	4	3%			4	3%
		2003-04 (n=181)	144	80%	26	14%	8	4%	3	2%	11	6%

Figure 6.21

Big River High School HSST Mathematics Proficiency Levels
By Grade Level, Ethnicity, and Gender, 2001-02 to 2003-04

Grade Level	Ethnicity	Gender	Year	Below Basic		Basic		Proficient		Advanced		% Proficient	
				Number	Percent	Number	Percent	Number	Percent	Number	Percent	Number	Percent
Grade 9	Black	Male	2001-02 (*n*=3)	2	67%	1	33%					0	0%
			2002-03 (*n*=2)	2	100%							0	0%
			2003-04 (*n*=3)	1	33%			2	67%			2	67%
		Female	2001-02 (*n*=3)	1	33%	1	33%	1	33%			1	33%
			2002-03 (*n*=6)	4	67%	2	33%					0	0%
			2003-04 (*n*=12)	6	50%	6	50%					0	0%
	Asian	Male	2001-02 (*n*=12)	3	25%	3	25%	4	33%	2	17%	6	50%
			2002-03 (*n*=14)	7	50%	3	21%	4	29%			4	29%
			2003-04 (*n*=19)	11	58%	5	26%	3	16%			3	16%
		Female	2001-02 (*n*=21)	4	19%	6	29%	11	52%			11	52%
			2002-03 (*n*=26)	14	54%	8	31%	4	15%			4	15%
			2003-04 (*n*=25)	10	40%	10	40%	5	20%			5	20%
	White	Male	2001-02 (*n*=54)	24	44%	15	28%	12	22%	3	6%	15	28%
			2002-03 (*n*=57)	31	54%	13	23%	6	11%	7	12%	13	23%
			2003-04 (*n*=46)	22	48%	12	26%	9	20%	3	7%	12	26%
		Female	2001-02 (*n*=67)	24	36%	21	31%	18	27%	4	6%	22	33%
			2002-03 (*n*=72)	23	32%	28	39%	20	28%	1	1%	21	29%
			2003-04 (*n*=101)	35	35%	38	38%	25	25%	3	3%	28	28%
	Hispanic/ Latino	Male	2001-02 (*n*=112)	92	82%	11	10%	9	8%			9	8%
			2002-03 (*n*=108)	75	69%	26	24%	6	6%	1	1%	7	6%
			2003-04 (*n*=115)	85	74%	22	19%	8	7%			8	7%
		Female	2001-02 (*n*=100)	73	73%	22	22%	5	5%			5	5%
			2002-03 (*n*=147)	90	61%	41	28%	15	10%	1	1%	16	11%
			2003-04 (*n*=146)	78	53%	50	34%	18	12%			18	12%

Figure 6.21 (Continued)

Big River High School HSST Mathematics Proficiency Levels
By Grade Level, Ethnicity, and Gender, 2001-02 to 2003-04

Grade Level	Ethnicity	Gender	Year	Below Basic		Basic		Proficient		Advanced		% Proficient	
				Number	Percent	Number	Percent	Number	Percent	Number	Percent	Number	Percent
Grade 10	Black	Male	2001-02 (*n*=1)			1	100%					0	0%
			2002-03 (*n*=1)			1	100%					0	0%
			2003-04 (*n*=2)	2	100%							0	0%
		Female	2001-02 (*n*=5)	3	60%	1	20%	1	20%			1	20%
			2002-03 (*n*=4)	2	50%	1	25%	1	25%			1	25%
			2003-04 (*n*=6)	6	100%							0	0%
	Asian	Male	2001-02 (*n*=12)	5	42%	4	33%	3	25%			3	25%
			2002-03 (*n*=9)	3	33%	4	44%	2	22%			2	22%
			2003-04 (*n*=14)	8	57%	6	43%					0	0%
		Female	2001-02 (*n*=15)	5	33%	5	33%	4	27%	1	7%	5	33%
			2002-03 (*n*=23)	5	22%	12	52%	4	17%	2	9%	6	26%
			2003-04 (*n*=23)	9	39%	8	35%	6	26%			6	26%
	White	Male	2001-02 (*n*=63)	23	37%	15	24%	22	35%	3	5%	25	40%
			2002-03 (*n*=50)	19	38%	12	24%	16	32%	3	6%	19	38%
			2003-04 (*n*=49)	24	49%	18	37%	5	10%	2	4%	7	14%
		Female	2001-02 (*n*=75)	19	25%	33	44%	19	25%	4	5%	23	31%
			2002-03 (*n*=67)	26	39%	21	31%	16	24%	4	6%	20	30%
			2003-04 (*n*=76)	28	37%	31	41%	16	21%	1	1%	17	22%
	Hispanic/ Latino	Male	2001-02 (*n*=78)	53	68%	16	21%	8	10%	1	1%	9	12%
			2002-03 (*n*=108)	86	80%	15	14%	6	6%	1	1%	7	6%
			2003-04 (*n*=90)	64	71%	20	22%	6	7%			6	7%
		Female	2001-02 (*n*=92)	55	60%	32	35%	5	5%			5	5%
			2002-03 (*n*=92)	67	73%	19	21%	5	5%	1	1%	6	7%
			2003-04 (*n*=128)	87	68%	31	24%	10	8%			10	8%

Figure 6.21 (Continued)

Big River High School HSST Mathematics Proficiency Levels
By Grade Level, Ethnicity, and Gender, 2001-02 to 2003-04

Grade Level	Ethnicity	Gender	Year	Below Basic		Basic		Proficient		Advanced		% Proficient	
				Number	Percent	Number	Percent	Number	Percent	Number	Percent	Number	Percent
Grade 11	Black	Male	2001-02 (*n*=2)	2	100%							0	0%
			2002-03 (*n*=3)	2	67%			1	33%			1	33%
			2003-04 (*n*=1)			1	100%					0	0%
		Female	2001-02 (*n*=7)	5	71%	2	29%					0	0%
			2002-03 (*n*=4)	3	75%	1	25%					0	0%
			2003-04 (*n*=4)	2	50%	2	50%					0	0%
	Asian	Male	2001-02 (*n*=12)	5	42%	3	25%	3	25%	1	8%	4	33%
			2002-03 (*n*=14)	7	50%	4	29%	3	21%			3	21%
			2003-04 (*n*=9)	2	22%	4	44%	1	11%	2	22%	3	33%
		Female	2001-02 (*n*=13)	6	46%	4	31%	3	23%			3	23%
			2002-03 (*n*=18)	6	33%	4	22%	6	33%	2	11%	8	44%
			2003-04 (*n*=19)	5	26%	9	47%	4	21%	1	5%	5	26%
	White	Male	2001-02 (*n*=63)	34	54%	16	25%	11	17%	2	3%	13	21%
			2002-03 (*n*=54)	27	50%	15	28%	9	17%	3	6%	12	22%
			2003-04 (*n*=50)	24	48%	9	18%	15	30%	2	4%	17	34%
		Female	2001-02 (*n*=53)	27	51%	15	28%	9	17%	2	4%	11	21%
			2002-03 (*n*=74)	36	49%	23	31%	11	15%	4	5%	15	20%
			2003-04 (*n*=63)	32	51%	14	22%	13	21%	4	6%	17	27%
	Hispanic/ Latino	Male	2001-02 (*n*=60)	48	80%	8	13%	2	3%	2	3%	4	7%
			2002-03 (*n*=65)	55	85%	9	14%	1	2%			1	2%
			2003-04 (*n*=95)	76	80%	13	14%	5	5%	1	1%	6	6%
		Female	2001-02 (*n*=80)	62	78%	15	19%	3	4%			3	4%
			2002-03 (*n*=90)	70	78%	17	19%	3	3%			3	3%
			2003-04 (*n*=86)	68	79%	13	15%	3	3%	2	2%	5	6%

Figure 6.22 displays the differences in results by grade level and high and low socio-economic status. Nearly 70% of Big River High School students were designated "High SES" families.

Figure 6.23 displays Mathematics proficiency results for those students requiring special education services.

Figure 6.22

Big River High School HSST Mathematics Proficiency Levels
By Grade Level and Socio-economic Status, 2001-02 to 2003-04

Grade Level	SES	Year	Below Basic		Basic		Proficient		Advanced		% Proficient	
			Number	Percent	Number	Percent	Number	Percent	Number	Percent	Number	Percent
Grade 9	High SES	2001-02 (*n*=247)	129	52%	58	23%	51	21%	9	4%	60	24%
		2002-03 (*n*=256)	123	48%	79	31%	46	18%	8	3%	54	21%
		2003-04 (*n*=342)	166	49%	115	34%	55	16%	6	2%	61	18%
	Low SES	2001-02 (*n*=125)	94	75%	22	18%	9	7%			9	7%
		2002-03 (*n*=176)	123	70%	42	24%	9	5%	2	1%	11	6%
		2003-04 (*n*=125)	82	66%	28	22%	15	12%			15	12%
Grade 10	High SES	2001-02 (*n*=235)	96	41%	78	33%	54	23%	7	3%	61	26%
		2002-03 (*n*=256)	130	51%	70	27%	47	18%	9	4%	56	22%
		2003-04 (*n*=277)	148	53%	91	33%	35	13%	3	1%	38	14%
	Low SES	2001-02 (*n*=106)	67	63%	29	27%	8	8%	2	2%	10	9%
		2002-03 (*n*=96)	77	80%	14	15%	3	3%	2	2%	5	5%
		2003-04 (*n*=109)	78	72%	23	21%	8	7%			8	7%
Grade 11	High SES	2001-02 (*n*=223)	131	59%	57	26%	28	13%	7	3%	35	16%
		2002-03 (*n*=245)	150	61%	56	23%	31	13%	8	3%	39	16%
		2003-04 (*n*=255)	158	62%	50	20%	37	15%	10	4%	47	18%
	Low SES	2001-02 (*n*=67)	58	87%	6	9%	3	4%			3	4%
		2002-03 (*n*=77)	56	73%	17	22%	3	4%	1	1%	4	5%
		2003-04 (*n*=71)	50	70%	15	21%	4	6%	2	3%	6	8%

Figure 6.23

Big River High School HSST Mathematics Proficiency Levels
By Grade Level and Special Education Identified, 2001-02 to 2003-04

Grade Level	Year	Below Basic		Basic		Proficient		Advanced		% Proficient	
		Number	Percent	Number	Percent	Number	Percent	Number	Percent	Number	Percent
Grade 9	2001-02 (*n*=21)	20	95%	1	5%					0	0%
	2002-03 (*n*=41)	38	93%	3	7%					0	0%
	2003-04 (*n*=33)	31	94%	1	3%	1	3%			1	3%
Grade 10	2001-02 (*n*=11)	10	91%			1	9%			1	9%
	2002-03 (*n*=7)	7	100%							0	0%
	2003-04 (*n*=21)	20	95%	1	5%					0	0%
Grade 11	2001-02 (*n*=3)	3	100%							0	0%
	2002-03 (*n*=5)	4	80%			1	20%			1	20%
	2003-04 (*n*=13)	11	85%	1	7%	1	8%			1	8%

As shown in the demographics section, Big River has a gifted program. Figure 6.24 displays the Mathematics proficiency results for the gifted students, by grade level, compared to those not in the program.

Figure 6.24

Big River High School HSST Mathematics Proficiency Levels By Grade Level and Gifted Designation, 2001-02 to 2003-04

Grade Level	Ability	Year	Below Basic		Basic		Proficient		Advanced		% Proficient	
			Number	Percent	Number	Percent	Number	Percent	Number	Percent	Number	Percent
Grade 9	Gifted	2001-02 (n=84)	20	24%	28	33%	31	37%	5	6%	36	43%
		2002-03 (n=63)	17	27%	26	41%	15	24%	5	8%	20	32%
		2003-04 (n=59)	11	19%	20	34%	26	44%	2	3%	28	47%
	Not Gifted	2001-02 (n=288)	203	70%	52	18%	29	10%	4	1%	33	11%
		2002-03 (n=369)	229	62%	95	26%	40	11%	5	1%	45	12%
		2003-04 (n=408)	237	58%	123	30%	44	11%	4	1%	48	12%
Grade 10	Gifted	2001-02 (n=72)	6	8%	27	38%	31	43%	8	11%	39	54%
		2002-03 (n=74)	18	24%	22	30%	26	35%	8	11%	34	46%
		2003-04 (n=62)	20	32%	23	37%	18	29%	1	2%	19	31%
	Not Gifted	2001-02 (n=269)	157	58%	80	30%	31	12%	1	0.4%	32	12%
		2002-03 (n=280)	190	68%	63	23%	24	9%	3	1%	27	10%
		2003-04 (n=326)	208	64%	91	28%	25	8%	2	1%	27	8%
Grade 11	Gifted	2001-02 (n=74)	32	43%	21	28%	17	23%	4	5%	21	28%
		2002-03 (n=72)	21	29%	27	38%	17	24%	7	10%	24	33%
		2003-04 (n=72)	32	44%	17	24%	16	22%	7	10%	23	32%
	Not Gifted	2001-02 (n=216)	157	73%	42	19%	14	6%	3	1%	17	8%
		2002-03 (n=250)	185	74%	46	18%	17	7%	2	1%	19	8%
		2003-04 (n=255)	177	69%	48	19%	25	10%	5	2%	30	12%

Figure 6.25 shows the proficiency results for students classified as English Proficient, English Learner, and those newly redesignated as English proficient, by grade level.

Figure 6.25

**Big River High School HSST Mathematics Proficiency Levels
By Grade Level and Language Proficiency, 2001-02 to 2003-04**

Grade Level	Language Proficiency	Year	Below Basic		Basic		Proficient		Advanced		% Proficient	
			Number	Percent	Number	Percent	Number	Percent	Number	Percent	Number	Percent
Grade 10	English Proficient	2001-02 (n=320)	176	55%	77	24%	58	18%	9	3%	67	21%
		2002-03 (n=273)	143	52%	80	29%	41	15%	9	3%	50	18%
		2003-04 (n=306)	142	46%	102	33%	56	18%	6	2%	62	20%
	English Learner	2001-02 (n=43)	47	90%	3	6%	2	4%			2	4%
		2002-03 (n=80)	69	86%	8	10%	3	4%			3	4%
		2003-04 (n=76)	64	84%	11	14%	1	1%			1	1%
	Redesignated Proficient	2002-03 (n=79)	34	43%	33	42%	11	14%	1	1%	12	15%
		2003-04 (n=85)	42	49%	30	35%	13	15%			13	15%
Grade 11	English Proficient	2001-02 (n=287)	120	42%	97	34%	62	22%	8	3%	70	24%
		2002-03 (n=243)	120	49%	68	28%	45	19%	10	4%	55	23%
		2003-04 (n=250)	137	55%	79	32%	31	12%	3	1%	34	14%
	English Learner	2001-02 (n=39)	43	80%	10	19%			1	2%	1	2%
		2002-03 (n=52)	47	90%	5	10%					0	0%
		2003-04 (n=56)	44	79%	10	18%	2	4%			2	4%
	Redesignated Proficient	2002-03 (n=59)	41	69%	12	20%	5	8%	1	2%	6	10%
		2003-04 (n=82)	47	57%	25	30%	10	12%			10	12%
Grade 12	English Proficient	2001-02 (n=250)	155	62%	58	23%	30	12%	7	3%	37	15%
		2002-03 (n=224)	133	59%	54	24%	29	13%	8	4%	37	17%
		2003-04 (n=228)	134	59%	49	21%	35	15%	10	4%	45	20%
	English Learner	2001-02 (n=33)	34	85%	5	13%	1	3%			1	3%
		2002-03 (n=48)	37	77%	8	17%	3	6%			3	6%
		2003-04 (n=44)	38	86%	5	11%			1	2%	1	2%
	Redesignated Proficient	2002-03 (n=50)	36	72%	11	22%	2	4%	1	2%	3	6%
		2003-04 (n=55)	37	67%	11	20%	6	11%	1	2%	7	13%

Study Questions for Where Are We Now?

As you review Big River's data, use either the margins in the text, this page, or print this page from the CD to write down your early thinking. These notes, of course, are only placeholders until all the data are analyzed. (Ch6Qs.pdf)

1. What are the student learning *strengths* and *challenges* for Big River High School?	
Strengths	*Challenges*

2. What are some *implications* for the Big River school improvement plan?

3. Looking at the data presented, what other student learning data would you want to answer the question *Where are we now?* for Big River High School?

What I Saw in the Example: Big River High School

Using the study questions as an outline, what I saw in the data for Chapter 6 appears below. When applicable, I have referenced the figure or page number that gave me my first impression of strengths and challenges. 🔍 (Ch6Saw.pdf)

Student Learning Strengths	*Student Learning Challenges*
English Language Arts: • Big River had a larger percentage of students scoring *Advanced* in ELA than the district at grade 11 in 2003-04. (Figure 6.8) • The percentage of students scoring *Below Basic* in ELA has decreased in all grades. These percentages were less than the district percentages in 2003-04. (Figure 6.8) • Except for Black students, the school had increases in the percent proficient by every disaggregation in 2003-04, at all grade levels. (Figures 6.12 and 6.13) • Cohort data shows a higher percent of students scored *Advanced* in ELA over time. (Figure 6.10) • The percentage of Hispanics scoring at proficient levels increased in the last year over the previous year, at all grade levels. (Figures 6.12) • Redesignated students had about 40% of the students proficient in ELA. (Figures 6.17)	*English Language Arts:* • The percentage of students scoring *Advanced* decreased in grades 10 and 11. (Figures 6.8 and 6.9) • Over half of the Big River students taking the ELA exam scored *Basic* or below. Only 38 to 46 percent scored *Proficient* or *Advanced*. (Figure 6.8) • Cohort data show more students scoring Below Basic in ELA over time, except 2003-04. (Figure 6.10) • The majority of students scoring *Below Basic* in ELA are males in each grade level. (Figure 6.13) • Over half the Hispanic and Black populations scored below proficiency in ELA. No Black student was proficient in ELA in grade 10: only one student was proficient in grade 11 in 2003-04. (Figure 6.12) • Even the students considered to be high SES are failing the ELA exam, but at half the rate of the low SES students. (Figures 6.14) • After grade 9, the school is "losing ground" with high SES students in ELA. (Figure 6.14) • Only two special education students at each grade level passed the ELA exam. (Figure 6.15) • Some of the gifted students scored below proficiency in ELA. (Figure 6.16) • English learners passed the ELA exam at very small percentages. (Figure 6.17)
Mathematics: • Schoolwide, some subgroup pcercentages, i.e., Hispanic, low SES, special education, not gifted, and redesignated English proficiency, increased in Math in 2003-04. (Figures 6.20, 6.22, 6.23, 6.24, and 6.25)	*Mathematics:* • Only 16% of ninth graders, 12% of tenth graders, and 17% of eleventh graders were proficient on the Math exam, scoring below the district. (Figure 6.9) • Over half scored *Below Basic* in Math in each grade level. (Figure 6.9) • Big River High School had a lower percentage of students proficient than the district in Math. (Figure 6.9) • Over half of the students at each grade level score *Below Basic* in Math. The scores are not getting better. (Figure 6.9) • No Black student was proficient in Math in grades 10 and 11 in 2003-04. Only 10% or fewer Hispanics were proficient at each grade level. (Figure 6.20) • Black and Hispanic students are being left behind in Math at all grade levels and both genders. (Figure 6.21) • Even high SES, gifted, and English proficient students performed poorly in Math. (Figures 6.22, 6.24, and 6.25). • Only one ninth and one eleventh grade special education student was proficient in Math. (Figure 6.15).

Implications for Big River's school improvement plan

- How is ELA being taught? How are students cycled through ELA classes? What is being taught? Do teachers know what is being measured on the test? What do the students know when they come to the high school?
- How is Math being taught? What is being taught? Do teachers know what is being measured on the test? What do the students know when they come to the high school?
- Are all teachers teaching to the standards?
- How is it that not all students are taking the test?
- Something must be done for special education students and for students of ethnicities, other than White.
- Staff needs to make sure that students and teachers see the importance of the proficiency test.
- Have the programs and schedules been evaluated?
- Students said in their questionnaires that they wish there was less homework. Do teachers collaborate on assignments and the amount of homework they assign? Is homework meaningful and classwork challenging?

Other desired student learning data or information

- What is the quality of teaching programs/schedule?
- Are special education students included in regular ELA and Math classes?

Analyzing required norm-referenced and/or criterion-referenced tests and disaggregating by grade level, gender, ethnicity, and lunch status is an excellent way to begin answering the question, "How are we doing?"

Summary

Answering the question, *Where are we now?*, takes the data analysis work into the student learning realm. Analyzing required norm-referenced and/or criterion-referenced tests and disaggregating by grade level, gender, ethnicity, socio-economic status, and special education is an excellent way to begin answering the question, *How are we doing?* Looking across measures can be useful and informative—another way to think about what students know and are able to do, giving us a glimpse at *how* students learn.

As one looks at the trends, she/he can begin to see discrepancies and areas for further and deeper analyses, which we follow in the next chapter. The study questions can help guide one to these next levels.

On the CD Related to this Chapter

▼ Study Questions Related to *Where Are We Now?* (Ch6Qs.doc)
These study questions will help you understand the information provided in Chapter 6. This template file can be printed for use with staff as you begin to explore your own student learning results.

▼ *Arguments For and Against Standardized Testing* (TestArgu.pdf)
This table summarizes the most common arguments for and against the use of standardized testing.

▼ *Standardized Test Score Terms, Their Most Effective Uses, and Cautions for Their Uses* (TestTerm.pdf)
This table shows the different standardized testing terms, their effective uses, and cautions for their uses.

▼ *Arguments For and Against Performance Assessments* (PerfArgu.pdf)
This table shows the most common arguments for and against the use of performance assessments.

▼ *Arguments For and Against Teacher Grading* (GradeArg.pdf)
This table shows the most common arguments for and against the use of teacher grading.

▼ *Terms Related to Analyzing Student Achievement Results, Descriptively, Their Most Effective Uses, and Cautions for Their Uses* (SAterms1.pdf)
This table shows the different terms related to analyzing student achievement results, descriptively, their effective uses, and cautions for their uses.

▼ *Terms Related to Analyzing Student Achievement Results, Inferentially, Their Most Effective Uses, and Cautions for Their Uses* (SAterms2.pdf)
This table shows the different terms related to analyzing student achievement results, inferentially, their effective uses, and cautions for their uses.

▼ *What I Saw in the Example* (Ch6Saw.pdf)
What I Saw in the Example is a file, organized by the student learning study questions, that summarizes what the author saw in the student learning data provided by Big River High School.

▼ Student Achievement Graphing Templates (HighSA.xls)
All of the *Microsoft Excel* files that were used to create the student achievement graphs in the Big River example (Chapter 6) appear on the CD. Use these templates by putting your data in the source data table and changing the title/labels to reflect your data. The graphs will build automatically. This file also explains how to use the templates.

▼ Student Achievement Data Summary Template (HighSA.doc)
This *Microsoft Word* file provides a template for creating your own school student achievement data summary like the one for the Big River example, using the graphing and table templates provided. Create your graphs and tables in the graphing templates, then copy and paste them into the *Student Achievement Data Summary Template.*

▼ *Questions to Guide the Analysis of Student Achievement Data* (QsStachv.doc)
This *Microsoft Word* file consists of questions to guide the interpretation of your student learning data. You can write your responses into this file.

Analyzing the Data:
What Are the Gaps? and What Are the Root Causes of the Gaps?

Gaps are the differences between *where the school wants to be* and *where the school is right now*. *Where the school wants to be* can be defined through the school's vision and goals.

A *vision* is what the school would look like, sound like, and feel like when it is carrying out its purpose. To be effective in getting all staff members implementing the same concepts, a vision must be spelled-out in specific terms that everyone can understand in the same way. *(The School Portfolio Toolkit: A Planning, Implementation, and Evaluation Guide for Continuous School Improvement* [Bernhardt, 2002], Chapter 5, beginning on page 97.)

Goals are the outcomes of the vision. Goals are stated in broad, general, abstract, and non-measurable terms. *(Objectives* are much more specific and require data so they can be measured.) Schools often want to attempt many goals, and very few get implemented. There should be only two to three school goals that reflect the results the school wants to achieve by implementing the vision. (See *Goal Setting* and *Gap Analysis and Objectives Activities* on CD.) (ACTGoals.pdf and ACTGap.pdf)

Where the school is right now are the results—specifically what the data say about strengths, challenges, and areas for improvement. To uncover *gaps*, one must review the data and dig deeper. Just looking at one level of analysis could be misleading. One must dig deeper to uncover those students not meeting the standards and where they rank on the scoring scale. The reason for digging deeper is that a large gap may not seem as large when one discovers that the students in the area with the largest gap scored only one or two points away from mastery, while the students not mastering the subtest with the smallest gap could be on the very bottom of the distribution—a long way from mastery.

Once school personnel see the gaps, they typically want to start implementing solutions *without discovering the root causes.*

Root causes are real reasons that "problems" or "challenges" exist. Schools must uncover the root causes of their undesirable results to alleviate the problem or to get desirable results that will last over time. (ACTRoot.pdf) If they do not understand the root causes, schools could be treating a symptom and never get to the real reason for the results. Gap and root cause analyses completed for Big River High School are on the pages that follow. Several activities/processes for working with staff to uncover root causes are on the CD. (ACTCause.pdf, ACTCycle.pdf, and CycleTmp.doc)

Please note the study questions on page 196 to assist in studying the data. (Ch7Qs.pdf) Also note that there is space in the margins on the data pages to write your impressions as you review the data. At the end of the chapter, I have shared what I saw in the data.

Where the school is right now are the results—specifically what the data say about strengths, challenges, and areas for improvement.

Root causes are real reasons that "problems" or "challenges" exist.

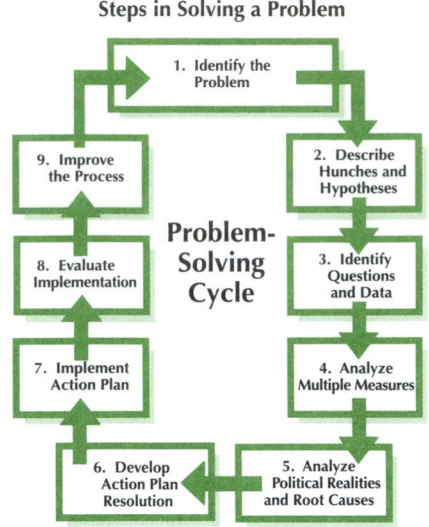

Steps in Solving a Problem

Problem-Solving Cycle

1. Identify the Problem
2. Describe Hunches and Hypotheses
3. Identify Questions and Data
4. Analyze Multiple Measures
5. Analyze Political Realities and Root Causes
6. Develop Action Plan Resolution
7. Implement Action Plan
8. Evaluate Implementation
9. Improve the Process

Our Example School: Big River High School

Big River High School teachers decided to use a problem-solving cycle to uncover root causes since not enough of their students were scoring *Proficient* and/or *Advanced* on the *High School Standards Test* (HSST). (ACTCycle.pdf) In the past, teachers merely looked at HSST scores and remediated the students falling behind. This time, they wanted to use data before jumping prematurely to unthought-out solutions. Teachers first stated the "problem" as objectively as they could. They then brainstormed 20 sincere reasons they think this problem exists, withholding any judgments, while encouraging all ideas. Twenty reasons allow for enough different ideas so as to not inhibit brainstorming. Limiting the list to fewer than 20 many mean some very good possibilities would not be included. The problem and the 20 brainstormed reasons follow.

Problem:

Not enough students are proficient in ELA and Math, as measured on the HSST.

Brainstormed reasons this problem exists:

1. Students do not think this test is important.
2. The students don't try to do well.
3. Too many students live in poverty.
4. There is too much student mobility in our school.
5. The students aren't prepared for high school.
6. Middle schools are not doing enough.
7. Many of our students are not fluent in English.
8. Even if the students don't speak English, they have to take the test in English.
9. There is a lack of parent support.
10. Students don't do their homework.
11. There is no district support.
12. There are budget problems at the school and district levels.
13. We don't know what data are important.
14. We don't know how to use the data.
15. We don't get the data soon enough to make a difference.
16. Not all our curriculum is aligned to the standards.
17. Teachers don't know how to set up lessons to teach to the standards.
18. We have too many new teachers and new administrators all at once.
19. We are not teaching to the standards.
20. We need more time to collaborate to improve instruction.

Staff members realized they first thought about all the external reasons students were not achieving. Ultimately they turned their thinking inward to what they know is closest to the contributing causes of their results. They felt that reasons 16 through 20 were probably very close to the root cause, or at least contributing causes.

Following the brainstorming, staff members determined the questions they needed to answer with data, before they can "solve" their problem. The questions and the data they needed to answer the questions are shown in Figure 7.1.

Figure 7.1

Questions	Data
1. Who are the students who are not performing?	Student achievement results by student groups.
2. What were the students' scores in middle school? Are we adding value to their education?	Big River ninth graders' student achievement results as grade eight students.
3. What do the students know and what do they not know?	Student achievement results by standards.
4. Are all teachers teaching to the standards?	Standards questionnaire.
5. How are we teaching Mathematics, ELA—actually everything?	Teacher reports about teaching strategies to grade-level teams.
6. What is the impact of our instruction?	We need to follow student achievement by teachers and by course
7. What do teachers think we need to do to improve our results?	Staff questionnaire and discussion.
8. What do students think we need to do to improve?	Student questionnaire and focus groups.
9. What do parents think we need to do to improve our results?	Parent questionnaire and follow-up focus groups of parents
10. How can we help students know how important this test is?	Teachers need to talk with students in focus groups to find out why they do not think the test is important. Teachers need to model in class how important the test is.
11. What does our data analysis tell us about what we need to do to improve?	Study data analysis results.

Question 1: Who are the students who are not performing?

Figures 7.2 and 7.3 show the number and percentage of students who scored at *Proficient* or *Advanced* levels, defined as "proficient" in this state. While showing the percentage of "proficient" students by NCLB student groups, the shaded cells in the figures represent the largest gaps (50% and below of that student group). These tables, while not doing so explicitly, also indicate the gaps—that is, the number and percentage of students not proficient.

Figure 7.2 shows that the only student groups that had over 50% of their group proficient in every grade level in ELA in 2003-04 were English Proficient, Gifted, and White. In grade nine, Asian, female, and high SES students additionally had more than 50% proficient in each of their student groups in 2003-04. In grade eleven, 50% of of Asian students were proficient.

The lowest percentages include students identified for special education services and English learners, with 6% and 3% of their small populations scoring proficient in 2003-04 (although these numbers can only be used inhouse as they are too small for legal comparisons).

Figure 7.3 shows that Math scores were even lower than ELA scores. No student group, at any grade level, had over 50% of its population scoring *Proficient*. The highest scoring student group was gifted ninth graders who had 47% of its population scoring *Proficient* or *Advanced* in 2003-04.

Figure 7.2

Summary of Big River High School English/Language Arts (ELA) HSST Number and Percentage Proficient, 2002-03 to 2003-04

Big River High School Grades 9–11			ELA Proficiency											
			Grade 9			Grade 10			Grade 11			School		
			Number Tested	Number Proficient	Percent Proficient	Number Tested	Number Proficient	Percent Proficient	Number Tested	Number Proficient	Percent Proficient	Number Tested	Number Proficient	Percent Proficient
Overall	All Students	2002-03	442	163	37%	396	146	37%	362	150	41%	1,200	459	38%
		2003-04	472	216	46%	415	160	39%	360	151	42%	1,247	527	42%
By Gender	Male	2002-03	185	53	29%	185	56	30%	165	54	33%	535	163	30%
		2003-04	185	58	31%	169	52	31%	170	63	37%	524	173	33%
	Female	2002-03	257	110	43%	211	90	43%	197	96	49%	665	296	45%
		2003-04	287	158	55%	246	108	44%	190	88	46%	723	354	49%
By Ethnicity	Black	2002-03	8	3	38%	6	2	33%	9	6	67%	23	11	48%
		2003-04	17	8	47%	8		0%	7	1	14%	32	9	28%
	Asian	2002-03	39	22	56%	34	25	74%	32	11	34%	105	58	55%
		2003-04	44	25	57%	37	16	43%	31	23	74%	112	64	57%
	White	2002-03	128	79	62%	128	80	63%	141	95	67%	397	254	64%
		2003-04	148	99	67%	132	82	62%	120	83	69%	400	264	66%
	Hispanic	2002-03	267	59	22%	228	39	17%	180	38	21%	675	136	20%
		2003-04	263	84	32%	238	62	26%	202	44	22%	703	190	27%
By Socio-economic Status	High SES	2002-03	266	133	50%	277	130	47%	272	136	50%	815	399	49%
		2003-04	345	184	53%	292	138	47%	284	134	47%	921	456	50%
	Low SES	2002-03	176	30	17%	114	14	12%	90	14	16%	380	58	15%
		2003-04	127	32	25%	120	22	18%	74	16	22%	321	70	22%
By SE Designation	SE Identified	2002-03	42	4	10%	39		0%	27	1	4%	108	5	5%
		2003-04	37	2	5%	36	2	6%	29	2	7%	102	6	6%
By Gifted Status	Gifted	2002-03	64	46	72%	74	56	76%	73	54	74%	211	156	74%
		2003-04	90	79	88%	89	74	83%	114	93	82%	293	246	84%
	Not Gifted	2002-03	378	117	31%	322	90	28%	289	96	33%	989	303	31%
		2003-04	465	220	47%	385	5	38%	318	130	41%	1,168	495	42%
By Language Proficiency	English Proficient	2002-03	277	140	51%	273	126	46%	250	132	53%	800	398	50%
		2003-04	386	255	66%	319	198	62%	317	184	58%	1,022	637	62%
	English Learner	2002-03	82		0%	64		0%	65	2	3%	211	2	1%
		2003-04	78	2	3%	52	2	4%	65	1	2%	195	5	3%
	Redesignated Proficient	2002-03	83	23	28%	59	20	34%	54	16	30%	196	59	30%
		2003-04	91	42	46%	61	23	38%	92	34	37%	244	99	41%

(*Note: Number Tested*=the number of students in that student group and grade level who took the test.

Number and Percent Proficient=the number and percentage of students who scored *Proficient* or *Advanced* on the test, divided by the number taking the test. Shaded cells represent the student groups and grade levels with 50% or fewer students scoring "proficient".)

WHAT ARE THE GAPS? AND WHAT ARE THE ROOT CAUSES OF THE GAPS?

187

Figure 7.3

Summary of Big River High School Mathematics
HSST Number and Percentage Proficient, 2002-03 to 2003-04

Big River High School Grades 9–11			Math Proficiency											
			Grade 9			Grade 10			Grade 11			School		
			Number Tested	Number Proficient	Percent Proficient	Number Tested	Number Proficient	Percent Proficient	Number Tested	Number Proficient	Percent Proficient	Number Tested	Number Proficient	Percent Proficient
Overall	All Students	2002-03	432	65	15%	354	61	17%	322	43	12%	1,108	169	15%
		2003-04	467	76	16%	388	46	12%	327	53	16%	1,182	175	15%
By Gender	Male	2002-03	181	24	13%	168	28	17%	136	17	13%	485	69	14%
		2003-04	183	25	14%	155	13	8%	155	26	17%	493	64	13%
	Female	2002-03	251	41	16%	186	33	18%	186	26	14%	623	100	16%
		2003-04	284	51	18%	233	33	14%	172	27	16%	689	111	16%
By Ethnicity	Black	2002-03	8		0%	5	1	20%	7	1	14%	20	2	10%
		2003-04	15	2	13%	8		0%	5		0%	28	2	7%
	Asian	2002-03	40	8	20%	32	8	25%	32	11	34%	104	27	26%
		2003-04	44	8	18%	37	6	16%	28	8	29%	109	22	20%
	White	2002-03	129	34	26%	117	39	33%	128	27	21%	374	100	27%
		2003-04	147	40	27%	125	24	19%	113	34	30%	385	98	25%
	Hispanic	2002-03	255	23	9%	200	13	7%	155	4	3%	610	40	7%
		2003-04	261	26	10%	218	16	7%	181	11	6%	660	53	8%
By Socio-economic Status	High SES	2002-03	256	54	21%	256	56	22%	245	39	16%	757	149	20%
		2003-04	342	61	18%	277	38	14%	255	47	18%	874	146	17%
	Low SES	2002-03	176	11	6%	96	5	5%	77	4	5%	349	20	6%
		2003-04	125	15	12%	109	8	7%	71	6	8%	305	29	10%
By SE Designation	SE Identified	2002-03	41		0%	7		0%	5	1	20%	53	1	2%
		2003-04	33	1	3%	21		0%	13	1	8%	67	2	3%
By Gifted Status	Gifted	2002-03	63	20	32%	74	34	46%	72	24	33%	209	78	37%
		2003-04	59	28	47%	62	19	31%	72	23	32%	193	70	36%
	Not Gifted	2002-03	369	45	12%	280	27	10%	250	19	8%	899	91	10%
		2003-04	408	48	12%	326	27	8%	255	30	12%	989	105	11%
By Language Proficiency	English Proficient	2002-03	273	50	18%	243	55	23%	224	37	17%	740	142	19%
		2003-04	306	62	20%	250	34	14%	228	45	20%	784	141	18%
	English Learner	2002-03	80	3	4%	52		0%	48	3	6%	180	6	3%
		2003-04	76	1	1%	56	2	4%	44	1	2%	176	4	2%
	Redesignated Proficient	2002-03	79	12	15%	59	6	10%	50	3	6%	188	21	11%
		2003-04	85	13	15%	82	10	12%	55	7	13%	222	30	14%

(*Note: Number Tested*=the number of students in that student group and grade level who took the test.
Number and Percent Proficient=the number and percentage of students who scored *Proficient* or *Advanced* on the test, divided by the number taking the test. Shaded cells represent the student groups and grade levels with 50% or fewer students scoring "proficient".)

Question 2: What were the students' scores in middle school? Are we adding value to their education?

An analysis was performed to study student achievement results for Big River ninth graders when they were eighth graders. The results show that Big River students performed better in both ELA and Math as ninth graders than they did as eighth graders. The number and percentage of students proficient in ELA went from 143 to 216 (almost 35% to 46%), and in Math from 43 to 76 (10% to 16%). The number and percentage of students scoring *Below Basic* in ELA decreased from 128 to 122 (31% to 25%), and in Math from 261 to 248 (approximately 63% to 51%). Staff felt that these data make it a little more obvious that there needs to be a partnership developed with the middle schools and the elementary schools. A summary of the results appears in Figure 7.4 below.

Figure 7.4

Summary of Big River High School Student Performance in Grade Eight, 2002-03, and Grade Nine, 2003-04

Grade Level	Year	ELA Proficient		Math Proficient	
Grade 8	2002-03	$n=143$	35%	$n=43$	10%
Grade 9	2003-04	$n=216$	46%	$n=76$	16%

Grade Level	Year	ELA Below Basic		Math Below Basic	
Grade 8	2002-03	$n=128$	31%	$n=261$	63%
Grade 9	2003-04	$n=122$	25%	$n=248$	51%

Question 3: What do the students know and what do they not know?

Figure 7.5 shows what little standards information there is available for the HSST. For the most part, ELA scores are improving by grade level, as can be seen by following the cohorts across grade levels. The exception is *Literary Response and Analysis* from grade nine to grade ten. In Math, only ninth-grade scores improved—by two-tenths of a point from 2002-03 to 2003-04.

Figure 7.5

Big River High School Percent Correct Performance on Standards 2002-03 to 2003-04

Subject and Grade Level			2002-03	2003-04
ELA	Grade 9	Literacy Response and Analysis	53.2	54.1
		Reading Comprehension	55.1	59.3
		Word Analysis and Vocabulary Development	49.5	66.0
		Total	**53.7**	**58.9**
	Grade 10	Literacy Response and Analysis	50.6	50.1
		Reading Comprehension	52.3	61.5
		Word Analysis and Vocabulary Development	57.2	67.4
		Total	**53.6**	**59.7**
	Grade 11	Literacy Response and Analysis	49.2	55.8
		Reading Comprehension	57.5	62.6
		Word Analysis and Vocabulary Development	64.1	65.7
		Total	**56.9**	**60.2**
Math	Grade 9	**Total**	**40.4**	**40.6**
	Grade 10	**Total**	**42.6**	**39.3**
	Grade 11	**Total**	**45.4**	**42.3**

Question 4: Are all teachers teaching to the standards?

According to the Standards Assessment Questionnaire, most teachers (70%) said they have read in depth or are very knowledgeable of the standards for their grade levels and content areas. Only 44% said the same for the grades that precede, and 56% said they know the standards for the grade levels that follow their grades. A little over half of the teachers (57%) indicated that they know well what it would look like, sound like, and feel like if they were teaching to the standards 100% of the time.

In open-ended comments, however, teachers mentioned other teachers not teaching to the standards and the need for professional learning in teaching to the standards. Teachers also wrote a lot about needing the time to communicate and collaborate about the standards.

Question 5: How are we teaching Math, ELA—actually everything?

Staff members determined that they could not answer this question right now, but they do want an honest analysis of what they are teaching and how they are teaching. Staff agreed that classroom observations, communication, and collaboration on what teachers are teaching need to be major pieces of their school improvement plan.

Question 6: What is the impact of our instruction?

Questions 3 and 5 will help staff answer this question officially. In the meantime, we have our HSST results that give us a grim look at our instructional impact.

The HSST results of our ninth graders compared to their scores as eighth graders (Figure 7.3) do indicate that we are making some progress with our students, as does our ELA standards analysis (Figure 7.3). We have to do something to improve math scores, however.

Question 7: What do teachers think we need to do to improve our results?

Teacher questionnaire results tell us that we need to create the time to communicate and collaborate to ensure student learning. Professional development will help us learn how to ensure basic skills while making learning fun for all of our students. In interviews, staff added that professional development in effective instructional strategies for working with students of all backgrounds and standards implementation, along with time to observe, communicate, and collaborate with each other, would help tremendously.

Question 8: What do students think we need to do to improve?

After reviewing the data from students, staff determined teachers need to conduct some focus group interviews with students to get a deeper understanding of what students need in order to improve their learning. In the student questionnaires, students said they want less homework and more interesting ways to learn. In the questionnaires, students did not feel that teachers ask them for feedback about their teaching, or that teachers provide information or materials to their parents to help them at home.

Question 9: What do parents think we need to do to improve our results?

From the questionnaire results, parents indicated that teachers do not ask for feedback about their teaching, or that the school does not provide materials or information to help their child learn at home. Parents also do not feel teachers contact parents about their child's progress in school or help with homework at school outside of class.

Question 10: How can we help students know how important this test is?

Teachers were a little surprised when they saw the staff questionnaire results that said that *teachers* do not believe the state test is an important measure of student learning. Teachers realize they have to be positive and consistent with their language and actions regarding the state test to help students know the importance of the test.

Question 11: What does our data analysis tell us about what we need to do to improve?

Below is a summary of the implications for the school improvement plan from Chapters 4 through 7.

Demographics:

▼ Do teachers have the professional learning needed to work with students with ethnic, language, and SES backgrounds different from their own? With the unemployment rate increasing, perhaps there will be an even higher need for understanding how to work with students who live in poverty.

▼ Are the new teachers, and those not fully credentialed, well supported to help them become effective teachers?

▼ The school needs to recruit more ethnic teachers, particularly Hispanics.

▼ Big River would do well to make sure teachers, by average years of teaching, are mixed by grade and content area.

▼ With an assumed shortage of Hispanic teachers, it might be good for the school/district to have a future teacher program.

▼ The behavior program and the dropout prevention program need to be evaluated, as does GEAR UP.

Continuous Improvement Continuums:

▼ Staff needs to review the mission and vision of the school and bring the new staff along.

▼ Staff needs to use the data warehouse to dig deeper to prevent student failures, and also to pull their data together in a systematic and systemic way for planning.

▼ Staff needs to continue to clarify and communicate student evaluation procedures.

▼ Staff needs to reinforce the teaching of standards.

▼ Staff needs to implement and evaluate the plan, and implement powerful professional development, partnership development, and leadership strategies.

▼ Staff needs to continue to meet regularly to ensure the implementation of the vision and plan, for cross-curricular planning, for collaboration and communication, and to ensure that new teachers are supported and feeling supported, to reinforce the teaching of standards, and to study student work and student data.

▼ Staff needs to do more work with the elementary and middle schools to create a continuum of learning that makes sense for the students.

▼ Staff needs professional learning related to teaching students who live in poverty and who are not native speakers of English, also related to studying student work and student data. The professional learning needs to be embedded into the workweek.

▼ Staff needs to evaluate partnerships and encourage new ones.

Questionnaires:

▼ Getting the same results for five years implies that either the questionnaire needs to be improved or the results need to be implemented.

▼ Teachers should be using the expectations of parents and students to go to college as a means of improving student achievement results.

▼ Teachers need to ask students for feedback about their teaching.

▼ Teachers need to think about adding more challenging classroom activities.

▼ Teachers need to make sure all student populations are being treated with respect (pay attention to the Black students).

▼ Staff needs to make sure Black students are feeling as if they are being assisted with their learning.

▼ All staff have to make the state test more important to students and to teachers.

▼ New teachers might need some support with classroom management.

▼ Staff needs to collaborate within and across curricular areas and grade levels.

▼ Staff wants communication to be improved across staff and between staff and administration.

▼ Staff needs to look at ways to increase parent contact regarding student progress, and to help parents know how to help their children learn at home.

▼ Staff needs to develop a system to get more parents to complete the questionnaire.

Standards Assessment:

Need to get all teachers knowing and implementing content standards, through:

▼ All staff needs to communicate and collaborate to make learning consistent across grade levels, to remember why they got into teaching in the first place, and to provide feedback on their teaching with one another.

▼ Staff seems to think professional learning on how to teach to the standards, feedback from classroom observations, demonstration lessons, and peer coaching will help everyone better know the standards.

▼ Staff would like all staff to care more about students and teach to the standards.

▼ Staff would like time to work with each other and students, and more administrative support.

▼ Staff wants more ways to improve students' basic skills.

Student Learning:

▼ How is ELA being taught? How are students cycled through ELA classes? What is being taught? Do teachers know what is being measured on the test? What do the students know when they come to the high school?

▼ How is Math being taught? What is being taught? Do teachers know what is being measured on the test? What do the students know when they come to the high school?

▼ Are all teachers teaching to the standards?

▼ How is it that not all students are taking the test?

▼ Something must be done for special education students and for students of ethnicities other than White.

▼ Staff need to make sure that students and teachers see the importance of the proficiency test.

▼ Have the programs and schedules been evaluated?

▼ Students said in their questionnaires that they wish there was less homework. Do teachers collaborate on assignments and the amount of homework they assign? Is homework meaningful and is classwork challenging?

What Are the Root Causes of Big River's Gaps?

After analyzing Big River's data, the gaps, and digging deeper to discover root causes, staff came up with the idea that there are many contributing causes. What emerged at the forefront of their thinking was the fact that staff did not have a clear direction that would create a continuum of learning that makes sense for *all* students. Many staff did not have the professional learning needed to teach students with backgrounds different from their own, or to know how to teach to the state content standards. The lack of communication and collaboration among staff members was also cited as a contributing cause.

Big River staff members used their next professional learning day to revisit their vision. The vision, the plan, and the strategies to implement that vision and plan appear in Chapter 8.

Study Questions for What Are the Gaps? and What Are the Root Causes of the Gaps?

As you review Big River's data, use either the margins in the text, this page, or print this page from the CD to write down your early thinking. (Ch7Qs.pdf) These notes, of course, are only hunches or placeholders until all the data are analyzed and verified with the staff.

1. What are Big River's *gaps*?

2. Do you feel that the *root causes* of their student learning results were uncovered? If the answer is *no*, what other analyses would you perform?

What I Saw in the Example: Big River High School

Using the study questions as an outline, what I saw in the data for Chapter 7 appears below. When applicable, I have referenced the figure or page number that gave me my first impression of strengths and challenges. (Ch7Saw.pdf)

What are the gaps?

The gaps in both English Language Arts and Mathematics, as measured by the HSST, are huge. No student group had 50% or more students proficient in Mathematics. In fact, over half of the students in each grade level scored *Below Basic*. Only White, gifted, English fluent students were proficient on the ELA at a high rate, at all grade levels.

What are the root causes of the gaps?

From all the data analyzed, it appears as though there are many contributing causes to the HSST scores being so low. Some of the causes seem to be centered on the lack of:

1. Instructional quality and coherence
2. Staff working together for the benefit of the students.
3. Caring for the well being of the students.
4. Consistency in the treatment of students.
5. Focus (vision).

Summary

Gap analyses are critical for answering the question, *What are the gaps?* Gap analyses help schools see the difference between *where they are* (current results) and *where they want to be* (vision and goals). To be effective, gap analyses must dig layers deep into the data to truly understand the results and to begin to uncover root causes.

Root causes, as used in this continuous school improvement planning model, refer to the deep underlying reasons for the occurrence of a specific situation—the gap. While a symptom may become evident from a needs assessment or gap analysis, the symptom (low student scores) is not the cause. To find a root cause, one often has to ask *Why?* at least five levels down to uncover the root cause of the symptom. One will know if she/he found the root cause when she/he can answer *no* to the following questions:

▼ Would the problem have occurred if the cause had not been present?

▼ Will the problem reoccur if the cause is corrected? (Preuss, 2003)

If the answers to these questions are *maybe,* you are probably looking at contributing causes, not one root cause. Most problems within schools are caused by systems rather than people. Improvement of the system will result in reduction or removal of the problem. Teams that include processes in their analyses tend not to jump to solutions or conclusions as quickly as those who do not. At some point, when searching for the root cause, one must realize that the "problem" is really a result. What we are trying to do with these analyses is to uncover how we get our results. These very same processes can be used to uncover how we get our successes.

Root causes are not easy to uncover, but the information that is uncovered is well worth the effort.

Big River staff used a quick but analytical brainstorming approach—the problem-solving cycle—to study why so many students are scoring *Below Basic.* (ACTCycle.pdf and CycleTmp.doc) The next chapter will show what they did with their information to create changes in next year's results.

On the CD Related to this Chapter

▼ *Goal Setting Activity* (ACTGoals.pdf)

By setting goals, a school can clarify its end targets for the school's vision. This activity will help a school set goals for the future.

▼ *Gap Analysis and Objectives Activity* (ACTGap.pdf)

The purpose of this activity is to look closely at differences between current results and where the school wants to be in the future. It is this gap that gets translated into objectives that guide the development of the action plan.

▼ *Root Cause Analysis Activity* (ACTRoot.pdf)

Root causes are the real causes of our educational problems. We need to find out what they are so we can eliminate the true cause and not just address the symptom. This activity asks staff teams to review and analyze data and ask probing questions to uncover the root cause(s).

▼ *Cause and Effect Analysis Activity* (ACTCause.pdf)

This activity will help teams determine the relationships and complexities between an effect or problem and all the possible causes.

▼ *Problem-Solving Cycle Activity* (ACTCycle.pdf)

The purpose of the *Problem-Solving Cycle Activity* is to get all staff involved in thinking through a problem before jumping to solutions. This activity can also result in a comprehensive data analysis design.

▼ *Problem-Solving Cycle Handout Template* (CycleTmp.doc)

This *Microsoft Word* file is the last three pages of the problem-solving cycle activity. Use this template to fill-in hunches and hypotheses about why the problem exists, determine the questions needed to answer with data to know more about the problem, and what data are needed to support those answers.

▼ Study Questions Related to the Gaps and the Root Causes of the Gaps (Ch7Qs.doc)

These study questions will help you better understand the information provided in Chapter 7. This template file can be printed for use with staffs as you analyze their data to determine the gaps and the root causes of the gaps.

▼ *What I Saw in the Example* (Ch7Saw.pdf)

What I Saw in the Example is a file, organized by the student learning study questions, that summarizes what the author saw in the student learning data provided by Big River High School.

▼ *Gap Analyses Data Table Templates* (HighGaps.doc)

All of the *Microsoft Word* files that were used to create the gap analyses data tables in the Big River example (Chapter 7) appear on the CD. Use these templates by putting your data in the data table and changing the title/labels to reflect your data.

▼ *No Child Left Behind* (NCLB) Templates

Table templates for analyzing student learning data for NCLB are provided on the CD.

◆ *NCLB Language Scores Template* (LangTbl.doc)

This *Microsoft Word* file is a table template to use in capturing your NCLB Language scores analysis.

◆ *NCLB Reading Scores Template* (ReadTbl.doc)

This *Microsoft Word* file is a table template to use in capturing your NCLB Reading scores analysis.

◆ *NCLB Math Scores Template* (MathTbl.doc)

This *Microsoft Word* file is a table template to use in capturing your NCLB Math scores analysis.

◆ *NCLB Student Achievement Reading Results Template* (ProfLaEl.doc)

This *Microsoft Word* file is a table template to use in summarizing your NCLB disaggregated student achievement Reading proficiency results.

◆ *NCLB Student Achievement Math Results Template* (ProfMaEl.doc)

This *Microsoft Word* file is a table template to use in summarizing your NCLB disaggregated student achievement Math proficiency results.

▼ Group Process Tools and Activities.

The files include read-only documents, examples, templates, tools, activities, and strategy recommendations. Many of the group process tools and activities can be used throughout the analysis of data.

◆ *Affinity Diagram Activity* (ACTAfnty.pdf)

The affinity diagram encourages honest reflection on the real underlying root causes of a problem and its solutions, and encourages people to agree on the factors. This activity assists teams in discussing and resolving problems, using a nonjudgmental process.

◆ *Fishbowl Activity* (ACTFish.pdf)

This activity can be used for dynamic group involvement. The most common configuration is an inner ring, which is the discussion group, surrounded by an outer ring, which is the observation group. Just as people observe the fish in the fishbowl, the outer ring observes the inner ring.

- *Forcefield Analysis Activity* (ACTForce.pdf)

  The *Forcefield Analysis Activity* helps staffs think about the ideal state for the school and the driving and restraining forces regarding that ideal state.

- *Placemat Activity* (ACTPlace.pdf)

  The *Placemat Activity* was developed to invite participants to share their knowledge about the school portfolio, data, a standard, an instructional strategy, a concept, etc.

- *T-Chart Activity* (ACTTChrt.pdf)

  A *T-Chart* is a simple tool to organize material into two columns. Use a T-Chart to compare and contrast information or to show relationships. Use it to help people see the opposite dimension of an issue.

- *"X" Marks the Spot Activity* (ACTXSpot.pdf)

  This activity helps staff understand levels of expertise or degrees of passion about a topic.

- *Quadrant Diagram Activity* (ACTQuadr.pdf)

  A quadrant diagram is a method to determine which solution best meets two goals at once, such as low cost and high benefit.

WHAT ARE THE GAPS? AND WHAT ARE THE ROOT CAUSES OF THE GAPS?

201

Analyzing the Data:
How Can We Get to Where We Want to Be?

We know the gaps in Big River's student achievement results, and we have a better idea of the contributing causes to the root causes. So now, *How can we get to where we want to be?* The answer to this question is the key to unlocking how the gaps will be eliminated. An action plan consisting of strategies, actions, person(s) responsible, due dates, timelines, and resources needs to be created to eliminate the root causes of the gaps.

Action plans need to clarify how decisions will be made, identify professional learning required for staffs to learn new skills and gain new knowledge, and incorporate the use of partners, such as parent, businesses, and the community, to achieve the vision, and spell-out how all parts of the plan will be evaluated. A school's leadership structure, professional development strategies, and partnership development plan are important components of the answer to the question, *How can we get to where we want to be?*

This chapter shows how Big River High School created a school improvement plan, using the data gathered and analyzed, to close their gaps and improve all student learning.

Our Example School: Big River High School
How Can We Get to Where We Want to Be?

The Big River Vision

The data (demographics, student learning, the *Continuous Improvement Continuums*, questionnaires, and gap analysis) showed Big River staff members that they needed to revisit their vision. The following are the *Guiding Principles*, core values and beliefs, purpose, mission, and vision that staff members created in the spring before implementing their plan that would commence in the fall of 2004. (BRVision.pdf)

Big River High School
Guiding Principles, May 2004

Core Values and Beliefs about what supports effective learning for Big River High School students.

Values and Beliefs

▼ We believe all students can learn. We need to find out student learning styles and interests, and teach to them.

▼ We believe parents, businesses, and the community are important to students' learning.

▼ We believe that using data will help us prevent student failures and ensure student success.

▼ Standards—essential standards for each content area must be determined, taught consistently within subject areas and across grade levels, and monitored.

▼ Variety of instruction—instruction should be engaging to the students, relevant, and meet the needs of all students, regardless of their backgrounds. Whenever possible, instruction should be project-based or hands-on and include an element of student choice.

▼ Variety of assessments—ongoing and consistent standards-based assessments and benchmarks are needed to know how students are doing all along the way and to calibrate the curriculum and instruction.

▼ Preparation for the state assessment—we have to show students, in all ways, that we believe the state assessment is important. We also have to prepare ourselves and the students for the assessment.

▼ The instruction and curriculum should prepare our students for all post-secondary paths and use real-world examples. The curriculum should be interesting, challenging, and rigorous, while practical for postsecondary life.

▼ Guidance/placement are important in helping teachers prepare all students for the next level of learning.

▼ Teachers must care for students and establish rapport with each and every student they have.

▼ Teachers, students, and parents need to be held accountable for student learning.

▼ Teachers must support each other to do the best job possible for all students. The climate of the school should be collaborative and about doing our best for the students.

A school's guiding principles will focus all staff in the same direction.

Purpose

Prepare students for the future.

Mission

*The mission of Big River High School is
to prepare our students to become productive citizens
with 21st century skills.*

Vision

Curriculum

▼ Interesting, exciting, relevant, and practical for postsecondary life,
varied, challenging, real-world, standards-based, flexible/changing
over time

▼ Meets the needs of all student cultural and socio-economic
backgrounds

▼ Responsive to student academic needs

▼ Standards-based

Instruction

▼ Relates to future goals of students

▼ Diverse, but consistent

▼ Standards-based

▼ Emphasis on motivating students to learn for the future

▼ In partnership with local businesses, universities, and community
organizations to keep content real-world and related to future goals

▼ Reaches all types of learners

▼ Engaging (interesting, exciting, fun)

▼ Interactive (hands-on, project-based, technology based)

▼ Varied, based on standards, benchmarks, and ongoing assessments

Assessment

▼ Varied, ongoing, and consistent standards-based assessments
and benchmarks

▼ Will prepare students for the state assessment

▼ Authentic, understood by students

▼ Student-parent-teacher conferences to report progress

Environment

▼ Safe and caring for students and teachers

▼ Personalized, with positive student-teacher rapport

▼ Values all students

▼ Positive attitude towards success

▼ Teachers supporting other teachers and collaborating to ensure learning for students

▼ Involves parents/educating parents in how to help their children learn

▼ Involves community members

▼ Happy, friendly place

Big River Vision Narrative

When the vision of Big River High School is implemented, one will see students of all ethnicities and socio-economic backgrounds working together on projects related to standards-based instruction and curriculum. All students are actively involved in learning. Students feel safe at this school and want to be present to learn. Teachers feel safe to experiment with instructional strategies and practical ways to meet the needs of all students and to prepare them to be productive citizens for the future world.

Teachers know what students know and are able to do in each content area as they start the year. Teachers and students know that teachers care for students and truly believe that all students can learn. Teachers and students also know the essential standards for each content area and that students will have many opportunities to demonstrate what they know.

Teachers form *Professional Learning Communities* and meet at least once a week to study student data and student work, and to share best practices and lessons. In addition, time is also allotted to observe and coach each other to encourage high quality teaching.

The School Improvement Plan

Big River's staff members determined that they had only one goal—

Our only goal is for all Big River High School students to reach Proficiency or Advanced in all the core subject areas, by 2013-14.

And to this end, there are three objectives:

Objective 1: *By the end of 2005, all teachers will be implementing the state content standards in their classrooms, as measured through classroom observations, standards implementation tools, lesson plans, and HSST results.*

Objective 2: *Staff will continuously improve the learning organization, as measured by the Continuous Improvement Continuums assessments, questionnaire results, the AYP, and HSST results.*

Objective 3: *Staff, students, parents, businesses, and the community will become actively involved in students' learning, as measured by questionnaire and HSST results.*

Staffs' review of data indicated that they had a long way to go with many students. Staff looked for pathways to improvement by reviewing the research on performance improvement, the implications for school improvement that came from their data analysis study, and by committing to improvement.

Staff members acknowledged that they needed—

1. *Instructional coherence*—to have all teachers teaching to the state standards and creating a continuum of learning for all students.

2. *A shared vision for school improvement*—staff members were glad they took the time to revisit their vision and committed Monday afternoon so all staff members could and would commit to teaching consistencies and school improvement.

3. *Data-driven decision making*—at all points along the way, staff members would gather data to know if they are making progress with moving all students to proficiency in all subject areas. It is no longer an option not to use data, and not to know if all students are learning as the year progresses.

Staff created a plan from the data analysis and the vision. The first draft of the *Big River School Plan* is shown in Figure 8.1. (SchlPlan.pdf)

Big River High School Plan for Improvement, 2004-05

Our Only Goal: *All students will reach proficiency or advanced in all the core subject areas, by 2013-14.*

Profiency 2003-04

Grade Nine	Grade Ten
English Language Arts: 46%	English Language Arts: 39%
Mathematics: 16%	Mathematics: 12%

Grade Eleven
English Language Arts: 42%
Mathematics: 16%

Objectives:

▼ By the end of 2005, all teachers will be implementing the state content standards in their classrooms, as measured through classroom observations, standards implementation tools, lesson plans, and HSST results.

▼ Staff will continuously improve the learning organization, as measured the *Continuous Improvement Continuum* assessments, questionnaire results, the AYP, and HSST results.

▼ Staff, students, parents, businesses, and the community will become actively involved in students' learning, as measured by questionnaire and HSST results.

Figure 8.1

Strategy/Action	Person Responsible	Measurement	Resources Needed	Due Date	Aug	Sept	Oct	Nov	Dec	Jan	Feb	Mar	Apr	May	Jun	Jul
I. By the end of 2005, all teachers will be implementing the state content standards in their classrooms, as measured through classroom observations, standards implementation tools, lesson plans, and HSST results.																
Make sure every teacher has knowledge of the state content standards and what it would look like, sound like, feel like if the standards are being implemented.																
♦ Make sure all teachers know the standards for their grade levels and content areas and the grades that precede and follow their grades.	Leadership Team Content Area Chairs Principal	Professional Learning Plan Lesson Plans EFF Standards Questionnaire, given and analyzed	Support with questionnaire administration and analysis	October 2004	X	X	X									
♦ Create and use a Professional Learning Plan— one that will provide teachers with focused professional learning that will deepen their content knowledge and their ability to provide instruction and assessment so all students can meet high academic standards.	Leadership Instructional Coaches	Development of Professional Learning Calendar	Time and materials	Ongoing	X	X	X	X	X	X	X	X	X	X		
Identify essential standards by content areas and grade levels.																
♦ Identify essential standards by content areas and grade levels.	Teachers Content and Grade Chairs	Minutes of Monday Team meetings, attendance records	Standards for all teachers, release time	October 2004	X	X	X									
♦ Make sure all students and parents know the standards.	Teachers	Lesson plans that include standards		Ongoing	X	X	X	X	X	X	X	X	X	X		
♦ Post essential standards on the website and in newsletters, in documents to feeder schools, and in classrooms.	Webmaster Content and Grade Chairs Principal	Standards posted on school website, in classrooms, included in newsletters home		Ongoing		X	X	X	X	X	X	X	X			
♦ Utilize student work to calibrate the implementation of the standards in each content area and to find (look for) problems.	Teachers Content and Grade Chairs	Assessment and calibration of student work	Student work protocol	Three times during the year		X			X				X			

HOW CAN WE GET TO WHERE WE WANT TO BE?

Big River High School Plan for Improvement, 2004-05 *(Continued)*

Strategy/Action	Person Responsible	Measurement	Resources Needed	Due Date	Aug	Sept	Oct	Nov	Dec	Jan	Feb	Mar	Apr	May	Jun	Jul
I. By the end of 2005, all teachers will be implementing the state content standards in their classrooms, as measured through classroom observations, standards implementation tools, lesson plans, and HSST results. *(Continued)*																
◆ Use ongoing assessments, including diagnostics at the beginning of the year, to identify students progress toward mastery.	Teachers Content and Grade Chairs	Lesson plans that include assessments; actual assessments	Assessment	Quarterly		X			X			X			X	
Make sure all teachers are implementing the state content standards across the curriculum.																
◆ Use ongoing reflection activities that will assess the degree to which teachers are implementing the vision and standards.	Content and Grade Chairs	Reflection activities completed by all teachers	Reflection model or format agreed on by teachers	Monthly		X	X	X	X	X	X	X	X	X	X	
◆ Share *Best Practices* in staff and Monday team meetings (teachers sharing research and how they have learned to enjoy teaching the essential standards and seeing success).	Content and Grade Chairs	Minutes of Monday meetings Notes/Handouts Attendance	Professional journals, teacher success stories	Monthly		X	X	X	X	X	X	X	X	X	X	
◆ Teachers demonstrate lessons so each teacher knows what it will look like, sound like, feel like when she/he is teaching to the standards.	Content and Grade Chairs	Demonstration lessons, peer observation	Documentation of demonstration lessons in a resource book	Monthly		X	X	X	X	X	X	X	X	X	X	
◆ Conduct observations using the Classroom Observation Tool (COF) so teachers know how to improve their implementation of the standards.	Content and Grade Chairs Principal	Classroom Observation Tool is used	System to allow for peer observations Substitutes	Monthly		X	X	X	X	X	X	X	X	X	X	
◆ Use peer coaching to support the implementation of the standards and the COF in every classroom.	Content and Grade Chairs	Classroom Observation Tool is used	System to allow for peer observations Substitutes	Monthly		X	X	X	X	X	X	X	X	X	X	
Make sure all teachers know how to meet the needs of a diverse population of students.																
◆ Provide professional learning to assist teachers in meeting the needs of students who live in poverty and /or with diverse backgrounds through differentiating instruction and project-based learning	Content and Grade Chairs Leadership	Minutes, notes, handouts from professional learning activities	Journals, books, articles	Ongoing	X	X	X	X	X	X	X	X	X	X	X	
◆ Assess the degree to which the professional learning is being implemented in the classroom.	Content and Grade Chairs Leadership	Classroom Observation Tool HSST results		Ongoing	X	X	X	X	X	X	X	X	X	X	X	
◆ Assess student learning styles and teaching style preferences of teachers.	Technology Coordinator	Completion of Inventories Evidence of use of results	Inventories	October 2004			X									

Figure 8.1 *(Continued)*

Big River High School Plan for Improvement, 2004-05 *(Continued)*

Strategy/Action	Person Responsible	Measurement	Resources Needed	Due Date	Timeline Aug	Sept	Oct	Nov	Dec	Jan	Feb	Mar	Apr	May	Jun	Jul
II. Staff will continuously improve the learning organization, as measured by comprehensive data anlaysis, including demographic analysis process assessment, the *Continuous Improvement Continuums* assessments, questionnaire results, the AYP, and HSST results.																
◆ Assess progress using the *Education for the Future Continuous Improvement Continuums* to determine progress.	Principal	Results reflected in a report	Outside Facilitator Time	September 2004		X										
◆ Administer student, staff, and parent questionnaires.	Technology Coordinator	Completion of questionnaires	Time	October 2004			X									
◆ Conduct a comprehensive data analysis.	Data Team Chair	Comprehensive data profile	Stipends	Summer work August Report	X											X
◆ Administer exit and alumni questionnaires and interviews	School Counselors	Completion of questionnaires and interviews		Alumni— October 2004 Exit—Ongoing		X	X	X	X	X	X	X	X	X		
◆ Follow up on— • Dropouts • Number of students going to college and how they do • Students who took jobs after graduation • Graduation rates • Charter and private school transfers	School Counselors	Report of findings	Time	September report for previous years		X										
◆ Conduct evaluation of dropout prevention programs.	School Counselors	Report of findings	Time	September report for previous years	X	X										X
◆ Ensure teachers are highly qualified.	Assistant Principal– Human Resources	Professional learning plans of teachers		Ongoing	X	X	X	X	X	X	X	X	X	X	X	

Figure 8.1 *(Continued)*

Big River High School Plan for Improvement, 2004-05 *(Continued)*

Strategy/Action	Person Responsible	Measurement	Resources Needed	Due Date	Timeline											
					Aug	Sept	Oct	Nov	Dec	Jan	Feb	Mar	Apr	May	Jun	Jul
III. Staff, students, parents, businesses, and the community will become actively involved in students' learning, as measured by questionnaire and HSST results.																
♦ Establish partnership plan for real partnerships with parents, feeder schools, universities, businesses, and the community to help students meet the standards and mission of Big River High School, and to make the school relevant through— • Service learning • Career awareness • Internships • Senior projects • Joint programs and course work • Student led conferences • Communication with parents about how parents can help	Assistant Principal for Curriculum	Plan is completed	Time	January 2005		X	X	X	X	X						
♦ Collaborate and calibrate standards implementation with feeder schools through— • Regular meetings to discuss standards and review student work and data, and share best practices • Align curriculum	Principal	Meetings occur HSST results improve	Meeting supplies	Monthly				X	X	X	X	X	X	X	X	
♦ Outreach to families.	School Counselors Principal	Materials, meeting minutes		Monthly				X	X	X	X	X	X	X		

Figure 8.1 (Continued)

The 2004-05 plan is a simple one designed to get all teachers teaching to the standards and implementing meaningful instructional practices to meet the needs of all learners. Teaching style and learning style inventories will be given to all teachers and students, respectively.

The action plan includes strategies for ensuring that the shared vision is implemented in every classroom. It includes strategies for ensuring the alignment of curriculum to the standards, as well as ensuring a continuum of learning within and across grade levels and content areas. Content area chairs are responsible for the standards implementation of their content areas. Staff will meet during early release Mondays every week, and will be coached and observed by colleagues and administration.

Content-area chairs and the principal will work closely with feeder elementary and middle school leaders about grade level expectations and subject matter readiness.

Integrated throughout the plan is the reliance on data to drive decisions. Data will be used to assess school processes and the system itself, standards implementation, student needs, and the results.

Partnerships with businesses, parents, universities, feeder schools, and the community will help Big River staff members meet the learning needs of students while they are achieving the mission of the school.

By the end of 2004-05, curriculum, instruction, and assessment will be aligned to essential content standards, and communication and collaboration will be at an all-time high. At the end of the year, staff members will reassess where they need to go next to implement the vision. The end result will be student achievement increases.

Implementing the Plan: The Leadership Structure

It is hard to create a comprehensive plan—no doubt. Making sure everyone on staff implements the plan in the manner intended is even harder. A leadership structure can ensure that a plan is truly implemented. Staff members knew that the Big River High School leadership structure must look like the vision and help them implement that shared vision and the state content standards.

The *Big River High School School Leadership Structure* emerged from the plan. (LeadPlan.pdf) The leadership structure and a narrative follow. The leadership structure focuses on the effective use of the Monday afternoon early release time staff has with each other.

Big River Leadership Structure, 2004-05

The Big River High School Leadership Structure emerged from the School Improvement Plan. (This information is in the plan; it has been extracted from the plan to clarify roles, responsibilities, and meeting times.) Big River staff is committed to the leadership structure, and to the meeting times, roles, and responsibilities.

Meeting Times for Staff

Big River staff was adamant about establishing early release time on Mondays to meet as a staff to ensure teaching to standards and the vision, and to participate in professional learning. The leadership team will meet additionally on the first and the third Wednesday of each month. The focus for 2004-05 is *standards*—learning them, implementing, assessing, and understanding the impact of teaching to them. Since our release time is 2 hours and 15 minutes long, an agenda will be provided by e-mail before each meeting. The dates and times are as follows:

Day	Time	Teams
1st Wednesday	3:45 to 5:00 PM	Leadership
1st Monday	1:30 to 3:45 PM	Content Areas by Grade Level
2nd Monday	1:30 to 3:45 PM	Cross-grade Level by Content
3rd Monday	1:30 to 3:45 PM	Content Areas by Grade Level
3rd Wednesday	3:45 to 5:00 PM	Leadership
4th Monday	1:30 to 3:45 PM	Cross-grade Level by Content
5th Monday	1:30 to 3:45 PM	All Staff

Roles and Responsibilities

It is each staff member's responsibility to implement the standards in her/his classroom. All staff members will meet in content area teams by grade level, cross-grade level content-area teams, with and without feeder school involvement, or as a full staff every week to further refine the implementation of the standards in each classroom. In addition, some staff members will participate on the leadership team. The roles and responsibilities of each team are defined below.

Content Area by Grade-level Teams

The purposes of content area by grade level teams are to maintain unity of curriculum, instruction, assessment, and to align and implement the standards in each content area within each grade level.

▼ Every teacher will participate in meetings with content area and grade-level colleagues.

▼ Teachers will coach and support the implementation of the standards and the vision in each other's classrooms.

▼ The content area by grade-level teams will advise the leadership team of progress and concerns of implementing standards by content area and grade level.

▼ Teachers will study and support each other's implementation of best practices.

▼ Support staff will be assigned to appropriate content-area teams.

▼ Each chairperson is responsible for ensuring the implementation of the plan.

Cross-grade Level by Content Teams

The purposes of the cross-grade-level teams are to maintain unity of curriculum, instruction, and assessment in each content area, specifically to:

▼ improve instruction and student achievement results schoolwide.

▼ ensure the implementation of standards within content areas and across the grade levels.

▼ advise the leadership team of progress and concerns of content area and cross-grade-level team meetings.

▼ advise the leadership team of progress and concerns of implementing the standards and assessments.

▼ coach and support the quality implementation of content areas.

- ▼ demonstrate the implementation of content standards for teachers in each subject area.

- ▼ review data and plan for improvement.

- ▼ disseminate content information from the school, district, state, and federal government.

Purposes of the Content Level by Grade Level and Cross-grade-level Content Meetings

The purposes of the content level by grade level and cross-grade-level content meetings include:

- ▼ review and clarify standards.

- ▼ discuss and implement the state-content standards.

- ▼ support the implementation of the standards in every classroom.

- ▼ share best practices.

- ▼ share examples.

- ▼ review data (student learning, questionnaire, demographics, school process, student learning style preferences).

- ▼ review and discuss student work.

- ▼ assess student work related to the standards.

- ▼ map the curriculum.

- ▼ help teachers format classroom tests to resemble the state assessment.

Leadership Team

The leadership team will meet on the first and third Wednesday of each month from 3:45 to 5:00, and other times as necessary. The purposes of the leadership team are to:

- ▼ improve instruction and student achievement results schoolwide.

- ▼ guide, enforce, and reinforce the school plan and vision.

- ▼ assist with the development of agendas for the grade-level and cross-grade-level meetings.

- ▼ ensure the implementation of standards and the vision within and across the grade levels.

- ▼ monitor progress and address concerns.

- ▼ be a resource for the implementation of standards and the school vision.

- ▼ review data and plan for improvement.

- ▼ disseminate content information from the district, state, and federal government.

- ▼ trouble-shoot the concerns of teams.

- ▼ enable others to act and model the way.

- ▼ encourage the heart.

All Staff

Whenever there is a fifth Wednesday of the month, staff will meet as a whole to celebrate and/or to assess progress. The leadership team will determine from staff what the celebrations will include.

Implementing the Plan:
The Professional Learning Calendar

The *Professional Learning Calendar* that reinforces the *Leadership Structure* and overall plan can help staff know if the plan is possible and what adjustments are necessary. It also serves as a document of commitment. It is one thing to see the activities in a plan; it is another thing to see the activities listed in chronological order, with the time commitments and expectations clearly laid out. Below is *Big River's Professional Learning Calendar for Fall 2004* (Figure 8.2), extracted from the overall plan (Figure 8.1). (PrDevCal.pdf)

Also on the CD is a table of *Powerful Professional Development Designs* and a folder of activities related to these designs. (Designs.pdf and Powerful Professional Development Designs Folder) Most school improvement plans that get implemented include at least thirty *Powerful Professional Development Designs* to assist with implementation.

Figure 8.2

Big River High School Professional Learning Calendar

Fall 2004		
Date	**Type of Meeting**	**Topics**
August 30 1:30 to 3:45 PM	All Staff	Set policies and continuous improvement processes in place for the year. Review the comprehensive data analysis from last year. Identify areas of concern to watch throughout the year.
September 1 3:45 to 5:00 PM	Leadership Team	Follow-up on the data analysis results from last year. Determine strategies for improvement. Review Classroom Observation Tool and develop strategies to share it with full staff.
September 6 1:30 to 3:45 PM	Content Areas by Grade Level	Ensure that every teacher knows the standards, and begin identifying essential content standards for each grade level and content area. Review student diagnostic assessments in the context of the standards.
September 13 1:30 to 3:45 PM	Cross-grade Level by Content	Continue identifying essential content standards for each grade level and content area, making sure the standards fall into place across grade levels.
September 15 3:45 to 5:00 PM	Leadership Team	Determine where each content area and grade level is with respect to identifying essential content standards. Suggest an agenda for next meetings.
September 20 1:30 to 3:45 PM	Content Areas by Grade Level	Continue identifying essential content standards for each grade level and content area. Align the curriculum and assessments to these standards. Develop lessons that focus on the standards. Share best practices and demonstration lessons.
September 27 1:30 to 3:45 PM	Cross-Grade Level by Content	Continue identifying essential content standards for each grade level and content area, making sure the standards fall into place across grade levels. Align the curriculum and assessments to these standards. Develop lessons that focus on the standards. Share best practices and demonstration lessons.
October 4 1:30 to 3:45 PM	Content Areas by Grade Level	Continue identifying essential content standards for each grade level and content area. Align curriculum and assessments to these standards. Develop lessons that focus on the standards. Determine who would like to have demonstration lessons in their classrooms.
October 6 3:45 to 5:00 PM	Leadership Team	Setup schedule for peer observations.
October 11 Professional Learning All Day	All Staff	Professional learning with nationally known facilitator. Topic: *Reaching students with diverse backgrounds through differentiating instruction and project-based learning.*
October 18 1:30 to 3:45 PM	Content Areas by Grade Level	Share what we are learning via classroom observations and peer coaching, with respect to implementing standards, differentiating instruction, and assessments. Keep refining lessons. Establish anchor papers for reviewing student work.
October 20 3:45 to 5:00 PM	Leadership Team	Review where each content area and grade level is with respect to identifying essential content standards—anyone need a little extra help? Are standards clearly posted?
October 25 1:30 to 3:45 PM	Cross-grade Level by Content	Review student work and calibrate the curriculum and essential standards.
November 1 1:30 to 3:45 PM	Content Areas by Grade Level	Continue calibrating the curriculum, essential standards, and lessons after the review of student work.
November 3 3:45 to 5:00 PM	Leadership Team	Create the agenda to review student work at the next cross-grade level by content meeting.
November 8 1:30 to 3:45 PM	Cross-grade Level by Content	Evaluate student work review and curriculum calibration; plan any necessary adjustments.
November 15 1:30 to 3:45 PM	Content Areas by Grade Level	Evaluate student work review and curriculum calibration; plan any necessary adjustments.
November 17 3:45 to 5:00 PM	Leadership Team	Make recommendations for the next cross-grade level by content on the basis of the content areas by grade-level meeting and classroom observations.
November 22 1:30 to 3:45 PM	Cross-grade Level by Content	Review student work; prepare to share process with full staff.
November 29 1:30 to 3:45 PM	All Staff	Stories of successful plans or those that need to be reworked in order to be successful in using project-based learning to differentiate instruction. Each grade level/content area responsible for at least one presentation.
December 1 3:45 to 5:00 PM	Leadership Team	Plan for getting staff ready to assess on the standards.
December 6 1:30 to 3:45 PM	Content Areas by Grade Level	Review results of the assessment by grade level and content area.
December 13 1:30 to 3:45 PM	Cross-grade Level by Content	Review results of the assessment across grade levels within content areas.
December 15 3:45 to 5:00 PM	Leadership Team	Establish plan for second semester.

In addition to the leadership structure and professional development calendar, a *Classroom Observation Tool* was created for assessing where each teacher is in implementing the state-content standards and vision. Staff knows the tool will evolve over time. The first draft of this tool follows as Figure 8.3. 🌀 (ObvTool.pdf)

Figure 8.3

Classroom Observation Tool Related to the Big River High School Vision

Teacher: _____ Class/Grade Level: _____

Class Period/Time of Day: _____ Topic: _____

Observer: _____ Date: _____

Number of Students: _____ Male _____ Female

General description of the room:
(seating arrangement, activities/learning areas, standards in view, bulletin boards, walls, etc.)

_____

_____

_____

Introductory activities:
How did the teacher introduce lesson/activity; was students' prior knowledge assessed?

_____

_____

_____

Succeeding activities:
What did the teacher do?

_____

_____

_____

What did the students do?

_____

_____

_____

What types of questions were asked? What types of responses were given? Was appropriate corrective feedback given after incorrect student responses?

_____

_____

_____

What types of teaching strategies were evident, i.e., student-centered learning, lecture, discussion, checking for understanding, guided practice, adapting instruction to student learning styles, pacing, cooperative learning, re-teaching, use of technology, closure?

_____

_____

_____

Figure 8.3 (Continued)

Classroom Observation Tool Related to the Big River High School Vision

Succeeding activities *(Continued)*:

How do teaching strategies address diversity within the classroom?

_____

_____

_____

What types of materials/resources were used? Did they support the instructional goals?

_____

_____

_____

Were standards of behavior in place, posted, and enforced consistently and fairly?

_____

_____

_____

Were routines and procedures in place, posted, and followed by the students?

_____

_____

_____

What types of assessments were evident? Did students receive frequent and appropriate assessment feedback so they could make adjustments on their own?

_____

_____

_____

Was respect among students and students, students and teacher evident?

_____

_____

_____

Did the teacher communicate positively with all students and indicate a belief that all students can meet the standards?

_____

_____

_____

Additional Comments:

_____

_____

_____

For discussion following the observation:

What strategies does the teacher use to work cooperatively with parents/guardians to help the students?

_____

_____

_____

How does the teacher work with colleagues to ensure student learning?

_____

_____

_____

Created by Joy Rose, Retired Principal, Westerville South High School, Westerville, Ohio

Implementing the Plan: The Partnership Plan

Similar to the leadership structure and professional learning calendar, a partnership plan can be extracted from the overall plan and needs to be reflected in the overall plan. 🔘 (PartPlan.pdf)

Big River did not have an official plan for partnerships. Big River staff and students like partnerships with businesses and the community, but have not actively sought *meaningful* partnerships. Staff would like stronger bonds with parents as well. During their creation of the school mission and vision, staff members committed to creating meaningful partnerships with parents, community, and business. The major intention with partnerships is to make learning more fun and relevant for the students, and as another way for students to meet the content standards. Staff members established a partnership team to create a partnership plan for the school by January 2005. Staff took a few moments to brainstorm what they wanted their partnership with parents, businesses, and the community to achieve and came up with these guidelines for the partnership team:

▼ Partnerships need to be a two-way street: both parties must contribute and both parties must benefit.

▼ Partnerships should include:
  ◆ career awareness.
  ◆ internships.
  ◆ mentoring.
  ◆ service learning.
  ◆ giving back to the community.
  ◆ learning standards in use.
  ◆ field trips/exposure.
  ◆ meeting a shortage or need; for example, our community has a teacher shortage, especially minority teachers. Perhaps a Future Teacher of America chapter could be established, along with tutoring in the middle and elementary schools, mentoring with feeder school students, or even the students in Big River.
  ◆ parents as learners.
  ◆ celebrations to honor and thank our partners for their contributions.
  ◆ evaluation of effectiveness and for continuous improvement.

▼ The school should provide opportunities for community members to volunteer—let them know how they can volunteer—use the *Partnership Evaluation Questionnaire* on the CD. 🔘 (PaEvalQ.pdf)

- ▼ The partnership team needs to develop a list of parents/guardians and community members who are willing to volunteer and/or provide their expertise as guest speakers for classes.

- ▼ Teachers need to let potential partners know when they would like support related to certain content standards.

- ▼ Teachers need to recognize alumni who have contributed or are contributing to the community.

- ▼ Partnerships need to help staff meet the mission and goal of the school.

- ▼ Partnerships should not be about:
  - ◆ money and stuff.
  - ◆ one-shot events/activities, unless there is a good reason.

Figure 8.4 is the *Big River High School Partnership Evaluation Questionnaire.* (PaEvalQ.pdf)

Figure 8.4

Education for the Future   **Partnership Evaluation**

The purpose of our partnership with your company/organization is to enhance students' attainment of learning standards. We would like to understand your role in the partnership, your perceptions of the impact of the partnership, and your satisfaction with our partnership program. Please complete the following questionnaire to the best of your ability.

	Not Clear	Minimally Clear	Somewhat Clear	Clear	Very Clear
1. How clear were the outcomes of the partnership?	①	②	③	④	⑤
2. How clearly did the partnership meet these outcomes?	①	②	③	④	⑤

3. What was your role in the partnership? _____
_____

4. With which grade level and content areas did you partner? _____
_____

What did you do and how satisfied were you with the partnership?

Grade Level	What You Did	Not Satisfied	Minimally Satisfied	Somewhat Satisfied	Satisfied	Very Satisfied
_____	_____	①	②	③	④	⑤
_____	_____	①	②	③	④	⑤
_____	_____	①	②	③	④	⑤
_____	_____	①	②	③	④	⑤

Comments: _____
_____
_____

5. What do you see as the benefits of this partnership to you and your company/organization?
_____
_____

6. What do you see as the benefits of this partnership to the students and to the school?
_____
_____

7. How could this partnership be improved?
_____
_____

8. Other Comments:
_____
_____
_____
_____

*Thank you for your time to partner, to improve our students' learning,
and for your time to complete this questionnaire.*

Evaluating the Plan

Also in the *Big River High School Action Plan* is a column indicating how strategies and activities will be monitored and evaluated. By condensing the measurement column into a comprehensive evaluation plan (Figure 8.5), the persons responsible for the measurement of the plan can see the overall evaluation and plan accordingly. (EvalPlan.pdf) If one looks only at the measurement of individual strategies and activities in isolation of each other, she/he could miss ways to efficiently measure the entire plan.

Figure 8.5

Big River High School Evaluation Plan

The first draft of the Big River High School Evaluation Plan is shown below. The evaluation of the Big River High School Improvement Plan is designed to measure adequate yearly progress (AYP) toward 100%.

Evaluation of the Plan

Big River's staff members determined that they had only one goal—

Our only goal is for all Big River High School students to reach Proficiency or Advanced in all the core subject areas, by 2013-14.

And to this end, there are three objectives—

Objective 1: *By the end of 2005, all teachers will be implementing the state content standards in their classrooms, as measured through classroom observations, standards implementation tools, lesson plans, and HSST results.*

Objective 2: *Staff will continuously improve the learning organization, as measured by the Continuous Improvement Continuums assessments, questionnaire results, the AYP, and HSST results.*

Objective 3: *Staff, students, parents, businesses, and the community will become actively involved in students' learning, as measured by questionnaire and HSST results.*

The gaps related to all students and subgroups meeting proficiency include:

Not proficient 2003-04, overall:

Grade Nine	*Grade Ten*	*Grade Eleven*
ELA: 54%	ELA: 61%	ELA: 58%
Math: 84%	Math: 88%	Math: 84%

Not proficient 2003-04, by subgroups:

Grade Nine ELA:

Black: 53%	Low SES: 74%
Asian: 43%	Special Education: 94%
White: 33%	Gifted: 12%
Hispanic: 68%	English Learner: 97%

Grade Nine Math:

Black: 87%	Low SES: 88%
Asian: 82%	Special Education: 95%
White: 73%	Gifted: 53%
Hispanic: 90%	English Learner: 98%

Grade Ten ELA:

Black: 100%	Low SES: 82%
Asian: 57%	Special Education: 94%
White: 38%	Gifted: 17%
Hispanic: 74%	English Learner: 97%

Grade Ten Math:

Black: 100%	Low SES: 93%
Asian: 84%	Special Education: 100%
White: 81%	Gifted: 69%
Hispanic: 92%	English Learner: 97%

Grade Eleven ELA:

Black: 86%	Low SES: 78%
Asian: 25%	Special Education: 93%
White: 31%	Gifted: 18%
Hispanic: 78%	English Learner: 98%

Grade Eleven Math:

Black: 100%	Low SES: 91%
Asian: 71%	Special Education: 93%
White: 70%	Gifted: 68%
Hispanic: 94%	English Learner: 97%

Figure 8.5 (Continued)

Big River High School Evaluation Plan

To meet the requirements of *No Child Left Behind,* Big River will move 9% of its students from non-proficient to proficient each year, as measured by the HSST.

Objective 1: *By the end of 2005, all teachers will be implementing the state content standards in their classrooms, as measured through classroom observations, standards implementation tools, lesson plans, and HSST results.*

The degree to which teachers implement the vision and the standards will be measured as follows:

- Each teacher will receive positive feedback with respect to implementing the vision and the standards by the end of the 2004-05 school year, as measured by the *Big River Classroom Observation Tool.*

- Minutes of content area by grade-level teams, cross-grade level by content teams, and leadership team meetings will show productive discussions and activities related to implementing the standards and the vision. The minutes will also show that teachers are in attendance at their respective meetings. Teachers' lesson plans will show the implementation of the standards and the vision.

- The standards implementation questionnaire will show all teachers knowing the standards and knowing how to teach to and assess the standards by the end of the 2004-05 school year.

- Student work will show what students know and are able to do.

- Principal's classroom observations will show that teachers know the standards and are implementing the standards and the vision.

- Principal's classroom observations will show that students know what they are supposed to be learning and are learning these things.

- All teachers will be in attendance at all professional learning sessions.

- All teachers will observe demonstration lessons provided by colleagues and will demonstrate at least one lesson that incorporates standards during 2004-05.

- All teachers will participate in peer coaching to implement the standards.

- Student scores on the HSST will improve because of teachers' focus on content standards.

Objective 2: *Staff will continuously improve the learning organization, as measured by the Continuous Improvement Continuums assessments, questionnaire results, the AYP, and HSST results.*

- The school will improve from the baseline assessment on the *Education for the Future Continuous Improvement Continuums* at least one level in all areas by June 2005.

- The *Education for the Future* staff questionnaire will show, by the end of school year 2004-05, that all staff agree there is a shared vision, one plan to get to the shared vision, strong communication, and an effective leadership structure. The staff questionnaire will also show that teachers believe teaching to the state-content standards will increase student learning.

- The *Education for the Future* student questionnaire will show that students feel teachers care about them, that school is fun, and that they are learning a lot. The questionnaire will also indicate that students know what they are supposed to be learning, that they are challenged by the work, and are trying as hard as they can to learn.

- The *Education for the Future* parent questionnaire will show that parents feel welcome at the school, that they know about their child's progress, that school-home communications are effective, and that they know what they can do to help their children learn at home.

- Student achievement results will improve in part because the learning organization is healthy.

Figure 8.5 (Continued)

Big River High School Evaluation Plan

Objective 3: *Staff, students, parents, businesses, and the community will become actively involved in students' learning, as measured by questionnaire and HSST results.*

Evidence of partnership involvement and communication will be assessed as follows:

- Parents' perceptions of home-school communications will improve by Spring 2005, as measured by the *Education for the Future* parent questionnaire.

- The number of parents attending parent events at the school, such as *Back to School Night,* will be steady and high.

- The number of partners contributing will increase each year.

- Evaluations of partner events will be satisfactory, as measured by instruments developed to assess the quality of the event.

- Students will be delighted with the relevance of their learning because it takes place in the community, as measured by the student questionnaire.

- Parents, community, and businesses feel that they are contributing and benefiting from their involvement with Big River High School, as measured by the partnership evaluation instrument.

- Ultimately, student learning, as measured by HSST, will increase because of partner involvement.

Summary

With the strengths, challenges, gap analyses, and root cause analyses complete, one can integrate findings to create a continuous school improvement plan that is informed by the data and a school vision, and that will lead to student achievement increases. A continuous school improvement plan that is based on quality data can eliminate root causes. Identifying and then eliminating the root causes of the gaps in student achievement by using the data will almost surely guarantee student learning increases.

A continuous school improvement plan includes objectives for reaching the school goals, strategies, and actions to achieve the objectives, person responsible, how each strategy and action will be measured, resources needed, due date, and timeline.

From the overall continuous school improvement plan, one can pull out a leadership structure, evaluation plan, professional development schedule/plan, and even a partnership plan that will reinforce roles, responsibilities, meeting times, and the overall approach to continuous improvement and evaluation.

> *A continuous school improvement plan includes objectives for reaching the school goals, strategies, and actions to achieve the objectives, person responsible, how each strategy and action will be measured, resources needed, due date, and timeline.*

On the CD Related to this Chapter

▼ *Big River Shared Vision* (BRVision.pdf)
This read-only file is the first draft of the *Big River Guiding Principles and Shared Vision,* shown on pages 205-207 in Chapter 8.

▼ *Big River School Plan for Improvement* (SchlPlan.pdf)
This read-only file is the first draft of the *Big River High School Plan* and is shown as Figure 8.1 in Chapter 8.

▼ *Planning Template* (APForm.doc)
A quality action plan to implement the vision consists of goals, objectives, strategies, actions, persons responsible, resources required, due dates, and timelines. A template with these components is provided in *Microsoft Word,* ready to be completed.

▼ *Big River Leadership Structure* (LeadPlan.pdf)
This read-only file is the Big River Leadership Structure, created from the overall action plan, and is shown on pages 214-217 in Chapter 8.

▼ *Big River Professional Learning Calendar* (PrDevCal.pdf)
This read-only file Big River's 2004-05 Fall/Winter Calendar, also shown as Figure 8.2 in Chapter 8.

▼ *Professional Learning Calendar Template* (PrDevCal.doc)
This *Microsoft Word* document is a template for creating your school Professional Learning Calendar.

▼ *Classroom Observation Tool* (ObvTool.pdf)

This read-only file is the first draft of the *Big River Classroom Observation Tool,* created for assessing where each teacher is in implementing the state-content standards and vision, and shown as Figure 8.3 in Chapter 8.

▼ *Big River Partnership Plan* (PartPlan.pdf)

This read-only file is the *Big River Partnership Plan,* created from the overall action plan, and is shown on pages 222-223 in Chapter 8.

▼ *Establishing a Partnership Plan* (EstPPlan.pdf)

This read-only file describes the steps in creating a partnership plan that will become a part of the continuous school improvement plan.

▼ *Partnership Evaluation Questionnaire* (PaEvalQ.pdf)

This read-only file, the *Big River High School Partnership Evaluation Questionnaire,* is used to assess community members' role in the partnership, perceptions of the impact of the partnership, and satisfaction with the partnership program, and is shown as Figure 8.4 in Chapter 8.

▼ *Big River Evaluation Plan* (EvalPlan.pdf)

This read-only file, the *Big River Evaluation Plan,* condenses the measurement column of the action plan into a comprehensive evaluation plan, and is shown as Figure 8.5 in Chapter 8.

▼ *Evaluating a Program Activity* (ACTEval.pdf)

The purpose of this activity is to get many people involved in creating a comprehensive evaluation design to determine the impact of a program and to know how to improve the program.

▼ *Powerful Professional Development Designs* (Designs.pdf)

This read-only file describes numerous ways to embed professional development into the learning community.

▼ *Powerful Professional Development Designs Folder*

Powerful Professional Development Designs are those that are embedded into the daily operations of a staff. They are ongoing and lead to improvement of instruction and increases in student learning.

◆ *Action Research Activity* (ACTRsrch.pdf)

Teachers and/or administrators raise questions about the best way to improve teaching and learning, systematically study the literature to answer the questions, implement the best approach, and analyze the results.

◆ *Cadres or Action Teams Activity* (ACTCdres.pdf)

Organizing cadres or teams allows for the delegation of responsibilities so teams of educators can study new approaches, plan for the implementation of new strategies or programs, and get work done without every staff member's involvement.

- *Case Studies Activity* (ACTCases.pdf)

  Staff members review case studies of student work, and/or of another teacher's example lessons, which can lead to quality discussions and improved practices.

- *Coaching Activity* (ACTCoach.pdf)

  Teachers form teams of two or three to observe each other, plan together, and to talk and encourage each other in meaningful ways, while reflecting on continuously improving instructional practices.

- *Examining Student Data: Teacher Analysis of Test Scores Table One* (Table1.doc)

  Examining student data consists of conversations around individual student data results and the processes that created the results. This approach can be a significant form of professional development when skilled team members facilitate the dialogue.

- *Examining Student Work Activity* (ACTSWork.pdf)

  Examining student work as professional development ensures that what students learn is aligned to the learning standards. It also shows teachers the impact of their processes.

- *Example Lessons: Birds of a Feather Unit Example* (UnitEx.pdf)

  Some teachers need to see what a lesson that implements all aspects of the school vision would look like. Providing examples for all teachers to see can reward the teacher who is doing a good job of implementing the vision and provide a template for other teachers. It is very effective to store summary examples in a binder or on a website for everyone to peruse at any time.

- *Example Lessons: Unit Template* (UnitTmpl.doc)

  This *Microsoft Word* template provides the outline for creating instructional units that implement the vision.

- *Immersion Activity* (ACTImrsn.pdf)

  Immersion is a method for getting teachers engaged in different content through hands-on experiences as a learner.

- *Journaling Activity* (ACTJourn.pdf)

  Journal writing helps teachers construct meaning for, and reflect on, what they are teaching and learning.

- *Listening to Students Activity* (ACTListn.pdf)

  Students' perceptions of the learning environment are very important for continuous improvement. Focus groups, interviews, and questionnaires can be used to discover what students are perceiving.

- *Needs Assessment: Professional Development Needs Related to Technology Example* (TechnEx.pdf)
  Needs assessments help staff understand the professional development needs of staff. At the same time, if done well, this tool can lead to quality staff conversations and sharing of knowledge.

- *Needs Assessment: Professional Development Plan Related to Technology Template* (TechTmpl.doc)
  This template provides the outline for doing your own professional development needs assessment.

- *Networks Activity* (ACTNtwrk.pdf)
  Purposeful grouping of individuals/schools to further a cause or commitment.

- *Partnerships: Creating Partnerships Activity* (ACTParts.pdf)
  Teachers partnering with businesses in the community, scientists, and/or university professors can result in real-world applications for student learning and deeper understandings of content for the teacher.

- *Process Mapping: Charting School Processes Activity* (ACTProcs.pdf)
  School processes are instruction, curriculum, and assessment strategies used to ensure the learning of all students. Mapping or flowcharting school processes can help staff members objectively look at how students are being taught.

- *Reflection Log Activity* (ACTLog.pdf)
  Reflective logs are recordings of key events in the educators' work days to reflect on improvement and/or to share learnings with colleagues.

- *Scheduling Activity* (ACTSchdl.pdf)
  A real test for whether or not a vision is realistic is to have teachers develop a day's schedule. This will tell them immediately if it is doable, or what needs to change in the vision and plan to make it doable.

- *School Meetings: Running Efficient Meetings* (Meetings.pdf)
  Staff, department, grade level, and cross-grade level meetings can promote learning through study or sharing best practice, while focusing on the implementation of the vision.

- *Self-Assessment: Teacher Assessment Tool Related to the School Vision* (AssessEx.pdf)
  Staff self-assessments on tools to measure progress toward the vision, such as the *Continuous Improvement Continuums,* will help them see where their school is as a system and what needs to improve for better results.

- *Self-Assessment: Teacher Assessment Tool Related to Our School Vision Template* (AssessEx.doc)

  This template file for self-assessments on tools to measure progress toward the vision, such as the *Continuous Improvement Continuums,* will help teachers see where their school is as a system and what needs to improve for better results.

- *Self-Assessment: Our School Shared Vision Implementation Rubric Example* (StRubric.pdf)

  Self-assessments on tools to measure progress toward the vision, such as the *Continuous Improvement Continuums,* will help teachers see where their school is as a system and what needs to improve for better results.

- *Self-Assessment: Our School Shared Vision Implementation Rubric Template* (StRubric.doc)

  This template file for self-assessments on tools to measure progress toward the vision, such as the *Continuous Improvement Continuums,* will help teachers see where their school is as a system and what needs to improve for better results.

- *Self-Assessment: Staff-Developed Rubric Activity* (ACTRubric.pdf)

  This activity for self-assessments on tools to measure progress toward the vision, such as the *Continuous Improvement Continuums,* will help teachers see where their school is as a system and what needs to improve for better results.

- *Shadowing Students Activity* (ACTShadw.pdf)

  Purposefully following students and systematically recording the students' instructional experiences is a wonderful job-embedded approach to understanding what students are experiencing in school.

- *Storyboarding Activity* (ACTStory.pdf)

  Storyboarding is an activity that will allow participants to share previous knowledge, while reflecting on the topic. It is a structure for facilitating conversations.

- *Study Groups Activity* (ACTStudy.pdf)

  Groups of educators meet to learn new strategies and programs, to review new publications, or to review student work together.

- *Teacher Portfolio Activity* (ACTTcher.pdf)

  Teacher portfolios can be built to tell the story of implementing the vision in the classroom, and its impact on student learning. Portfolios are excellent for reflection, understanding, and showing progress. Portfolios can be used for many things including self-assessment, employment, supervision to replace traditional teacher evaluation, and peer collaboration.

- *Train the Trainers Activity* (ACTTrain.pdf)

  Train the Trainers is an approach to saving time and money. Individuals are trained and return to the school or school district with a commitment to train others.

- *Tuning Protocols Activity* (ACTTune.pdf)

  A tuning protocol is a formal process for reviewing, honoring, and fine tuning colleagues' work through presentation and reflection.

Analyzing the Data:
Conclusions and Recommendations

The main purpose of *Using Data to Improve Student Learning in High Schools* is to show analyses of a real high school's data, using a continuous school improvement planning model to understand, explain, and continuously improve learning for all students.

In this book, an analysis of data has been presented. Many of you might consider the analysis to be massive. However, this example was created using only the state criterion-referenced assessments, some perceptions, some demographics, and some process data. The data shown here and on the CD, therefore, are not exhaustive. More comprehensive data analyses would use other measures of student learning in addition to state assessments, such as grades, authentic assessments, and additional process measures such as degree of program or process implementation. Additionally, comprehensive data analyses would have multiple years of data—ideally, we want to follow students throughout their K-12 education experiences. This is not very realistic for all schools and districts at this point in time. Three years of consistent measures are good—five years are better. Most schools have plenty of data. Most do not need to gather more data—where effort is needed is in organizing, graphing, analyzing, and using what they already have.

What the Example Shows

From the example, I hope you can see how much a person can learn about a school through data—even when only little data are available. I hope you can also see that one person alone cannot analyze all the data. Everybody sees something different in the results, so many perspectives are necessary and valuable.

The demographic analyses of this school show us that we could get a very good understanding of the context of education for students at Big River. The way the school organizes itself to provide for its students is shown in the demographic data, and it tells a story. My hope is that school personnel reviewing these data will take the time to comprehensively analyze their own system's demographic data. There are times when others must read about your school. Remember how easy it would be, when reviewing this school's data, to start "making up" parts of the story when it is not complete. Your best defense against others drawing incorrect or incomplete assumptions about your school is to provide complete analyses.

With regard to perceptions data, we viewed five different types of perceptual data—a *Continuous Improvement Continuum* assessment, student, staff, and parent climate questionnaire data, and standards data implementation. These data helped the school see itself from different perspectives. A major caution in looking at the questionnaire results is to make sure one does not over-interpret differences in subgroups—even though a gap in averages appears, there might not be a *real* difference if both averages indicate agreement. It just might be the degree of the agreement that is different. Real differences would show agreement-disagreement. We are not concerned with looking for "significant differences." We want to know about "educational or perceptual differences," because these differences are significant in the learning of students.

The *Continuous Improvement Continuums* are a powerful self-analysis tool. These assessments help whole staffs talk the same talk and walk the same walk. Over time, they show staffs that they are making improvement, which keeps them moving ahead.

In analyzing student learning results, Big River used its state high school standards test (HSST). Because we are only looking at high school data, we do not know about the educational experiences of students before these grade levels that contributed to the grade level results. We also do not know how well the students did after high school. One can see through this example, however, that analyzing data over time for each grade level can give powerful information about which students are not being reached.

As far as gap analyses are concerned, Big River High School was able to indicate gaps. It was not able to find *one* root cause, which is very common.

If working directly with a school staff, one would be able to analyze processes more comprehensively. All programs or processes used to deliver instruction could be described and eventually coded in the data warehouse so impact can be determined, since the way in which instruction is delivered is the one element over which schools have complete control. Demographic, perceptual, and student learning data show some process impact and data.

Data Warehouses

Done well, data analysis is a massive activity requiring the technical support of knowledgeable people and a data warehouse. Districts are coming on board with acquiring data warehouses that will enable the storage of a large number of data elements, and the analysis of data quickly, easily, accurately, and meaningfully. (See *Designing and Using Databases for School Improvement* [Bernhardt, 2000].) On the CD are two articles entitled *Databases Can Help Teachers with Standards Implementation* (Bernhardt, 1999), and *Data Tools for School Improvement* (Bernhardt, 2005), summarizing how databases can help with standards implementation. (Dbases.pdf and DataTools.pdf)

> *Done well, data analysis is a massive activity requiring the technical support of knowledgeable people and a data warehouse.*

School districts or schools that do not have such a tool right now must begin looking and preparing to buy a data warehouse, because they need one. It simply is no longer an option not to have one. When looking for a database or data warehouse, districts need to keep at least six considerations in mind:

1. *Accessibility at different levels.* We would like the data stored at the district, possibly even regional or state levels, and have it accessible from the school and classroom levels. Small districts can form consortia.

2. *Build graphs automatically.* We want to be able to look over the data tables to check for accuracy; however, we want the data analysis tool to build graphs as well. Because we want staffs to review the data, it is wise to put the data in picture form so everyone can see the resulting information in the same way. Trends are often easier to detect in graphs rather than in tables. However, sometimes we need tables to display the data. (The CD has graphing templates for use with a data analysis tool or paper data.)

3. *Disaggregation on the fly.* When performing analyses that are starting to show interesting data, we want to be able to analyze quickly and easily at the next deeper levels. The easier and quicker this is to do, the deeper one can get into the data, and the more likely we are to get to root causes.

4. *Point and click or drag and drop technology that is intuitive.* We want anyone to be able to use the database without requiring a manual every time it is used.

5. *The ability to create standard reports with a click of a button.* Some reports have to be created every year, such as a School Accountability Report Card or a Title 1 report. If the same information is required each year, the programming should allow one to push a button the next year to create the report without spending a lot of time on it.

6. *The ability to follow cohorts.* Following the same groups of students as they progress through their educational careers will provide a great deal of information about one's school processes.

For the analyses in this book, I used a data warehouse tool called *EASE-E Data Analyzer* by *TetraData (www.tetradata.com)*. With this tool, I am able to analyze an entire district's data and all of its schools at the same time, as quickly and easily as analyzing one school. I do the analyses for all the schools at the same time, and then use graphing templates, such as the ones provided on the accompanying CD, to build the graphs quickly and easily. (*Point of clarification:*

EASE-E builds graphs. I use graphing templates for the fastest production. Teachers and administrators can also access specific school and classroom data from this warehouse.)

Because of their commitment to help make data analysis easier, especially for schools, *TetraData* has included the analyses made in this work as standard queries and the school profiles as standard reports. In other words, if you own *EASE-E Data Analyzer,* you will be able to create a school report similar to Big River's, with a few clicks of buttons. You will have to verify that what you named as elements are similar to those in this study.

Who Does the Data Analysis Work?

For the types of data analyses shown here in the example, or described above as comprehensive data analyses, it would be ideal if someone at the district level did the major analyses. With a good strong data analysis tool, the district person can analyze the data for all the schools, at all grade levels, for all the subtests, disaggregated by demographics, in one query. A clerk can then copy and paste the individual results into charting templates, perhaps even into the templates provided on the CD with this book.

With a strong data analysis tool, standard queries and standard reports, such as a school report card, can be created for each of the schools by one person. Our passion with data analysis is getting the results into the hands of teachers and giving them professional development in understanding the results and the time to study the *results* of the analyses, instead of having them use their time performing the analyses. In our ideal world, at minimum, teachers would start the school year with historical data on each student in their class(es). They would have the demographic data and would know what the students know and what they need to know. Also in our ideal world, teachers would be using ongoing measurements in their classrooms to make sure all students are progressing and mastering the standards/outcomes.

Let's say your district does not have a data warehouse and provides only the state assessment results on paper; you can still use these data in meaningful ways. At minimum, schools can use the templates on the CD to graph the content and proficiency levels over time. If there have been positive improvements in the school, you should see increases in scores. If the school is making a positive impact on students, student cohort scores should increase over time.

> *Our passion with data analysis is getting the results into the hands of teachers and giving them professional development in understanding the results and the time to study the results of the analyses, instead of having them use their time performing the analyses.*

> *A school's performance cannot improve without the building administrator(s) being totally dedicated to and engaged in this process.*

The Role of the Administrator

Research shows that there are three preconditions to school/district performance improvement: instructional coherence, a shared vision for school improvement, and data-driven decision making (Armstrong, 2002). Data are necessary, but not sufficient. All three—instructional coherence, a shared vision, and data-driven decision making—must work together. We believe the link for these three preconditions is the administrator. The administrator must lead the way, challenging processes through the study of school results, inspiring the shared vision, enabling others to act through planning, modeling the way through consistent actions, and encouraging the heart by reminding teachers of the purpose of the school, why they got into teaching in the first place, and celebrating successes (Kouzes & Posner, 2002). A school's performance cannot improve without the building administrator(s) being totally dedicated to and engaged in this process.

Evaluation

Just a word about evaluation. *Continuous Improvement and Evaluation* is required to assess the alignment of all parts of the system to the vision and to check the results the learning organization is getting compared to what is being implemented. If schools or districts conduct the analyses described in this book, they will have a fairly comprehensive evaluation. An evaluation does not have to be different from data analysis. You might organize an evaluation around school goals, objectives, or even purpose and vision, by asking the basic question, *What do we have as evidence that we are doing these things?* This might take reorganizing the data already analyzed, or simply answering questions, using the data already analyzed.

Summary: Review of Steps in Using Data to Improve Student Learning in High Schools

Continuous school improvement planning for increasing student learning can be organized through answering a series of logical questions.

One of the first questions we want to answer is *Who are we?* Demographic data can answer this question. The answers set the context for the school, have huge implications for the direction the continuous school improvement plan will take, and can help explain how the school gets the results it is getting. In fact, there is no way any school can understand another number without the context.

The second question, *How do we do business?*, tells us about perceptions of the learning environment from student, staff, and parent perspectives. Understanding these perceptions can help a school know what is possible and what is appropriate, needed, and doable in the continuous school improvement plan.

Answering the question, *How are we doing?* takes the data analysis work into the student learning realm. Analyzing required norm-referenced and/or criterion-referenced tests is an excellent way to begin answering this question. Looking across all measures can be useful and informative—another way to think about what students know and are able to do, giving us a glimpse of *how* students learn.

Gap analyses are critical for answering the question, *What are the gaps?* Gap analyses help schools see the differences between where they are (current results) and where they want to be (vision and goals). To be effective, gap analyses must dig layers deep into the data to truly understand the results and to begin to uncover root causes.

A root cause, as used in this continuous school improvement planning model, refers to the deep underlying reason for the occurrence of a specific situation, the gap. While a symptom may become evident from a needs assessment or gap analysis—the symptom (low student scores) is not the cause. To find a root cause, one often has to ask *why* at least five levels down to uncover the root reason for the symptom. Root causes are not easy to uncover, but the information that is uncovered in the process of uncovering root causes is well worth the effort.

With the strengths, challenges, gap analyses, and root cause analyses complete, one can integrate findings to create a continuous school improvement plan that is informed by the data, and that will lead to student achievement increases. Additionally, a continuous school improvement plan based on data will eliminate root causes.

Continuous School Improvement Planning through Answering Logical Questions

- Who are we?
- How do we do business?
- Where are we now?
- Why do we exist?
- Where do we want to be?
- What are the gaps?
- How can we get to where we want to be?
- How will we implement?
- How will we evaluate our efforts?

A continuous school improvement plan to eliminate root causes can answer the question, *How will we get there?* A continuous school improvement plan focused on data lays out the strategies and activities to implement. Required professional development, a leadership structure, a design for partnerships with parents, communities, and businesses, and the evaluation of the plan are vital components of the plan.

Gather your schoolwide data, graph it in a manner similar to the examples in this book; this will give you a good look at where your school is right now. To understand what to improve in your system, you have to know as much about your systems as you possibly can; study your demographic data, and your perceptual and student learning results, along with your current processes.

Time and time again, the differences in results by classroom or by school come down to the fact that some teachers are teaching to the standards and some are not. I can almost guarantee that if all teachers in your school know what the students know when they start a grade level and subject area, focus their effective instructional strategies on teaching what they want students to know and be able to do to meet the standards, measure in an ongoing fashion to know if the students are improving, student learning results for all students will increase in a very short period of time.

Final Notes

In the past, the usual way typical school personnel dealt with school data was to analyze the dickens out of their annual state assessment results, develop a plan to increase the lowest scores, and then wait for the next year's results to come out to know if their plan made a difference. Many found they could improve their assessment results in that area, only to discover that other subject-area scores declined. With *No Child Left Behind,* this approach is no longer plausible. To move all students to proficiency, school personnel must have a complete understanding of the whole system the students experience and work on improving the system that creates the results.

In the example, we started with demographic and perceptual data, which gave us a view of the system that student learning data alone cannot give. There were definite student learning issues that would be missed had we only looked at student learning results. My recommendations for getting student learning increases at the schoolwide level include the following:

▼ Gather and analyze your demographic data to understand clearly the students you are serving and who is teaching them, by grade level and by content area. Make sure your processes are set up for success.

▼ Listen to the *voices* of students, parents, and staff through questionnaires.

▼ Analyze your student achievement results by student groups, by grade level, and by following cohorts.

▼ Align and monitor your curriculum and instructional strategies to meet content standards.

▼ Incorporate into all teaching ongoing assessments related to standards acquisition (e.g., diagnostics, benchmarking, grade level indicators).

▼ Pull these data together to learn what needs to change to get different results.

▼ Create a vision that is shared and a plan to implement the vision and close the gaps.

The data are not the hardest part of creating this scenario. Getting staffs to work together to share and implement a shared vision and plan takes strong and consistent leadership from the school administrator(s) and leadership teams, as well as the district leadership teams.

Best wishes to you as you continuously improve your systems for the students. You are creating the future in which the next generation will live.

On the CD Related to this Chapter

▼ *Databases Can Help Teachers with Standards Implementation* (Dbases.pdf)
This read-only article, by Victoria L. Bernhardt, describes how databases can help with standards implementation.

▼ *Data Tools for School Improvement* (DataTools.pdf)
This read-only article, by Victoria L. Bernhardt, describes how data tools can help schools analyze and use data effectively.

> *It's easy to get the players. Getting 'em to play together, that's the hard part.*
>
> **Casey Stengel**

Appendix A
Overview of the CD Contents

The Appendix provides a list of the files as they appear on the accompanying CD-ROM. These files are listed by section, along with a description of the file's content and file type. (This list appears as the Index file [Index.pdf] on the CD.)

▼ **WHAT DATA ARE IMPORTANT?**

The files in this section support Chapter 2 in the book and provide an overview of what data are important in understanding if a school is effectively carrying out its purpose and assessing if *all* students are learning.

Multiple Measures of Data Graphic   MMgraphc.pdf   Acrobat Reader
> This is Figure 2.1 in a PDF (portable document file) for printing.

Summary of Data Intersections   IntrscTbl.pdf   Acrobat Reader
> This is Figure 2.2 in a PDF for your use with staff.

Data Discovery Activity   ACTDiscv.pdf   Acrobat Reader
> The purpose of this activity is to look closely at examples of data and to discover specific information and patterns of information, both individually and as a group.

Intersections Activity   ACTIntrs.pdf   Acrobat Reader
> The purpose of this activity is to motivate school improvement teams to think about the questions they can answer when they cross different data variables. It is also designed to help teams focus their data-gathering efforts so they are not collecting everything and anything.

Creating Intersections Activity   ACTCreat.pdf   Acrobat Reader
> This activity is similar to the *Intersections Activity*. The purpose is to have participants "grow" their intersections.

Data Analysis Presentation   DASlides.ppt   Microsoft PowerPoint
> This *Microsoft PowerPoint* presentation is an overview to use with your staffs in getting started with data analysis. The script of the presentation can be found under "view notes" and by setting the print option to "notes pages." Handouts can be created by setting the print option to "handouts" (three slides to a page).

Articles

These read-only articles, by Victoria L. Bernhardt, will be useful in workshops or in getting started on data with staff.

Multiple Measures   MMeasure.pdf   Acrobat Reader
This article by Victoria L. Bernhardt, in read-only format, summarizes why, and what, data are important to continuous school improvement.

Intersections: New Routes Open when One
     Type of Data Crosses Another   Intersct.pdf   Acrobat Reader
This article by Victoria L. Bernhardt, in read-only format, published in the *Journal of Staff Development* (Winter 2000), discusses how much richer your data analyses can be when you intersect multiple data variables.

No Schools Left Behind   NoSchls.pdf   Acrobat Reader
This article by Victoria L. Bernhardt, in read-only format, published in *Educational Leadership* (February 2003), summarizes how to improve learning for *all* students.

Study Questions Related to *What Data are Important?*   Ch2Qs.doc   Microsoft Word
> These study questions will help you better understand the information provided in Chapter 2. This template file can be printed for use with staff as they think through the data questions they want to answer and the data they will need to gather to answer the questions.

▼ GETTING STARTED ON DATA ANALYSIS FOR CONTINUOUS SCHOOL IMPROVEMENT

The files in this section support Chapter 3 in the book and provide an overview of how a school can get started with comprehensive data analysis work.

Continuous School Improvement Planning via the School Portfolio Graphic	CSIPlang.pdf	Acrobat Reader

This read-only graphic displays the questions that can be answered to create a continuous school improvement plan. The data that can answer the questions, and where the answers would appear in the school portfolio, also appear on the graphic. In the book, it is Figure 3.1.

Continuous School Improvement Planning via the School Portfolio Description	CSIdscr.pdf	Acrobat Reader

This read-only file shows Figure 3.1, along with its description.

The School Portfolio Presentation	SPSlides.ppt	Microsoft PowerPoint

This *Microsoft PowerPoint* presentation is an overview to use with your staffs in getting started on the school portfolio. The script of the presentation can be found under "view notes" and by setting the print option to "notes pages." Handouts can be created by setting the print option to "handouts" (three slides to a page).

Study Questions Related to *Getting Started*	Ch3Qs.doc	Microsoft Word

These study questions will help you better understand the information provided in Chapter 3. This template file can be printed for use with staff as you begin continuous school improvement planning. Answering the questions will help staff determine the data needed to answer the questions discussed in this chapter.

▼ ANALYZING THE DATA: *WHO ARE WE?*

The files in this section support Chapter 4 in the book and are tools to create a demographic profile of your school in order to answer the question, *Who are we?*

Study Questions Related to *Who Are We?*	Ch4Qs.doc	Microsoft Word

These study questions will help you better understand the information provided in Chapter 4. This template file can be printed for use as you study the case study or to use with staff as you study your own demographic data.

Demographic Graphing Templates	HighDemog.xls	Microsoft Excel

All of the *Microsoft Excel* files that were used to create the demographic graphs in the Big River example in Chapter 4 appear on the CD in this section. Use these templates by putting your data in the data source table and changing the title/labels to reflect your data. Your graphs will build automatically. This file also explains how to use the templates.

School Data Profile Template	HighProfil.doc	Microsoft Word

This *Microsoft Word* file provides a template for creating your own school data profile like the one in the example, using the graphing and table templates provided. Create your graphs in the graphing and table templates, then copy and paste them into the *School Profile Template*.

School Profile	ProfilSc.doc	Microsoft Word

The *School Profile* is a template for gathering and organizing data about your school, prior to graphing. Please adjust the profile to add data elements you feel are important for describing the context of your school. This information is then graphed and written into a narrative form. If creating a school portfolio, the data graphs and narrative would appear in *Information and Analysis*. (If you already have your data organized and just need to graph it, you might want to skip this step and use the graphing templates described above.)

Community Profile   ProfilCo.doc   Microsoft Word

The *Community Profile* is a template for gathering and organizing data about your community, prior to graphing. Please adjust the profile to add data elements you feel are important for describing the context of your community. It is important to describe how the community has changed over time, and how it is expected to change in the near future. This information is then graphed and written into a narrative form. If creating a school portfolio, the data graphs and narrative would appear in *Information and Analysis*. (If you already have your data organized and just need to graph it, you might want to skip this step and use the graphing templates described on the previous page.)

Administrator Profile   ProfilAd.doc   Microsoft Word

The *Administrator Profile* is a template for gathering and organizing data about your school administrators, prior to graphing. Please adjust the profile to fully describe your administrators. This information is then graphed and written into a narrative form. If creating a school portfolio, the data graphs and narrative will appear in *Information and Analysis* and *Leadership* sections. (If you already have your data organized and just need to graph it, you might want to skip this step and use the graphing templates described on the previous page.)

Teacher Profile   ProfilTe.doc   Microsoft Word

The *Teacher Profile* is a template for gathering and organizing data about your school's teachers, prior to graphing. Please adjust the profile to fully describe your teachers. The synthesis of this information is then graphed and written into a narrative form. If creating a school portfolio, the data graphs and narrative would appear in *Information and Analysis*. (If you already have your data organized and just need to graph it, you might want to skip this step and use the graphing templates described on the previous page.)

Staff (Other than Teacher) Profile   ProfilSt.doc   Microsoft Word

The *Staff (Other than Teacher)Profile* is a template for gathering and organizing data about school staff who are not teachers, prior to graphing. Please adjust the profile to fully describe your non-teaching staff. The synthesis of this information is then graphed and written into a narrative form. If creating a school portfolio, the data graphs and narrative would appear in *Information and Analysis*. (If you already have your data organized and just need to graph it, you might want to skip this step and use the graphing templates described on the previous page.)

History Gram Activity   ACTHstry.pdf   Acrobat Reader

A team-building activity that will "write" the history of the school, which could help everyone see what staff has experienced since coming to the school and how many school improvement initiatives have been started over the years. It is helpful for understanding what it will take to keep this current school improvement effort going.

Questions to Guide the Analysis of Demographic Data   QsDemogr.doc   Microsoft Word

This *Microsoft Word* file provides a guide for interpreting your demographic data. Adjust the questions to better reflect the discussion you would like to have with your staff about the gathered demographic data.

What I Saw in the Example   Ch4Saw.pdf   Acrobat Reader

What I Saw in the Example is a file, organized by the demographic study questions, that summarizes what the author saw in the demographic data provided by Big River High School.

Demographic Data to Gather to Create the Context of the School   DemoData.pdf   Acrobat Reader

This file defines the types of demographic data that are important to gather to create the context of the school and describe *Who are we?*

The files in this section support Chapter 5 in the book and include tools to help staff understand the organization and climate of the school from the perspective of students, staff, and parents. The resulting analyses can help answer the question, *How do we do business?*

Continuous Improvement Continuums for Schools	CICs.pdf	Acrobat Reader

This read-only file contains the seven *School Portfolio Continuous Improvement Continuums* for schools. These can be printed as is and also enlarged for posting individual staff opinions during staff assessments.

Continuous Improvement Continuums for Districts	CICsDstrct.pdf	Acrobat Reader

This read-only file contains the seven *School Portfolio Continuous Improvement Continuums* for assessing the district level. These can be printed as is and also enlarged for posting individual staff opinions during staff assessments.

Big River School Baseline CIC Results	BRBase.pdf	Acrobat Reader

This read-only file is the summary of Big River's baseline assessment on the *School Portfolio Continuous Improvement Continuums.*

Continuous Improvement Continuum Tools

These files are tools for assessing on the CICs and for writing the CIC report.

Continuous Improvement Continuums Self-Assessment Activity	ACTCIC.pdf	Acrobat Reader

Assessing on the *Continuous Improvement Continuums* will help staffs see where their systems are right now with respect to continuous improvement and ultimately will show they are making progress over time. The discussion has major implications for the *Continuous School Improvement (CSI) Plan.*

Coming to Consensus	Consenss.pdf	Acrobat Reader

This read-only file provides strategies for coming to consensus, useful when assessing on the *Continuous Improvement Continuums.*

Continuous Improvement Continuums Report Example	ExReprt1.pdf	Acrobat Reader

This read-only file shows a real school's assessment on the *School Portfolio Continuous Improvement Continuums,* as an example.

Continuous Improvement Continuums Report Example for Follow-Up Years	ExReprt2.pdf	Acrobat Reader

This read only file shows a real school's assessment on the *School Portfolio Continuous Improvement Continuums* over time, as an example.

Continuous Improvement Continuums Baseline Report Template	ReptTemp.doc	Microsoft Word

This *Microsoft Word* file provides a template for writing your school's report of its assessment on the *School Portfolio Continuous Improvement Continuums.*

Continuous Improvement Continuums Graphing Templates	CICGraph.xls	Microsoft Excel

This *Microsoft Excel* file is a template for graphing your assessments on the seven *School Portfolio Continuous Improvement Continuums.*

Study Questions Related to *How Do We Do Business?*	Ch5Qs.doc	Microsoft Word

These study questions will help you better understand the information provided in Chapter 5. This template file can be printed for use with staff as you answer the question, *How do we do business?,* through analyzing Big River's perceptual data.

What I Saw in the Example	Ch5Saw.pdf	Acrobat Reader

What I Saw in the Example is a file, organized by the perceptual study questions, that summarizes what the author saw in the perceptual data provided by Big River High School.

Analysis of Questionnaire Data Table	QTable.doc	Microsoft Word

This *Microsoft Word* file is a tabular guide for interpreting your student, staff, and parent questionnaires, independently and interdependently. It will help you see the summary of your results and write the narrative.

Full Narratives of Questionnaire Results Used in the Example

Big River Student Questionnaire Results	StuNarr.doc	Microsoft Word

This template file is the full narrative of student questionnaire results used in the school example.

Big River Staff Questionnaire Results	StfNarr.doc	Microsoft Word

This template file is the full narrative of staff questionnaire results used in the school example.

Big River Parent Questionnaire Results	ParNarr.doc	Microsoft Word

This template file is the full narrative of parent questionnaire results used in the school example.

Education for the Future Questionnaires

These PDF files are for content review purposes only—*not* intended for use in questionnaire administration. For more information about administering and analyzing *Education for the Future* questionnaires, please visit *http://eff.csuchico.edu/questionnaire_resources/*.

Student (Kindergarten to Grade 3) Questionnaire	StQKto3.pdf	Acrobat Reader

This read-only file is the *Education for the Future* perception questionnaire for students in kindergarten through grade three.

Student (Grades 1 to 12) Questionnaire	StQ1to12.pdf	Acrobat Reader

This read-only file is the *Education for the Future* perception questionnaire for students in grades one through twelve.

Student (Middle/High School) Questionnaire	StQMidHS.pdf	Acrobat Reader

This read-only file is the *Education for the Future* perception questionnaire for middle and high school students.

Teaching Staff Questionnaire	TeachStaffQ.pdf	Acrobat Reader

This read-only file is the *Education for the Future* perception questionnaire for teaching staff.

Organizational Learning Questionnaire	OrgLearnQ.pdf	Acrobat Reader

This read-only file is the *Education for the Future* perception organizational learning questionnaire for staff.

Administrator Questionnaire	AdminQ.pdf	Acrobat Reader

This read-only file is the *Education for the Future* perception questionnaire for administrators.

Parent Questionnaire	ParntK12Q.pdf	Acrobat Reader

This read-only file is the *Education for the Future* perception questionnaire for parents of kindergarten through grade twelve students.

High School Parent Questionnaire	ParntHSQ.pdf	Acrobat Reader

This read-only file is the *Education for the Future* perception questionnaire for parents of high school students.

Alumni Questionnaire	AlumniQ.pdf	Acrobat Reader

This read-only file is the *Education for the Future* perception questionnaire for high school graduates.

How to Analyze Open-ended Responses	OEanalz.pdf	Acrobat Reader

This read-only file discusses how to analyze responses to the open-ended questions on questionnaires.

Questions to Guide the Analysis of Perceptions Data	PerceptQ.doc	Microsoft Word

This *Microsoft Word* file is a tabular guide for interpreting your perceptions data. You can change the questions if you like or use the file to write in the responses. It will help you write the narrative for your results.

▼ ANALYZING THE DATA: *WHERE ARE WE NOW?*

The tools in this section support Chapter 6 in the book, help staffs determine the results of their current processes, particularly student achievement results, and can help staffs answer the question, *Where are we now?*

Study Questions Related to *Where Are We Now?*   Ch6Qs.doc   Microsoft Word

These study questions will help you better understand the information provided in Chapter 6. This template file can be printed for use with staff as you begin to explore your own student learning results.

Arguments For and Against Standardized Testing   TestArgu.pdf   Acrobat Reader

This table summarizes the most common arguments for and against the use of standardized testing.

Standardized Test Score Terms   TestTerm.pdf   Acrobat Reader

This table shows the different standardized testing terms, their most effective uses, and cautions for their uses.

Arguments For and Against Performance Assessments   PerfArgu.pdf   Acrobat Reader

This table shows the most common arguments for and against the use of performance assessments.

Arguments For and Against Teacher Grading   GradeArg.pdf   Acrobat Reader

This table shows the most common arguments for and against the use of teacher grading.

Terms Related to Analyzing Student Achievement
Results, Descriptively   SAterms1.pdf   Acrobat Reader

This table shows the different terms related to analyzing student achievement results, descriptively, their most effective uses, and cautions for their uses.

Terms Related to Analyzing Student Achievement
Results, Inferentially   SAterms2.pdf   Acrobat Reader

This table shows the different terms related to analyzing student achievement results, inferentially, their most effective uses, and cautions for their uses.

What I Saw in the Example   Ch6Saw.pdf   Acrobat Reader

What I Saw in the Example is a file, organized by the student learning study questions, that summarizes what the author saw in the student learning data provided by Big River High School.

Student Achievement Graphing Templates   HighSA.xls   Microsoft Excel

All of the *Microsoft Excel* files that were used to create the student achievement graphs in the Big River example (Chapter 6) appear on the CD. Use these templates by putting your data in the data table and changing the title/labels to reflect your data. The graphs will build automatically. This file also explains how to use the templates.

Student Achievement Data Summary Template   HighSA.doc   Microsoft Word

This *Microsoft Word* file provides a template for creating your own school student achievement data summary like the one in the Big River example (Chapter 6), using the graphing and table templates provided. Create your graphs and tables in the graphing template, then copy and paste them into the *Student Achievement Data Summary Template*.

Questions to Guide the Analysis of Student Achievement Data   QsStachv.doc   Microsoft Word

This *Microsoft Word* file consists of questions to guide the interpretation of your student learning data. You can write your responses into this file.

▼ ANALYZING THE DATA: *WHAT ARE THE GAPS?* AND
   WHAT ARE THE ROOT CAUSES OF THE GAPS?

The tools in this section support Chapter 7 in the book and help staffs analyze their data to determine the gaps and the root causes of the gaps. These files and tools can help answer the questions, *What are the gaps?* and *What are the root causes of the gaps?*

Goal Setting Activity	ACTGoals.pdf	Acrobat Reader

By setting goals, a school can clarify its end targets for the school's vision. This activity will help a school set goals for the future.

Gap Analysis and Objectives Activity	ACTGap.pdf	Acrobat Reader

The purpose of this activity is to look closely at differences between current results and where the school wants to be in the future. It is this gap that gets translated into objectives that guide the development of the action plan.

Root Cause Analysis Activity	ACTRoot.pdf	Acrobat Reader

Root causes are the real causes of our educational problems. We need to find out what they are so we can eliminate the true cause and not just address the symptom. This activity asks staff teams to review and analyze data, and ask probing questions to uncover the root cause(s).

Cause and Effect Analysis Activity	ACTCause.pdf	Acrobat Reader

This activity will help teams determine the relationships and complexities between an effect or problem and all the possible causes.

Problem-Solving Cycle Activity	ACTCycle.pdf	Acrobat Reader

The purpose of the *Problem-Solving Cycle Activity* is to get all staff involved in thinking through a problem before jumping to solutions. This activity can also result in a comprehensive data analysis design.

Problem-Solving Cycle Handout Template	CycleTmp.doc	Microsoft Word

This Microsoft Word file is the last three pages of the problem-solving cycle activity. Use this template to fill-in hunches and hypotheses about why the problem exists, determine the questions needed to answer with data to know more about the problem, and what data are needed to support those answers.

Study Questions Related to the Gaps and the Root Causes of the Gaps	Ch7Qs.doc	Microsoft Word

These study questions will help you better understand the information provided in Chapter 7. This template file can be printed for use with staff as you analyze their data to determine the gaps and the root causes of the gaps.

What I Saw in the Example	Ch7Saw.pdf	Acrobat Reader

What I Saw in the Example is a file, organized by the demographic study questions, that summarizes what the author saw in the demographic data provided by Big River High School.

Gap Analyses Data Table Templates	HighGaps.doc	Microsoft Word

All of the *Microsoft Word* files that were used to create the gap analyses data tables in the Big River example (Chapter 7) appear on the CD. Use these templates by putting your data in the data table and changing the title/labels to reflect your data.

No Child Left Behind (NCLB) Templates

Table templates for analyzing student learning data for NCLB are provided on the CD.

NCLB Language Scores Template	LangTbl.doc	Microsoft Word

This *Microsoft Word* file is a table template to use in capturing your *No Child Left Behind* (NCLB) Language scores analysis.

NCLB Reading Scores Template	ReadTbl.doc	Microsoft Word

This *Microsoft Word* file is a table template to use in capturing your *No Child Left Behind* (NCLB) Reading scores analysis.

NCLB Math Scores Template	MathTbl.doc	Microsoft Word

This *Microsoft Word* file is a table template to use in capturing your *No Child Left Behind* (NCLB) Math scores analysis.

NCLB Student Achievement Reading Results Template	ProfLaEl.doc	Microsoft Word

This *Microsoft Word* file is a table template to use in summarizing your *No Child Left Behind* (NCLB) disaggregated student achievement Reading proficiency results.

NCLB Student Achievement Math Results Template	ProfMaEl.doc	Microsoft Word

This *Microsoft Word* file is a table template to use in summarizing your *No Child Left Behind* (NCLB) disaggregated student achievement Math proficiency results.

Group Process Tools and Activities

The files include read-only documents, examples, templates, tools, activities, and strategy recommendations. Many of the group process tools and activities can be used throughout the analysis of data.

Affinity Diagram Activity	ACTAfnty.pdf	Acrobat Reader

The affinity diagram encourages honest reflection on the real underlying root causes of a problem and its solutions, and encourages people to agree on the factors. This activity assists teams in discussing and resolving problems, using a nonjudgmental process.

Fishbowl Activity	ACTFish.pdf	Acrobat Reader

The *Fishbowl Activity* can be used for dynamic group involvement. The most common configuration is an inner ring, which is the discussion group, surrounded by an outer ring, which is the observation group. Just as people observe the fish in the fishbowl, the outer ring observes the inner ring.

Forcefield Analysis Activity	ACTForce.pdf	Acrobat Reader

The *Forcefield Analysis Activity* helps staffs think about the ideal state for the school and the driving and restraining forces regarding that ideal state.

Placemat Activity	ACTPlace.pdf	Acrobat Reader

The *Placemat Activity* was developed to invite participants to share their knowledge about the school portfolio, data, a standard, an instructional strategy, a concept, etc.

T-Chart Activity	ACTTChrt.pdf	Acrobat Reader

A *T-Chart* is a simple tool to organize material into two columns. Use a T-Chart to compare and contrast information or to show relationships. Use it to help people see the opposite dimension of an issue.

"X" Marks the Spot Activity	ACTXSpot.pdf	Acrobat Reader

This activity helps staff understand levels of expertise or degrees of passion about a topic.

Quadrant Diagram Activity	ACTQuadr.pdf	Acrobat Reader

A quadrant diagram is a method to determine which solution best meets two goals at once, such as low cost and high benefit.

▼ ANALYZING THE DATA: *HOW CAN WE GET TO WHERE WE WANT TO BE?*

The files in this section support Chapter 8 in the book, helping staffs answer the question, *How can we get to where we want to be?* through comprehensive planning to implement the vision and eliminate the gaps, using powerful professional development, leadership, partnership development, and continuous improvement and evaluation.

Big River Shared Vision   BRVision.pdf   Acrobat Reader

This read-only file is Big River's Guiding Principles and Shared Vision, also shown on pages 205-207 in Chapter 8.

Big River School Plan for Improvement   SchlPlan.pdf   Acrobat Reader

This read-only file is the first draft of the Big River School Plan and is shown as Figure 8.1 in Chapter 8.

Planning Template   APForm.doc   Microsoft Word

A quality action plan to implement the vision consists of goals, objectives, strategies/actions, persons responsible, resources needed, due dates, and timelines. A template with these components is provided in *Microsoft Word,* ready to be completed.

Big River Leadership Structure   LeadPlan.pdf   Acrobat Reader

This read-only file is the Big River Leadership Structure, created from the overall action plan, and is shown on pages 214-217 in Chapter 8.

Big River Professional Learning Calendar   PrDevCal.pdf   Acrobat Reader

This read-only file is Big River's 2004-05 Fall/Winter Professional Learning Calendar, also shown as Figure 8.2 in Chapter 8.

Professional Learning Calendar Template   PrDevCal.doc   Microsoft Word

This *Microsoft Word* document is a template for creating your school Professional Learning Calendar.

Classroom Observation Tool   ObvTool.pdf   Acrobat Reader

This read-only file is the first draft of the *Big River Classroom Observation Tool,* created for assessing where each teacher is in implementing the state-content standards and vision, and shown as Figure 8.3 in Chapter 8.

Big River Partnership Plan   PartPlan.pdf   Acrobat Reader

This read-only file is the Big River Partnership Plan, created from the overall action plan, and is shown on pages 222-223 in Chapter 8.

Establishing a Partnership Plan   EstPPlan.pdf   Acrobat Reader

This read-only file describes the steps in creating a partnership plan that will become a part of the continuous school improvement plan.

Partnership Evaluation Questionnaire   PaEvalQ.pdf   Acrobat Reader

This read-only file is used to assess community members' role in the partnership, perceptions of the impact of the partnership, and satisfaction with the partnership program, and is shown as Figure 8.4 in Chapter 8.

Big River Evaluation Plan   EvalPlan.pdf   Acrobat Reader

This read-only file, the Big River Evaluation Plan, condenses the measurement column of the action plan into a comprehensive evaluation plan, and is shown as Figure 8.5 in Chapter 8.

Evaluating a Program Activity   ACTEval.pdf   Acrobat Reader

The purpose of this activity is to get many people involved in creating a comprehensive evaluation design to determine the impact of a program and to know how to improve the program.

| Powerful Professional Development Designs | Designs.pdf | Acrobat Reader |

This read-only file describes numerous ways to embed professional development into the learning community.

Powerful Professional Development Designs Folder

Powerful Professional Development Designs are those that are embedded into the daily operations of a staff. They are ongoing and lead to improvement of instruction and increases in student learning.

| Action Research Activity | ACTRsrch.pdf | Acrobat Reader |

Teachers and/or administrators raise questions about the best way to improve teaching and learning, systematically study the literature to answer the questions, implement the best approach, and analyze the results.

| Cadres or Action Teams Activity | ACTCdres.pdf | Acrobat Reader |

Organizing cadres or teams allows for the delegation of responsibilities so teams of educators can study new approaches, plan for the implementation of new strategies or programs, and get work done without every staff member's involvement.

| Case Studies Activity | ACTCases.pdf | Acrobat Reader |

Staff members review case studies of student work, and/or of another teacher's example lessons, which can lead to quality discussions and improved practices.

| Coaching Activity | ACTCoach.pdf | Acrobat Reader |

Teachers form teams of two or three to observe each other, plan together, and to talk and encourage each other in meaningful ways, while reflecting on continuously improving instructional practices.

| Examining Student Data: *Teacher Analysis of Test Scores Table One* | Table1.doc | Microsoft Word |

Examining student data consists of conversations around individual student data results and the processes that created the results. This approach can be a significant form of professional development when skilled team members facilitate the dialogue.

| Examining Student Work Activity | ACTSWork.pdf | Acrobat Reader |

Examining student work as professional learning ensures that what students learn is aligned to the learning standards. It also shows teachers the impact of their processes.

| Example Lessons: *Birds of a Feather Unit Example* | UnitEx.pdf | Acrobat Reader |

Some teachers need to see what a lesson that implements all aspects of the school vision would look like. Providing examples for all teachers to see can reward the teacher who is doing a good job of implementing the vision and provide a template for other teachers. It is very effective to store summary examples in a binder or on a website for everyone to peruse at any time.

| Example Lessons: *Unit Template* | UnitTmpl.doc | Microsoft Word |

This template provides the outline for creating instructional units that implement the vision.

| Immersion Activity | ACTImrsn.pdf | Acrobat Reader |

Immersion is a method for getting teachers engaged in different content through hands-on experiences as a learner.

| Journaling Activity | ACTJourn.pdf | Acrobat Reader |

Journal writing helps teachers construct meaning for, and reflect on, what they are teaching and learning.

| Listening to Students Activity | ACTListn.pdf | Acrobat Reader |

Students' perceptions of the learning environment are very important for continuous improvement. Focus groups, interviews, and questionnaires can be used to discover what students are perceiving.

| Needs Assessment: *Professional Development Needs Related to Technology Example* | TechnEx.pdf | Acrobat Reader |

Needs assessments help staff understand the professional development needs of staff. At the same time, if done well, this tool can lead to quality staff conversations and sharing of knowledge.

Needs Assessment: *Professional Development Needs*
  Related to Technology Template   TechTmpl.doc   Microsoft Word

This template provides the outline for doing your own professional development needs assessment.

Networks Activity   ACTNtwrk.pdf   Acrobat Reader

Purposeful grouping of individuals/schools to further a cause or commitment.

Partnerships: *Creating Partnerships Activity*   ACTParts.pdf   Acrobat Reader

Teachers partnering with businesses in the community, scientists, and/or university professors can result in real world applications for student learning and deeper understandings of content for the teacher.

Process Mapping: *Charting School Processes Activity*   ACTProcs.pdf   Acrobat Reader

School processes are instruction, curriculum, and assessment strategies used to ensure the learning of all students. Mapping or flowcharting school processes can help staff members objectively look at how students are being taught.

Reflection Log Activity   ACTLog.pdf   Acrobat Reader

Reflective logs are recordings of key events in the educators' work days to reflect on improvement and/or to share learnings with colleagues.

Scheduling Activity   ACTSchdl.pdf   Acrobat Reader

A real test for whether or not a vision is realistic is to have teachers develop a day's schedule. This will tell them immediately if it is doable, or what needs to change in the vision and plan to make it doable.

School Meetings: *Running Efficient Meetings*   Meetings.pdf   Acrobat Reader

Staff, department, grade level, and cross-grade level meetings can promote learning through study or sharing best practice, while focusing on the implementation of the vision.

Self-Assessment: *Teacher Assessment Tool Related*
  to the School Vision   AssessEx.pdf   Acrobat Reader

This read-only file shows staff assessments on tools to measure progress toward the vision, such as the *Continuous Improvement Continuums,* will help teachers see where their school is as a system and what needs to improve for better results.

Self-Assessment: *Teacher Assessment Tool Related*
  to Our School Vision   AssessEx.doc   Microsoft Word

This template file for staff assessments on tools to measure progress toward the vision, such as the *Continuous Improvement Continuums,* will help teachers see where their school is as a system and what needs to improve for better results.

Self-Assessment: *Our School Shared Vision*
  Implementation Rubric Example   StRubric.pdf   Acrobat Reader

Self-assessments on tools to measure progress toward the vision, such as the *Continuous Improvement Continuums,* will help teachers see where their school is as a system and what needs to improve for better results.

Self-Assessment: *Our School Shared Vision*
  Implementation Rubric Template   StRubric.doc   Microsoft Word

This template file for staff assessments on tools to measure progress toward the vision, such as the *Continuous Improvement Continuums,* will help teachers see where their school is as a system and what needs to improve for better results.

Self-Assessment: *Staff-Developed Rubric Activity*   ACTRubric.pdf   Acrobat Reader

This activity for staff assessments on tools to measure progress toward the vision, such as the *Continuous Improvement Continuums,* will help teachers see where their school is as a system and what needs to improve for better results.

Shadowing Students Activity   ACTShadw.pdf   Acrobat Reader

Purposefully following students and systematically recording the students' instructional experiences is a wonderful job-embedded approach to understanding what students are experiencing in school.

Storyboarding Activity   ACTStory.pdf   Acrobat Reader

Storyboarding is an activity that will allow participants to share previous knowledge, while reflecting on the topic. It is a structure for facilitating conversations.

Study Groups Activity   ACTStudy.pdf   Acrobat Reader

Groups of educators meet to learn new strategies and programs, to review new publications, or to review student work together.

Teacher Portfolio Activity   ACTTcher.pdf   Acrobat Reader

Teacher portfolios can be built to tell the story of implementing the vision in the classroom, and its impact on student learning. Portfolios are excellent for reflection, understanding, and showing progress. Portfolios can be used for many things including self-assessment, employment, supervision to replace traditional teacher evaluation, and peer collaboration.

Train the Trainers Activity   ACTTrain.pdf   Acrobat Reader

Train the trainers is an approach to saving time and money. Individuals are trained and return to the school or school district with a commitment to train others.

Tuning Protocols Activity   ACTTune.pdf   Acrobat Reader

A tuning protocol is a formal process for reviewing, honoring, and fine-tuning colleagues' work through presentation and reflection.

▼ ANALYZING THE DATA: *CONCLUSIONS AND RECOMMENDATIONS*

The files in this section support Chapter 9 in the book and help staffs evaluate their programs and processes.

Databases Can Help Teachers with Standards Implementation   Dbases.pdf   Acrobat Reader

This read-only article, by Victoria L. Bernhardt, describes how databases can help with standards implementation.

Data Tools for School Improvement   DataTools.pdf   Acrobat Reader

This read-only article, by Victoria L. Bernhardt, describes how data tools can help schools analyze and use data effectively.

Appendix B
Continuous Improvement Continuums for Schools

These *Education for the Future Continuous Improvement Continuums*, adapted from the *Malcolm Baldrige Award Program for Quality Business Management*, provide an authentic means for measuring schoolwide improvement and growth. Schools use these Continuums as a vehicle for ongoing self-assessment. They use the results of the assessment to acknowledge their accomplishments, to set goals for improvement, and to keep school districts and partners apprised of the progress they have made in their school improvement efforts.

Understanding the Continuums

These Continuums, extending from *one* to *five* horizontally, represent a continuum of expectations related to school improvement with respect to an *Approach* to the Continuum, *Implementation* of the approach, and the *Outcome* that results from the implementation. A *one* rating, located at the left of each Continuum, represents a school that has not yet begun to improve. *Five*, located at the right of each Continuum, represents a school that is one step removed from "world class quality." The elements between *one* and *five* describe how that Continuum is hypothesized to evolve in a continuously improving school. Each Continuum moves from a reactive mode to a proactive mode—from fire fighting to prevention. The *five* in *outcome* in each Continuum is the target.

Vertically, the *Approach, Implementation,* and *Outcome* statements, for any number one through five, are hypotheses. In other words, the implementation statement describes how the approach might look when implemented, and the outcome is the "pay-off" for implementing the approach. If the hypotheses are accurate, the outcome will not be realized until the approach is actually implemented.

Using the Continuums

Use the *Continuous Improvement Continuums* (CICs) to understand where your school is with respect to continuous improvement. The results will hopefully provide that sense of urgency needed to spark enthusiasm for your school improvement efforts.

The most beneficial approach to assessing on the Continuums is to gather the entire staff together for the assessment. When assessing on the Continuums for the first time, plan for three hours to complete all seven categories.

Start the assessment by stating or creating the ground rules, setting the tone for a safe and confidential assessment, and explaining why you are doing this. Provide a brief overview of the seven sections, taking each section one at a time, and having each staff member read the related Continuum and make independent assessments of where she/he believes the school is with respect to *Approach, Implementation,* and *Outcome.* We recommend using individual 8 1/2 x 11 copies of the Continuums for individual assessments. (CICs.pdf) Then, have each staff member note where she/he believes the school is with a colorful sticker or marker on a large poster of each Continuum. The markers allow all staff to see how much they are in agreement with one another. If only one color is used for the first assessment, another color can be used for the next assessment, and so forth, to help gauge growth over time, or you can plan to use two different charts for gauging progress over time such as in the photos below.

When all dots or marks have been placed on the enlarged Continuum, look at the agreement or disagreement of the ratings. Starting with *Approach,* have staff members discuss why they believe the school is where they rated it. Keep discussing until the larger group comes to consensus on one number that reflects where the school is right now. You might need to make a quick check on where staff is with respect to coming to consensus, using a thumbs up, thumbs down "vote." Keep discussing the facts until consensus is reached. (Consenss.pdf) Do not average the results—it does not produce a sense of urgency for improvement. We cannot emphasize this enough! Keep discussing until agreement is reached by everyone on a number that represents where "we" are right now. When that consensus is reached, record the number and move to *Implementation* and then *Outcome.* Determine *Next Steps.* Proceed in the same way through the next six categories.

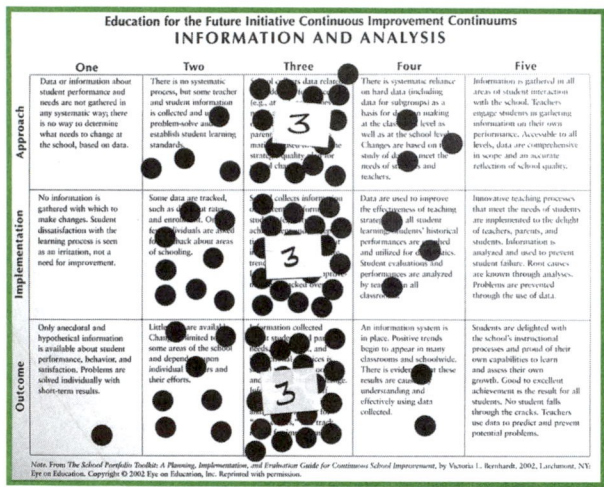

Fall Assessment

Spring Assessment

During the assessments, make sure someone records the discussions of the Continuum assessments. Schools might want to exchange facilitators with a neighboring school or district to have someone external to the school facilitate the assessments. This will enable everyone in the school to participate and provide an unbiased and competent person to lead the consensus-building piece. Assessing over time will help staff see that they are making progress. The decision of how often to assess on the *Continuous Improvement Continuums* is certainly up to the school. We recommend twice a year—about mid-fall and mid-spring—when there is time (or has been time) to implement next steps.

Using these Continuums will enable you and your school to stay motivated, to shape and maintain your shared vision, and will assist with the continuous improvement of all elements of your school. Take pictures of the resulting charts. Even if your consensus number does not increase, the dots will most probably come together over time showing shifts in whole staff thinking.

Remember that where your school is at any time is just where it is. The important thing is what you do with this information. Continuous improvement is a never-ending process which, when used effectively, will ultimately lead your school toward providing a quality program for all children.

School Continuous Improvement Continuums
INFORMATION AND ANALYSIS

	One	Two	Three	Four	Five
Approach	Data or information about student performance and needs are not gathered in any systematic way; there is no way to determine what needs to change at the school, based on data.	There is no systematic process, but some teacher and student information is collected and used to problem solve and establish student learning standards.	School collects data related to student performance (e.g., attendance, achievement) and conducts surveys on student, teacher, and parent needs. The information is used to drive the strategic quality plan for school change.	There is systematic reliance on hard data (including data for subgroups) as a basis for decision making at the classroom level as well as at the school level. Changes are based on the study of data to meet the needs of students and teachers.	Information is gathered in all areas of student interaction with the school. Teachers engage students in gathering information on their own performance. Accessible to all levels, data are comprehensive in scope and an accurate reflection of school quality.
Implementation	No information is gathered with which to make changes. Student dissatisfaction with the learning process is seen as an irritation, not a need for improvement.	Some data are tracked, such as drop-out rates and enrollment. Only a few individuals are asked for feedback about areas of schooling.	School collects information on current and former students (e.g., student achievement and perceptions), analyzes and uses it in conjunction with future trends for planning. Identified areas for improvement are tracked over time.	Data are used to improve the effectiveness of teaching strategies on all student learning. Students' historical performances are graphed and utilized for diagnostics. Student evaluations and performances are analyzed by teachers in all classrooms.	Innovative teaching processes that meet the needs of students are implemented to the delight of teachers, parents, and students. Information is analyzed and used to prevent student failure. Root causes are known through analyses. Problems are prevented through the use of data.
Outcome	Only anecdotal and hypothetical information is available about student performance, behavior, and satisfaction. Problems are solved individually with short-term results.	Little data are available. Change is limited to some areas of the school and dependent upon individual teachers and their efforts.	Information collected about student and parent needs, assessment, and instructional practices is shared with the school staff and used to plan for change. Information helps staff understand pressing issues, analyze information for "root causes," and track results for improvement.	An information system is in place. Positive trends begin to appear in many classrooms and schoolwide. There is evidence that these results are caused by understanding and effectively using data collected.	Students are delighted with the school's instructional processes and proud of their own capabilities to learn and assess their own growth. Good to excellent achievement is the result for all students. No student falls through the cracks. Teachers use data to predict and prevent potential problems.

School Continuous Improvement Continuums
STUDENT ACHIEVEMENT

	One	Two	Three	Four	Five
Approach	Instructional and organizational processes critical to student success are not identified. Little distinction of student learning differences is made. Some teachers believe that not all students can achieve.	Some data are collected on student background and performance trends. Learning gaps are noted to direct improvement of instruction. It is known that student learning standards must be identified.	Student learning standards are identified, and a continuum of learning is created throughout the school. Student performance data are collected and compared to the standards in order to analyze how to improve learning for all students.	Data on student achievement are used throughout the school to pursue the improvement of student learning. Teachers collaborate to implement appropriate instruction and assessment strategies for meeting student learning standards articulated across grade levels. All teachers believe that all students can learn.	School makes an effort to exceed student achievement expectations. Innovative instructional changes are made to anticipate learning needs and improve student achievement. Teachers are able to predict characteristics impacting student achievement and to know how to perform from a small set of internal quality measures.
Implementation	All students are taught the same way. There is no communication with students about their academic needs or learning styles. There are no analyses of how to improve instruction.	Some effort is made to track and analyze student achievement trends on a school-wide basis. Teachers begin to understand the needs and learning gaps of students.	Teachers study effective instruction and assessment strategies to implement standards and to increase their students' learning. Student feedback and analysis of achievement data are used in conjunction with implementation support strategies.	There is a systematic focus on implementing student learning standards and on the improvement of student learning schoolwide. Effective instruction and assessment strategies are implemented in each classroom. Teachers support one another with peer coaching and/or action research focused on implementing strategies that lead to increased achievement and the attainment of the shared vision.	All teachers correlate critical instructional and assessment strategies with objective indicators of quality student achievement. A comparative analysis of actual individual student performance to student learning standards is utilized to adjust teaching strategies to ensure a progression of learning for all students.
Outcome	There is wide variation in student attitudes and achievement with undesirable results. There is high dissatisfaction among students with learning. Student background is used as an excuse for low student achievement.	There is some evidence that student achievement trends are available to teachers and are being used. There is much effort, but minimal observable results in improving student achievement.	There is an increase in communication between students and teachers regarding student learning. Teachers learn about effective instructional strategies that will implement the shared vision, including student learning standards, and meet the needs of their students. They make some gains.	Increased student achievement is evident schoolwide. Student morale, attendance, and behavior are good. Teachers converse often with each other about preventing student failure. Areas for further attention are clear.	Students and teachers conduct self-assessments to continuously improve performance. Improvements in student achievement are evident and clearly caused by teachers' and students' understandings of individual student learning standards, linked to appropriate and effective instructional and assessment strategies. A continuum of learning results. No students fall through the cracks.

School Continuous Improvement Continuums
QUALITY PLANNING

	One	Two	Three	Four	Five
Approach	No quality plan or process exists. Data are neither used nor considered important in planning.	The staff realize the importance of a mission, vision, and one comprehensive action plan. Teams develop goals and timelines, and dollars are allocated to begin the process.	A comprehensive school plan to achieve the vision is developed. Plan includes evaluation and continuous improvement.	One focused and integrated schoolwide plan for implementing a continuous improvement process is put into action. All school efforts are focused on the implementation of this plan that represents the achievement of the vision.	A plan for the continuous improvement of the school, with a focus on students, is put into place. There is excellent articulation and integration of all elements in the school due to quality planning. Leadership team ensures all elements are implemented by all appropriate parties.
Implementation	There is no knowledge of or direction for quality planning. Budget is allocated on an as-needed basis. Many plans exist.	School community begins continuous improvement planning efforts by laying out major steps to a shared vision, by identifying values and beliefs, the purpose of the school, a mission, vision, and student learning standards.	Implementation goals, responsibilities, due dates, and timelines are spelled out. Support structures for implementing the plan are set in place.	The quality management plan is implemented through effective procedures in all areas of the school. Everyone commits to implementing the plan aligned to the vision, mission, and values and beliefs. All share responsibility for accomplishing school goals.	Schoolwide goals, mission, vision, and student learning standards are shared and articulated throughout the school and with feeder schools. The attainment of identified student learning standards is linked to planning and implementation of effective instruction that meets students' needs. Leaders at all levels are developing expertise because planning is the norm.
Outcome	There is no evidence of comprehensive planning. Staff work is carried out in isolation. A continuum of learning for students is absent.	The school community understands the benefits of working together to implement a comprehensive continuous improvement plan.	There is evidence that the school plan is being implemented in some areas of the school. Improvements are neither systematic nor integrated schoolwide.	A schoolwide plan is known to all. Results from working toward the quality improvement goals are evident throughout the school. Planning is ongoing and inclusive of all stakeholders.	Evidence of effective teaching and learning results in significant improvement of student achievement attributed to quality planning at all levels of the school organization. Teachers and administrators understand and share the school mission and vision. Quality planning is seamless and all demonstrate evidence of accountability.

School Continuous Improvement Continuums
PROFESSIONAL DEVELOPMENT

	One	Two	Three	Four	Five
Approach	There is no professional development. Teachers, principals, and staff are seen as interchangeable parts that can be replaced. Professional development is external and usually equated to attending a conference alone. Hierarchy determines "haves" and "have-nots."	The "cafeteria" approach to professional development is used, whereby individual teachers choose what they want to take, without regard to an overall school plan.	The shared vision, school plan, and student needs are used to target focused professional development for all employees. Staff is inserviced on relevant instructional and leadership strategies.	Professional development and data-gathering methods are used by all teachers and are directed toward the goals of the shared vision and the continuous improvement of the school. Teachers have ongoing conversations about student achievement data. Other staff members receive training in their content areas. Systems thinking is considered in all decisions.	Leadership and staff continuously improve all aspects of the learning organization through an innovative, data-driven, and comprehensive continuous improvement process that prevents student failures. Effective job-embedded professional development is ongoing for implementing the vision for student success. Traditional teacher evaluations are replaced by collegial coaching and action research focused on student learning standards. Policies set professional development as a priority budget line-item. Professional development is planned, aligned, and lead to the achievement of student learning standards.
Implementation	Teacher, principal, and staff performance is controlled and inspected. Performance evaluations are used to detect mistakes.	Teacher professional development is sporadic and unfocused, lacking an approach for implementing new procedures and processes. Some leadership training begins to take place.	Teachers are involved in year-round quality professional development. The school community is trained in shared decision making, team building concepts, effective communication strategies, and data analysis at the classroom level.	Teachers, in teams, continuously set and implement student achievement goals. Leadership considers these goals and provides necessary support structures for collaboration. Teachers utilize effective support approaches as they implement new instruction and assessment strategies. Coaching and feedback structures are in place. Use of new knowledge and skills is evident.	Teams passionately support each other in the pursuit of quality improvement at all levels. Teachers make bold changes in instruction and assessment strategies focused on student learning standards and student learning styles. A teacher as action researcher model is implemented. Staffwide conversations focus on systemic reflection and improvement. Teachers are strong leaders.
Outcome	No professional growth and no staff or student performance improvement. There exists a high turnover rate of employees, especially administrators. Attitudes and approaches filter down to students.	The effectiveness of professional development is not known or analyzed. Teachers feel helpless about making schoolwide changes.	Teachers, working in teams, feel supported and begin to feel they can make changes. Evidence shows that shared decision making works.	A collegial school is evident. Effective classroom strategies are practiced, articulated schoolwide, are reflective of professional development aimed at ensuring student achievement, and the implementation of the shared vision, that includes student learning standards.	True systemic change and improved student achievement result because teachers are knowledgeable of and implement effective, differentiated teaching strategies for individual student learning gains. Teachers' repertoire of skills are enhanced, and students are achieving. Professional development is driving learning at all levels.

School Continuous Improvement Continuums
LEADERSHIP

	One	Two	Three	Four	Five
Approach	Principal as decision maker. Decisions are reactive to state, district, and federal mandates. There is no knowledge of continuous improvement.	A shared decision-making structure is put into place and discussions begin on how to achieve a school vision. Most decisions are focused on solving problems and are reactive.	Leadership team is committed to continuous improvement. Leadership seeks inclusion of all school sectors and supports study teams by making time provisions for their work.	Leadership team represents a true shared decision-making structure. Study teams are reconstructed for the implementation of a comprehensive continuous improvement plan.	A strong continuous improvement structure is set into place that allows for input from all sectors of the school, district, and community, ensuring strong communication, flexibility, and refinement of approach and beliefs. The school vision is student focused, based on data, and appropriate for school/community values, and meeting student needs.
Implementation	Principal makes all decisions, with little or no input from teachers, the community, or students. Leadership inspects for mistakes.	School values and beliefs are identified; the purpose of school is defined; a school mission and student learning standards are developed with representative input. A structure for studying approaches to achieving student learning standards is established.	Leadership team is active on study teams and integrates recommendations from the teams' research and analyses to form a comprehensive plan for continuous improvement within the context of the school mission. Everyone is kept informed.	Decisions about budget and implementation of the vision are made within teams, by the principal, by the leadership team, and by the full staff as appropriate. All decisions are communicated to the leadership team and to the full staff.	The vision is implemented and articulated across all grade levels and into feeder schools. Quality standards are reinforced throughout the school. All members of the school community understand and apply the quality standards. Leadership team has systematic interactions and involvement with district administrators, teachers, parents, community, and students about the school's direction. Necessary resources are available to implement and measure staff learning related to student learning standards.
Outcome	Decisions lack focus and consistency. There is no evidence of staff commitment to a shared vision. Students and parents do not feel they are being heard. Decision-making process is clear and known.	The mission provides a focus for all school improvement and guides the action to the vision. The school community is committed to continuous improvement. Quality leadership techniques are used sporadically.	Leadership team is seen as committed to planning and quality improvement. Critical areas for improvement are identified. Faculty feel included in shared decision making.	There is evidence that the leadership team listens to all levels of the organization. Implementation of the continuous improvement plan is linked to student learning standards and the guiding principles of the school. Leadership capacities for implementing the vision among teachers are evident.	Site-based management and shared decision making truly exists. Teachers understand and display an intimate knowledge of how the school operates. Teachers support and communicate with each other in the implementation of quality strategies. Teachers implement the vision in their classrooms and can determine how their new approach meets student needs and leads to the attainment of student learning standards. Leaders are standards-driven at all levels.

School Continuous Improvement Continuums
PARTNERSHIP DEVELOPMENT

	One	Two	Three	Four	Five
Approach	There is no system for input from parents, business, or community. Status quo is desired for managing the school.	Partnerships are sought, but mostly for money and things.	School has knowledge of why partnerships are important and seeks to include businesses and parents in a strategic fashion related to student learning standards for increased student achievement.	School seeks effective win-win business and community partnerships and parent involvement to implement the vision. Desired outcomes are clearly identified. A solid plan for partnership development exists.	Community, parent, and business partnerships become integrated across all student groupings. The benefits of outside involvement are known by all. Parent and business involvement in student learning is refined. Student learning *regularly* takes place beyond the school walls.
Implementation	Barriers are erected to close out involvement of outsiders. Outsiders are managed for least impact on status quo.	A team is assigned to get partners and to receive input from parents, the community, and business in the school.	Involvement of business, community, and parents begins to take place in some classrooms and after school hours related to the vision. Partners begin to realize how they can support each other in achieving school goals. School staff understand what partners need from the partnership.	There is a systematic utilization of parents, community, and businesses schoolwide. Areas in which the active use of these partnerships benefit student learning are clear.	Partnership development is articulated across all student groupings. Parents, community, business, and educators work together in an innovative fashion to increase student learning and to prepare students for the 21st Century. Partnerships are evaluated for continuous improvement.
Outcome	There is little or no involvement of parents, business, or community at-large. School is a closed, isolated system.	Much effort is given to establishing partnerships. Some spotty trends emerge, such as receiving donated equipment.	Some substantial gains are achieved in implementing partnerships. Some student achievement increases can be attributed to this involvement.	Gains in student satisfaction with learning and school are clearly related to partnerships. All partners benefit.	Previously non-achieving students enjoy learning with excellent achievement. Community, business, and home become common places for student learning, while school becomes a place where parents come for further education. Partnerships enhance what the school does for students.

School Continuous Improvement Continuums
CONTINUOUS IMPROVEMENT AND EVALUATION

	One	Two	Three	Four	Five
Approach	Neither goals nor strategies exist for the evaluation and continuous improvement of the school organization or for elements of the school organization.	The approach to continuous improvement and evaluation is problem solving. If there are no problems, or if solutions can be made quickly, there is no need for improvement or analyses. Changes in parts of the system are not coordinated with all other parts.	Some elements of the school organization are evaluated for effectiveness. Some elements are improved on the basis of the evaluation findings.	All elements of the school's operations are evaluated for improvement and to ensure congruence of the elements with respect to the continuum of learning students experience.	All aspects of the school organization are rigorously evaluated and improved on a continuous basis. Students, and the maintenance of a comprehensive learning continuum for students, become the focus of all aspects of the school improvement process.
Implementation	With no overall plan for evaluation and continuous improvement, strategies are changed by individual teachers and administrators only when something sparks the need to improve. Reactive decisions and activities are a daily mode of operation.	Isolated changes are made in some areas of the school organization in response to problem incidents. Changes are not preceded by comprehensive analyses, such as an understanding of the root causes of problems. The effectiveness of the elements of the school organization, or changes made to the elements, is not known.	Elements of the school organization are improved on the basis of comprehensive analyses of root causes of problems, client perceptions, and operational effectiveness of processes.	Continuous improvement analyses of student achievement and instructional strategies are rigorously reinforced within each classroom and across learning levels to develop a comprehensive learning continuum for students and to prevent student failure.	Comprehensive continuous improvement becomes the way of doing business at the school. Teachers continuously improve the appropriateness and effectiveness of instructional strategies based on student feedback and performance. All aspects of the school organization are improved to support teachers' efforts.
Outcome	Individuals struggle with system failure. Finger pointing and blaming others for failure occurs. The effectiveness of strategies is not known. Mistakes are repeated.	Problems are solved only temporarily and few positive changes result. Additionally, unintended and undesirable consequences often appear in other parts of the system. Many aspects of the school are incongruent, keeping the school from reaching its vision.	Evidence of effective improvement strategies is observable. Positive changes are made and maintained due to comprehensive analyses and evaluation.	Teachers become astute at assessing and in predicting the impact of their instructional strategies on individual student achievement. Sustainable improvements in student achievement are evident at all grade levels, due to continuous improvement.	The school becomes a congruent and effective learning organization. Only instruction and assessment strategies that produce quality student achievement are used. A true continuum of learning results for all students and staff. The impact of improvements is increasingly measurable.

Glossary of Terms

The Glossary provides brief definitions of data analysis and testing terms used throughout *Using Data to Improve Student Learning in High Schools*.

▼ **Achievement**

The demonstration of student performance measured against learning goals, learning objectives, or standards.

▼ **Achievement Gap**

The difference between how well low-income and minority children perform on standardized tests, as compared with their peers. For many years, low-income and minority children have been falling behind their white peers in terms of academic achievement.

▼ **Accountability**

The act of being responsible to somebody else or to others. It also means capable of being explained.

▼ **Action**

Specific steps, tasks, or activity used to implement a strategy.

▼ **Action Plan**

The part of continuous school improvement planning that describes the tasks that must be performed, when they will be performed, who is responsible, and how much they will cost to implement.

▼ **Action Research**

Teachers and/or administrators raise questions about the best way to improve teaching and learning, systematically study the literature to answer the questions, implement the best approach(es), and analyze the results.

▼ **Adequate Yearly Progress (AYP)**

An individual state's measure of yearly progress toward achieving state academic standards. *Adequate Yearly Progress* is the minimum level of improvement that states, school districts, and schools must achieve each year to fulfill the requirement of the *No Child Left Behind Act*.

▼ **Affinity Diagram**

A visual picture or chart of reflective thinking. The result is that more participants are likely to deal with problems that emerge.

▼ **Aggregate**

Combining the results of all groups that make up the sample or population.

▼ **Alignment**

An arrangement of groups or forces in relation to one another. In continuous school improvement planning, we align all parts of the system to the vision. With curriculum, we align instruction and materials to student learning standards.

▼ **Analysis**

The examination of facts and data to provide a basis for effective decisions.

▼ Analysis of Variance (ANOVA)

ANOVA is an inferential procedure to determine if there is a significant difference among sample means.

▼ Anticipated Achievement Scores

An estimate of the average score for students of similar ages, grade levels, and academic aptitude. It is an estimate of what we would expect an individual student to score on an achievement test.

▼ Articulation

The varied process of integrating the district/school aligned curriculum across disciplines and between grade levels and connecting it to real-life situations; also presenting it to all stakeholders and implementing it district/school wide.

▼ Assessment

Gathering and interpretation of student performance, primarily for the purpose of enhancing learning. Also used for the improvement of a program and/or strategies.

▼ Authentic Assessment

Refers to a variety of ways to assess a student's demonstration of knowledge and skills. Authentic assessments may include performances, projects, exhibitions, and portfolios.

▼ Bar Graph

A pictorial representation that uses bars to display data, usually frequencies, percentages, and averages.

▼ Baseline Data

Information collected to comprise a reference set for comparison of a second set of data collected at a later time; used to interpret changes over time, usually after some condition has been changed for research purposes that sets the standard for any research that follows in the same project.

▼ Benchmark

A standard against which something can be measured or assessed.

▼ Brainstorming

The act of listing ideas without judgment. Brainstorming generates creative ideas spontaneously.

▼ Cadres or Action Teams

Groups or teams of educators who agree to accept responsibility to study new approaches, plan for the implementation of new strategies or programs, and get work done without every staff member's involvement.

▼ Case Studies

Reviewing student's work, and/or another teacher's example lessons, which can lead to quality discussions and improved practices.

▼ Cause and Effect

The relationship and complexities between a problem or effect and the possible causes.

▼ Coaching

Teachers form teams of two or three to observe each other, plan together, and talk and encourage each other in meaningful ways while reflecting on continuously improving instructional practices.

▼ Cognitive Abilities or Skills Index

An age-dependent, normalized standard score based on a student's performance on a cognitive skills test with a mean of 100 and standard deviation of 16. The score indicates a student's overall cognitive ability or academic aptitude relative to students of similar age, without regard to grade level.

▼ Cohort

A group of individuals sharing a particular statistical or demographic characteristic, such as the year they were in a specific school grade level. Following cohorts over time helps teachers understand the effects particular circumstances may have on results. Matched cohort studies follow the same individuals over time, and unmatched cohort studies follow the same group over time.

▼ Cohort Analysis

The reorganization of grade level data to look at the groups of students progressing through the grades together over time.

▼ Collaboration

Evidence of two of more concerned groups (i.e., teachers, aides, itinerant and resource teachers, parents, community representatives, etc.), working together to improve the school program.

▼ Collaborative

Working jointly with others, especially in an intellectual endeavor.

▼ Comprehensive Action Plan

Defining the specific actions needed to implement the vision, setting forth when the actions will take place, designating who is responsible for accomplishing the action, how much it will cost, and where to get the funds.

▼ Confidence Interval

Used in inferential statistics, a range of values that a researcher can estimate, with a certain level of confidence, where the population parameter is located.

▼ Congruent

Corresponding to, or consistent with, each other or something else.

▼ Consensus

Decision making where a group finds a proposal acceptable enough that all members can support it; no member actively opposes it.

▼ Content Standard

Description of the knowledge or skills that educators want students to learn.

▼ Continuous

In the context of continuous school improvement, continuous means the ongoing review of the data, the implementation of the plan, and the progress being made.

▼ Continuous Improvement

Keeping the process of planning, implementing, evaluating, and improving alive over time.

▼ Continuous Improvement and Evaluation

The section of the school portfolio that assists schools to further understand where they are and what they need to do to move forward in the big picture of continuous school improvement.

▼ Continuous Improvement Continuums (CICs)

As developed by *Education for the Future Initiative,* CICs are seven rubrics that represent the theoretical flow of systemic school improvement. The *Continuous Improvement Continuums* take the theory and spirit of continuous school improvement, interweave educational research, and offer practical meaning to the components that must change simultaneously and systematically.

▼ Continuous School Improvement

By *continuous school improvement,* we mean measuring and evaluating processes on an ongoing basis to identify and implement improvement.

▼ Continuous School Improvement Plan

A plan for improvement, based on data, that will help create and manage change. The process of answering the following questions: *Who are we? How do we do business? What are our strengths and areas for improvement? Why do we exist? Where do we want to be? What are the gaps? What are the root causes of the gaps? How can we get to where we want to be? How will we implement? How will we evaluate our efforts?*

▼ Control Groups

Control groups serve as a baseline in making comparisons with treatment groups and are necessary when general effectiveness of the treatment is unknown. During an experiment, the control group is studied the same as the experimental groups, except that it does not receive the treatment of interest.

▼ Convenience Sampling

Convenience sampling is done when one wants to survey people who are ready and available, and not hassle with trying to get everyone in the population ready and willing to complete the questionnaire.

▼ Correlation

A statistical analysis that helps one see the relationship of scores in one distribution to scores in another distribution. Correlation coefficients have a range of −1.0 to +1.0. A correlation of around zero indicates no relationship. Correlations of .8 and higher indicate strong relationships.

▼ Criteria

Characteristics or dimensions of student performance.

▼ Criterion-referenced Tests

Tests that judge how well a test taker does on an explicit objective, learning goal, or criteria relative to a pre-determined performance level. There is no comparison to any other test takers.

▼ Culture

Attitudes, values, beliefs, goals, norms of behavior, and practices that characterize a group.

▼ Curriculum Alignment

A curriculum in which what is taught, how it is taught, and how it is assessed is intentionally based on, but not limited to, the state *Core Curriculum Content Standards and Assessment*—the sequence of learning in an aligned curriculum is articulated and constantly discussed, monitored, and revised.

▼ Curriculum Development and Implementation

The way content is designed and delivered. Teachers must think deeply about the content, student-learning standards, and how it must be managed and delivered, or put into practice.

▼ **Curriculum Implementation**

Putting the curriculum into practice.

▼ **Curriculum Mapping and Webbing**

Approaches that require teachers to align the curriculum and student learning standards by grade levels, and then across grade levels, to ensure a continuum of learning that makes sense for all students.

▼ **Data Cleansing**

The process of ensuring that all values in a database are consistent and correctly recorded.

▼ **Data-driven Decision Making**

Making decisions based on demographic, student learning, perceptions, and school process data. True data-driven decision making has the guiding principles of the learning organization at the center of every decision.

▼ **Data Mining**

Techniques for finding patterns and trends in large data sets. The process of automatically extracting valid, useful, previously unknown, and ultimately comprehensible information from large databases. Just doing common data analysis is not data mining.

▼ **Data Table**

The source of data for tables and graphs. In building graphs with a software program, one would need to create a data table from which to create the graphs or tables.

▼ **Data Warehouse**

A single, large database that has collected relevant information from several other sources into a single, accessible format designed to be used for decision making. The data warehouse is created to house data imported from many other data sources that are not designed to work together or to share information.

▼ **Database**

A storage mechanism for data that eliminates redundancy and conflict among multiple data files. Data is entered once and is then available to all programs that need it.

▼ **Deciles**

The values of a variable that divide the frequency distribution into ten equal frequency groups. The ninth decile shows the number (or percentage) of the norming group that scored between 80 and 89 NCE, for example.

▼ **Demographics**

Statistical characteristics of a population, such as average age, number of students in a school, percentages of ethnicities, etc. Disaggregation with demographic data allows us to isolate variations among different subgroups.

▼ **Derived Score**

A score that is attained by performing some kind of mathematical operation on a raw score for comparison within a particular grade (e.g., T-scores, NCE, etc.).

▼ **Descriptive Statistics**

Direct measurement (i.e. mean, median, percent correct) of each member of a group or population. Descriptive statistics can include graphing.

▼ Diagnostic

Assessment/evaluation carried out prior to instruction that is designed to determine a student's attitude, skill, or knowledge in order to identify specific student needs.

▼ Diagnostic Tests

Usually standardized and normed, diagnostic tests are given before instruction begins to help the instructor(s) understand student learning needs. Many different score types are used with diagnostic tests.

▼ Different Ways of Knowing (DWOK)

A standards-based, interdisciplinary, arts-infused curriculum that promotes collaborative learning and higher–order thinking.

▼ Disaggregate

Separating the results of different groups that make up the sample or population.

▼ Disaggregated Data

To *disaggregate* means separating the results of different groups or separating a whole into its parts. In education, this term means that test results are sorted into groups of students by gender, those who are economically disadvantaged, by racial and ethnic minority groups, disabilities, or by English fluency. This practice allows administrators and teachers to see more than just the average score for the school. Instead, administrators and teachers can see how each student group is performing.

▼ Diverse/Diversity

The inclusion of differences based on gender, race, disability, age, national origin, color, economic status, religion, geographic regions, and other characteristics. Achieving diversity requires respect of differences; valuing differences; supporting, encouraging, and promoting differences; and affirmation initiatives, such as recruitment, placement, and retention.

▼ Educationally Significant

Gains in student achievement, school, or program results can be considered educationally significant, even though they are not statistically significant.

▼ Evaluation

Making judgments about the quality of overall student performance for the purpose of communicating student achievement. Evaluation also is the study of the impact of a program or process.

▼ Examining Student Data

Conversations around individual student data results and the processes that created the results. This approach can be a significant form of professional development when skilled team members facilitate the discussions.

▼ Examining Student Work

Ensures that what students learn is aligned to the learning standards. It also shows teachers the impact of their actions.

▼ Exemplars

Models or examples of excellent work that meet stated criteria or levels of performance.

▼ Experimental Design

The detailed planning of an experiment, made beforehand, to insure the data collected is appropriate and obtained in a way that will lead to an objective analysis, with valid inferences. Preferably, the design will maximize the amount of information that can be gained, given the amount of effort expended.

▼ Fluency

The capacity to read text accurately and quickly.

▼ Flow Chart

A flowchart illustrates the steps in a process. By visualizing the process, a flow chart can quickly help identify bottlenecks or inefficiencies where a process can be streamlined or improved.

▼ Focus Group

A group convened to gather information about processes or practices that need to be examined.

▼ Formative

Assessments at regular intervals of a student's progress, with accompanying feedback in order to help the student's performance and to provide direction for improvement of a program for individual students or for a whole class.

▼ Frequency

The number of times a given score occurs in a distribution.

▼ Frequency Distribution

Describes how often observations fall within designated categories. It can be expressed as numbers, percents, and deciles, to name just a few possibilities.

▼ Gain Score

The difference between two administrations of the same test. Gain scores are calculated by subtracting the previous score from the most recent score. One can have negative gains, which are actually losses.

▼ Gaps

The difference between where the school is now and where the school wants to be in the future. It is this gap that gets translated into goals, objectives, strategies, and actions in the action plan.

▼ Goals

Achievements or end results. Goal statements describe the intended outcome of the vision and are stated in terms that are broad, general, abstract, and non-measurable. Schools should have only two or three goals.

▼ Grade-level Analysis

Looking at the same grade level over time.

▼ Grade-level Equivalent

The grade and month of the school year for which a given score is the actual or estimated average. Based on a 10-month school year, scores would be noted as 6.1 for grade six, first month, 8.10 for grade eight, tenth month, etc.

▼ Grades

Subjective scores given by teachers to students for performance.

▼ Guiding Principles

The vision of the school, or district, that is based on the purpose and mission of the organization, created from the values and beliefs of the individuals to make up the organization. Everything that is done in the organization ought to be aligned to its guiding principles.

▼ Holistic

Emphasizing the organic or functional relation between parts and the whole.

▼ Horizontal Articulation or Coordination

Indicates that the curriculum is carefully planned within grade levels. In effect, this would mean that every primary grade throughout the school/district will teach the same curriculum—also every grade six social studies class; every grade ten health class; every grade twelve physics class, and so on.

▼ Inferential Statistics

Statistical analysis concerned with the measurement of only a sample from a population and then making estimates, or inferences, about the population from which the sample was taken; inferential statistics help generalize the results of data analyses.

▼ Information and Analysis

Establishes systematic and rigorous reliance on data for decision making in all parts of the organization. This section of the school portfolio sets the context of the learning organization.

▼ Intersections

Analyzing the intersections or overlapping of measures (demographics, perceptions, school processes, student learning) enables schools to predict what they must do to meet the needs of all the students they have, or will have in the future.

▼ Interval Scale

Intervals are meaningful with a relative zero point. Can calculate mode, median, mean, range, standard deviation, etc.

▼ Item Analysis

Reviewing each item on a test or assessment to determine how many students missed the particular item. A general term for procedures designed to access the usefulness of a test item.

▼ Latent Trait Scale

A scaled score obtained through one of several mathematical approaches collectively known as Latent-trait procedures or Item Response Theory. The particular numerical values used in the scale are arbitrary, but higher scores indicate more knowledgeable test takers or more difficult items.

▼ Leadership

Providing needed assistance to schools to think through and plan for their vision, shared decision making, and other structures that will work with their specific population.

▼ Learner-Centered

An environment created by educators focusing on the needs and learning styles of all students.

▼ Learning

A process of acquiring knowledge, skills, understanding, and/or new behaviors.

▼ Learning Environment

Any setting or location, inside or outside the school, used to enhance the instruction of students.

▼ Learning Goal

A target for learning: a desired skill, knowledge, or behavior.

▼ Line Graph

Line graphs give a lot of flexibility and are exceptionally good for showing a series of numbers over time. Line graphs can display complex data more effectively than bar graphs.

▼ Matched Cohorts

Looking at the same students (individual, not groups) progressing through the grades over time.

▼ **Maximum**

The highest actual score or the highest possible score on a test.

▼ **Mean**

Average score in a set of scores; calculated by summing all the scores and dividing by the total number of scores.

▼ **Means**

Methods, strategies, actions, and processes by which a school plans to improve student achievement.

▼ **Measures**

A way of evaluating something; how we know we have achieved the objective.

▼ **Median**

The score that splits a distribution in half: 50 percent of the scores lie above and 50 percent of the scores lie below the median. If the number of scores is odd, the median is the middle score. If the number of scores is even, one must add the two middle scores and divide by two to calculate the median.

▼ **Minimum**

The lowest score or the lowest possible score on a test.

▼ **Mission**

A brief, clear, and compelling statement that serves to unify an organization's efforts. A mission has a finish line for its achievement and is proactive. A mission should walk the boundary between the possible and impossible.

▼ **Mobility**

The reference to the movement of students in and out of a school or district.

▼ **Mode**

The score that occurs most frequently in a scoring distribution.

▼ **Multiple Measures**

Using more than one method of assessment, gathered from varying points of view, in order to understand the multifaceted world of school from the perspective of everyone involved.

▼ **N**

The number of students in the group being described, such as the number taking a test or completing a questionnaire.

▼ **Needs Assessment**

Questions that help staff understand their professional development needs. At the same time, if done well, this assessment can lead to quality staff conversations and sharing of knowledge.

▼ **No Child Left Behind (NCLB)**

The No Child Left Behind Act of 2001 reauthorized the 1965 Elementary and Secondary Education Act. NCLB calls for increased accountability for states, school districts, and schools; choices for parents and students; greater flexibility for states, school districts, and schools regarding Federal education funds; establishing a Reading First initiative to ensure every child can read by end of grade three; and improving the quality of teachers.

▼ **Nominal Scale**

Qualitative, categorical information. Numbers represent categories, e.g., 1=male, 2=female.

▼ Normal Curve
The bell-shaped curve of the normal distribution.

▼ Normal Curve Equivalent (NCE)
Equivalent scores are standard scores with a mean of 50, a standard deviation of 21.06, and a range of 1 to 99.

▼ Normal Distribution
A distribution of scores or other measures that in graphic form has a distinctive bell-shaped appearance. In a normal distribution, the measures are distributed symmetrically about the mean. Cases are concentrated near the mean and decrease in frequency, according to a precise mathematical equation, the farther one departs from the mean. Also known as a normal curve.

▼ Normalized Standard Score
A transformation procedure used to make scores from different tests more directly comparable. Not only are the mean and the standard deviation of the raw score distribution changed, as with a linear standard score transformation, but the shape of the distribution is converted to a normal curve. The transformation to a normalized z-score involves two steps: 1) compute the exact percentile rank of the raw score; and 2) determine the corresponding z-score for that exact percentile rank from a table of areas under the normal curve.

▼ Norming Group
A representative group of students whose results on a norm-referenced test help create the scoring scales with which others compare their performance. The norming group's results are professed to look like the normal curve.

▼ Norm-referenced Test
Any test in which the score acquires additional meaning by comparing it to the scores of people in an identified norming group. A test can be both norm- and criterion-referenced. Most standardized achievement tests are referred to as norm-referenced.

▼ Norms
The distribution of test scores and their corresponding percentile ranks, standard scores, or other derived scores of some specified group called the norming group. For example, this may be a national sample of all fourth graders, a national sample of all fourth-grade males, or perhaps all fourth graders in some local district.

▼ Norms versus Standards
Norms are not standards. Norms are indicators of what students of similar characteristics did when confronted with the same test items as those taken by students in the norming group. Standards, on the other hand, are arbitrary judgments of what students should be able to do, given a set of test items.

▼ Objectives
Goals that are redrafted in terms that are clearly tangible. Objective statements are narrow, specific, concrete, and measurable. When writing objectives, it is important to describe the intended results, rather than the process or means to accomplish them, and state the time frame.

▼ Observation
Teacher and observer agree on what is being observed, the type of information to be recorded, when the observation will take place, and how the information will be analyzed. The observee is someone implementing strategies and actions that others want to know. Observer might be a colleague, a supervisor, or a visitor from another location.

▼ Open-ended Response Items

Questions that require students to combine content knowledge and application of process skills in order to communicate an answer.

▼ Ordinal

Ordinal provides information about size or direction; numbers ordered along underlying dimension, but no information about distance between points.

▼ Outcome

Successful demonstration of learning that occurs at the culmination point of a set learning experiences.

▼ Over Time

No less than three years.

▼ Parameter

A parameter is a population measurement that characterizes one of its features. An example of a parameter is the mode. The mode is the value in the population that occurs most frequently. Other examples of parameters are a population's mean (or average) and its variance.

▼ Partnerships

Teachers developing relationships with parents, businesses in the community, scientists, and/or university personnel to help students achieve student learning standards, and to bring about real world applications for student learning and deeper understandings of content.

▼ Pearson Correlation Coefficient

The most widely-used correlation coefficient determines the extent to which two variables are proportional to each other; measures the strength and direction of a linear relationship between the x and y variables.

▼ Percent Correct

A calculated score implying the percentage of students meeting and exceeding some number, usually a cut score, or a standard. Percent passing equals the number passing the test divided by the number taking the test.

▼ Percent Proficient

Percent Proficient, Percent Mastery, or Percent Passing are terms that represent the percentage of students who pass a particular test at a level above a cut score, as defined by the test creators or the test interpreters.

▼ Percentile

A point on the normal distribution below which a certain percentage of the scores fall. For example, if 70 percent of the scores fall below a raw score of 56, then the score of 56 is at the 70th percentile. The term *local percentile* indicates that the norm group is obtained locally. The term *national percentile* indicates that the norm group represents a national group.

▼ Percentile Rank (PR)

Percentage of students in a norm group (e.g., national or local) whose scores fall below a given score. Range is from 1 to 99. A 50th percentile ranking would mean that 50 percent of the scores in the norming group fall below a specific score.

▼ Perceptions Data

Information that reflects opinions and views of questionnaire respondents.

▼ Performance Assessment

Refers to assessments that measure skills, knowledge, and ability directly—such as through performance. In other words, if you want students to learn to write, you assess their ability on a writing activity.

▼ Performance Standard

Identification of the desired level of proficiency at which educators want a content standard to be mastered.

▼ Pie Chart or Pie Graph

A graph in a circular format, used to display percentages of something, such as the percentage of a school or district population, by ethnicity.

▼ Population

Statisticians define a population as the entire collection of items that is the focus of concern. Descriptive Statistics describe the characteristics of a given population by measuring each of its items and then summarizing the set of measures in various ways. Inferential Statistics make educated inferences about the characteristics of a population by drawing a random sample and appropriately analyzing the information it provides.

▼ Press Release

Article written by school public information official or an education reporter for a local newspaper.

▼ Process Mapping

School processes are instruction, curriculum, and assessment strategies used to ensure the learning of all students. Mapping or flow charting school processes can help staff objectively look at how students are being taught.

▼ Processes

Measures that describe what is being done to get results, such as programs, strategies, and practices.

▼ Professional Development

Planned learning activities that help staff members, teachers, and administrators change the manner in which they work, i.e., how they make decisions; gather, analyze, and use data; plan, teach, and monitor achievement; evaluate personnel; and assess the impact of new approaches to instruction and assessment on students.

▼ Program Evaluation

The examination of a program to understand its quality and impact.

▼ Purpose

The aim of the organization; the reason for existence.

▼ Quality Planning

Developing the elements of a strategic plan including a vision, mission, goals, action plan, outcome measures, and strategies for continuous improvement and evaluation. Quality planning is a section of the school portfolio.

▼ Quality

A standard for excellence.

▼ Quartiles

Three quartiles—Q1, Q2, Q3—divide a distribution into four equal groups (Q1=25th percentile; Q2=50th percentile; Q3=75th percentile).

▼ Query

A request one makes to a database that is returned to the desktop. Understanding and knowing how to set up queries or to ask questions of the database is very important to the information discovery process.

▼ Quota Sampling

Divides the population being studied into subgroups such as male and female, or young, middle, and old, to ensure that you set a quota of responses.

▼ Range

A measure of the spread between the lowest and the highest scores in a distribution, calculated by subtracting the lowest score from the highest score.

▼ Ratio

A proportional relationship between two different numbers or quantities.

▼ Raw Scores

A person's observed score on a test or subtest. The number of questions answered correctly on a test or subtest. A raw score is simply calculated by adding the number of questions answered correctly.

▼ Regression

An analysis that results in an equation that describes the nature of the relationship among variables. Simple regressions predict an object's value on a criterion variable when given its value on one predictor variable. Multiple regressions predict an object's value on a criterion variable when given its value on each of several predictor variables.

▼ Relational Database

A type of database that allows the connection of several databases to each other. The data and relations between them are stored in table form. Relational databases are powerful because they require few assumptions about how data are related and how they will be extracted from the database.

▼ Relationships

Looking at two or more sets of analyses to understand how they are associated or what they mean to each other.

▼ Reliability

The consistency with which an assessment measures what it intends to measure.

▼ Research

The act of methodically collecting information about a particular subject to discover facts or to develop a plan of action based on the facts discovered.

▼ RIT Scale Scores

Named for George Rasch, who developed the theory of this type of measurement, RIT scores are scaled scores that come from a series of tests created by the Northwest Evaluation Association (NWEA). The tests that draw from an item bank are created to align with local curriculum and state standards.

▼ Root Cause

As used in the continuous school improvement plan, root cause refers to the deep underlying reason for a specific situation. While a symptom may be made evident from a needs assessment or gap analysis—the symptom (low student scores) is not the cause. To find a root cause or causes one often has to ask Why? at least five levels down to uncover the root reasons for the symptom.

▼ Rubric

A scoring tool that rates performance according to clearly stated levels of criteria. The scales can be numeric or descriptive.

▼ Sample

In statistical terms, a random sample is a set of items that have been drawn from a population in such a way that each time an item is selected, every item in the population has an equal opportunity to appear in the sample. In practical terms, it is not so easy to draw a random sample.

▼ Scaled Scores

A mathematical transformation of a raw score. It takes the differences in the difficulty of test forms into consideration and is useful for teaching changes over time.

▼ School Improvement Planning

Planning to implement the vision requires studying the research, determining strategies that will work with the students, and determining what the vision would look like, sound like, and feel like when the vision is implemented, and how to get all staff members implementing the vision.

▼ School Portfolio

A professional development tool that gathers evidence about the way work is done in the school and a self-assessment tool to ensure the alignment of all parts of the learning organization to the vision. A school portfolio can also serve as a principal portfolio.

▼ School Processes

Instruction, curriculum, and assessment strategies used to ensure the learning of all students.

▼ School Profile

A two to four page summary that presents a picture of a school. Usually includes demographic and achievement information, as well as analysis of other available data.

▼ Scientifically-based Research

The revised *Elementary and Secondary Education Act,* recently approved by Congress and also known as the *No Child Left Behind Act of 2001,* mandates that educators base school programs and teaching practices on Scientifically Based Research. This includes everything from teaching approaches to drug abuse prevention. Scientifically Based Research means research that involves the application of rigorous, systematic, and objective procedures to obtain reliable and valid knowledge relevant to education activities and programs.

▼ Self-assessment

Assessment by the individual performing the activity.

▼ Shared Decision Making

A process whereby all stakeholders within a school are engaged and meaningfully involved in the planning and decision-making process of that school.

▼ Simple Sample

A smaller version of the larger population that can be considered representative of the population. One classroom of students can be a simple sample, or one school in the district. This is typically used when administering a very large questionnaire.

▼ Skewed Distribution

Most of the scores are found near one end of the distribution. When most of the scores are grouped at the lower end, it is positively skewed. When most of the scores are grouped at the upper end, it is negatively skewed.

▼ Snowball Sampling

Relies on members of one group completing the questionnaire to identify other members of the population to complete the questionnaire.

▼ Socioeconomic Status (SES)

An indication of the level of poverty in which a student lives. Most school districts use whether or not a student qualifies for free/reduced lunch as an indicator. Other school districts use more complex equations that include mother's level of education and the like.

▼ Standard

A guideline or description that is used as a basis for judgment—exemplary performance; an objective ideal; a worthy and tangible goal.

▼ Standard Deviation

Measure of variability in a set of scores. The standard deviation is the square root of the variance. Unlike the variance, the standard deviation is stated in the original units of the variable. Approximately 68 percent of the scores in a normal distribution lie between plus one and minus one standard deviation. The more scores cluster around the mean, the smaller the variance.

▼ Standard Scores

A group of scores having a desired mean and standard deviation. A z-score is a basic standard score. Other standard scores are computed by first converting a raw score to a z-score (sometimes normalized), multiplying the transformation by the desired standard deviation, and then adding the desired mean to the product. The raw scores are transformed this way for reasons of convenience, comparability, and ease of interpretation.

▼ Standardized Tests

Tests that are uniform in content, administration, and scoring. Standardized tests can be used for comparing results across classrooms, schools, school districts, and states.

▼ Standards

Consistent expectations of all learners.

▼ Standards-based Assessments

A collection of items that indicate how much students know and/or are able to do with respect to specific standards.

▼ Stanines

A nine-point normalized standard score scale. It divides the normal curve distribution of scores into nine equal points: 1 to 9. The mean of a stanine distribution is 5, and the standard deviation is approximately 2.

▼ Statistically Significant

Statistical significance of a result is the probability that the observed relationship in a sample occurred by pure chance; indicates that there is at least a 95% probability of the result that did not happen by chance.

▼ Strategies

Procedures, methods, or techniques to accomplish an objective.

▼ Stratified Random Sample

One which divides the population into subgroups, and then a random sample is selected from each of the groups. This approach would be used when you want to make sure that you hear from all the groups of people you want to study.

▼ Student Achievement Data

Information that reflects a level of knowledge, skill, or accomplishment, usually in something that has been explicitly taught.

▼ Study Groups

Teams or groups of educators meet to learn new strategies or programs, to review new publications, or to review student work together.

▼ Summative

Assessment or evaluation designed to provide information; used in making judgments about a student's achievement at the end of a period of instruction.

▼ Symptom

A symptom is the outward (most visible) indicator of a deeper root cause.

▼ System

A system is the sum of the interactions between and among its component parts. School districts are systems.

▼ Systemic

Affecting or relating to a system as a whole.

▼ Systematic

Refers to approaches that are repeatable and that use data and information so that improvement and learning are possible.

▼ Systems Perspective

Viewing the school or school district as a whole or perceiving the combination of related structures/components of the school and community (i.e., indicators and standards for school improvement), organized into a complex whole.

▼ Systems Thinking

Systems thinking would have continuous improvement teams focusing on improving how the parts of the system interact and support one another towards achievement of common goals.

▼ T-Chart

Used to compare and contrast information or to show relationships. It is used to help people see the opposite dimension of an issue.

▼ T-Scores

A calculated standard score with a mean of 50 and a standard deviation of 10. T-scores are obtained by the following formula: $T=10z+50$. T-scores are sometimes normalized.

▼ Table

A data structure comprised of rows and columns, like a spreadsheet.

▼ Teacher Portfolios

The process and product of documenting a teacher as learner; includes reflections, observations, and evidence. Portfolios can be used for many things, such as, self-assessment, employment, supervision to replace traditional teacher evaluation, and for peer collaboration.

▼ Tests of Significance

Procedures that use samples to test claims about population parameters. Significance tests can estimate a population parameter, with a certain amount of confidence, from a sample.

▼ Trends

Direction that is given from a learning organization's data. Usually need three years of data to see a trend.

▼ Triangulation

The term used for combining three or more student achievement measures to get a more complete picture of student achievement.

▼ Validity

The degree to which an assessment strategy measures what it is intended to measure.

▼ Values and Beliefs

The core of who we are, what we do, and how we think and feel. Values and beliefs reflect what is important to us; they describe what we think about work and how we think it should operate. Core values and beliefs are the first step in reaching a shared vision.

▼ Variance

A measure of the dispersion, or variability, of scores about their mean. The population variance is calculated by taking the average of the squared deviations from the mean—a deviation being defined as an individual score minus the mean.

▼ Variation

All systems and processes vary. It is essential to understand what type of variation is present before trying to correct or improve the system. Two types of variation are *common cause* and *special cause.* Special cause variation must be eliminated before a system can be improved.

▼ Vertical Articulation or Alignment

Indicates that the curriculum is carefully planned and sequenced from beginning learning and skills to more advanced learning and skills. Vertical articulation speaks to what is taught from pre-school through upper grades and is sometimes noted simply as "K-12 Curriculum."

▼ Vision

A specific description of what the learning organization will be like when the mission is achieved. A vision is a mental image. It must be written in practical, concrete terms that everyone can understand and see in the same way.

▼ z-Scores

A standard score with a mean of zero and a standard deviation of one. A z-score is obtained by the following formula: z = raw score (x) minus the mean, divided by the standard deviation (sd). A z-score is sometimes normalized.

References and Resources

The references used in this book, along with other resources that will assist busy school administrators and teachers in conducting quality data analyses, appear below.

Airasian, P. W. (1994). *Classroom assessment.* New York, NY: McGraw-Hill, Inc.

Ammerman, M. (1998). *The root cause analysis handbook: A simplified approach to identifying, correcting, and reporting workplace errors.* New York, NY: Quality Resources.

Annenberg Foundation. (2003). *Rethinking accountability: Voices in urban education.* Providence, RI: Author.

Ardovino, J., Hollingsworth, J., & Ybarra, S. (2000). *Multiple measures: Accurate ways to assess student achievement.* Thousand Oaks, CA: Corwin Press, Inc.

Armstrong, J. (2002). *What is an accountability model?* Denver, CO: Education Commission of the States. Available: http://www.ecs.org.

Armstrong, J., & Anthes, K. (2001). How data can help: Putting information to work to raise student achievement. In *American School Board Journal,* 38-41.

Arter, J. (1999). *Teaching about performance assessment.* Portland, OR: Northwest Regional Educational Laboratory.

Arter, J., & The Classroom Assessment Team, Laboratory Network Program. (1998). *Improving classroom assessment: A toolkit for professional developers: Alternative Assessment.* Aurora, CO: MCREL.

Arter, J., & Busick, K. (2001). *Practice with student-involved classroom assessment.* Portland, OR: Assessment Training Institute, Inc.

Arter, J., & McTighe, J. (2001). *Scoring rubrics in the classroom: Using performance criteria for assessing and improving student performance.* In Guskey, T.R., & Marzano, R.J. (Series Eds.). *Experts in Assessment.* Thousand Oaks, CA: Corwin Press, Inc.

Aschbacher, P. R., & Herman, J. L. (1991). *Guidelines for effective score reporting.* (CSE Technical Report No. 326). Los Angeles, CA: University of California, Center for Research on Evaluation, Standards and Student Testing (CRESST).

Baldrige National Quality Program. (2004). *Education criteria for performance excellence.* Gaithersburg, MD: National Institute of Standards and Technology. Available: www.quality.nist.gov

Barth, P., Haycock, K., Jackson, H., Mora, K., Ruiz, P., Robinson, S., & Wilkins, A. (Eds.). (1999). *Dispelling the myth: High poverty schools exceeding expectations.* Washington, DC: Education Trust in Cooperation with the Council of Chief State School Officers and partially funded by the U.S. Department of Education.

Bernhardt, V. L. (2005). Data tools for school improvement. *Educational Leadership,* 62(5), 66-69.

Bernhardt, V. L. (2004). Data analysis. In L. Easton (Ed.), *Powerful Designs for Professional Development.* Oxford, OH: National Staff Development Council (NSDC).

Bernhardt, V. L. (2004). *Data analysis for continuous school improvement* (2nd ed.). Larchmont, NY: Eye on Education, Inc.

Bernhardt, V. L. (2004). *Using data to improve student learning in middle schools.* Larchmont, NY: Eye on Education, Inc.

Bernhardt, V. L. (2003). No schools left behind. *Educational Leadership, 60*(5), 26-30.

Bernhardt, V. L. (2003). *Using data to improve student learning in elementary schools.* Larchmont, NY: Eye on Education, Inc.

Bernhardt, V. L. (2002). *The school portfolio toolkit: A planning, implementation, and evaluation guide for continuous school improvement.* Larchmont, NY: Eye on Education, Inc.

Bernhardt, V. L. (2000). *Designing and using databases for school improvement.* Larchmont, NY: Eye on Education, Inc.

Bernhardt, V. L. (2000). Intersections: New routes open when one type of data crosses another. *Journal of Staff Development, 21*(1), 33-36.

Bernhardt, V.L. (1999, June). *Databases can help teachers with standards implementation.* Monograph No. 5. California Association for Supervision and Curriculum Development (CASCD).

Bernhardt, V. L. (1999). *The school portfolio: A comprehensive framework for school improvement* (2nd ed.). Larchmont, NY: Eye on Education, Inc.

Bernhardt, V. L., von Blanckensee, L., Lauck, M., Rebello, F., Bonilla, G., & Tribbey, M. (2000). *The example school portfolio, A companion to the school portfolio: A comprehensive framework for school improvement.* Larchmont, NY: Eye on Education, Inc.

Blythe, T., & Associates. (1998). *The teaching for understanding guide.* San Francisco, CA: Jossey-Bass, Inc.

Bobko, P. (2001). *Correlation and regression: Applications for industrial/organizational psychology and management.* (2nd ed.). Thousand Oaks, CA: Sage Publications, Inc.

Carr, N. (2001). Making data count: Transforming schooling through data-driven decision making. *American School Board Journal,* 34-37.

Cawelti, G. (Ed.). (1999). *Handbook of research on improving student achievement* (2nd ed.). Arlington, VA: Educational Testing Service.

Chenoweth, T., & Everhart, R.B. (1993). *The restructured school: How do you know if something is happening* (Report No. ISSN-0032-0684). East Lansing, MI: National Center for Research on Teacher Learning. (ERIC Document Reproduction Service No. EJ462413)

Clarke, D. (1997). *Constructive assessment in mathematics: Practical steps for classroom teachers.* Berkeley, CA: Key Curriculum Press.

Clune, B., & Webb, N. (2001-02). WCER Highlights. Madison, WS: University of Wisconsin-Madison, Wisconsin Center for Education Research.

Cohen, M. (2001). *Transforming the American high school.* Washington, DC: Aspen Institute.

Commission on Instructionally Supportive Assessment. (2001). *Building tests to support instruction and accountability.* Available: http://www.aasa.org.

Conzemius, A., & O'Neill, J. (2001). *Building shared responsibility for student learning.* Alexandria, VA: Association for Supervision and Curriculum Development.

Creighton, T. B. (2001). *Schools and data: The educator's guide for using data to improve decision-making.* Thousand Oaks, CA: Corwin Press, Inc.

Creswell, J. W. (2003). *Research design: Qualitative, quantitative, and mixed methods approaches.* Thousand Oaks, CA: SAGE publications.

Dann, R. (2002). *Promoting assessment as learning.* New York, NY: RoutledgeFalmer.

Darling-Hammond, L., Berry, B., & Toreson, A. (2001). Does Teacher Certification Matter? Evaluating the Evidence. *Educational Evaluation and Policy Analysis,* 23(1), 57-77.

Deming, W. E. (1986). *Out of the crisis.* Cambridge, MA: MIT Press.

Dickinson, T. (Ed). (2001). *Reinventing the middle school.* New York, NY: Routledge Falmer.

DuFour, R., & Eaker, R. (1998). *Professional learning communities at work: Best practices for enhancing student achievement.* Alexandria, VA: Association for Supervision and Curriculum Development.

Eaker, R., DuFour, R., & Burnett, R. (2002). *Getting started: Reculturing schools to become professional learning communities.* Bloomington, IN: National Educational Service.

Education Trust. (2002). *Dispelling the myth: Lessons from high-performing schools.* Washington, DC: Author.

Educators in Connecticut's Pomperaug Regional School District 15. (1996). *A teacher's guide to performance-based learning and assessment.* Alexandria, VA: Association for Supervision and Curriculum Development.

Ellis, A. K. (2001). *Teaching, learning, and addressing together.* Larchmont, NY: Eye on Education, Inc.

Elmore, R. F. (2000). *Building a new structure for school leadership.* Washington, DC: The Albert Shanker Institute.

English, F. W. (2000). *Deciding what to teach and test: Developing, aligning, and auditing the curriculum.* Thousand Oaks, CA: Corwin Press, Inc.

Falk, B. (2000). *The heart of the matter: Using standards and assessment to learn.* Portsmouth, NH: Heinemann.

Fullan, M. (2001). *Leading a culture of change.* New York, NY: Jossey-Bass/Pfeiffer.

Fullan, M. (2002). *Changing forces with a vengeance.* New York, NY: RoutledgeFalmer.

Garmston, R.J., & Wellman, B.M. (1999). *The adaptive school: A sourcebook for developing collaborative groups.* Norwood, MA: Christopher-Gordon Publishers, Inc.

Glatthorn, A. A. (1999). *Performance standards & authentic learning.* Larchmont, NY: Eye on Education, Inc.

Glatthorn, A. A., & Fontana, J. (Eds.). (2000). *Coping with standards, tests, and accountability: Voices from the classroom.* Washington, DC: National Education Association.

Gredler, M. (1999). *Classroom assessment and learning.* Needham Heights, MA: Allyn & Bacon.

Gupta, K. (1999). *A practical guide to needs assessment.* San Francisco, CA: Jossey-Bass, Inc.

Guskey, T. (2000). *Evaluating professional development.* Thousand Oaks, CA: Corwin Press, Inc.

REFERENCES

287

Guskey, T. R., & Bailey, J. M. (2001). Developing grading and reporting systems for student learning. In Guskey, T.R. & Marzano, R.J. (Series Eds.). *Experts in assessment.* Thousand Oaks, CA: Corwin Press, Inc.

Haladyna, T. M., Nolan, S. B., & Haas, N. S. (1991). Raising standardized achievement test scores and the origins of test score pollutions. *Educational Researcher,* 20(5), 2-7.

Haycock, K. (1999). *Results: Good teaching matters.* Oxford, OH: National Staff Development Council.

Henry, G. (1997). *Creating effective graphs: Solutions for a variety of evaluation data.* Editor-in-chief. New Directions for Evaluation, a publication of the American Evaluation Association..

Henry, T. (2001, June 11). Lawmakers move to improve literacy, the 'new civil right.' *USA Today,* pp. A1-2.

Herman, J. L., & Golan, S. (1991). *Effects of standardized testing on teachers and learning—another look.* (CSE Technical Report No. 334). Los Angeles, CA: University of California, Center for Research on Evaluation, Standards and Student Testing (CRESST).

Holcomb, E. L. (1999). *Getting excited about data.* Thousand Oaks, CA: Corwin Press, Inc.

Holly, P.J. (2003). *Conceptualizing a new path: Data-driven school improvement series.* Princeton, NJ: Educational Testing Service.

Hord, S. (2003). *Learning, leading together: Changing schools through professional learning communities.* Austin, TX: Southwest Educational Development Laboratory.

Isaac, S., & William, B. M. (1997). *Handbook in research and evaluation for education and the behavioral sciences* (3rd ed.). San Diego, CA: Educational and Industrial Testing Services.

Johnson, D. W., & Johnson, R. T. (2002). *Introduction: Cooperative learning and assessment.* Needham Heights, MA: Allyn & Bacon.

Johnson, R. S. (2002). *Using data to close the achievement gap: How to measure equity in our schools.* Thousand Oaks, CA: Corwin Press, Inc.

Joint Commission Resources. (2002). *Root cause analysis in healthcare: Tools and techniques.* Indianapolis, IN: Joint Commission Resources.

Kachigan, S. K. (1991). *Multivariate statistical analysis: A conceptual introduction* (2nd ed.). New York, NY: Radius Press.

Kain, D. L. (1996). *Looking beneath the surface: Teacher collaboration through the lens of grading practices.* Teachers College Record, Summer, 569-587.

Kifer, E. (2000). *Large-scale assessment: Dimensions, dilemmas, and policy.* Thousand Oaks, CA: Corwin Press, Inc.

Killion, J. (2002). *Assessing impact: Evaluating staff development.* Oxford, OH: National Staff Development Council.

Koretz, D., Stecher, B., Klein, S., & McCaffrey, D. (1994). The Vermont portfolio assessment program: Finding and implications. *Educational Measurement: Issues and Practice,* 13(3), 5-16.

Kosslyn, S. (1994). *Elements of graph design.* New York, NY: W. H. Freeman and Company.

Kouzes, J. M., & Posner, B. Z. (2002). *The leadership challenge: How to keep getting extraordinary things done in organizations.* (2nd Ed.). San Francisco, CA: Jossey-Bass Publishers.

Krueger, R. A. (2000). *Focus groups: A practical guide for applied research.* (3rd ed.). Thousand Oaks, CA: Sage Publications, Inc.

Kubiszyn, T., & Borich, G. (1996). *Educational testing and measurement: Classroom application and practice.* (5th ed.) New York, NY: HarperCollins.

Lambert, L. (2003). *Leadership capacity for lasting school improvement.* Alexandria, VA: Association for Supervision and Curriculum Development.

Lambert, L. (1998). *Building leadership capacity in schools.* Alexandria, VA: Association for Supervision and Curriculum Development.

Lazear, D. (1998). *The rubrics way: Using MI to assess understanding.* Tucson, AZ: Zephyr Press.

Linn, R. L., Baker, E. L., & Dunbar, S. B. (1991). *Complex, performance-based assessment: Expectations and validation guide.* (CSE Technical Report No. 331). Los Angeles, CA: University of California, Center for Research on Evaluation, Standards and Student Testing (CRESST).

Lissitz, R. W., & Schafer, W. D. (2002). (Eds.). *Assessment in educational reform: Both means and ends.* Needham Heights, MA: Allyn & Bacon.

Marzano, R. J. (2000). *Transforming classroom grading.* Alexandria, VA: Association for Supervision and Curriculum Development.

Marzano, R. J., Pickering, D., & McTighe, J. (1993). *Assess student outcomes: Performance assessment using dimensions of learning model.* Alexandria, VA: Association for Supervision and Curriculum Development.

Marzano, R. J., Pickering, D., & Pollock, J. E. (2001). *Classroom instruction that works: Research-based strategies for increasing student achievement.* Alexandria, VA: Association for Supervision and Curriculum Development.

McIntyre, C.V. (1992). *Writing effective news releases: How to get free publicity for yourself, your business, or your organization.* Colorado Springs, CO: Piccadilly Books.

McMillian, J. H. (2001). *Classroom assessment: Principles and practice for effective instruction* (2nd ed.). Needham Heights, MA: Allyn & Bacon.

McMillian, J. H. (2001). *Essential assessment concepts for teachers and administrators.* In Guskey, T.R. & Marzano, R.J. (Series Eds.). Experts in Assessment. Thousand Oaks, CA: Corwin Press, Inc.

McREL. (1995-2002). *Classroom assessment, grading, and record keeping.* Aurora, CO: Author.

McTighe, J., & Ferrara, S. (1998). *Assessing learning in the classroom.* Washington, DC: National Education Association.

Merrow, J. (2001). *"Good enough" schools are not good enough.* Lanham, MD: Scarecrow Press.

Microsoft. (2003). Available: http://www.microsoft.com.

National Association of Secondary School Principals. (2004). *Breaking ranks II: Strategies for leading high school reform.* Reston, VA: Author.

National Education Association. (2001). *School dropouts in the United States: A policy discussion.* Washington, DC: Author.

National Staff Development Council (NSDC) *Journal of research in professional learning.* [online]. Available from *http://www.nsdc.org/library/publications/research/index.cfm.*

National Staff Development Council. (2002, October). Scientifically-based research as defined by NCLB. *Results*. Oxford, OH: Author.

Newman, F. (Ed.). (1992). *Student engagement and achievement in American secondary schools*. New York: Teachers College Press.

Noguera, P.A. (2004). Transforming high schools. *Educational Leadership*, Volume 61, No. 8.

Northley, S. (2005). *Handbook on differentiated instruction for middle and high schools*. Larchmont, NY: Eye on Education.

Northwest Evaluation Association (NWEA). (2002). Available: http://www.nwea.org.

O'Connor, K. (1999). *The mindful school: How to grade for learning*. Arlington Heights, IL: Skylight Professional Development.

Oshry, B. (2000). *Leading systems: Lessons from the power lab*. San Francisco, CA: Berrett-Koehler Publishers.

Oosterhof, A. (1999). *Developing and using classroom assessments* (2nd ed.). Upper Saddle River, NJ: Prentice Hall, Inc.

Parsons, B. A. (2002). *Evaluative Inquiry: Using evaluation to promote student success*. Thousand Oaks, CA: Corwin Press, Inc.

Patten, M. L. (1997). *Understanding research methods: An overview of the essentials*. Los Angeles, CA: Pyrczak Publishing.

Payne, R. K., & Magee, D. S. (1999). *Meeting standards and raising test scores when you don't have much time or money*. Highlands, TX: RFT Publishing Company.

Perone, V. (Ed.). (1991). *Expanding student assessment*. Alexandria, VA: Association for Supervision and Curriculum Development.

Peterson, K. D. (1999). *Shaping school culture: The heart of leadership*. San Francisco, CA: Jossey-Bass Publishers.

Peterson, R. A. (2000). *Constructing effective questionnaires*. Thousand Oaks, CA: Sage Publications, Inc..

Popham, W. J. (1999). *Classroom assessment: What teachers need to know* (2nd ed.). Needham Heights, MA: Allyn & Bacon.

Popham, W. J. (2001). Standardized achievement tests: Misnamed and misleading. *Education Week*, 21(3), 46.

Preuss, P. G. (2003). *School leader's guide to root cause analysis: Using data to dissolve problems*. Larchmont, NY: Eye on Education, Inc.

Quellmalz, E., & Burry, J. (1983). Analytic scales for assessing students' expository and narrative writing skills. (CSE Technical Report No. 5). Los Angeles, CA: University of California, Center for Research on Evaluation, Standards and Student Testing (CRESST).

Rauhauser, B., & McLennan, A. (1995). *America's schools: Making them work*. Chapel Hill, NC: New View.

Rauhauser, B., & McLennan, A. (1994). *America's schools: Meeting the challenge through effective schools research and total quality management*. Lewisville, TX: School Improvement Specialists.

Rauhauser, B., & McLennan, A. (1995). *Research design: Qualitative, quantitative, and mixed methods approaches*. Thousand Oaks, CA: SAGE publications.

Rogers, S., & Graham, S. (2000). *The high performance toolbox: Succeeding with performance tasks, projects, and assessments* (3rd ed.). Evergreen, CO: Peak Learning Systems.

Sanders, J. R. (2000). *Evaluating school programs: An educator's guide.* Thousand Oaks, CA: Corwin Press, Inc.

Schafer, W. D., & Lissitz, R. W. (1987). Measurement training for school personnel: Recommendations and reality. *Journal of Teacher Education,* 38(3), 57-63.

Schmoker, M. (2001). *The results fieldbook: Practical strategies from dramatically improved schools.* Alexandria, VA: Association for Supervision and Curriculum Development.

Senge, P., Cambron-McCabe, N. H., Lucas, T., Smith, B., Dutton, J., & Kleiner, A. (2000). *Schools that learn: A fifth discipline fieldbook for educators, parents, and everyone who cares about education.* New York, NY: Doubleday Dell Publishing Group, Inc.

Senge, P., Kleiner, A., Roberts, C., Ross, R. B., & Smith, B. (2000). *The fifth discipline fieldbook: Strategies and tools for building a learning organization.* New York, NY: Doubleday Dell Publishing Group, Inc.

Shepard, L. A. (2000). *The role of classroom assessment in teaching and learning.* (CSE Technical Report No. 517). Los Angeles, CA: University of California, Center for Research on Evaluation, Standards and Student Testing (CRESST).

Smith, J. K., Smith, L. F., & DeLisi, R. (2001). *Natural classroom assessment: Designing seamless instruction & assessment.* In Guskey, T.R. & Marzano, R.J. (Series Eds.). Experts in Assessment. Thousand Oaks, CA: Corwin Press, Inc.

Solomon, P. (2002). *The assessment bridge: Positive ways to link tests to learning, standards, and curriculum improvement.* Thousand Oaks, CA: Corwin Press, Inc.

Statistica. (2003). Available: http://www.statsoft.com.

Stiggins, R. J. (2000). *Student-Involved classroom assessment* (3rd ed.). Englewood Cliffs, NJ: Prentice Hall.

Stiggins, R. J. (1999). Assessment, student confidence, and school success. *Phi Delta Kappan,* November, 191-198.

Stigler, J. W., & Hiebert, J. (1999). *The teaching gap: Best ideas from the world's teachers for improving education in the classroom.* New York, NY: The Free Press.

Strong, R. W., Silver, H. F., & Perini. M. J. (2001). *Teaching what matters most: Standards and strategies for raising student achievement.* Alexandria, VA: Association for Supervision and Curriculum Development.

TetraData. (2002). Available: http://www.Tetradata.com.

Trice, A. D. (2000). *A handbook of classroom assessment.* Needham Heights, MA: Allyn & Bacon.

Tufte, E. R. (2001). *The visual display of quantitative information.* (2nd ed.). Cheshire, CT: Graphics Press.

Tufte, E. R. (1997). *Visual explanations: Images and quantities, evidence and narrative.* Cheshire, CT: Graphics Press.

Tufte, E. R. (1990). *Envisioning information.* Cheshire, CT: Graphics Press.

U. S. Department of Education. *No child left behind.* Available: http://www.ed.gov.

Visual Mining, Inc. (2003). Available: http://www.visualmining.com.

Wahlstrom, D. (1999). *Using data to improve student achievement: A handbook for collecting, analyzing, and using data.* Virginia Beach, VA: Successline Publications.

Wellman, B., & Lipton, L. (2004). *Data-driven dialogue: A facilitator's guide to collaborative inquiry.* Sherman, CT: MiraVia, LLC.

Whitaker, T., Whitaker, B., & Lumpa, D. (2000). *Motivating and inspiring teachers: The educational leader's guide for building staff morale.* Larchmont, NY: Eye on Education.

Wiggins, G. (1998). *Educative assessment: Designing assessments to inform and improve student performance.* San Francisco, CA: Jossey-Bass, Inc.

Wiggins, G., & McTighe, J. (1998). *Understanding by design.* Alexandria, VA: Association for Supervision and Curriculum Development.

Wilson, L. W. (2002). *Better instruction through assessment: What your students are trying to tell you.* Larchmont, NY: Eye on Education, Inc.

Wittrock, M. C., & Baker, E. L. (Eds.). (1991). *Testing and cognition.* Englewood Cliffs, NJ: Prentice Hall.

Wormeli, R. (2003). *Day one & beyond: Practical matters for new middle-level teachers.* Portland, ME: Stenhouse Publishers.

Worthen, B. R., White, K. R., Fan, X., & Sudweeks, R. R. (1999). *Measurement and assessment in the schools* (2nd ed.). Needham Heights, MA: Allyn & Bacon.

Yero, J. L. (2002). *Teaching in mind: How teacher thinking shapes education.* Hamilton, MT: MindFlight Publishing.

Yin, R. K. (2003). *Case study research: Design and methods.* (3rd ed.). Thousand Oaks, CA: Sage Publications, Inc.

Zemelman, S., Daniels, H., & Hyde, A. (1998). *Best practice: New standards for teaching and learning in America's schools* (2nd ed.). Portsmouth, NH: Heinemann.

Zepeda, S.J. (1999). *Staff development practices that promote leadership in learning communities.* Larchmont, NY: Eye on Education.

Zmuda, A., Kuklis, R., & Kline, E. (2004). *Transforming schools: Creating a culture of continuous improvement.* Alexandria, VA: Association for Supervision and Curriculum Development.

Index

EYE ON EDUCATION and EDUCATION FOR THE FUTURE INITIATIVE
END-USER LICENSE AGREEMENT

READ THIS

You should carefully read these terms and conditions before opening the software packet(s) included with this book ("Book"). This is a license agreement ("Agreement") between you and EYE ON EDUCATION. By opening the accompanying software packet(s), you acknowledge that you have read and accept the following terms and conditions. If you do not agree and do not want to be bound by such terms and conditions, promptly return the Book and the unopened software packet (s) to the place you obtained them for a full refund.

1. License Grant

EYE ON EDUCATION grants to you (either an individual or entity) a nonexclusive license to use the software and files (collectively, the "Software") solely for your own personal or business purposes on a single computer (whether a standard computer or a workstation component of a multiuser network). The Software is in use on a computer when it is loaded into temporary memory (RAM) or installed into permanent memory (hard disk, CD-ROM, or other storage device). EYE ON EDUCATION reserves all rights not expressly granted herein.

2. Ownership

EYE ON EDUCATION is the owner of all rights, title, and interests, including copyright, in and to the compilation of the Software recorded on the CD-ROM ("Software Media"). Copyright to the individual programs recorded on the Software Media is owned by the author or other authorized copyright owner of each program. Ownership of the Software and all proprietary rights relating thereto remain with EYE ON EDUCATION and its licensers.

3. Restrictions On Use and Transfer

(a) You may only (i) make one copy of the Software for backup or archival purposes, or (ii) transfer the Software to a single hard disk, provided that you keep the original for backup or archival purposes. You may not (i) rent or lease the Software, (ii) copy or reproduce the Software through a LAN or other network system or through any computer subscriber system or bulletin-board system, or (iii) adapt or create derivative works based on the Software.

(b) You may not reverse engineer, decompile, or disassemble the Software. You may transfer the Software and user documentation on a permanent basis, provided that the transferee agrees to accept the terms and conditions of this Agreement and you retain no copies. If the Software is an update or has been updated, any transfer must include the most recent update and all prior versions.

4. Restrictions On Use of Individual Programs

You must follow the individual requirements and restrictions detailed for each individual program on the Software Media. These limitations are contained in the individual license agreements recorded on the Software Media. By opening the Software packet, you will be agreeing to abide by the licenses and restrictions for these individual programs that are detailed on the Software Media. None of the material on this Software Media or listed in this Book may ever be redistributed, in original or modified form, for commercial purposes.

5. Limited Warranty

(a) EDUCATION FOR THE FUTURE INITIATIVE warrants that the Software and Software Media are free from defects in materials and workmanship under normal use for a period of thirty (30) days from the date of purchase of this Book. If EDUCATION FOR THE FUTURE INITIATIVE receives notification within the warranty period of defects in materials or workmanship, EDUCATION FOR THE FUTURE INITIATIVE will replace the defective Software Media.

(b) **EYE ON EDUCATION, EDUCATION FOR THE FUTURE INITIATIVE, AND THE AUTHOR OF THIS BOOK DISCLAIM OTHER WARRANTIES, EXPRESSED OR IMPLIED, INCLUDING WITHOUT LIMITATION IMPLIED WARRANTIES OF MERCHANTABILITY AND FITNESS FOR A PARTICULAR PURPOSE WITH RESPECT TO THE SOFTWARE AND FILES, AND/OR THE TECHNIQUES DESCRIBED IN THIS BOOK. EYE ON EDUCATION DOES NOT WARRANT THAT THE FUNCTIONS CONTAINED IN THE SOFTWARE WILL MEET YOUR REQUIREMENTS OR THAT THE OPERATION OF THE SOFTWARE WILL BE ERROR FREE.**

(c) This limited warranty gives you specific legal rights, and you may have other rights that vary from jurisdiction to jurisdiction.

6. Remedies

(a) EYE ON EDUCATION's entire liability and your exclusive remedy for defects in materials and workmanship shall be limited to replacement of the Software Media, which may be returned to EDUCATION FOR THE FUTURE INITIATIVE with a copy of your receipt at the following address: EDUCATION FOR THE FUTURE INITIATIVE, ATTN: Brad Geise, 400 West 1st. St., Chico, CA 95929-0230, or call 1-530-898-4482. Please allow three to four weeks for delivery. This Limited Warranty is void if failure of the Software Media has resulted from accident, abuse, or misapplication. Any replacement Software Media will be warranted for thirty (30) days.

(b) In no event shall EYE ON EDUCATION, EDUCATION FOR THE FUTURE INITIATIVE, or the author be liable for any damages whatsoever (including without limitation damages for loss of business profits, business interruption, loss of business information, or any other pecuniary loss) arising from the use of or inability to use the Book or the Software, even if EYE ON EDUCATION, EDUCATION FOR THE FUTURE INITIATIVE, or the author has been advised of the possibility of damages.

(c) Because some jurisdictions do not allow the exclusion or limitation of liability for consequential or incidental damages, the above limitation or exclusion may not apply to you.

7. U.S. Government Restriction Rights

Use, duplication, or disclosure of the Software by the U.S. Government is subject to restrictions stated in paragraph (c) (1)(ii) of the Rights in Technical Data and Computer Software clause of DFARS 252.227-7013, and in subparagraphs (a) through (d) of the Commercial Computer—Restricted Rights clause at FAR 52. 227–19, and in similar clauses in the NASA FAR supplement, when applicable.

8. General

This Agreement constitutes the entire understanding of the parties and revokes and supersedes all prior agreements, oral or written, between them and may not be modified or amended except in writing signed by both parties hereto that specifically refers to this Agreement. This Agreement shall take precedence over any other documents that may be in conflict herewith. If any one or more provisions contained in this Agreement are held by any court or tribunal to be invalid, illegal, or otherwise unenforceable, each and every other provision shall remain in full force and effect.

INSTALLATION INSTRUCTIONS

 **Windows**

Step 1 Set up a folder on your desktop (or in your documents folder) labeled *High Data Tools* for capturing the files that you wish to download.

Step 2 Make sure your monitor is set to 800 by 600 or higher to view the entire CD contents. (When you are on the main menu page of the CD and cannot see the top menu bar, your monitor must be moved to a higher setting. Do this by going into *Start / Settings / Control Panel / Display.* Open *Display,* and click on *Settings.* Move the arrow on the screen area to at least 800 by 600 pixels.)

Step 3 The CD should start automatically. The introduction will run up to the *Main Menu* page. If the CD does *not* start automatically, follow steps 3a. and 3b. below:

    3a. Open/Explore *My Computer* and Open/Explore the CD *High.*

    3b. With the CD contents showing, click on *Click Here.exe.* The CD will begin.

Step 4 After the introduction, you will come to the *Main Menu.* If you do not have *Adobe Reader* v.5 or above, download it by pressing *Adobe Acrobat.* After installing, go back to the *Main Menu.*

Step 5 By placing your cursor on the section titles, you will be able to see what is on the CD. Click on the section that you want to know more about and read the descriptions of the files in that section.

Step 6 To download the tools from that section, press the *Download* button.

Step 7 When *Extract Archive Files* appears, click *Next.*

Step 9 Note: When *Destination Directory* appears, click *Browse* to locate the folder in which you want the files to download. If you put a folder entitled *High Data Tools* on your desktop, you will see it in the *Desktop Folder.* (This may vary slightly depending upon the version of *Windows* you are using.)

Step 9 Open *The High Data Tools* folder and click *Next.* The files will extract and ask you if it is okay to download. Click *Yes* and the files will extract into your *High Data Tools* folder. Click *Finish.*

Step 10 Go back to the *INFO* window. Select the *Back to Main Menu* button to return to the *Main Menu.*

Step 11 Continue exploring and downloading. You must quit the CD to view the documents that you download.

 **Mac**

Step 1 Create a folder on your desktop (or your hard drive) labeled *High Data Tools* for capturing the files that you wish to download.

Step 2 Make sure your monitor is set to 800 by 600 or higher to view the entire CD contents. (When you are on the main menu page of the CD and cannot see the top menu bar, your monitor must be moved to a higher setting. Change the settings in the *Monitors Control Panel.*)

Step 3 Open the CD by double-clicking the CD icon on your desktop. Select the icon for *OS 9* or *OS X,* depending upon which operating system you use. The CD will begin.

Step 4 By placing your cursor on the section titles, you will be able to see what is on the CD. Click on the section that you want to know more about and read the descriptions of the files.

Step 5 To download the tools from that section, press the *Download* button.

Step 6 When a dialog box appears, click *Continue.*

Step 7 Note: A *Save* window will appear. Locate your *High Data Tools* folder, or if you did not make a folder when you started, create a new folder. Save the section's files to the *High Data Tools* folder.

Step 8 Go Back to *INFO* window. Select the *Back to Main Menu* button to return to the *Main Menu.*

Step 9 Continue exploring and downloading. You must quit the CD to view the documents that you download.

Please see our website for more information:

http://eff.csuchico.edu/home/

To contact *Education for the Future,* call:

(530) 898-4482